The African Book of Names

5,000+ Common and Uncommon Names from the African Continent

Askhari Hodari, Ph.D.

Health Communications, Inc.
Deerfield Beach, Florida
www.bcibooks.com

929.4
HoD

Library of Congress Cataloging-in-Publication Data
is available through the Library of Congress.

© 2009 Askhari Hodari, Ph.D.

ISBN-13: 978-0-7573-0779-9
ISBN-10: 0-7573-0779-5

Publisher: Health Communications, Inc.
        3201 S.W. 15th Street
        Deerfield Beach, FL 33442-8190

Cover design by Andrea Perrine Brower
Inside book design and formatting by Dawn Von Strolley Grove

A12005 580428

Millions didn't make it . . .

. . . for those who did.

"I have a dream. A dream when we—[children of Africa]—will address each other the same way our forefathers addressed each other—that is by the African name. Pass the word around about how sweet, charming, and beautiful the names of our forefathers are."

—*Kipkemboi Murgor*

"No people can be spiritually and culturally secure until they answer to a name of their own choosing—a name that instantaneously relates that people to the past, the present, and the future."

—*John Henrik Clarke*

Contents

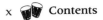

Acknowledgments

"To whom much is given, much is expected."
—*The Bible, Luke 12:48*

he *African Book of Names* is a community collaboration and represents the efforts and spirits of many. This project matured and was completed because of . . .

My sisters: Dr. Kendra Corr Roberson and Yvonne McCalla Sobers. i[1] do not have enough pages to list the tangible and intangible contributions these strong, determined, intelligent, independent, creative, loyal women made to this project. Briefly, let me express gratitude to them for editing the manuscript from first to final draft; helping with the tedious task of categorizing names by theme; formatting references; and, most essentially, calling this book "our book" and saying things like, "I am here for whatever you need" and "anything for you."

The assistance of each continental or diasporic Afrikan[2] who helped me locate, source, and pronounce Afrikan names: Hloniphile Nyide (an indigenous Zulu who was with me the night my name changed); Ahmed Obafemi (Zulu and other South Afrikan names); Nahbila Sonia Tutuwan (names from Cameroon); the Bali Cultural Association (West Afrikan names); Dr. Arletha Livingston (Khamitic or KMT names); Dr. Mutulu Shakur and Dr. Alison Irvine Sobers (linguist). Additionally, my comrades and fellow Black Studies practitioners Dr. Makungu Akinyela and Dr. Akinyele Umoja provided information on New Afrikan[3] naming rituals.

Sterne Library's Heather Martin and Eddie Luster were invaluable to the progression of this project. Also helpful were the staff of Howard University's Founder's Library; Dwight Green, Major Bowens, Bridget Turner, and Lonnie Jones of the Homewood Public Library; Gail Short, and student assistants, Theodore Foster, Alexis Morris, and Kimberly Rodgers.

Rita Rosenkranz of the Rita Rosenkranz Literary Agency and Allison Janse of Health Communications were enthused, open, and supportive from start to finish. Rita is the type of agent to hold a project in both her hands, not just one. . . .

i appreciate . . .

Each person who amiably shared his or her Afrikan name with me.

All those persons, younger and older, who have trusted me with naming or renaming them.

The counsel and encouragement from the best friends of my writing life: Sis./Dr. Kendra Corr Roberson, Sis. Yvonne McCalla Sobers, Baba Kalamu ya Salaam, Sis. Pearl Cleage, Sis. Boatema Sonyika, and Sis. Sunny Sumter.

The general goodwill of Sis. Rukia Lumumba, Baba Ahmed Obafemi, Sis. Sanovia Muhammad, Sis. Alizinya Myemyela (Tess McGhee), Mfundishi Tayari Casel, Sis. Aminata Umoja, Bro./Dr. Mutulu Shakur, Bro. Oliver Hilaire Sobers, Esq., Bro./Dr. Tony Medina, Bro. Kenyatta Becktemba, and the following members of de Griot Space Online Writing Workshop: Bro. Quentin Huff, Sis. Melanie Norris, Bro. Andrew Reeves, Sis. Stephanie Purdy, and Sis. M. Yvonne Lee.

My family—the Johnson and McClellan clans. My aunts act more like my mothers than my aunts, and my uncles treat me more like a daughter than a niece. Most essentially: my mama and my daddy. Both developed in me a sustained and celebratory love of Afrika. i want to especially thank my parents and other biological relatives for understanding my need for a name that clearly and unapologetically identifies me as a child of Afrika. It was not easy for me to give up the name my parents gave me all those years ago, and i still carry the spirit of that name close to my heart.

To everyone who has been waiting for me to finish this book—here it is!

Introduction: Born Again

In the Beginning

The bird flies, but always returns to earth.

—*Senegal, Gambia*

I adore African names. They feel elegant to my ear and enthuse my tongue. I appreciate their sounds and meanings, which are different from the names of North America. Each time a person calls me by my African name, he or she reminds me my roots are indeed in Africa.

In the last twenty years, I have been blessed to have been consulted in the naming of hundreds of babies and in the renaming of hundreds of children and adults. Naming in African societies is more of a communal process than in other societies; in fact, it is common for parents, young people, or adults to consult with community members or African Studies practitioners before bestowing a name upon an infant, or upon themselves.

In the case of a child born eight years ago, we named him *Jasir Dia*. Each time a person speaks to Jasir, they are calling him a "fearless champion," and a "winner." We believe his name helps and influences Jasir's life, and we expect him to become all that his name implies long after his parents and other family members have passed on.

Recently, we named an infant male *Qadir Rai Lumumba*. When we call to him, we are saying, "competent, healthy one who is gifted." In the case of a child born five years ago, we named her *Zindzhi Niasha Nubia Haderah*. When her family and friends call to her, they are saying, "warrior with purposeful life," "I have seen it," and "lioness." The circumstances surrounding her birth and desired characteristics influenced our choice of name for her. Zindzhi was born as her mother was leaving earth. So, while three of her names reflect desired characteristics, we chose one of her names, *Nubia*, to tie Zindzhi's birth to her mother, and to honor the unforgettable woman who passed on before us.

We named another man-child *Mujasi Zibusiso*, ("courageous fighter," "blessing.") In addition, as I write this, our community is awaiting the arrival of a girl child whom we will name *Sadmia* ("she suits me," "well

1

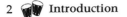

matched"). The name that awaits this baby is the name of her maternal aunt, who passed on before us.

After Birth: Renaming Later in Life

Let each bird cry according to its kind.

—*Niger, Nigeria*

Choosing an African name does not have to happen shortly after birth. Across the world, individuals take on new names during the life cycle. In Mali, the Bobo people characteristically give children as many as three different names during a life cycle. The Bobo give children a name seven days after birth, another name when they begin to walk, and another name when they complete an initiation or rites of passage ritual. (The Bobo use their second and third names during special or religious events). Many African individuals receive new names when marrying, or when reaching an important milestone or achievement.

New names can represent new stages of development. Sojourner Truth, Muhammad Ali, Kareem Abdul-Jabbar, and El Haj Malik El Shabazz (Malcolm X) all took on new names as adults. I have helped a number of people change their names to African names later in life, because they believed the names they were given at birth were "slave names" and that claiming an African name would link them to their motherland or ancestral home.

Therefore, with my help, Cleve Bowie became Tahleb Obike ("seeker of truth," "strong household"); Chris Johnson became Kojo Ayinde ("unconquerable," "we asked for him and he came"); Tiffany Hawkins became Kimya Shekayo Amachi ("quiet passion," "who knows what God will bring us through this one"); and Will Anderson became Jasiri Kafele ("fearless one," "worth dying for"). These individuals requested new names as they became more politically mature. We chose their names essentially for meaning, but also for aesthetic value. Tess McGhee became Aliyinza Ilizi Khanyiswa Myemyela ("she will be able to handle it," "charm against lions," "she reflects the light," "smile"). Aliyinza had a naming ceremony during her pregnancy. We choose a new name for her to guide her birthing journey and to bless the way of the forthcoming child.

Everlasting Life: Why African Names?

*If you understand the beginning well,
the end will not trouble you.*

—*Ghana (Ashanti)*

I promote the use of African names for several reasons. First, the importance of African culture is often minimized, leading to the exclusion of African names from many name books. This negligence deprives parents, researchers, students, and other readers of the philosophy and wisdom of African societies. Also, since many traditional and modern African societies tend to rely on and emphasize oral communication more than written communication, I want to contribute to as much of a written record of African names as possible, particularly since Africans are no longer in one rather large area, but are scattered across the planet.

Numerous names in this book are based on my experience with, personal knowledge of, and longtime, passionate interest in Africana. I learned many names as I traveled to different places on the African continent. Other names I learned when I studied Kiswahili[3]. Still, other names came to me during the six years I was a professor of Black Studies at the university level. Naturally, I have also been collecting, studying, and gathering African names from books, novels, and literature. As a result of the richness of the African continent, my *personal* collection now exceeds 7,000 African names.

Each African name book I have studied has something to offer. Likewise, each book has vulnerabilities. Thus, *The African Book of Names* borrows best practices from each name book to strengthen, not to compete with, extant African name literature. My goal has been to build upon the foundation other African name books have established by creating a balanced and comprehensive text. However, an exhaustive text would require more than one volume because of the countless African names that exist, many in languages and from cultures with which I am not familiar.

If you're looking for an African name, you can choose one of the more than 5,000 names from a range of cultures and languages in this book. I celebrate Africa's cultural contributions by sharing a broad array of potential first, last, organization, and business names from at least thirty-seven

African countries and at least seventy of Africa's ethnolinguistic groups.

While the birth of a baby is a joyous time that creates a need to choose a name, *The African Book of Names* does not focus solely on baby names. Individuals of any age can embrace this collection to select names for themselves, organizations, events, or other entities.

It has been my honor, privilege, and duty to design *The African Book of Names* to guide, inform, instruct, inspire, and interest. Let it be known this book is guided by a spiritual, social, political, and academic acknowledgment of Africa as the absolute birthplace of humankind. Indeed, *The African Book of Names* unapologetically celebrates Africa as a beating heart of the world.

Asante/Thank you,

Askhari Hodari, Ph.D.
Birmingham, Alabama
October 2008

PART 1

So Loved the World:
Embracing African Names

*If you allow yourself to forget the sound
of your town's horn you get lost in the gathering.*
—*Ghana (Akan)*

For the first time in history, 2008 witnessed the election of a United States president with an African name—Barack Obama (*Barack*, meaning "blessed," *Obama* meaning "bending or bent"). In 2006, people celebrated a United States Olympic gold medalist with an African name—speed skater Shani Davis (*Shani*, meaning "amazing child").

Other celebrities with African names include, but are not limited to, former UN Secretary General Kofi Annan ("born on Friday," "fourth in family"); New Jersey Poet Laureate Amiri Baraka ("prince," "blessing"); supermodel Iman ("faith"); world champion basketball player Rasheed Wallace ("rightly guided"); boxer Laila Ali ("born at night," "exalted"); recording artist Sade ("direct from God"); Grammy award-winning recording artists Nitanju Bolade Casel ("protect and possess trust," "honor arrives"); and Aisha Khalil ("alive," "friend") of the internationally renowned a capella ensemble Sweet Honey in the Rock; Cosby Show alumnae Malcolm Jamal-Warner ("gift from god"); and screen actors Omar Epps ("the highest") and Sanaa Lathan ("art").

Equally important, Black celebrities have given their children culturally harmonious African names offering a rich sense of their history:

- Stevie Wonder, double-digit Grammy award-winning recording artist, named his daughter *Aisha* ("life").
- Screen actor Danny Glover named his daughter *Mandisa* ("sweet").
- Multiple Grammy-winning recording artist Gladys Knight named her daughter *Kenya* ("artist").

According to the Social Security Administration's data, over the last hundred years, the most popular names given to female children in the United States were: Mary, Linda, Lisa, Jennifer, Jessica, Ashley, and Emily. Census records show that one hundred years ago, the twenty most popular names were largely the same for Blacks and whites. In recent years, more than 40 percent of the names given to Black females were names that were not given to *any* white female born in the same year. Currently, only a few names are frequently found within both Black and white populations, but Black names (and subcultures) began to differ from white people's during the 1960s, when Blacks began once again wearing African clothes and also increased their use of African names.

What's My Name? Reintroducing African Names to the World

The purity of your name is worth
more than the purity of your body.

—*Tunisia*

A few years before I was born, heavyweight boxer Cassius Clay rejected his name, saying "Cassius Clay" lacked "divine meaning." "Cassius Clay is a slave name," he said. "I didn't choose it, and I didn't want it. I am Muhammad Ali, a free name—it means 'beloved of God'—and I insist people use it when speaking to me and of me."

True to his word, Ali verbally and physically insisted on the use of his new name. When Floyd Patterson called Ali "Clay," Ali publicly punished Patterson for twelve rounds, neglecting to knock out an obviously hurt Patterson. Then, during a 1967 pre-fight press conference, Ernie Terrell refused to call Ali by his rightful name, instead referring to the people's champ as "Cassius Clay." Ali told Terrell he would punish him just as he head punished Patterson. Ali beat on Terrell for fifteen rounds, hurting him badly, but not knocking him out. He even held Terrell up while battering him with punches. Ali repeatedly (and loudly) asked Terrell, "What's my name? What's my name, fool?"

"Get used to me," Ali said. "Black, confident, cocky—my name, not yours. My religion, not yours. My goals, my own. Get used to me." Shortly after the fight, Muhammad Ali apologized for taunting Terrell during the fight. He did so, Ali said, so that people would respect his beliefs and his name. Muhammad

Ali was one of many who paved the way for other African-descended people to reject European names and adopt African names. Today, the name Muhammad Ali remains one of the most recognized names in the world.

In 1971, one of my favorite professional basketball players legally changed his name to Kareem Abdul-Jabbar. Discussing the change, Abdul-Jabbar said he was latching on to something that was part of his heritage. A French planter named Alcindor brought Abdul-Jabbar's family to America. However, his people were Yoruba, a culture that survived slavery. "All I needed to know [was] that, hey, I was somebody, even if nobody else knew about it. When I was a kid, no one would believe anything positive that you could say about Black people. And that's a terrible burden on Black people, because they don't have an accurate idea of their history, which has been either suppressed or distorted," said Abdul-Jabbar. In choosing a new name, Kareem Abdul-Jabbar indicated he intended to be generous, kind, and possess religious devotion and courage. As author Richard Moore said, "Slaves and dogs are named by their masters. Free men name themselves."

Born Again

Family names are like flowers; they blossom in clusters.

—Africa

I was born the year Tommy Smith and John Carlos raised black-gloved fists on the victory stand at the Mexico City Olympics; the year the heavyweight champion of the world (Muhammad Ali) refused to be drafted to fight in the Vietnam War; and the same year someone murdered Martin Luther King Jr. Like Muhammad Ali, I was not born with the name I now wear.

At birth, I was named after my father and my mother. Those names were unique, but not African. In 1989, I completed an African Rites of Passage program with twenty-two other young women. During our traditional naming ceremony, our Great Mother, an elder, whispered the name *Askari* in my ear. Immediately, I felt she was singing a song just for me. I felt intimately at home in my new name. I had always wanted an African name—now I finally had one. The decision to keep and use my African name was an easy decision, but discarding the names given to me by my father and mother was not easy to do. It was, however, necessary.

Deep down in my African soul, I knew the European names I carried were not my names. I enjoy hearing and writing my names now. I feel connected to my past, present, and future. I believe the spirit world saved these names for me. And, each time someone calls me by my name, I feel a duty to soldier on, to be brave and strong. Whenever I am having a difficult time, I repeat my entire name to myself, over and over, to remind myself that I must earn my name each and every day and that I am blessed to be alive.

The names of my family tree, apart from Johnson and McClellan, include Burrell, Graham, Samuel, and Henry. It is easy to see these names do not identify my family and families of African-descended people as children of Africa, whereas Wong, Patel, Takahashi, Petrov, Schmidt, or Nowak provide immediate clues to ethnic origin. Clearly, the African holocaust or Maafa is largely responsible for the phenomenon by which my family and families of African-descended people have and pass on names that do not identify us as children of Africa.

In addition to being an act of cultural resistance, for me, taking an African name was a way to redress the theft of my ancestors from the African continent.

Did You Know?

Estimates of the number of Africans stolen from Africa range from 20 to 60 million, with many scholars agreeing on higher numbers within that range.

Scholars have identified six countries as the principal areas from which Africans were kidnapped (Lewin 1996):

Nigeria	24%	Guinea Bissau	11%
Angola	24%	Sierra Leone	6%
Ghana	16%	Other	6%
Senegal/Gambia	13%		

Six major colonial empires colonized and divided Africa and then forced their own cultural idiosyncrasies on Africa: France, Britain, Germany, Italy, Portugal, and Spain. These European empires established national boundaries that in turn had an adverse influence on African naming. In fact, one of the legacies of the so-called scramble for Africa is inconsistency in the spelling and pronunciations of African names. Some names have been Europeanized beyond African recognition.

Often, I remember how passionately Kunta Kinte held onto his African name in *Roots*, the record-breaking and prize-winning miniseries. For me, the most memorable moments of *Roots* were those scenes during which Kunta Kinte refused to embrace the slave name, Toby, even as he was being whipped by an overseer:

> "I want to hear you say it. Your name is Toby. What's your name?"
> "Kunta. Kunta Kinte."
> "When the master gives you something, you take it. He give you a name. It is a nice name. Toby. I want to hear it. Who are you?"

After watching Kunta Kinte's act of cultural resistance, I knew I would not continue to wear the names of the English (Johnson) and Irish (McClellan) slaving families who used to own my biological families.

Lost and Found

They ate our food, and forgot our names.

—Ghana

Unquestionably, European colonial powers forced continental Africans to use foreign names. In Azania[4], for instance, an all-white government passed racist laws requiring South Africans to have Christian names in order to be eligible for employment and education. In other words, Christian names were synonymous with European names such as Emily, George, James, Rebecca, Richard, or Steven—names that have no African importance and names that do not speak to an African past or future.

In an effort to restore authenticity and integrity to African naming practices, the Democratic Republic of the Congo's (DRC) government changed personal and place names. Beginning in 1972, all children in the DRC were baptized with African names and citizens were required to abandon foreign names. Joseph Mobutu, the president at the time, changed his name to Mobutu Sese Seko Kuku Ngbendu wa za Banga, meaning "the all-powerful warrior who, because of his endurance and inflexible will to win, will go from conquest to conquest, leaving fire in his wake." The government also changed the name of Elizabethville to Lubumbashi.

Other African countries followed in an effort to resist and reverse the impact of colonization. This process took two fundamental forms: replacing foreign, European names with African names, or adopting African spellings for foreign names. Countries such as Mali, Ghana, and Zambia all changed their names after realizing independence.

Across an ocean, enslaved Africans like Kunta Kinte had frequently refused to take on the new names slave masters gave them. Given that enslaved children were often separated from their parents, naming was a strategy used to try to trace the whereabouts of children when they or their parents were sold. Parents, therefore, named their children after family members, or for a specific place.

Similarly, enslaved Africans preserved their languages by using a dual-naming system. Black children frequently had two names—one name given by the "master," and a secret "basket" or "day" name given by the family. These basket names, like nicknames of today, were usually derived from African words. *Anyika, Mesu, Seba, Tulu*, and *Tuma* are examples of Gullah "basket" names. *Reena, Mingo*, and *Fanny* are examples of nicknames and names with African origins.

This dual-naming system began in Africa and survived slavery and imperialism. In today's Africa, there are still persons, such as the Basuto people of Lesotho, who will not share their secret names. I have heard stories of Basuto women waiting years before revealing their secret names to their husbands. Many African children have at least one name that is protected by a layer of other names. Even in diasporic societies, some people retain a private nickname known to family and community, and then an official name that outside authorities use. This practice stems from the belief that names are sacred and possess spiritual power.

The Familiar: Naming Patterns

After emancipation from slavery, many freed women and men took on the surnames of their former owners. Some Blacks in the United States took on the surname Freeman, while others adopted the names of popular figures such as former presidents Washington, Jefferson, and Jackson. Today, Blacks in North America have the power to exercise more creativity and self-determination when naming.

Intentionally or not, it is common for Blacks to use or create names with patterns that recall African languages and sounds. For example, Blacks have a tendency toward names that include the following sound or letter combinations: *de*, *la*, *ra*, *sha*, and *ta*. Oftentimes, Blacks add the following sounds to the beginning of an existing name, or an "a" is added to the end of the name:

◆ de	◆ ja	◆ ra
◆ la	◆ ni	◆ sha
◆ tri	◆ wa	

Examples of names in this category include:

◆ DeAndre	◆ RaKesha	◆ ShaShawn
◆ LaRon	◆ RaShonda	◆ TaNesha
◆ Latonya		

Logically speaking, the notion of American is more monolithic in concept than in reality. Bowing to pressure, individuals and groups who are not in the numerical majority often choose between celebrating their own culture by giving their children distinctive names, or helping their children blend. For decades, Jewish and Asian people and families have changed their names, hoping to improve their economic prospects in the face of discrimination, as have other ethnic groups who have just as rich a history in America as Europeans.

For more than two decades, I have been keeping colorful handwritten lists of African names in my journals. I have saved these names for the children of Africa who, like Kunta Kinte and me, had their ancestral names stolen from them, or were given the non-African names of their slavers.

What Is in a Name?
Themes Common to African Naming

A name or nickname influences one's character.

—*Benin*

Whenever I learn a new African name, I learn more about African beliefs, culture, and philosophy. For the most part, African naming practices are more elaborate than naming practices in other parts of the world. Certainly, these practices offer learning about Africa, her people, and culture. African names link African people to ethnic groups, a place, a time, or circumstance. My African name ties me to my initiation or rites of passage; to the other community members involved in my naming ceremony; to my biological brother, Khary; and to Eastern and Southern Africa.

On such a diverse continent, the people of Africa differ from each other with regard to language, religion, philosophy, music, and appearance. Africa's indigenous people come in all different sizes, skin colors, and shapes. They govern themselves in a myriad of ways, speak thousands of different languages, and worship different indigenous and imported gods.

Despite enormous cultural variety throughout Africa, there are central themes common to African naming.

Day, Time, or Order of Birth

Quite often in African cultures, a name evidences the day of birth, time of birth, or the birth order. For example:

Akua	Wednesday.
Doto	Second of twins.
Layla	Born at night.
Mosi	First born.
Nina	First female child.

Conditions or Circumstances of Birth and Reactions to Birth

Conditions of and reactions to birth vary. The people of Nigeria say, "We consider the state of our affairs before we name a child." The following names evidence these assorted states of affairs:

Alfryea	Born during good times.
Alanyo	A child born at a time when parents were separated.
Chifini	Child born after the mother has buried several young ones.

Falala	Born into abundance.
Kijita	Child born after the death of her father.
Lesa	Child born unexpectedly.

Location of Birth

Africans frequently reference geography and landscape when selecting names. The Yoruba people say, "Rivers dry up but not their names." Recognizing this, many times names document the place or area of birth:

Afiba	By the sea.
Jiri	Forest of wild fruits.
Kusi	South.
Sanga	From the valley.
Shartati	Most beautiful mountain.
Zizwe	Child born in a foreign land.

Event or Season of Birth

As with location, African names also document the season of birth or events happening during the time of birth:

Arusi	Born during time of wedding.
Bejide	Child born during the rains.
Chozi	Tear, born after a funeral.
Demokrasi	Born during nationalist revolution.
Khephu	Born during snow conditions.
Rabia	Spring.

Religious and Spiritual Concepts

All available information suggests Afridiasporic people have some concept of God. There is no record of an African society devoid of a God concept (Mbiti 1972).

Certainly, one of the biggest categories of names relates to (1) the image of God; (2) the nature of God; (3) the activities of God; and (4) the relationships between God and woman and man. African names emphasize God as one who manifests through action rather than speech (what God does, rather than what God says). Following are examples of African names related to God, religion, faith, or spirituality:

Ekedi	The existence of the creator is shown by what he does.
Nathi	God is with us.
Kemba	She is full of faith.
Basha	Act of God.
Chima	God has the answer.
Sheyi	See what God did for me.
Suku	He who supplies the needs of his creatures.

Deceased Persons, Relatives, and Royalty

In Ethiopia, the people say, "One's name remains about the grave." Africans often name their children after deceased persons, relatives, celebrities, or royalty. Common names of this type include:

Nefertiti	The beautiful one has arrived.
Nofoto	Child born in the image of her grandmother.
Nzinga	From the river.
Ramses	Sun-born.
Sesi	Sister.
Shaka	Stomach disorder.
Cleopatra	Famous.

Physical Characteristics

Not surprisingly, numerous Africans use names to describe physical appearance. When someone has a special or peculiar physical quality, he or she is likely to receive names such as:

Kabibi	Fat and beautiful child.
Mashavu	Little baby with chubby cheeks.
Najla	Having big eyes.
Shakila	Shapely, well-rounded.
Tabasamu	A beautiful smile.
Yozi	The one with big sleepy eyes.

Desired Characteristics

Frequently, Africans take the character, behavior, and attitude of the name bearer into account when selecting names. A Moroccan proverb reads, "a good name is more valuable than a velvet garment." Accordingly, African names speak to desired characteristics. In a sense, these types of names are waiting for the person:

Hodari	Brave; courageous.
Ime	Patient.
Jinaki	Self-confident; proud.
Kashka	Friendly.
Okaome	One who says and does what he says.
Zuberi	Strong.

Animals and Other Living Creatures

Sometimes, names of animals or other living creatures represent the physical attributes or personal qualities of individuals.

Fezela	Scorpion (a hurtful person, a mischievous person).
Kasuku	Parrot (talkative person).
Musota	Snake (sly and mischievous person).
Nama	Lion (strong, powerful person).
Nkuku	Rooster (early riser).
Rasha	Gazelle (graceful runner).
Tausi	Peacock (person full of pride).
Zekle	Cock (quarrelsome).

With 16 percent of the world's population residing on the African continent, Africa has given birth to millions of lyrical, intriguing, and significant names—thousands of which are listed here in *The African Book of Names*.

Come After Me: How I Chose the Names

All heads are the same, but not all thoughts are the same.
—*Ghana (Twi)*

You will find in *The African Book of Names* a preference for names innate to Africa. Arabic names are included, however, because Arabic has influenced African languages to the point where many Arabic names are regarded as African.

Sound and Rhythm

With regard to name selection, my idiosyncrasies and personal preferences shape *The African Book of Names*. A word artist, I began by selecting names because of how they felt on my tongue, and I moved toward names that excited my tongue—names I liked hearing and saying over and over again. Names such as:

Rasha	(gazelle).
Dejenaba	(affectionate).
Jasisi	(to spy).
Hararah	(passion).
Elela	(to see clearly).
Farashuu	(butterfly).

Pronunciation

During name selection, ease of pronunciation was a consideration. Many African names are easy to pronounce. However, I was careful not to neglect names because of difficult pronunciation. Some names (African or not) are difficult to pronounce at first, but pronunciation often becomes easier with practice. Therefore, many names have been included in this collection despite perceived difficulty of pronunciation. Names such as:

Nto	(war).
Enobakhare	(the king's word).
Byomere	(one who is rich).
Chafulumisa	(speed, swiftness).
Uramukiwe	(who will be next).
Xoxo	(frog).

The pronunciation guide will help with some names. Then, there are a few names, like Ugobungqongqo, which even I could not pronounce. But how could I leave out a Zulu name meaning "he who bends down even majesties"?

Meaning

The African Book of Names takes a unique approach by focusing on meaning while still maintaining the integrity of sound, region, and gender distinction.

In order to preserve the integrity of African names, I did not attempt to bend or create meanings for names. In the case of each name, I tried to provide meanings as originally intended. Further, so a large number of names can be shared, I kept meanings simple, and did not go into tremendous detail.

Some African names have several meanings depending on the origin of the name or the local culture. Thus, please do not accept meanings as exclusive or absolute. Where I have erred in meaning, I intended no disrespect. I have researched names to the best of my competence.

Further, a number of names may seem offensive to those unfamiliar with African naming culture. In fact, some naming books exclude names perceived as negative. I have chosen to be more inclusive.

For instance, *Shaka* means stomachache, stomach pain, or displeasure. It is difficult to imagine naming a child "displeasure." However, Shaka Zulu is one of Africa's fiercest and most respected warriors. He certainly created displeasure for his enemies.

I attempted to be comprehensive in treating names or multiple meanings so readers can thoroughly study the naming practices of Africa. Various African cultures give children uncomplimentary names for a variety of logical, social-political, and spiritual reasons.

African parents select some names perceived as negative to fight off evil and wrongdoing. For example, a mother might name her child *Ukeh* (poison) to make an infant less appealing to spiritual forces that might mean the child harm. Many times, parents who have previously lost children (to death) select names intended to trick spirits into ignoring the present child. Similarly, sometimes, Africans confer names such as *Janvagha* (feeding death or enemies), *Chijohfom* (I live among enemies) or *Nkunda* (I love those who hate me) upon a child as a way of subtlety warning and alerting enemies that their ill intentions are known. Some of these names—*Makani* (death go ahead and finish us), for instance—exist as challenges.

Names also reflect an African tendency to describe matters exactly as they are. *Asya* (born during time of grief), *Jenmie* (people hate me when I am poor), and *Siwata* (born during time of conflict with another group) are examples.

I believe the use of African names must be guided by a love of and appreciation for African culture. However, it is not my duty to judge what may or may not be an appropriate name. *The African Book of Names* provides a diverse selection of names. The rest is up to readers.

Familiarity and Popularity

This collection includes African names (allowing for spelling variations) that readers would expect to see in any general African name book. Names such as:

◆ *Aisha*	Life.
◆ *Jamal*	Gift from God.
◆ *Jamilah*	Elegant.
◆ *Jelani*	Mighty one.
◆ *Kenya*	Artist.
◆ *Kenyatta*	Musician.
◆ *Kofi*	Born on Friday.
◆ *Kwame*	Born on Saturday.
◆ *Malik*	King, master, he who owns.
◆ *Omar*	The highest.
◆ *Sekou*	Fighter.

New York, with its multiethnic population, has quite a few popular African names included in the total population. The most popular African names in New York City during 2006 were:

FEMALES		MALES	
Name	# of Times Used	Name	# of Times Used
Nia	59	Amir	72
Aaliyah	49	Malik	50
Fatoumata	47	Omar	28
Sanaa	41	Omari	25
Imani	38	Khalil	19
Aminata	28	Jabari	17
Layla	23	Jamar	14
Ayanna	22	Ajani	13
Fatima	17	Sekou	13
Sade	17	Abdul	12
Akeelah	15	Amadou	12
Mariama	15	Jamir	11
Aisha	13	Moussa/Musa	11
Kenya	13	Ahmed	10
Amani	12	Ali	10
Amina	12	Jelani	10
Amira	12	Raheem	10
Zahara	11		
Nana	10		

In addition to common names, I also gravitate toward less familiar names. Thus, *The African Book of Names* presents a broad, unconditional selection of names.

Your Will Be Done:
What to Consider as You Choose a Name

The hunter's name is always connected
to the meat of the elephant.

—*Ghana*

arranged the African names alphabetically by subject, and then alphabetically within each subject. I developed a list of more than 100 themes from the names and then modified the list as needed to be more inclusive or exclusive. The Contents lists all themes/subject headings.

You may want to consider the following in choosing a name that an individual will carry as a form of identity for a lifetime.

Family Tree

You can consider names already in your immediate and extended family, as societies in Africa regularly honor the dead by naming the living after the dead. Think of those persons you already love and feel closely connected to. I encourage you to speak to relatives or close community to see if there are family names (not of African descent) that you can be adopt or adapt. For instance:

- Allison can become *Alisiri*.
- Angela can become *Angalia*.
- Amanda can become *Amandah*.
- Ethan can become *Etan*.
- Emma can become *Ema* or *Eme*.
- Gina or Jeanna can become *Jina* or *Ngina*.
- Hannah can become *Hana* or *Hanaa*.
- Harold or Harry can become *Hari*.
- Isabelle can become *Isabele* or *Isibili*
- Jason can become *Jasir*.
- Jeffrey can become *Jafari*.
- Janeen can become *Janaan*.
- Kenneth can become *Kenyatta*.
- Lisa can become *Lesa*.
- Malcolm can become *Malik*.
- Olivia can become *Olova*.
- Robert can become *Roblai*.
- Thomas or Tom can become *Thandiwe* or *Toma*.

You many consider community family names as well. Many Black people name their children after leaders such as Kwame Nkrumah, Winnie Mandela, and more. People are named after distinguished persons to instill the newly named individual with the desire to emulate the characteristics of the person whose name they wear. Are there special people or names you want to honor? When exploring family trees, also ask yourself the following questions:

- ◆ Is the chosen name harmonious with the family surname?
- ◆ Should the names of siblings sound similar?

Spirituality and Religion

Parents may affirm their spiritual or religious beliefs through the name they give to a child, as African-descended people are traditionally spiritual. According to Stewart (1996), names with broad spiritual meanings tend to work better than names that are so specific as to limit children who may outgrow certain beliefs or decide to follow different directions during their life cycle.

Origin

Naming is an opportunity to express ethnic pride. Some names are clearly associated with groups, languages, or backgrounds, so as you prepare to select names, consider cultures for which you have an affinity and therefore might like the name to represent.

Some names are African, but recognizable as non-African, including names such as *Ava, Ada, Brook, China, Fanta, Fela, Jon, Linda, Lola, Nina, Tina, Yoko, Yolanda,* and *Zina.* There are also English words that can easily be adapted into African names with similar sounds (and meanings). As examples:

Muziki means music
Suga means sugar
Rozi and *Iliroza* mean rose
Soja means soldier

When choosing, consider using African countries, lakes, rivers, or adapted English words as names. Or, take a word from an African language dictionary and use it as a name. There are millions of available African names from a myriad of sources.

Gender

Africans use a plethora of African names for both genders. Therefore, gender specificity (as far as it exists) need not limit name choice. According to legend, the great Zulu warrior Nozishada was given a typical female name because his father wanted a daughter. In my view, it is acceptable to ignore gender specificity, while still respecting and preserving African culture.

Across cultures, parents tend to find it easier to name females than males. Data suggests parents often want to give their girl children names to reflect femininity, love, and individuality. On the other hand, parents frequently want their male children to have names to convey a sense of masculinity, strength, and virility. Because, for instance, women can be strong and men can be loving, I have made a determined effort to supply an equitable number of female, male, and unisex names in all categories (where possible). I denoted gender-specific names with an F or M.

Number

In the United States, where I live, people usually have three names—a first, middle, and last name. A person is usually called by the first name. Only a few people know a person's middle name, and the middle name is used rather infrequently. The last name, or surname, is often the name of the father, reflecting a patriarchal system of naming.

How many names would you like the child, individual, or business to have? Traditional Africans do not confine themselves to three names—a first, middle, and last name. Many African people have four, five, and even six or seven names. Giving many names is more the rule than the exception and there is no end to the giving of names, so that a person may acquire a sizeable collection of names during a lifetime.

For example, the Congolese shot-blocking NBA player Dikembe Mutombo (the man with the largest shoe size in the NBA, along with Shaquille O'Neal) has seven names. Born in the Congo, Mutombo's full name is: *Dikembe Mutombo Mpolondo Mukamba* Jean Jacque *Wamutombo*. In order, these names are his uncle's name, his family surname, his grandfather's name, his nickname given by his village, his name given at birth, and his hometown village. Like Mutombo, I have seven African names.

Sound and Rhythm

Listen to the rhythm and the way a name sounds when said aloud. Say the name along with the other names that may precede or succeed the name. Consider whether the name sounds too similar to other names in the family or close community. Also ask yourself these questions:

◆ How does the name sound when you whisper it and when you say the name aloud?

◆ Do you want to only consider names starting with a certain letter of the alphabet?

◆ Are the desired numbers of syllables present in the name? (There are some who believe long first names go well with short last names and vice versa.)

◆ Does the name rhyme?

◆ Are there negative concepts or terms similar to, or rhyming with the name? (Parents especially need be aware of undesirable hidden rhymes or jokes associated with the names.)

◆ Will the sound of the name age well? (Some names sound nice for babies, but may not sound suitable for older adults.)

Once you have selected a name or names, say the name over and over again. You will probably not tire of hearing the right name.

Pronunciation

Write the selected name out and pronounce the name to see if the name rolls off the tongue. Some readers want names short and easy to pronounce. Other readers are attracted to polysyllabic names. The chosen name need not be easy to pronounce, but the name you select should begin to come naturally to you.

Spelling

Choosing the spelling of a name offers opportunities to avoid common spellings and also offers a way for a name to stand out. As an example, my rather popular name is traditionally spelled "Askari." I added an "h" to 1) help my Askhari stand apart from other Askaris; and 2) to contribute to the similarity between my own name and Khary, the birth name of my biological brother.

With spelling, be creative, cautious, and respectful. There is the possibility that a nontraditional spelling of a name will change the meaning or affect the ability of others to correctly pronounce the name. Work for phonetic harmony between the spelling and actual pronunciation of a name.

Popularity

Consider the popularity of a name during name selection. Choosing a trendy name may mean sitting in a room full of people with the same name. Also, popular names don't always age well. Certain names are "in" at times and "out" at others. You will want to pick a name that will grow with the person or entity being named.

To determine popularity of a specific name, visit the United States Social Security Administration's URL: http://www.ssa.gov/OACT/babynames/. The Social Security Administration's database is far from comprehensive and does not include most African names. The popularity of many names can be determined to some degree, however, by searching the database by name, state, or year. Again, for a variety of reasons, including home and other unrecorded births, most African names will not be present in the database.

Uniqueness

Many African societies name individuals according to rules and norms. These names tend to indicate the time the child was born or circumstances of birth. They may also locate individuals in space and time. This conventional naming system produces high-occurrence names. Many readers will be more comfortable with conventional, often used names, such as *Aisha, Shaka*, or *Kwame*.

And yet, some readers want uncommon or exotic-sounding names that stand out. Uncommon names emphasize individuality and convey identity.

Nicknames and Initials

According to the Baby Centre, four out of ten parents have nicknames for their children. Historically, people in Black communities use shortened names. Nickname usage is a direct survivor of continental African naming practices. Therefore, consider the following questions:

- ◆ What do initials spell out or represent?
- ◆ Is there the potential for undesirable letter combinations?
- ◆ Do shortened versions of the selected names sound good?
- ◆ Do you want all members of your family to have the same initials?

Meaning

Meanings give you opportunities to make significant statements. In the spirit of continental Africans, you may choose a name that represents day, time, or order of birth, location of birth, condition or circumstance of birth, or desired or physical characteristics.

You can choose themes to represent the entire family. In the name you give to an individual, express your life philosophy or the hopes, beliefs, joys, and worries of your community.

Alternately, the meaning of a non-African name can be used to find an African name. For example, the German name William means "protector," or "protection." Yet, instead of naming a child William, the child could be named *Arisi, Asim,* or *Kafil,* all of which mean "protector." Or, instead of the popular name, Hannah, meaning "grace of god," a child could be named *Nyasha*. Another popular non-African name is Matthew, meaning "gift of god." The African name *Noni* also means "gift from God."

Sometimes names reveal or confirm themselves to you during dreams, visions, or walks. Often, naming is simply a matter of listening. The name you are choosing should evoke positive or pleasant feelings and feel "right." I trust each reader finds at least one name that brings a smile, an "aha moment," or a sense of satisfaction.

By Their Fruits, You Will Know Them: Contextualizing Africa

Africa, my Africa, I have never known you
but my face is full of your blood.

—*David Diop*

 frica was an elder when Europe was in infancy. Africans managed socially responsible and civilized nations for thousands and thousands of years before the first European ever "wore a shoe or lived in a house with a window." Africans gave the world its first tool, machine, method of transportation, and organized society.

"What is Africa to me?" becomes a salient question in restoring our African names. Countee Cullen asked this question in his poem *Heritage*, drawing attention to our need to uncover truths that Africans brought to the Americas, truths that need to be retained or rediscovered.

Paul Kofi (spelled *Cuffee* at the time) was the first African to formally change his name in recorded United States history. A nineteenth-century Boston shipbuilder, he discarded his slaver's name, Slocum, in favor of his father's name, *Kofi*, a name from Ghana (meaning "born on Friday"). Well known for financing the repatriation of United States Blacks to Sierra Leone, Kofi wrote to the thousands of Africans left behind, "Be not fearful to come to Africa, which is your country by right. Africa, not America, is your country and your home."

For hundreds of years, Africans who involuntary immigrated to North America did not regard, nor immediately embrace, America as their home. Rather, as scholar W. E. B. Dubois wrote:

> From the fifteenth through the seventeenth centuries, the Africans imported to America regarded themselves as temporary settlers destined to return eventually to Africa. Their increasing revolts against the slave system, which culminated in the eighteenth century, showed a feeling of close kinship to the motherland and even well into the nineteenth century they called their organizations "African" as witness the "African Unions" of New York and Newport, and the African Churches of Philadelphia and New York, such as the African Methodist Episcopal Church.

The Rastafarian movement, emerging in Jamaica in the 1930s, also encouraged members to recognize Africa as home. This movement, now worldwide, is based on teachings of Marcus Garvey who is regarded as a prophet whose philosophy of race, culture, and politics helped to inspire a new worldview in Africa and the African diaspora. Rastafarians rejected the European culture as brainwashing while in captivity, and embraced the African culture that was taken from them on the slave ships and the plantations. Ethiopian names (such as *Makonnen* or *Yeshiemebet*) tend to be popular in Rastafarian communities, but Rastafarians are generally eclectic in choosing African names.

The words "Africa" and "African" signify tremendous cultural, physical, political, social, and human variety. Africa, with so many countries, languages, and ethnic groups, is a mix of wealth and poverty; technology and tradition; health and sickness; peace and conflict; and potential and actual. Africa, the second largest continent, has contributed knowledge, culture, and people to every other continent in the known world. When discussing the importance of Africa, W. E. B. Dubois wrote:

> Always Africa is giving us something new: On its black bosom arose one of the earliest, if not the earliest, of self-protecting civilizations, and grew so mightily that it still furnishes superlatives to thinking and speaking men. Out of its dark and more remote forest vastnesses came, if we may credit many recent scientists, the first welding of iron, and we know that agriculture and trade flourished there when Europe was a wilderness.

Unquestionably, Africa is culturally rich and relevant. *The African Book of Names* vibrates with the culture of Africa and encourages Blacks in America and the diaspora to recover and reconstruct their African heritage and affirm their African origins by selecting African names. Please accept the invitation to do so by turning the page.

PART 2

Let My People Go: Authentic African Names

African Names Listed Alphabetically by Theme

A cat goes to a monastery, but still remains a cat.
—*Congo*

☥ Ability, Skill, and Talent

If we put a hammer in every person's hand,
could they all become blacksmiths? —*Ghana*

Name	Pronunciation	Meaning	Origin	Gender
AKILI	ah-KEE-lee	Competent, capable.	Kenya, Tanzania (Kiswahili)	M
ALIYINZA	ah-lee-yeen-zah	She will be able to handle it.	Uganda (Soga)	F
BEJIYA	beh-JEE-yah	I never do anything beyond me.	Nigeria (Ishan)	
BINGWA	BEHNG-wah	Competent, capable.	Kenya, Tanzania	
CHIJIOKE	CHEE-jee-oh-keh	God given talent.	Nigeria (Igbo)	M
DLULU	dhh-LOOH-lah	Surpass; go beyond.	Azania	M
DUNA	doo-nah	He will be able to do everything when he grows up.	Cameroon (Mubako)	M
EREVU	EH-reh-voo	Clever, talented.	Kenya, Tanzania (Kiswahili)	
ETUDAYE	eh-too-dah-yeh	Do not underestimate or belittle the ability of a man until you have experienced him.	Nigeria (Igarra)	M
FARISI	fah-REE-see	Competent, capable.	Kenya, Tanzania	

Name	Pronunciation	Meaning	Origin	Gender
IYA	EE-yah	Can do.	West Africa (Hausa)	
JALIA	jah-lee-ah	To grant; enable, empower.	Kiswahili	F
KADIRI	KAH-dee-ree	Capable.	Kenya, Tanzania (Kiswahili)	M
KANKO	KAHN-koh	You are able to do.	Nigeria (Hausa)	M
KUWENZA	KOO-weh-zah	Very capable.	East Africa (Kiswahili)	M
KUWEZA	koo-WEH-zah	Very capable.	Kenya, Tanzania	
LUMUMBA	loo-moom-bah	One who is gifted.	DRC	M
MAHIRI	mah-hee-ree	Skillful; clever.	Kenya, Tanzania	
MAKIRI	mah-KEE-ree	Skillful; clever.	Kiswahili	M
MOMA	mmoh-mah	Proficient.	Uganda (Ganda)	M
MSANAA	m-SAH-nah	A skillful man.	Kenya, Tanzania	M
NAHWEDGA	nah-WEHD-gah	Keep within your limits.	Cameroon (Mubako)	F
NATASA	NAH-tah-sah	Skillful.	East Africa (Kiswahili)	F
NGOTI	ngoh-tee	The expert.	Azania	M
NONGOTI	nohn-GOH-tee	The expert.	Azania	F
SANIFU	sah-NEE-foo	To compose.	Kiswahili	
SANII	sah-NEE-ee	To make with skill..	Kiswahili	
TABIA	tah-BEE-ah	Talents.	East Africa (Kiswahili)	F
TAHA	TAH-hah	Skillful.	East Africa (Kiswahili)	M
TENDAJI	TEHN-dah-jee	Makes things happen.	Kenya, Tanzania (Kiswahili)	M
UJAZO	oo-JAH-zoh	Capacity.	Kiswahili	
ZOTSHOLO	zoht-SHOH-loh	Expert, a skilled person.	Azania (Xhosa)	

Absence and Departure

Fruit falls where there are no gatherers. —Tanzania

Name	Pronunciation	Meaning	Origin	Gender
BOAHIN MAA	bwa-HEEN-mah	One who has left her own community; expatriate.	Ghana (Ewe)	F
BOKUNA	boh-koon-nah	You have lost your brother or sister.	Cameroon (Mubako)	F
CHAROVA	tch-ah-roh-vah	The one who has disappeared.	Zimbabwe, Mozambique, Zambia (Shona)	M
CHATULUKA	chah-too-LOO-kah	A departure.	Malawi (Ngoni)	M
CHIPITA	chee-pee-tah	It has gone.	Malawi (Ngoni)	M
DAHKOBA	dah-koh-bah	You cannot leave your bed.	Cameroon (Mubako)	M
DIIYGANE	dee-YAH-neh	Exiled, the little exile.	Azania (Zulu)	
HAAJAR	HAH-jahr	He abandoned.	North Africa (Arabic)	M
KASIYA	kah-SEE-yah	Departure.	Malawi (Ngoni)	M
KONO	KOH-noh	Left behind.	Sierra Leone (Mandinka)	M
KUNLEMIA	koon-LEH-mee-ah	My brothers have abandoned me.	Cameroon (Mubako)	F
KUREMBERA	koo-rehm-BEH-rah	To disappear slowly in the horizon.	Rwanda, Burundi (Kinyarwanda, Kirundi)	
KWENDE	KWEHN-deh	Let's go.	Malawi (Ngoni)	M
LEHKUNA	leh-KOO-nah	You have abandoned your brothers and sisters.	Cameroon (Mubako)	F
LIKIZO	lee-KEE-zoh	Vacation; leave.	Kiswahili	
MALEKANO	mah-leh-KAH-noh	To part from one another.	Zambia (Bemba)	
MALOMO	MAH-loh-moh	Don't go away any more.	Nigeria (Yoruba)	
MAREHEMU	mah-reh-HEH-moo	The departed.	Kiswahili	

Name	Pronunciation	Meaning	Origin	Gender
MASAMBA	mah-SAHM-bah	Leave.	Malawi (Yao)	M
OJEALO	oh-jeh-AH-loh	He who goes and must return.	Nigeria (Igbo)	M
SEMUGENZI	sseh-moo-gehn-zee	The departed.	Uganda (Ganda)	M
TALIIWO	tah-lee-woh	He is not there.	Uganda (Ganda, Soga)	M
TSALANI	tsah-LAH-nee	Goodbye.	Malawi (Ngoni)	M
VALEMIA	vah-leh-MEE-ah	She has died and left me alone.	Cameroon (Mubako)	F
ZIZIMIA	zee-zee-MEE-ah	To sink; disappear.	Kiswahili	

Abundance and Prosperity

The owner of a cheerful heart will find joy ever increasing. —Kenya

Name	Pronunciation	Meaning	Origin	Gender
ADESUWA	ah-deh-SOO-wah	In the center of prosperity.	Nigeria (Edo)	F
AGAMA	ah-GAHM-mah	More than, or too much.	Nigeria (Eleme)	
AHONJA	ah-HOHN-jah	Prosperity.	West Africa	
AINEBYONA	ah-ee-neh-bjoh-oh-nah	Endowed with everything.	Uganda (Kiga, Nyankore)	
BANJI	BAHN-jee	Many.	Zambia (Tonga)	
BANNI	bah-nee	Too much something.	Cameroon (Mubako)	
BANYINA	bah-yeen-ah	Too much something.	Cameroon (Mubako)	F
BASI	BAH-see	Enough—that will do!	Kiswahili	
BINGI	bee-ngee	They are many.	Uganda (Ganda, Kiga, Nyankore)	M
DOLO	DOH-loh	Great multitude, abundance.	Azania (Xhosa)	

Name	Pronunciation	Meaning	Origin	Gender
ENEZEZELO	eh-neh-zeh-ZEH-loh	Addition.	Azania (Zulu)	
ENYO	EHN-yoh	Enough children.	West Africa	
FALALA	fah-LAH-la	Born into abundance.	Ghana (Fulani)	F
FANAKA	fah-nah-KAH	Prosperity.	Kenya, Tanzania (Kiswahili)	F
FANIKIA	fah-NEE-kee-ah	Prosperity.	Kenya, Tanzania (Kiswahili)	F
GHANIMA	GAH-nee-mah	Abundance, plenty.	Kenya, Tanzania (Kiswahili)	
JORE	joh-reh	Full.	Sudan (Bari)	F
KANYA	kah-ndjh-ah	An abundance.	Uganda (Ganda)	M
KEHFUN	KEH-foon	One who has brought prosperity.	Cameroon (Mubako)	M
KIZO	KEE-zoh	Abundant, plentiful.	Kenya, Tanzania	
KUTOSHA	koo-TOH-shah	Enough!	Kiswahili	
LOLO	LOH-loh	Prosperity.	Nigeria	
MUNANIRE	moo-nah-nee-REH	Has more than his share.	Uganda (Luganda)	M
MUNGI	moon-gee	One that has a lot.	Uganda (Ganda)	M
NAFAIKA	nah-fah-EE-kah	Prosperity.	Kenya, Tanzania	
NAFISIKA	nah-fee-SEE-kah	One who is well-off.	Kenya, Tanzania	
NAKI MWERO	nah-tch-ee-mweh-eh-roh	An abundance.	Uganda	
NENGI	NEHN-gee	Plentiful, abundant.	Zimbabwe	
NINGI	NEEN-gee	Abundant, plentiful.	Azania	
NOGOMO	noh-goh-moh	One who is prosperous.	Central Africa	M
NONDYEBO	non-dyeh-boh	Mother of plenty.	Azania (Xhosa)	F
NUFAIKA	noo-fah-EE-kah	Prosperity.	Kenya, Tanzania	
OKORO	oh-KOH-roh	The boy born in the midst of plenty.	Nigeria (Ishan)	M

Name	Pronunciation	Meaning	Origin	Gender
OLONA	oh-LOH-nah	The most.	Azania (Xhosa)	
OMOZUWA	oh-moh-ZOO-wah	A child chooses prosperity.	Nigeria (Edo)	M
ONGEZA	ohn-GEH-zah	To increase the numbers.	Azania (Zulu)	
SHIBA	SHEE-bah	Abundance; satiated.	Kiswahili	F
SOYINI	soh-YEE-nee	Richly endowed.	West Africa	F
TELE	TEH-leh	In abundance.	Kiswahili	
UBUNENGI	oo-boo-NEHN-gee	Abundant, plentiful.	Zimbabwe	
UBUNINZI	oo-boo-NEEN-zee	Abundant, plentiful.	Azania	
UFANISI	oo-fah-NEE-see	Prosperity.	Kenya, Tanzania	
UJAZI	oo-JAH-zee	Abundance.	Kiswahili	
UNGI	OON-gee	Plentiful, to have a multitude.	Kiswahili	
UNWANA	oon-WAH-nah	Another one.	Southern Africa (Tsonga)	
USITAWI	oo-see-TAH-wee	Prosperity.	Kiswahili	
UWANDI	oo-WAHN-dee	Plentiful, abundant.	Zimbabwe	
VAMILE	vah-MEE-leh	Abundant, plentiful.	Azania	
WINGI	WEEN-gee	Abundance.	Kiswahili	
WOTEBBA	woh-TEH-bah	I have had enough.	Cameroon (Mubako)	F
YUSUF	yoo-SOOF	He shall add to his powers.	East Africa (Kiswahili)	M
ZAID	ZAH-eed	Abundance.	Kiswahili	M
ZANDILE	zahn-DEE-leh	They have multiplied.	Azania (Zulu)	F
ZANI	zah-nee	They are enough.	Azania (Xhosa)	M
ZUNA	ZOO-nah	Abundance and riches.	Central Africa	
ZUWA	ZOO-wah	A child chooses prosperity.	Nigeria (Edo)	M

Adoration and Admiration

The way to the beloved is not thorny. —Cameroon

Name	Pronunciation	Meaning	Origin	Gender
ABIBA	ah-bee-bah	Beloved.	DRC (Bembe)	F
ALAKE	ah-lah-KEH	One to be petted, made much of.	Nigeria (Yoruba)	F
ALI	ah-LEE	Exalted.	East Africa (Kiswahili)	M
ALIYA	ah-lee-AH	Exalted.	East Africa (Kiswahili)	F
AMADIKA	ah-mah-DEE-kah	Beloved one.	Zimbabwe	F
AMONKE	ah-mohn-KEH	To know her is to pet her.	Nigeria (Yoruba)	F
AZIZI	ah-ZEE-zee	Adored, cherished child.	East Africa (Kiswahili)	M
BUKIWE	boo-kee-weh	Adorable.	Azania (Xhosa)	F
CHICHA	CHEE-chah	Beloved.	West Africa	M
DAUDI	dah-OO-dee	Beloved one.	East Africa (Kiswahili)	M
DAWUD	dah-OOD	Beloved.	North Africa (Arabic)	M
FATOU	FAH-too	Beloved by all.	West Africa	F
HABIBU	hah-BEE-boo	Beloved.	Kenya, Tanzania	
HALIFI	hah-LEE-fee	Beloved one.	Kenya, Tanzania	
IBADA	ee-BAH-dah	The adored one.	Kiswahili	
KARISA	kah-REE-sah	To be impressive; admirable.	Zimbabwe (Ndebele)	M
KENNA	kehn-nah	Pride; to be admired.	Azania (Xhosa)	F
KITOGA	kee-toh-gah	Beloved child of the family.	DRC (Rega)	M
LUNGILE	loon-GEE-leh	The admirable one.	Azania	
MUDIWA	moo-DEE-wah	Beloved.	Zimbabwe (Shona)	F
NALO	nah-loh	Lovable, beloved daughter.	West Africa	F
NOLUNGILE	noh-loon-GEE-leh	The admirable one.	Azania	F

Name	Pronunciation	Meaning	Origin	Gender
OBIOHA	oh-bee-OH-ah	Dear to his people.	Nigeria (Igbo)	M
RAISA	rah-EE-sah	Exalted.	East Africa (Kiswahili)	F
THANDIWE	tahn-DEE-weh	Beloved.	Azania (Zulu)	M

Advice and Counsel

Even the clever one is advised. —Kenya

Name	Pronunciation	Meaning	Origin	Gender
BALOZI	bah-LOH-zee	Consul, commissioner.	Kiswahili	
BAMBA	BAHM-bah	Counsel.	Kiswahili	
BARAB WIRIZA	bah-rahb-wee-REE-zah	They give advice.	Rwanda, Burundi (Kinyarwanda, Kirundi)	
DIWANI	dee-WAH-nee	A councilor.	Kiswahili	
ELETSA	eh-LEHT-sah	Advisor, thinker.	Southern Africa (Tsonga)	
ELULEKI	eh-loo-LEH-kee	Counselor, advisor.	Azania (Zulu)	
JINJINA	jeen-JEEN-nah	Consider other's advice.	West Africa (Hausa)	
MLULEKI	m-loo-LEH-kee	The advisor.	Azania	M
MOELETSI	moh-eh-leh-tsee	Counselor.	Azania (Sotho)	M
MUTESA	moo-teh-eh-sah	A counselor.	Uganda (Ganda)	M
MUTIRA	MOH-tee-rah	Counselor or advisor.	Kenya (Agikuyu)	M
NOMLULEKI	nohm-loo-leh-kee	The advisor.	Azania	F
NTIGINAMA	n-tee-geen-ah-mah	God doesn't ask for advice.	Rwanda, Burundi (Kinyarwanda, Kirundi)	
RASHIDI	rah-SHEE-dee	Of good council.	East Africa (Kiswahili)	M
SHAURI	shah-OO-ree	Advice.	East Africa (Kiswahili)	M

Africa and Africans

If it only depended on those who went to Europe,
Africa would have been destroyed long ago. —Ghana

Name	Pronunciation	Meaning	Origin	Gender
ABIDU	ah-BEE-doo	Very Black at birth.	Nigeria (Ishan)	
BILAL	bee-LAHL	A Black man.	North Africa (Arabic)	M
CHAGO	CHAH-goh	One who is proud of his African traditional attire.	East Africa	M
CHEUSI	cheh-OO-zee	The dark one.	Africa	F
CHIFITA	chee-FEE-tah	A person dark in complexion.	Zambia (Bemba)	
CHOKWE	CHOHK-weh	Ethnic group of Central Africa, city in southern Mozambique.	Central Africa	
EBI	EH-bee	Dark.	Nigeria (Bini)	
FULANI	foo-LAH-nee	Traditionally nomadic group of West Africa.	West Africa	
IZIBILI	ee-zee-BEE-lee	Very Black child.	Nigeria (Ishan)	
JAWN	JAHWN	Black.	North Africa (Arabic)	M
JUWAYN	joo-wahn	Black.	North Africa (Arabic)	F
MORWANA	mohr-wah-nah	Bushman.	Azania (Sotho)	
MUIRU	MOO-ee-roo	Black one.	Kenya (Agikuyu)	M
MWAA FRIKA	mwah-ah-FREE-kah	Person of African descent.	East Africa	M
NJIRU	njee-ROO	Black one.	Kenya (Agikuyu)	M
NONTZIKIZI	nohnt-zee-KEE-zee	Female baby with a dark complexion.	Azania (Xhosa)	F
NYOKABI	NYOH-kah-bee	Of the Maasai people.	Kenya (Agikuyu)	F

Name	Pronunciation	Meaning	Origin	Gender
TIKUR	tee-koor	Black.	Ethiopia	
WAMUIRU	wah-moh-ee-roh	Dark-skinned beauty.	Kenya (Agikuyu)	F
WOKABI	WOH-kah-bee	She is of the Maasai.	Kenya (Agikuyu)	F

Age, Elders, and Experience

Every time an old man dies, it is as if a library has burnt down. —*West Africa*

Name	Pronunciation	Meaning	Origin	Gender
ANTO	AHN-toh	This one has missed the good old days.	Ghana	
ETOMI	eh-TOH-mee	We have lived long to witness.	Nigeria (Ishan)	
GUGILE	goo-GEE-leh	The aging one.	Azania	M
KEBBA	KEHB-bah	Old man.	Gambia	M
KIZEE	KEE-zeh-eh	Old woman.	Kenya	F
MAALIK	MAH-leek	Experience.	East Africa (Kiswahili)	M
MAARIFA	mah-REE-fah	Experience.	Kiswahili	
MADALA	mah-DAH-lah	The elder.	Azania (Xhosa)	M
MATALA	mah-TAH-lah	The old one.	Lesotho (South Sotho)	
MUKADDE	moo-kahd-deh	Elder, parent, old person.	Uganda (Ganda)	
MUKULU	moo-koo-loo	Adult, elder, grown-up.	Uganda (Ganda)	
MUKURU	moo-koo-roo	Elder; important person.	Burundi, Rwanda	
MUSUKEBBA	moo-soo-KEHB-bah	Senior wife; elderly woman.	Gambia	F
MZEE	m-zeh	Sir; elder; old man.	Kenya, Tanzania (Kiswahili)	M
NOGUGILE	noh-goo-gee-leh	The aging one.	Azania	F

Name	Pronunciation	Meaning	Origin	Gender
UJUZI	oo-JOO-zee	Experience.	Kiswahili	
UZEE	OO-zee	Old age.	Kiswahili	
WAIRA	wah-ee-rah	One who is of old times.	Uganda (Soga)	M

Air, Breath, and Wind

Wind is never caught by hand. —Lesotho

Name	Pronunciation	Meaning	Origin	Gender
ANGA	AHN-gah	Air, atmosphere.	Kiswahili	
KADA	KAH-dah	Blow of slight breeze.	West Africa (Hausa)	
KASKAZI	kahs-KAH-zee	North wind.	Kiswahili	
KIIMA	KEE-mah	To inhale.	Gambia (Mandinka)	
MAPHEFO		A child born on a windy day.	Azania (Nguni)	
MARASHI	mah-rah-shee	Sweet air, perfume.	Kenya, Tanzania	
MATILAI	mah-tee-lah-ee	East wind.	Kiswahili	
MPEPHO	MPEH-poh	A breath of fresh air; refreshing.	Azania (Xhosa)	M
MUKKA	mook-kah	Breath, air which one breathes.	Uganda (Ganda)	M
MWELA	MWEH-lah	Wind; air.	Zambia (Bemba)	
NASIIM	NAH-seem	Fresh air.	East Africa (Kiswahili)	F
NUMFASHI	noo-fah-shee	Breath.	West Africa (Hausa)	
NYALLA	n-YAH-lah	Wind or breeze.	Cameroon (Mubako)	M
NYAMIYAGA	n-YAHM-ee-yah-gah	Of winds.	Rwanda, Burundi (Kinyarwanda, Kirundi)	
SEKIZIMU	sseh-tch-e-zee-moo	The whirlwind.	Uganda (Ganda)	M
SEMPEWO	ssehm-peh-woh	Air; wind; breeze.	Uganda (Ganda)	M

Name	Pronunciation	Meaning	Origin	Gender
UME	OO-meh	Breath.	Nigeria (Igbo)	M
VUNGUZA	voon-GOO-zah	Strong wind.	Azania (Zulu)	

Alertness and Observation

Seeing excels hearing. —West Africa

Name	Pronunciation	Meaning	Origin	Gender
AMSHA	AHM-shah	To awaken someone.	Kiswahili	
ANGALENI	ahn-gah-LEH-nee	Beware, look out!	Namibia (Ovambo)	
ANGALIA	ahn-gah-LEE-ah	To observe, to watch.	Kiswahili	
ANGAZA	ahn-GAH-zah	To keep one's eyes open.	Kiswahili	
BANDORA	bahn-DOH-rah	They watch me.	Rwanda, Burundi (Kinyarwanda, Kirundi)	M
BANNI	BAHN-nee	We are watching to see what happens.	Cameroon (Mungaka)	
BANNIJEYE	bahn-nee-JEH-yeh	We are watching to see what happens.	Cameroon (Mungaka)	
BEHGHA	beh-gah	I have seen.	Cameroon (Mubako)	M
CACA	KAH-kah	Plainly seen or heard.	Azania (Xhosa)	
ELELA	eh-LEH-lah	To see clearly.	Southern Africa (Tsonga)	
HAFIDHA	HAH-fee-dah	Mindful.	East Africa (Kiswahili)	F
HAMU	HAH-moo	Be alert.	Kiswahili	
JASISI	jah-SEE-see	To spy.	Kiswahili	
JASUSI	jah-SOO-see	Spy.	Kiswahili	
JONGIWE	john-GEE-weh	Look at me.	Azania (Xhosa)	
KALIIMI	kah-lee-mee	A lookout; spy.	Uganda (Ganda)	M
KALUNDI	kah-loon-dee	Tended to; kept in view.	Uganda (Ganda)	M

Name	Pronunciation	Meaning	Origin	Gender
KAMPIBE	kahm-PEE-beh	Go and look.	Malawi (Ngoni)	M
KATASSI	kah-tahs-see	Little scout; little spy.	Uganda (Ganda)	F
KESHA	KEH-shah	To stay awake; keep watch.	Kiswahili	
KIMACHO	KEE-mah-choh	Observant; alert.	Kenya, Tanzania (Kiswahili)	F
KIONI	KEE-OH-nee	She who sees.	Kenya (Agikuyu)	F
KOROSI	koh-roh-see	To observe.	Gambia (Mandinka)	
KUMBE	KOOM-beh	Behold!	Kiswahili	
KURAMU KAHO	koo-rah-moo-KAH-oh	To wake up.	Rwanda, Burundi (Kinyarwanda, Kirundi)	
KURARAMA	koo-rah-RAH-mah	To look up.	Rwanda, Burundi (Kinyarwanda, Kirundi)	
LINGIRA	leen-gee-rah	Spy; look out for.	Uganda (Soga)	M
MASO MAKALI	mah-soh-mah-KAH-lee	Sharp eyes.	Tanzania (Nyakyusa)	M
MUKESSI	moo-kehs-see	Spy.	Uganda (Ganda)	M
MUSAMBA	moo-sahm-bah	Eye opener.	DRC (Rega)	M
NAKA	NAH-kah	Take notice.	Azania (Zulu)	
NAMU JULIRWA	nah-moo-joo-lee-rwah	Witness; martyr.	Uganda (Ganda)	
NDAHNYO	n-dahn-yoh	I shall see.	Cameroon (Mungaka)	M
NOVUKILE	noh-voo-kee-leh	The alert one.	Azania	F
NUBIA	noo-bee-ah	I have seen it.	Cameroon (Mubako)	
ONANI	oh-NAH-nee	Look.	Malawi (Ngoni)	M
PAKI	PAH-kee	Witness, observer, one who watches.	Azania (Xhosa)	M
PEPUKAYI	peh-poo-KAH-yee	Wake up.	Zimbabwe (Shona)	M
RAHEEDA	rah-HEE-dah	Sagacious, discerning.	North Africa (Arabic)	

Name	Pronunciation	Meaning	Origin	Gender
RANA	RAH-nah	Watch over, wonder.	North Africa (Arabic)	
RANYA	RAHN-yah	To observe, look upon.	North Africa (Arabic)	
SHAHIDI	shah-HEE-dee	Witness or eyewitness.	Africa	M
SIJAONA	SEE-jah-oh-nah	I have not seen.	East Africa (Kiswahili)	F
TACUMA	tah-coo-mah	Alert.	DRC	M
TALENI	tah-LEH-nee	Look, observe!	Namibia (Ovambo)	
TAONA	tah-oh-nah	We have seen.	Zimbabwe, Mozambique, Zambia (Shona)	
TAYE	TAH-yeh	Has seen.	Ethiopia	M
TIONE	tee-OH-neh	Let us see.	Malawi	
UUKA	oo-OO-kah	Wake up; arise.	Azania (Xhosa)	
VUKANI	voo-KAH-nee	Wake up!	Azania	M
VUSA	VOO-sah	To awaken.	Azania (Zulu)	

Ancestors and Angels

A tree cannot stand without roots. —DRC

Name	Pronunciation	Meaning	Origin	Gender
AAKHUTERA	ah-ah-koo-TEH-rah	The ancestor of God is my guide.	Egypt/Khamit	
ABSAMA	ahb-sah-mah	Having good ancestors.	Somalia	
BABU	bah-BOO	Ancestor.	Kiswahili	
BADIMO	bah-DEE-moh	Ancestral spirits.	Azania (North Sotho)	
DARWESHI	dahr-WEH-shee	Saintly.	East Africa (Kiswahili)	M
IBAORISHA	ee-bah-oh-REE-shah	I respect the deified ancestors.	Nigeria (Yoruba)	
IBARISHA	ee-bah-REE-shah	I respect the ancestors.	Nigeria (Yoruba)	

Name	Pronunciation	Meaning	Origin	Gender
INGELOSI	eeng-eh-loh-see	Angel.	Azania	
JIBRI	JEE-bree	Angel of Allah.	North Africa (Arabic)	
MALAIKA	mah-lah-EE-kah	Angel.	Kenya, Tanzania	
MKALE	m-KAH-leh	An ancestor.	Kiswahili	
MZIMU	m-ZEE-moo	Spirit of dead person.	Kiswahili	

Anger

Anger and madness are brothers. —Africa

Name	Pronunciation	Meaning	Origin	Gender
CHIWANDA	chee-WAHN-dah	Mad.	Malawi (Yao)	M
DIRIYE	dee-ree-yeh	Hot-headed; impetuous.	Somalia	
GHADHABU	gahd-HAH-boo	Anger.	Kiswahili	
HASIRA	hah-SEE-rah	Anger.	Kiswahili	
IWEGBOLU	ee-wehg-boh-loo	May anger cease.	Nigeria	
KASIRANI	kah-see-RAH-nee	Anger.	Kiswahili	
KASIRIKA	kah-see-REE-kah	To be angry.	Kiswahili	
NDAKAZA	N-dah-KAH-zah	I anger.	Rwanda, Burundi (Kinyarwanda, Kirundi)	M
RAAIWE	rah-ah-ee-weh	Give up anger.	Nigeria (Igbo)	
SEKALALA	seh-kah-lah-lah	One that becomes angry.	Uganda (Ganda)	M
SESHAFI	seh-SHAH-fee	Angry woman.	Egypt/Khamit	F

Animals and Creatures

The failure to travel in groups habit
of snakes makes it easy for humans
to kill them with machetes. —West Africa

Name	Pronunciation	Meaning	Origin	Gender
AKASI	ah-KAH-see	Horse.	Nigeria (Ishan)	
ASAD	AH-sahd	Lion; strong.	North Africa (Arabic)	M
AVU	AH-voo	Dove.	Azania (Xhosa)	
AZINZA	ah-ZEEN-zah	Mermaid.	Togo (Mina)	
BAKAME	bah-KAH-meh	Rabbit.	Rwanda, Burundi (Kinyarwanda, Kirundi)	M
BATHA	BAH-tah	Spider's web.	Azania (Xhosa)	
BATTE	bah-teh	Elephant.	Uganda (Luganda)	M
BAUNA	bah-oo-nah	Buffalo.	West Africa (Hausa)	
BETOTO	beh-TOH-toh	Owl.	Azania (Sotho)	
BHADI	BHAH-dee	Springbuck, butterfly.	Azania (Xhosa)	
BHODLA	bohd-lah	Roar like a lion.	Azania (Zulu)	
BUIBUI	bwi-bwi	Spider.	Kiswahili	
CHANDU	CHAHN-doo	Octopus.	Kiswahili	
COYAH	koh-yah	Snake.	Guinea	
DANGALA	dahn-GAH-lah	Baboon.	Azania (Zulu)	
DLULAMITHI	dhh-LOOH-lah-mee-tee	Giraffe (above the trees).	Azania (Zulu)	
DUDU	DOO-doo	Insect.	Kiswahili	
DUMCULU	doom-koo-loo	Black wasp.	Azania (Xhosa)	
EBU	EE-boo	Spider's web.	Azania (Nguni)	
FARASHUU	FAH-rah-shoo	Butterfly.	Kenya, Tanzania (Kiswahili)	F
FEZELA	feh-ZEH-lah	Scorpion.	Azania (Nguni)	
FINYEZI	feen-YEH-zee	Firefly.	Azania (Zulu)	
FIRIFIROO	fee-ree-fee-roh	Butterfly.	Gambia (Mandinka)	
FUDU	FOO-doo	Tortoise.	Azania (Zulu)	

Name	Pronunciation	Meaning	Origin	Gender
GAMKA	GAHM-kah	Lions.	Azania (Khoikhoin)	
GASARASI	gah-sah-rah-see	Antelope.	Rwanda, Burundi, DRC (Huti, Tutsi, Twa)	M
GATARE	gah-tah-reh	Small lion.	Rwanda, Burundi, DRC (Huti, Tutsi, Twa)	M
GENDE	GEHN-deh	Queen of an ant community.	Azania (Xhosa)	F
GIWA	GEE-wah	Elephant.	West Africa (Hausa)	
GOLELA	goh-leh-lah	Animals gathering place.	Azania (Swazi)	
GOYA	goh-yah	Wild cat.	Southern Africa (Tsonga)	
GUNJU	GOON-joo	Wild cat.	Uganda (Ganda)	
HAYDARA	hah-ee-DAH-rah	Lioness; strength.	North Africa (Arabic)	F
HORERA	hoh-REH-rah	Kitten.	Kiswahili	F
IBUBESI	ee-boo-BEH-see	Lion.	Azania (Zulu)	M
IMBUZI	eem-BOO-zee	Cat.	Azania (Nguni)	
IMFEZI	ee-FEH-zee	Cobra.	West Africa (Yoruba)	
IMPISI	eem-PEE-see	Hyena.	Azania (Zulu)	
INAMA	ee-NAH-mah	Wild animals.	Zambia (Bemba)	
INGWE	eeng-weh	Leopard.	Azania (Zulu)	
JATOO	JAH-too	Lion.	Gambia (Mandinka)	M
JEKAMANZI	jeh-kah-MAHN-zee	Dragonfly.	Azania (Nguni)	
JIKE	JEE-keh	Female animal.	Kiswahili	
KADA	KAH-dah	Crocodile.	West Africa (Hausa)	
KAKEMBO	kah-kehm-boh	Small monkey.	Uganda (Ganda)	M
KAMBUJI	kahm-BOO-jee	Goat.	Malawi (Ngoni)	M
KAMHUKA	kahm-hoo-kah	Little animal.	Zimbabwe, Mozambique, Zambia (Shona)	M
KAMPOGO	kahm-poh-goh	Antelope.	Rwanda, Burundi, DRC (Huti, Tutsi, Twa)	F

Name	Pronunciation	Meaning	Origin	Gender
KANONI	kah-NOH-nee	Little bird.	Tanzania (Ulaya)	F
KANYONI	kah-ndjh-oh-nee	A small bird.	Rwanda, Burundi, DRC (Huti, Tutsi, Twa)	
KASUKU	kah-SOO-koo	Parrot.	Kiswahili	
KATSE	KAHT-seh	Cat.	Azania (North Sotho)	
KHOLA	KOH-lah	Deer.	Kiswahili	F
KHOLWASI	khol-WAH-see	Flamingo.	Malawi (Ngoni)	
KINYONGA	keen-YOHN-gah	Chameleon.	Kiswahili	
KIPANGA	KEE-pahn-gah	Falcon.	East Africa (Kiswahili)	M
KOLA	KOH-lah	Snail.	Tanzania	
KOMONDO	kah-mohn-doh	Small tiger.	Rwanda, Burundi, DRC (Huti, Tutsi, Twa)	F
KOMUNTALE	koo-moon-tah-leh	Born in lion country.	Uganda (Rutooro)	F
KWENA	KWEH-nah	Crocodile.	Azania (North Sotho)	
LENCHO	LEHN-choh	Lion.	Ethiopia, Kenya (Oromo)	M
LISIMBA	lee-SEEM-bah	Lion.	Malawi (Yao)	M
LUBAYA	loo-BAH-yah	Young lioness.	Kiswahili	F
LUVEVE	loo-veh-veh	Moves like a butterfly from place to place.	Azania (Xhosa)	
MACHUI	mah-CHOO-ee	Like a leopard.	Kiswahili	
MAUDUA	mah-oo-doo-ah	Spider's web.	Azania (Sotho)	
MBOGO	m-BOH-goh	Buffalo.	Kenya (Agikuyu)	M
MSAMAKI	m-sah-MAH-kee	Like a fish.	Tanzania (Kiswahili)	M
MUSOTA	moo-soh-tah	Snake.	Uganda (Ganda)	M
MUTENITENI	moo-TEH-nee-TEH-nee	Firefly.	DRC	F

Name	Pronunciation	Meaning	Origin	Gender
NADJAMBA	nahd-JAHM-bah	Elephant; fearless person.	Namibia (Ovambo)	
NAMA	NAH-mah	Lion.	Zambia (Bemba)	
NAMBOGO	nahm-boh-goh	The buffalo.	Uganda (Ganda)	F
NANGOLO	nahn-GOH-loh	Zebra.	Namibia (Ovambo)	
NANTALE	nah-ntah-leh	Lioness.	Uganda (Luganda)	F
NDEGI	NDEH-gee	Bird.	Kiswahili	
NDEMBO	n-DEHM-boh	Elephant.	Malawi (Yao)	M
NDIWA	NDEE-wah	Dove.	Kiswahili	
NDLOVU	n-DLOH-voo	Elephant.	Azania (Nguni)	
NGO	n-GOH	Leopard.	Zambia (Bemba)	
NGOMBE	n-GOHM-beh	Cow.	Malawi (Yao)	M
NGONGA	n-gahn-gah	Eagle.	Angola (Ovimbundu)	M
NGUNDA	n-GOOD-dah	Dove.	Malawi (Yao)	M
NGUNI	n-GOON-nee	Honey bird.	Zambia (Bemba)	
NJAGI	n-JAH-gee	Zebra.	Kenya	
NJAU	n-jow	Young bull.	Kenya (Agikuyu)	M
NJE	n-JEH	Lion, courage.	Cameroon (Bassa)	
NJOFU	ndjh-oh-foo	Elephant.	Tanzania (Chaga)	M
NKUKU	n-koo-koo	Rooster.	Malawi (Yao)	M
NOKADHIHI	noh-kah-DHEE-dhee	Small ant.	Namibia (Ovambo)	
NONYANA	nohn-YAH-nah	Bird.	Azania (Sotho)	
NSOMBA	n-SOHM-bah	Fish.	Malawi (Yao)	M
NTARE	n-TAH-reh	Lion.	Rwanda, Burundi (Kinyarwanda, Kirundi)	M
NYANI	n-YAH-nee	Baboon.	Kiswahili	

Name	Pronunciation	Meaning	Origin	Gender
NYIRA MONDO	n-yee-rah-mohn-doh	Panther.	Rwanda, Burundi (Kinyarwanda, Kirundi)	F
NYIREJ	NYEE-rehj	Little fish.	Sudan (Shulla)	F
NZOGU	nzoh-goo	Elephant.	DRC (Rega)	M
ONI	OH-nee	Bird.	Azania (Nguni)	
PAA	PAH	Gazelle.	Kiswahili	
PAKA	PAH-kah	Cat.	Kiswahili	
PANYA	PAHN-yah	Mouse.	Kiswahili	
POPO	POH-poh	Butterfly.	Kiswahili	
RASHA	RAH-shah	Gazelle.	North Africa (Arabic)	
RINA	REE-nah	Hornet.	West Africa (Hausa)	
SANURA	sah-NOO-rah	Kitten.	Kiswahili	F
SEGOKGO	seh-gohk-goh	Spider.	Azania (Sotho)	
SEKITU LEGE	sseh-tch-ee-too-leh-geh	Zebra.	Uganda (Ganda)	M
SEMPALA	ssehm-pah-lah	An antelope.	Uganda (Ganda)	M
SENGO	ssehn-goh	Leopard.	Uganda (Ganda)	M
SENKIMA	ssehn-tch-ee-mah	Monkey.	Uganda (Ganda)	M
SENTASHYA	sehn-TAH-shah	Sparrow.	Rwanda, Burundi (Kinyarwanda, Kirundi)	M
SEOKGO	seh-ohk-goh	Spider.	Azania (Sotho)	
SERU RUBELE	seh-roo-roo-beh-leh	Butterfly.	Azania (North Sotho)	
SHUMBA	SHOOM-bah	Lion.	Zimbabwe (Shona)	M
SIAFU	see-AH-foo	Ant.	Kiswahili	
SIMBA	SEHM-bah	Lion.	Kiswahili	
SIRI	SEE-ree	Tiger.	Nigeria	

Name	Pronunciation	Meaning	Origin	Gender
SONO	SOH-noh	Elephant.	Ghana (Akan)	M
SULUWO	soo-LOO-woh	Wolf.	Gambia	
SUNDIATA	soon-dee-AH-tah	Hungry lion.	Guinea	M
TAI	TAH-ee	An eagle.	Kiswahili	
TALI	TAH-lee	Lion.	Azania (North Sotho)	
TAU	TAH-oo	Lion.	Botswana (Tswana)	M
TAUSI	tah-OO-see	Peacock.	Kiswahili	F
THETHE	teh-teh	Grasshopper.	Azania (Nguni)	
THUTIWA	too-tee-wah	Giraffe.	Azania (Sotho)	
TLOWANA	ttloh-wah-nah	Little elephant.	Azania (Sotho)	
TOLI	TOH-lee	A sparrow.	West Africa	F
TSHWENE	tch-weh-neh	Baboon.	Azania (Sotho)	
TWIGA	twee-gah	Giraffe.	Kiswahili	
UFUDO	oo-FOO-doh	Tortoise.	Azania (Nguni)	
UGO	OO-goh	Eagle.	Nigeria (Igbo)	M
URUSA MAGWE	oo-roo-sah-MAHG-weh	Panther.	Rwanda, Burundi (Kinyarwanda, Kirundi)	
VEMVANE	vehm-vah-neh	Butterfly.	Azania (Zulu)	
VUZIMANZI	voo-zee-mahn-zee	Water snake.	Azania (Nguni)	
WABAYI	wah-BAH-yee	Raven.	Azania (Nguni)	
WANGARI	WAHN-gah-ree	Leopard.	Kenya (Agikuyu)	F
XOXO	TSOH-tsoh	Frog.	Azania (Nguni)	
YOLA	YOH-lah	Firefly.	Nigeria (Hausa)	F
ZAKARA	zah-KAH-rah	Rooster.	West Africa (Hausa)	
ZAKI	ZAH-kee	Lion.	West Africa (Hausa)	
ZIZI	zee-zee	Animal shelter.	Kiswahili	F

Appropriateness

Blow your horn in a herd of elephants;
crow in the company of cockerels;
bleat in a flock of goats. —*Malawi*

Name	Pronunciation	Meaning	Origin	Gender
FANELE	fah-NEH-leh	Appropriate.	Azania (Zulu)	
KAGYA	kah-jah	That is appropriate.	Uganda (Ganda)	
KALUGYE	kah-loo-jeh	Appropriate.	Uganda (Ganda)	M
KUFAA	KOO-faah	Appropriate.	Kiswahili	
KUNTA	KOON-tah	To fit; male surname.	Gambia (Mandinka)	M
OMOLARA	oh-MOH-lah-rah	Child born at the right time.	Benin	
SADMIA	sahd-mee-ah	Suits me, well matched.	Cameroon (Mubako)	F
ZIDLELA	zeed-LEH-lah	Appropriate.	Azania (Zulu)	

Aroma

Who is brave enough to tell the lion that his breath smells? —*Morocco*

Name	Pronunciation	Meaning	Origin	Gender
EWUNIKI	eh-woo-nee-kee	Fragrant.	East Africa	F
MALIASHI	mah-ljah-tch-ee	Nice smell.	DRC (Rega)	F
MANUKATO	mah-noo-KAH-toh	Perfume.	Kiswahili	
MNUKIO	m-noo-KEE-oh	A sweet smell.	Kiswahili	
MNUKO	m-NOO-koh	A bad smell.	Kiswahili	
NAMUGA	nah-moo-gah	Perfume.	Uganda (Ganda)	F
NUKILIA	noo-KEE-lee-ah	To follow a scent.	Kiswahili	
REHAAN	REH-ha-ahn	Beautiful scent.	North Africa (Arabic)	M

Name	Pronunciation	Meaning	Origin	Gender
REHAANA	reh-HAH-ah-nah	Beautiful scent.	North Africa (Arabic)	F
USENDE	u-SEHN-deh	Perfume, fragrance.	Azania (Zulu)	

Arrival and Presence

Before one replies, one must be present. —*Senegal, Gambia*

Name	Pronunciation	Meaning	Origin	Gender
ABABUO	ah-bah-BOO-oh	Child that keeps coming back.	Ghana (Ewe)	F
ABAYIE	ah-bah-YEE-eh	This birth has come in good time.	Ghana (Akan)	
AKHONA	ah-KOH-nah	They are present.	Azania (Zulu)	
ALUNA	ah-LOO-nah	Come here.	Kenya (Mwera)	F
ANDWELE	and-WEH-leh	God brings me.	Tanzania	M
ANOWI	ah-NOH-wee	Came to stay.	Nigeria (Igbo)	M
APARA	ah-PAH-rah	Child that comes and goes.	Nigeria (Yoruba)	M
ARYAIJA	ah-ree-yah-ee-dzah	God will come.	Uganda (Kiga, Nyankore, Nyoro, Toro)	
AYIZE	ah-YEE-zeh	Let it come.	Azania (Zulu)	
BANJOKO	BAN-joh-koh	Stay with me, and go no more.	Nigeria (Yoruba)	
BEKELE	boo-KEH-leh	He has come into being.	Ethiopia	M
BIZA	BEE-zah	Invitation.	Azania (Xhosa)	
BUKELWA	boo-kehl-wah	One who attracts attention.	Azania (Xhosa)	F
BWERANI	bweh-RAH-nee	Come (you are welcome).	Malawi (Ngoni)	M
BYANI	BYAH-nee	Come back.	Azania (Zulu)	
CHABWERA	chah-BWEH-rah	He has arrived.	Malawi (Ngoni)	M

Name	Pronunciation	Meaning	Origin	Gender
DURODEMI	doo-roh-DEH-mee	Stay with me.	Nigeria (Yoruba)	
EJAITA	eh-jah-EE-tah	Let them stay.	Nigeria (Urhobo)	
FIKA	FEE-kah	Arrive.	Azania	M
FIKILE	fee-KEE-lee	She has arrived; come.	Azania (Zulu)	F
FILIJE	fee-lee-jeh	Leave it here.	Gambia	
FINYELELA	FEEN-yeh-leh-lah	To reach, to arrive.	Kiswahili	
GALELEKILE	gah-leh-leh-KEE-leh	He has arrived.	Azania (Xhosa)	M
GARAYI	gah-rah-yee	Stay put in place.	Zimbabwe, Mozambique, Zambia (Shona)	M
GUMIRA	goo-mee-rah	Stay where you are.	Rwanda, Burundi, DRC (Huti, Tutsi, Twa)	M
ITA	EE-tah	The invited one.	Kiswahili	
KAIRE	kah-ee-reh	May the little one return.	Uganda (Soga)	F
KAIZA	kah-ee-zah	The little one who returns.	Uganda (Soga)	F
KARIBU	kah-REE-boo	Come in!	Kiswahili	
KIGERI	kee-geeh-ree	One who arrives.	Rwanda, Burundi, DRC (Huti, Tutsi, Twa)	M
KUFIKA	koo-FEE-kah	To arrive.	Kiswahili	
MAJILIO	mah-jee-LEE-oh	Coming.	Kiswahili	
MALAMO	mah-lah-moh	Do not go away again.	Nigeria (Yoruba)	
MAREJEO	mah-reh-jeh-oh	Return.	Kiswahili	
MAVELA	mah-VEH-lah	The one who appears.	Azania	M
MBWELERA	m-bweh-LEH-rah	Return.	Malawi (Ngoni)	M
MTAKUJA	m-tah-koo-jah	Come back.	Tanzania (Kiswahili)	F
NADA	NAH-dah	Finally, she has arrived.	Azania (Xhosa)	F
NAKYAJJA	nnah-tch-ahj-jah	It came, it arrived, it happened.	Uganda (Ganda)	F

Name	Pronunciation	Meaning	Origin	Gender
NALUZZE	nnah-looz-zeh	A return.	Uganda (Ganda)	F
NDATEBA	n-dah-teh-bah	Quick to come back.	Rwanda, Burundi (Kinyarwanda, Kirundi)	M
NJOKI	n-JOH-kee	She who has returned.	Kenya (Agikuyu)	F
NUBIDLA	noo-BEED-lah	Gone and come back.	Cameroon (Mubako)	M
OBADELE	oh-bah-DEH-leh	The king arrives at the house.	Nigeria (Yoruba)	M
ONONYE	oh-nohn-yeh	Stay with me.	Nigeria	
PETIRI	PEH-tee-ree	Here we are.	Zimbabwe (Shona)	M
SONDISA	sohn-DEE-sah	Bring him near to us.	Zimbabwe (Shona)	M
TEZI	TEH-zee	One who stays.	Azania (Zulu)	
THENGA	TEHNG-gah	Bring him.	Malawi (Yao)	M
THOLAKELE	toh-lah-keh-leh	Found.	Azania (Zulu)	F
VELI	VEH-lee	One who appears.	Azania	M
VELILE	veh-LEE-leh	One who appears.	Azania	F
VELISWA	veh-LEES-wah	One who appears.	Azania	F
ZANAZO	zah-nah-zoh	Come with him.	Azania (Zulu)	
ZANIGE	zah-NEE-geh	Come.	Zambia (Tumbuka	M
ZIRAJE	zee-raah-jeh	They are coming.	Rwanda, Burundi, DRC (Huti, Tutsi, Twa)	M
ZUKA	ZOO-kah	To appear suddenly; to come onto the scene as an upstart.	Kiswahili	

Art and Creativity

The creator of a dance
should not be excluded from it. —*Ghana*

Name	Pronunciation	Meaning	Origin	Gender
ADWIN	AHD-ween	Creative, imaginative.	West Africa	
CHIUMBO	chee-OOM-boh	Small creation.	Kenya (Mwera)	M
DALA	DAH-lah	Be creative; create something new.	Azania (Xhosa)	M
DOLI	DOH-lee	Doll.	East Africa (Kiswahili)	F
EMARA	eh-MAH-rah	Conception.	Southern Africa (Tsonga)	
KENYA	KEHN-yah	Artist.	East Africa	
KUUMBA	KOO-oom-bah	Creativity.	East Africa (Kiswahili)	M
MOTAKI	moh-tah-kee	Artist.	Azania (Sotho)	
MUUMBA	moo-OOM-bah	Creator.	Zimbabwe (Shona)	
OKIKE	oh-KEE-keh	Creation.	Nigeria (Igbo)	
SANAA	SAH-naa	Art.	East Africa (Kiswahili)	F
SEITU	seh-ee-too	Artist.	East Africa	

Aunts and Uncles

If you never offer palm wine to your uncle,
you will not know many proverbs. —Benin

Name	Pronunciation	Meaning	Origin	Gender
BAMBOD	bahm-bohd	Junior paternal uncle.	Cameroon (Mungaka)	M
BINKI	BEEN-kee	Aunt.	Gambia (Mandinka)	F
ETEVI	eh-TEH-vee	Aunt.	Ghana	F
FAKEBA	fah-KEH-bah	Father's elder brother.	Gambia	M
MAKAZI	mah-KAH-zee	Aunt (maternal).	Azania	F

Name	Pronunciation	Meaning	Origin	Gender
MALUME	mah-LOOM-meh	Uncle (maternal).	Azania	M
MALUM EKAZI	mah-loo-meh-KAH-zee	Aunt (maternal).	Azania	F
MJOMBA	m-JOHM-bah	Uncle.	Kiswahili	M
SHANGAZI	shahn-GAH-zee	Paternal aunt.	Kiswahili	F
TANGWI	TAHNG-wee	Paternal aunt.	Cameroon (Mungaka)	F
UBABEKAZI	oo-bah-beh-KAH-zee	Father's sister; aunt.	Azania (Zulu)	F
UMALUME	oo-mah-loo-meh	Maternal uncle.	Azania (Zulu)	M

Authenticity

He who has named his child "stop fighting"
does not make bullets. —Ghana

Name	Pronunciation	Meaning	Origin	Gender
ASILIA	ah-see-LEE-ah	Genuine; honest.	Kenya, Tanzania	
EKWUEME	eh-kwoo-EH-meh	He says, he does.	Nigeria (Igbo)	M
HALISI	hah-LEE-see	Genuine.	Kiswahili	
KIMAADA	kee-mah-AH-dah	Genuine.	Kiswahili	
MAGSIA	mahg-SEE-ah	One never clones himself or herself.	Cameroon (Mubako)	F
MPAMY ABIGWI	mpah-mee-ah-bee-gwee	A man who stands by his word.	Rwanda (Rufumbira)	M
ODMI	OHD-mee	Brings as it were true lineage.	Cameroon (Mubako)	F
OKAOME	oh-kah-OH-meh	One who says, and does what he says.	Nigeria (Igbo)	

Name	Pronunciation	Meaning	Origin	Gender
THABITI	tah-BEE-tee	A true man.	Kenya (Mwera)	M
UMUNTU	oo-MOON-too	A real person.	Rwanda, Burundi (Kinyarwanda, Kirundi)	

Beauty and Appearance

Everyone has God-given beauty. —Ghana

Name	Pronunciation	Meaning	Origin	Gender
ACHAMA	ah-chah-mah	One that is light-skinned is beautiful.	Nigeria (Igbo)	F
ADAJINMA	ah-dah-JEEN-mah	Beauty holding daughter.	Nigeria (Igbo)	F
ADANMA	ah-DAHN-mah	Beautiful, loving daughter.	Nigeria (Igbo)	F
ADAOMA	ah-dah-OH-mah	Good-looking daughter.	Nigeria (Igbo)	F
AHSAKI	ah-sah-kee	Beautiful.	West Africa	F
AHUMMA	ah-HOOM-ah	Beautiful body.	Nigeria (Igbo)	
AMAHLE	ah-MAH-leh	The beautiful ones.	Azania (Zulu)	
ANIKA	ah-NEE-kah	Pretty; elegant.	North Africa (Arabic)	F
ARIYO	ah-REE-oh	Looking good or well.	Nigeria	
AYANNA	ah-YAHN-nah	Beautiful blossom.	East Africa	F
AZIZA	ah-ZEEZ-zah	Exquisite child.	Somalia	F
BAKABAKA	bah-kah-BAH-kah	Pretty woman.	Azania (Zulu)	
BHELU	BEH-loo	Very handsome person.	Azania (Zulu)	
BINTI	BEEN-tee	Girl, daughter; daughter of a beautiful son.	Kenya, Tanzania, Azania (Xhosa)	F
BOMBA	BOHM-bah	Pretty.	Southern Africa (Tsonga)	
BONTLE	BOHNT-leh	Beauty.	Azania (Tswana)	
BOTSE	boht-see	Pretty woman.	Azania (Sotho)	F

Name	Pronunciation	Meaning	Origin	Gender
BUHLE	boo-leh	He reflects beauty internally and externally.	Azania (Xhosa)	M
BULE	BOO-leh	Beauty.	Azania (Xhosa)	F
BUSUMA	boo-SOO-mah	Beauty.	Zambia (Bemba)	
DADA	DAH-dah	Child with curly hair.	Nigeria (Yoruba)	F
ENHLE	EHN-leh	Beautiful.	Azania (Nguni)	
FABU	FAH-boo	A beautiful woman.	Ethiopia	F
FANISWA	fah-NEE-swah	She looks like one of us.	Azania	F
FANTA	FAHN-tah	Beautiful day.	Guinea	F
FARIH	FAH-ree	Light-complexioned.	West Africa	
GAMAL	GAH-mahl	Handsome.	Egypt/Khamit	M
GEZA	GEH-zah	Handsome young man.	Azania (Zulu)	
GHADAH	GAH-dah	Beautiful.	North Africa (Arabic)	F
GUNE	goo-neh	Big-headed one.	Sudan (Bari)	M
HALIYAMTU	hah-lee-AHM-too	A person's appearance tells about his personality.	Africa	M
HASIINA	hah-SEE-ee-nah	Beautiful; attractive.	Kiswahili	F
HASIJNA	HAH-seej-nah	Beautiful.	East Africa (Kiswahili)	F
HUSANI	hoo-SAH-nee	Handsome young man.	Kiswahili	M
HUSNA	HOOS-nah	Most beautiful.	Kiswahili	F
ILA	EE-lah	Birthmark.	Kiswahili	
IMOSE	ee-MOH-seh	Beauty.	Nigeria (Bini)	
INDADEEKA	n-DAH-DEE-kah	She who pleases the eye.	Somalia	F
IRIBAGIZA	ee-ree-bah-GEE-zah	Beauty incarnated.	Rwanda, Burundi (Kinyarwanda, Kirundi)	F
IRUKA	ee-ROO-kah	Face is paramount.	Nigeria (Igbo)	F
ITEKU	ee-TEH-koo	Big-headed child.	Nigeria (Ishan)	

Name	Pronunciation	Meaning	Origin	Gender
JAMAR	JAH-mar	Handsome.	North Africa (Arabic)	M
JAMIR	JAH-meer	Handsome.	North Africa (Arabic)	M
KAJUMBA	kah-JOOM-bah	Beautiful.	Uganda (Ganda)	
KAMEKE	kah-MEH-keh	Small eyes.	Angola (Ovimbundu)	
KEINBA	keh-een-bah	The beautiful one.	Nigeria	
KESSE	KEH-see	Fat at birth.	Ghana (Fante, Ashanti)	M
KIFIMBO	kee-FEEM-boh	A very thin baby.	East Africa (Kiswahili)	
KITOKA	kee-toh-kah	Beauty.	DRC (Kongo)	F
KUHLE	koo-leh	It is beautiful.	Azania (Zulu)	
LINDELIHLE	lehn-deh-lee-leh	The beautiful one.	Azania	
LULLA	LOOL-lah	Beautiful as pearl.	Ethiopia	F
MAANAMI	maah-nah-mee	One who is beautiful.	West Africa	F
MAHA	MAH-hah	Beautiful eyes.	Sudan	F
MASHAVU	mah-SHAH-voo	Little baby with chubby cheeks.	East Africa (Kiswahili)	F
MASILO	mah-see-loh	Son of a beautiful daughter.	Azania (Sotho)	M
MASOPA KYINDI	mah-soh-pahk-YEEN-dee	Eyes like hard porridge.	Tanzania (Nyakyusa)	M
MUJWALA	moo-jwah-lah	Well-dressed.	Uganda (Ganda)	M
MWARI	MWAH-ree	Son of a beautiful daughter.	Kiswahili	
MWIZA	MWEE-zah	Beautiful.	Rwanda	
MXOLISA	moo-ksoh-lee-sah	Beautiful.	Azania (Xhosa)	
NABULUNGI	nah-boo-loon-GHEE	Beautiful one.	Uganda (Ganda, Luganda)	F
NAFRE	NAH-freh	Beautiful creation.	Egypt/Khamit	
NAFRINI	nah-free-nee	She brings beauty.	Egypt/Khamit	F
NAHYUMA	nah-yoo-mah	A beautiful woman who makes me happy.	Cameroon (Mubako)	F

Name	Pronunciation	Meaning	Origin	Gender
NAJLA	NAHJ-lah	Having big eyes.	North Africa (Arabic)	F
NAKAWA	NAH-kah-wah	Beautiful; good-looking.	Kenya, Tanzania (Kiswahili)	F
NAKISAI	nah-kee-SAH-ee	Beautify.	Zimbabwe (Shona)	F
NAKKAZI	nahk-kah-zee	Big woman.	Uganda (Ganda)	F
NALUNGO	nah-LOON-goh	Beautiful.	Central Africa	F
NAMUTIBE	nnah-moo-tee-beh	Beautiful.	Uganda (Ganda)	F
NDIMHLE	n-DEEMH-leh	I am handsome.	Azania (Xhosa)	M
NEFERTITI	NEHF-uhr-TEE-tee	The beautiful one has arrived.	Egypt/Khamit	F
NNENMA	n-NEHN-mah	Mother of beauty.	Nigeria (Igbo)	F
NOBUHLE	noh-boo-leh	The cute one.	Azania (Zulu)	F
NOMBLE	NOM-bleh	Beauty.	Azania (Xhosa)	F
NOMDEDE	nohm-DEH-deh	Woman with big buttocks.	Azania	F
NUBITI	noo-BEE-tee	Golden lady.	Egypt/Khamit	F
NWADINMA	n-wah-deen-mah	The child is beautiful.	Nigeria (Igbo)	
NYIME	n-yee-meh	Beauty.	Nigeria (Eleme)	
NZINGHA	n-zeen-gah	Beautiful.	Central Africa	F
OMOROSE	oh-moh-ROH-seh	My beautiful child.	Benin	F
OPURU	oh-POO-roo	A fat, cheerful child.	Nigeria (Ishan)	F
PANYAZA	pahn-YAH-zah	Attractive girl with large eyes.	Azania (Zulu)	F
PEHTEMA	peh-TEH-mah	Divided thoughts—she has broken my heart with beauty.	Cameroon (Mubako)	F
REMBA	REHM-bah	Beautiful.	Kenya, Tanzania	
RUBE RANZIZA	roo-beh-rahn-ZEE-zah	The one who is attractive to the beautiful ones.	Rwanda, Burundi (Kinyarwanda, Kirundi)	
RUNAKO	roo-NAH-koh	Handsome.	Zimbabwe (Shona)	M

Name	Pronunciation	Meaning	Origin	Gender
SABERA	sah-BEH-rah	Attractive.	Rwanda, Burundi (Kinyarwanda, Kirundi)	
SEWELA	seh-weh-lah	Daughter of a beautiful son.	Azania (Sotho)	F
SHAKILA	shah-KEE-lah	Shapely; well-rounded.	East Africa (Kiswahili)	F
SHAKILYA	shah-KEEL-yah	Well-shaped.	Kiswahili	
SHIBA	SHEE-bah	Beautiful lady.	Ethiopia	F
SIHLE	see-leh	Beautiful.	Azania (Nguni)	
SIMOSIHLE	see-moh-see-leh	Beautiful feeling.	Azania (Zulu)	F
TABASAMU	TAH-bah-sah-moo	A beautiful smile.	East Africa (Kiswahili)	F
TANASHATI	tah-NAH-shah-tee	Well-dressed.	East Africa (Kiswahili)	F
TANDRA	tahn-drah	Beauty marks; moles.	Madagascar	
THANDEKA	tahn-deh-kah	She is lovable, lovely to look at.	Azania (Xhosa)	F
TOMBI	TOHM-bee	Lovely girl.	Southern Africa	M
TURKIYA	toor-KEE-yah	Beautiful.	Kiswahili	F
UGOOMA	oo-GOH-mah	Good-looking.	Nigeria (Igbo)	
URUJENI	oo-roo-jeh-nee	Beauty.	Rwanda, Burundi, DRC (Huti, Tutsi, Twa)	F
UZURI	oo-ZUHR-ree	Beauty.	Kiswahili	
VATI	VAH-tee	Birthmark.	Southern Africa (Tsonga)	
VIZURI	vee-ZOO-ree	Beautiful, pretty.	Kiswahili	
WAMWERU	WAH-mweh-rah	Light-skinned.	Kenya (Agikuyu)	F
WONGA	WOHN-gah	A handsome figure.	Azania (Xhosa)	
YOZI	YOH-zee	The one with big, sleepy eyes.	Azania (Zulu)	
ZAINA	zah-EE-nah	Beautiful daughter.	North Africa (Arabic)	
ZAINABU	zah-ee-NAH-boo	Beautiful.	East Africa (Kiswahili)	F

Name	Pronunciation	Meaning	Origin	Gender
ZANTA	ZAHN-tah	Beautiful girl.	Kiswahili	F
ZERA	ZEH-rah	Beauty, blooms, dawn.	East Africa (Kiswahili)	F
ZIBERA	zee-beh-eh-rah	They look good, they are more favorable.	Rwanda, Burundi, DRC (Huti, Tutsi, Twa)	M
ZINA	ZEEN-ah	Beauty.	Kiswahili	
ZINHLE	ZEHND-leh	The girls are good, beautiful.	Azania (Zulu)	F
ZINTLE	ZEHNT-leh	Beautiful girl.	Azania (Nguni)	F

Beginnings and Endings

If you understand the beginning well,
the end will not trouble you. —*Ghana*

Name	Pronunciation	Meaning	Origin	Gender
AGIK	ah-geek	The end.	Uganda (Acholi)	F
ALOHYA	ah-loh-yah	Where is the source?	Cameroon (Mungaka)	
ANZA	AHN-zah	Beginning.	Kiswahili	
ASILI	ah-SEE-lee	Original.	Kiswahili	
AWALI	ah-WAH-lee	The beginning; first.	Kiswahili	
CHATHA	CHAT-hah	An ending.	Malawi (Ngoni)	M
DABU	DAH-boo	Origin.	Azania (Zulu)	
DABUKO	dah-BOO-koh	Traditional custom, origin.	Azania (Zulu)	
KUTHA KWAKULU	koo-tah-kwah-KOO-loo	The end of man.	Malawi (Yao)	M
LEHDOGHA	leh-DOH-gah	The farm has ended.	Cameroon (Mubako)	M
MANDE	MAHN-deh	First day.	Uganda (Ganda)	F
MATSIMELA	maht-see-MEH-lah	Roots.	Lesotho (Sotho)	M
MNOMBO	m-nohm-boh	Origin.	Azania (Xhosa)	M

Name	Pronunciation	Meaning	Origin	Gender
MWAKA	MWAH-kah	Born at year's opening.	East Africa (Kiswahili)	F
MWISHO	MWEE-shoh	Last one, end.	Kiswahili	
NTONO	n-toh-noh	Beginning.	Uganda (Ganda)	
ZERE	ZEH-reh	Descendent of; seed of.	Ethiopia (Amharic)	M

Belonging and Possession

Have you noticed how some dog owners look more and more like their dogs and how it is more and more difficult to tell who belongs to whom and lives for whom? —*Ethiopia*

Name	Pronunciation	Meaning	Origin	Gender
ABENAKYO	ah-beh-nah-tch-oh	May she have it with her, may she possess it.	Uganda (Soga)	F
AFUNA	ah-foo-nah	S/he procures; the one who obtains.	Uganda (Ganda, Kiga, Nyankore)	
AKANNI	ah-KAHN-nee	Our encounter brings possessions.	Nigeria (Yoruba)	M
ALAMAZE	ah-lah-MAH-zeh	She has everything.	Ethiopia	F
ANSEH	ahn-seh	Has nothing, owes nothing.	Cameroon (Mubako)	
AYAZIKA	ah-yah-zee-kah	Who lends out one's possessions.	Uganda (Soga)	
BALINA	bah-lee-nah	They have.	Uganda (Ganda)	M
BANGANI	bahn-GAH-nee	Claim, possess.	Azania (Xhosa)	M
BANGILE	bahn-GEE-leh	The one who came to possess.	Azania (Xhosa)	M
BOBBILLA	bohb-BEEL-lah	The village has been regained.	Cameroon (Mubako)	
BUYISILE	booh-yee-SEE-leh	He has retrieved what was lost.	Azania (Xhosa)	M

Name	Pronunciation	Meaning	Origin	Gender
DANGMIA	dahng-MEE-ah	Has acquired me.	Cameroon (Mubako)	
DANYEBBA	dahn-YEHB-bah	Has acquired property.	Cameroon (Mubako)	
ENWERE	ehn-WEH-reh	The owner; one who owns.	Nigeria (Igbo)	M
IFEANYI	ee-feh-AHN-yee	Our beloved possession.	Nigeria	
JANDJE	JAHND-jeh	My.	Namibia (Ovambo)	
JIPATIA	jee-pah-TEE-ah	To acquire.	Kiswahili	
KANENE	kah-NEH-neh	A little thing in the eye is big.	Angola (Ovimbundu)	
KIGHA	kee-gah	It cannot be taken.	Cameroon (Mubako)	
KISAYE	kee-SAH-yeh	Belonging to God.	Uganda (Ganda)	F
KOMA	KOH-mah	Belonging to the people.	Ghana	F
LAHNDAMUN	lahn-dah-moon	The state of one's house is best known by her.	Cameroon (Mungaka)	F
LEYIGHA	leh-yee-gah	His compound has been left to me alone.	Cameroon (Mubako)	F
MAKAMI	mah-KAH-mee	He seizes.	Nigeria (Hausa)	M
MALINGA	mah-lehn-gah	A girl does not belong to one person.	DRC (Rega)	F
MAUNDA	mah-oon-dah	Our own child.	Ethiopia	F
MUNDA	MOON-dah	Ours.	Sierra Leone	
MWENYI	mweh-ndjh-ee	The owner.	DRC (Rega)	M
NAN GOSOLE	nahn-goh-soh-leh	The unattainable is more highly prized than the thing in hand.	Angola (Ovimbundu)	
NASIGA	nah-SEE-gah	Belonging to the old compound.	Cameroon (Mubako)	F
NDUWI MANA	n-doo-wee-mah-nah	I belong to God.	Rwanda, Burundi, DRC (Huti, Tutsi, Twa)	M

Name	Pronunciation	Meaning	Origin	Gender
NGABILE	n-gah-BEE-leh	I have got it.	East Africa (Nyakyusa)	F
NJIDEKA	n-jah-deh-kah	Possession or ownership.	Nigeria (Igbo)	F
NKEM	n-KEHM	My precious possession.	Nigeria	
NOZAKHE	noh-ZAH-keh	She will possess her possessions; she will take care of her own.	Azania (Xhosa)	F
NTOZAKE	n-toh-ZAH-kee	She comes with her own things.	Azania (Zulu)	F
NTOZAKHE	n-toh-zah-kee	His own things.	Zimbabwe (Ndebele)	M
NYANDA	n-yahn-dah	Mine.	Sierra Leone	
OBAKHO	oh-BAH-koh	Yours.	Azania (Zulu)	
OBAMI	oh-BAH-mee	This is mine.	Azania (Zulu)	
OBENU	oh-BEH-noo	Yours.	Azania (Zulu)	
OKWAM	OH-kwahm	My own.	Azania (Xhosa)	
OKWAMI	oh-KWAH-mee	Mine.	Azania (Zulu)	
OKWENU	oh-KWEH-noo	Yours.	Azania (Zulu)	
OKWETHU	oh-KWEH-too	Ours.	Azania (Zulu)	
OWENU	oh-WEH-noo	Yours.	Azania (Zulu)	
OWETHU	oh-weh-thoo	Ours.	Azania (Zulu)	
SENTARE	seh-ehn-tah-reh	The owner of lions.	Rwanda, Burundi, DRC (Huti, Tutsi, Twa)	M
TIBYANGYE	tee-bee-ahn-jeh	Everything belongs to God.	Uganda (Runyankore)	M
UBAKA	oo-BAH-kah	Ownership is great.	Nigeria (Igbo)	M
WAGAO	wah-GAH-oh	Yours.	Azania (North Sotho)	
WAROHA	wah-ROH-hah	Ours.	Azania (North Sotho)	
WUBBA	WOOB-bah	I now have dominion.	Cameroon (Mubako)	M
YENEE	yah-nay	Mine.	Ethiopia	F
YUMMUN	YOOM-moon	Somebody's thing.	Cameroon (Mungaka)	

Birth Circumstance

To give birth is to lengthen one's knees. —Azania

Name	Pronunciation	Meaning	Origin	Gender
ABEGUNDE	ah-beh-GOON-deh	Born during holiday.	Nigeria (Yoruba)	M
ALANYO	ah-lah-ndjh-oh	A child born at time when parents were separated.	Uganda, Kenya (Luo)	F
IGE	EE-geh	Delivered feet first.	Central Africa	
IGO	EE-goh	Delivered feet first.	Nigeria (Yoruba)	F
JIMIYU	JEE-mee-yoo	Born in a dry season.	Uganda (Ganda, Abaluhya)	M
KHADIJA	kah-DEE-jah	Born prematurely.	East Africa (Kiswahili)	F
KHADUA	kah-DOO-ah	Child born prematurely.	North Africa (Arabic)	
KHUDUEGO	koo-dweh-goh	Born on the day of a political disturbance; riots.	Botswana (Tswana)	M
LUMO	LOO-moh	Born face downwards.	Ghana (Ewe)	
NAMUSISI	mah-moo-see-see	Mother was pregnant during earthquake.	Uganda (Luganda)	F
PASUA	pah-SOO-ah	Born by cesarean operation.	East Africa (Kiswahili)	

Birth Order

Birth is the only remedy against death. —West Africa

Name	Pronunciation	Meaning	Origin	Gender
ADIAGA	ah-dee-AH-gah	First daughter.	Nigeria (Efik)	F
ADIAHA	ah-dee-AH-hah	First born daughter.	Nigeria (Igbo)	F
AFAFA	ah-FAH-fah	First daughter of second husband.	West Africa	F
AJULO	ah-djoo-loh	Second born.	Sudan, Ethiopia (Anuak)	F

Name	Pronunciation	Meaning	Origin	Gender
AKO	AH-koh	The first son.	West Africa	M
ALABA	ah-lah-BAH	Second child born after twins.	Nigeria (Yoruba)	F
AMOT	ah-moht	First born.	Sudan, Ethiopia (Anuak)	F
ANAN	AH-nahn	Fourth born child.	West Africa	
ANANE	ah-NAH-neh	The fourth son.	Ghana (Akan)	M
ANKOMA	ahn-KOH-mah	Last born of parents.	Ghana (Akan)	
ARUBAA	ah-ROO-bah	Fourth born.	Kiswahili	
AWOTWE	A-WOH-tweh	Eighth born.	Ghana (Akan)	
BAAKO	BAH-koh	First born.	Nigeria (Yoruba)	M
BADU	bah-DOO	Tenth child.	Ghana (Akan)	
BOFEJANE	boh-feh-JAH-neh	Youngest child, the last one.	Azania (Xhosa)	
DEDE	DEH-deh	First daughter.	Ghana (Ga)	F
FEH	FEH	A baby born after a set of twins.	Cameroon (Mungaka)	
FUSI	FOO-see	Child born next after twins.	Azania (Zulu)	
IDOWU	ee-DOH-woo	Born after twins.	Nigeria (Yoruba)	
KIJAI	kee-jah-ee	The first girl born in the family.	Uganda (Ateso)	F
KISSA	kees-SAH	Born after twins.	Cameroon	
KIZZA	keez-SAH	Born after twins.	Uganda (Ganda, Luganda)	M
KONYI	koh-ndjh-ee	First born son.	Sudan (Bari)	M
KUKU	koo-koo	First born.	Sudan (Nuba)	M
KUNTO	koon-toh	Third child.	Ghana (Twi)	F
LODU	LOH-doo	Second born male.	Sudan (Bari)	M
MAANKOH	mah-AHN-koh	A child followed by a set of twins, usually an additional name.	Cameroon (Mubako)	F

Name	Pronunciation	Meaning	Origin	Gender
MATHOMO	mah-TOH-moh	First born.	Azania (North Sotho)	
MOSI	MOH-see	First born.	Tanzania (Kiswahili)	M
MSRAH	m-srah	Sixth born.	Ghana (Akan)	
MWANAWA	mwah-NAH-wah	First born child.	Tanzania (Zaramo)	F
NAHNYENI	nahn-YEH-nee	The third of a set of triplets.	Cameroon (Mubako)	F
NAJJA	NAHJ-jah	Second born.	Uganda (Ganda)	F
NAKI	NAH-kee	First girl in the family.	Ghana	F
NALU	nah-loo	Fifth born.	Sudan (Nuba)	
NINA	nee-nah	First female child in the family.	Cameroon (Mungaka)	F
NKRUMAH	n-KROO-mah	Ninth born.	Ghana (Akan)	
NSOAH	n-soh-AH	Seventh born.	Ghana (Akan)	M
OKPARA	ohk-PAH-rah	First son.	Nigeria (Igbo)	M
OLLOR	OHL-lohr	Second son.	Nigeria (Eleme)	M
ONUA	oh-NOO-ah	Second daughter.	Nigeria (Eleme)	F
OPARA	oh-PAH-rah	My first male child.	Nigeria	M
OSARO	oh-SAH-roh	First son.	Nigeria (Eleme)	M
OSILA	oh-SEE-lah	First daughter.	Nigeria (Eleme)	F
SAMKEA	sahm-kee-ah	The third of a set of triplets.	Cameroon (Mubako)	M
SHAMISE	shah-MEE-seh	First born.	Egypt/Khamit	
SIA	SEE-ah	First born daughter.	Sierra Leone (Kono)	F
TETE	TEH-teh	First son.	Ghana (Ga)	
TIA	tee-yah	Third born.	Sudan (Nuba)	M
TOTO	toh-toh	Second born.	Sudan (Nuba)	F
UDOH	OO-doh	Second child.	Nigeria	
UJULO	oo-joo-loh	Second born.	Sudan (Anuak)	M

Name	Pronunciation	Meaning	Origin	Gender
YEYE	YEH-yeh	Second daughter.	Nigeria (Eleme)	F
ZAMBGA	zahmb-gah	First born.	West Africa (Bassa)	M

Blessings

*When you stand with the blessing of your mother
and God, it matters not who stands
against you.* —*West Africa*

Name	Pronunciation	Meaning	Origin	Gender
ABAINE	ah-bah-ee-neh	Blessed with relatives or friends.	Uganda (Ganda, Kiga, Nyankore)	
AKIN	AH-kehn	Blessing.	Nigeria	
AKINIYI	ah-kee-NEE-yee	A blessing.	Nigeria	
ALAMAKO	ah-lah-mah-KOH	God bless this child.	Guinea (Malinke)	F
ASHAIRE	ah-shah-EE-reh	Life's blessing.	New Afrika	
BARACK	bah-RAHK	Blessed, blessing.	Arabic	
BARAKA	bah-RAH-kah	Blessing, mystical blessings.	Kenya, Tanzania	
BARAKOO	bah-rah-KOH	Blessing.	Gambia (Mandinka)	
BARIKI	bah-REE-kee	Blessed.	Kenya, Tanzania	
BARKE	BAH-keh	Blessings.	East Africa (Kiswahili)	F
BOMA	BOH-mah	Blessing.	Nigeria	
BROOK	BROOHK	Blessed one.	Ethiopia	
BUSISIWE	boo-see-see-weh	Blessed.	Azania (Nguni, Sotho, Zulu)	
CHIGOZI	chee-GOH-zee	God blesses.	Nigeria	
CHINUA	CHEE-noo-ah	God's own blessing.	Nigeria (Igbo)	M
CHINUE	CHEE-weh	God's own blessing.	Nigeria (Igbo)	F
DARNISO	dahr-NEE-soh	Blessed one.	Azania	

Name	Pronunciation	Meaning	Origin	Gender
DIARRA	dee-AH-rah	Blessing, offering.	West Africa	
DOMME	DOHM-meh	I have been blessed.	Ghana (Akan)	
IRE	EE-reh	Blessing.	Nigeria (Yoruba)	
IVEREM	ee-VEH-rem	Blessing, favor.	Nigeria (Tiv)	F
IZE	EE-zeh	Blessing.	Nigeria (Igarra)	F
KIBWE	keeb-weh	Blessed.	DRC	M
MUKISA	moo-kee-sah	Blessing, fortune, luck.	Uganda (Ganda)	
MWA	MWAH	Blessing, grace.	West Africa	
NGOZI	n-GOH-zee	Blessing.	Nigeria (Igbo)	M
NIMA	NEE-mah	Blessing.	North Africa (Arabic)	M
NTSI KELELO	n-tsee-keh-leh-loh	Blessing.	Azania (Xhosa)	M
OKAKA	oh-KAH-kah	Blessing.	Nigeria (Eleme)	
OLUSHOLA	oh-LOO-shoh-lah	God has blessed me.	Nigeria (Yoruba)	M
PREYE	preh-yeh	God's gift or blessing.	Nigeria (Igbo)	M
SIBUSISO	see-boo-see-soh	Blessing.	Azania (Zulu)	M
SISAY	see-say	A blessing.	Ethiopia (Amharic)	
TEREHAS	teh-reh-hahs	Blessed.	Ethiopia	F
TUSAJIGWE	too-SAH-jee-gweh	We are blessed.	Tanzania (Nyakyusa)	F
UKAHI	oo-KAH-hee	We know you came with God's blessings.	Nigeria (Ishan)	

Body Parts

*It is the owner of the body
who looks out for the body. —Haiti*

Name	Pronunciation	Meaning	Origin	Gender
AMABELE	ah-mah-BEH-leh	Breasts.	Azania (Xhosa)	
AMBUNDA	ahm-BOON-dah	Back; hips.	Namibia (Ovambo)	
ASHIPALA	ah-shee-PAH-lah	Face.	Namibia (Ovambo)	
CHIKOSI	chee-KOH-see	Neck.	Malawi (Ngoni)	M
FUZI	FOO-zee	Shoulder.	Kiswahili	
KAMWENDO	kah-MWEHN-doh	Leg.	Malawi	
KAPASA	kah-PAH-sah	Penis.	Zambia (Bemba)	
KIARA	KEE-ah-rah	Finger.	Kenya (Agikuyu)	M
KWANYA	KWAN-yah	Brain.	West Africa (Hausa)	
MAFUPA	mah-FOO-pah	Bones.	Zambia (Bemba)	
MEMBE	MEHM-beh	Penis.	Zambia (Bemba)	
MWILI	MWEE-lee	Body.	Kiswahili	
NAMATSI	nah-maht-see	Ears.	Namibia (Ovambo)	
NUA	noo-ah	Eye.	Cameroon (Mubako)	M
NYENDWA	n-yehnd-wah	Vagina.	Zambia (Bemba)	F
NYINDO	n-ndjh-een-doh	Nose.	Uganda (Ganda)	M
SHIKESHO	shee-KEH-shoh	Wrist.	Namibia (Ovambo)	
SOLLOO	sohl-loh	Clitoris.	Gambia (Mandinka)	
UCHI	OO-chee	Nakedness.	Kiswahili	

Brothers and Sisters

*When your sister does your hair,
you do not need a mirror. —Africa*

Name	Pronunciation	Meaning	Origin	Gender
ADRI	adh-ree	Brother.	Uganda (Lugbara)	M
ADRIKO	adh-ree-koh	Without brothers.	Uganda (Lugbara)	M

Name	Pronunciation	Meaning	Origin	Gender
BHUTI	BOO-tee	Brother.	Azania (Xhosa)	
CAAMEN	kaah-mehn	Brother.	Gambia (Wolof)	M
DADA	dah-dah	Sister (Dada Nubia or Da Nubia).	Africa (Kiswahili)	F
DADE	DAH-deh	Sister.	Azania (Zulu)	F
DADIYE	dah-DEE-yeh	His sister.	Kiswahili	F
DARIKA	dah-REE-kah	Brotherhood.	West Africa (Hausa)	
DOOKEE	doh-keh	Young brother.	Gambia (Mandinka)	
DOOMAA	dooh-maah	Brother or sister.	Gambia (Mandinka)	
FOWABO	foo-WAH-boh	His, her, their brother.	Azania (Zulu)	M
FOWENU	foh-WEHN-noo	Your brother.	Azania (Zulu)	
KAKA	KAH-kah	Brother (Kaka Khary or Ka Khary); elder brother.	Kiswahili	M
KANYANYA	kah-ndjh-ah-ndjh-ah	Little sister.	Uganda (Ganda)	F
KUMBEGA	koom-BEH-gah	Brotherliness can never end.	Cameroon (Mubako)	M
KUNGABA	koon-GAH-bah	Brotherliness is affected by bad situations.	Cameroon (Mubako)	M
KUNJUMA	koon-joo-mah	Brotherhood is good.	Cameroon (Mubako)	M
KWAGA-LANA	KWAH-gah-lah-nah	Brotherly love.	Kenya, Tanzania (Kiswahili)	M
LEBKUNGA	lehb-KOON-gah	You cannot buy brotherliness.	Cameroon (Mubako)	F
NAHKUNA	nah-KOO-nah	My brother cannot be bad for me.	Cameroon (Mubako)	F
NWANNEDI	n-wahn-neh-dee	Brotherhood lives.	Nigeria (Igbo)	M
NYAKUNA	n-yah-koo-nah	I have mixed brotherliness.	Cameroon (Mubako)	M
NYEMKUNA	n-yehm-koo-nah	One cannot beg for, or borrow, a brother.	Cameroon (Mubako)	M

Name	Pronunciation	Meaning	Origin	Gender
SARE	SAH-reh	Incision made during a ritual of blood brotherhood.	Kiswahili	
SESI	seh-see	Sister.	Azania (Sotho)	F
UHUTI	oo-HOO-tee	My sister.	Kiswahili	F
UMBU	OOM-boo	Sister.	Kiswahili	F

Calm

Don't think there are no crocodiles just because the water is calm. —Malawi

Name	Pronunciation	Meaning	Origin	Gender
ANTEBBA	ahn-tehb-bah	Calm and beautiful bride.	Cameroon (Mubako)	F
AZOLA	a-ZOH-lah	His arrival brought calmness to the home.	Azania (Xhosa)	M
BANYUGGA	bahn-yoog-gah	Your insults will not upset me.	Cameroon (Mubako)	M
BIDBILA	beed-bee-lah	Calm has been restored in the home (name given to child after a family reconciliation).	Cameroon (Mubako)	M
BITEBBA	bee-teh-bah	The home is now calm.	Cameroon (Mubako)	M
CHAVELELA	chah-vee-LEH-lah	Calm, console, comfort.	Southern Africa (Tsonga)	
DAMBA	DAHM-bah	To become calm.	Azania (Xhosa)	
DIDAKEJE	dee-dah-KEH-jeh	Tranquil.	West Africa (Yoruba)	
FWASA	FWAH-sah	Be calm.	Zambia (Tumbuka)	M
GUNDJILENI	goon-jee-leh-nee	Calm down!	Namibia (Ovambo)	
HALEEMA	hah-LEE-mah	Calm, serene.	North Africa (Arabic)	
JOYA	JOH-yah	Shows restraint in the face of provocations from others.	Zambia (Tumbuka)	M

Name	Pronunciation	Meaning	Origin	Gender
KATENDE	kah-tehn-deh	The little one that is relaxed, little one that is at peace.	Uganda (Ganda)	M
KIMYA	KEEM-yah	Calm, quiet.	Kenya, Tanzania	
LAINISHA	lah-NEE-shah	To make smooth.	Kiswahili	
LUAM	loo-AHM	Calm; peaceful.	Eritrea, Ethiopia (Tigrinya)	F
MAKINI	mah-KEE-nee	Calm, serene.	East Africa (Kiswahili)	F
MZOLISI	m-zoh-LEE-see	The one who brings calmness.	Azania (Xhosa)	M
NACALA	nah-KAH-lah	Calm, peace, tranquility.	Mozambique	F
NITSUWA	neet-soo-wah	Calm.	West Africa (Hausa)	
NOKUZOLA	noh-koo-ZOH-lah	The confidently calm one.	Azania (Xhosa)	F
NUGA	NOO-gah	Nothing pains me.	Cameroon (Mubako)	M
NYUGA	n-yoo-gah	Nothing pains me.	Cameroon (Mubako)	M
NZOLO	n-ZOH-loh	Calmness.	Azania (Xhosa)	M
RELE	REH-leh	Calm.	West Africa (Yoruba)	
RUZUNA	roo-ZOO-nah	Calm; composed.	Kiswahili	F
SAKINA	SAH-kee-NAH	Tranquility; calm.	Kenya, Tanzania (Kiswahili)	F
SHUARI	shoo-AH-ree	Calm, placid.	Kiswahili	
SHUWARI	shoo-WAH-ree	Calm, placid.	Kiswahili	
SHWARI	SHAHWAH-ree	Calm.	Kiswahili	
TOFFA	TOH-fah	The country is calm.	Benin	M
TULIA	too-LEE-ah	Be calm.	Kiswahili	
TULIVU	too-LEE-voo	Tranquility.	Kenya, Tanzania	
ZODWA	ZOHD-wah	Tranquil; alone.	Azania (Zulu)	F
ZOLANI	zoh-LAHN-nee	Be calm.	Azania (Xhosa)	M
ZOLEKA	zoh-LEH-kah	She is calm; at peace.	Azania (Xhosa)	

Name	Pronunciation	Meaning	Origin	Gender
ZOLEWA	ZOH-leh-lwah	Everywhere she goes, storms will calm.	Azania (Xhosa)	F
ZOLIE	zoh-lee	To make calm.	Azania (Xhosa)	F
ZOLISA	zoh-LEE-sah	Bring about calmness.	Azania (Xhosa)	M
ZOZO	zoh-zoh	The calm, meek one.	Azania (Xhosa)	

Celebration

Even in the monastery there is occasion for song and merriment. —Ethiopia

Name	Pronunciation	Meaning	Origin	Gender
ABIODUN	ah-BEE-oh-doon	Born during a festival, holiday.	Nigeria (Yoruba)	M
BIKI	BEE-kee	Celebration.	West Africa (Hausa)	
BIRORI	bee-ROH-ree	Festivities.	Rwanda, Burundi (Kinyarwanda, Kirundi)	
CHEGA	CHE-gah	Holiday.	East Africa (Kiswahili)	M
CHEJA	CHE-jah	Holiday.	East Africa (Kiswahili)	M
DUMO	DOO-moh	One who is celebrated.	Azania	M
EIDI	eh-EE-dee	Festival, festivity.	Kenya, Tanzania	
EJAJA	ee-JAH-jah	Be jovial, merry.	Azania (Zulu)	
FARETI	fah-REH-tee	Parade.	West Africa (Hausa)	
JOMBOO	johm-boh	Celebration.	Gambia (Mandinka)	
JUURA	joo-rah	To celebrate.	Gambia (Mandinka)	
JUURI	joo-ree	To celebrate.	Gambia (Mandinka)	
KUDYAUKU	koo-YAH-oo-koo	Feast.	Malawi (Ngoni)	M
MAGOMA	mah-goh-MAH	Celebration.	East Africa (Kiswahili)	M
MKHOSI	m-KOH-see	The celebration.	Azania	M

Name	Pronunciation	Meaning	Origin	Gender
MWAKA	MWAH-kah	Born on New Year's Eve.	Uganda (Luganda)	M
NAFASI	nah-FAH-see	To love good times.	Kenya, Tanzania	
NOMKHOSI	nohm-koh-see	The celebration.	Azania	F
SHANGILA	shahn-GEE-lah	Celebrate.	East Africa (Kiswahili)	F
SHANGWE	shahn-GWEH	Celebration.	East Africa (Kiswahili)	F
SIKUKUU	see-KOO-koo-oo	A festival.	Kiswahili	
SULLE	SOOL-leh	Feast.	Mali	
TAMASHA	tah-MAH-shah	Happy occasion.	East Africa (Kiswahili)	F
YOHANA	yoh-HAH-nah	Congratulations.	Eritrea	M

Celestial

Nobody shows heaven to a child. —Ghana

Name	Pronunciation	Meaning	Origin	Gender
ABIJURU	ah-bee-joo-roo	Those who are destined for heaven.	Rwanda, Burundi, DRC (Huti, Tutsi, Twa)	
ADDAE	ah-DAH-eh	Morning sun.	Ghana (Akan)	M
ADHIAMBO	ah-dee-ahm-boh	The sun.	Central Africa	
AHISHA	ah-HEE-shah	The day star.	Azania (Xhosa)	
ALIHAWAA	ah-lee-hah-wah	All the space above earth.	Gambia (Mandinka)	
ALJANNA	ahl-jahn-nah	Paradise.	West Africa (Hausa)	
AMEN	AH-mehn	I am one with heaven.	Egypt/Khamit	
AMENSUA	ah-mehn-soo-ah	Knowing heaven, I am great.	Egypt/Khamit	
ANTWAR	ahnt-wah	Moonbeams, sunbeams.	North Africa (Arabic)	
ANYANWU	ahn-YAHN-woo	Sunshine.	Nigeria (Igbo)	M
ARJANA	ahr-JAH-nah	Heaven.	Gambia (Wolof)	

Name	Pronunciation	Meaning	Origin	Gender
BADRU	BAH-droo	Born at full moon.	Tanzania (Kiswahili)	M
BALELA	bah-LEH-lah	Clear skies.	Azania (Zulu)	
BARISA	bah-REE-sah	Sunrise.	Somalia	
CHAPHA	CHAH-pah	Touched with the first rays of the sun.	Azania (Xhosa)	
CHERIKA	cheh-REE-kah	The moon.	Ethiopia (Amharic)	
CWATHA	chwah-THAH	Cloudless.	Azania (Zulu)	
DIAH	DEE-ah	Born during full moon.	Somalia	M
DIKELA	dee-KEH-lah	Setting of the sun.	Southern Africa (Tsonga)	
DUTUVA	doo-TOO-vah	Overcast, cloudy.	Southern Africa (Tsonga)	
DYAMBU	dYAHM-boo	Day, sunlight.	Southern Africa (Tsonga)	
EFURU	eh-foo-roo	Daughter of heaven.	West Africa	
EKERA	eh-KEH-rah	The afterworld.	Ethiopia (Oromo)	
ELUMANJO	eh-loo-MAHN-joh	Heaven knows the evildoers.	Nigeria (Igbo)	
ENUDIKE	eh-noo-DEE-keh	Heaven holds the power.	Nigeria (Igbo)	M
GASUH	gah-swah	Chief of the moon.	Cameroon (Mubako)	M
GGULU	goo-loo	Heaven; sky.	Uganda (Ganda)	M
GHAZALA	gah-ZAH-lah	Rising sun.	North Africa (Arabic)	F
GHENET	geh-neht	Paradise.	Ethiopia	
GORE DENNA	goh-reh-deh-NAH	Black cloud; storm cloud.	Zimbabwe (Shona)	M
GULU	GOO-loo	Heaven.	Uganda	
HALA	HAH-lah	Ring around the moon or sun.	North Africa (Arabic)	F
IGULU	ee-goo-loo	Sky; heaven.	Uganda (Soga)	M
IGWE	EE-weh	Heavenly.	Nigeria (Igbo)	M
ILANGA	ee-LAHN-gah	The sun.	Azania (Zulu)	
ISIO	ee-SEE-oh	Stars.	Nigeria (Urhobo)	

Name	Pronunciation	Meaning	Origin	Gender
IZULU	ee-ZOO-loo	Sky.	Azania (Zulu)	
JANNA	JAH-nah	Paradise, heaven.	Kenya, Tanzania (Kiswahili)	F
JATA	JAH-tah	Star.	Kenya (Agikuyu)	F
JECHA	JEH-cha	Sunrise.	East Africa (Kiswahili)	M
JONGI LANGA	ohn-GEE-jlahn-gah	He will shoot for the sun; he faces the sun, stares at the sun.	Azania (Xhosa)	M
JURU	joo-roo	Sky.	Rwanda, Burundi, DRC (Huti, Tutsi, Twa)	M
KALIHE JURU	kah-lee-heh-JOO-roo	The one from the sky.	Rwanda, Burundi (Kinyarwanda, Kirundi)	
KAMARIA	kah-mah-REE-ah	Like the moon.	West Africa	
KASUBA	kah-SOO-bah	The sun.	Zambia (Bemba)	
KAUKAB	kah-oo-kab	Star.	Kiswahili	F
KHANYILE	KAHN-yee-leh	The one who shines like a star.	Azania (Xhosa)	M
KHITANTA	khee-TAHN-tah	Heaven gives as I give.	Egypt/Khamit	
KHORANHLAI	koh-rahn-lah-ee	She who brings sun.	Southern Africa	F
KHWEZI	K-WEH-zee	Morning star.	Azania (Xhosa)	M
KIANGA	kee-AHN-gah	Sunshine, sunbeams.	East Africa (Kiswahili)	F
KIRE	tch-ee-reh	Cloud.	Uganda (Ganda)	F
KIYUMBA	kee-YOOM-bah	Morning sun is sweet, but becomes bitter in the afternoon.	Uganda	M
KOMU SHANA	kohm-OO-SHAH-nah	Born when the sun was shining.	Uganda (Runyankore)	F
KWEEZI	kweh-eh-zee	The moon.	Rwanda, Burundi, DRC (Huti, Tutsi, Twa)	M

Name	Pronunciation	Meaning	Origin	Gender
LANDGA LIBALELE	lahn-dah-lee-bah-LEH-leh	The hot sunshine.	Azania	M
LANGA	LAHN-gah	Sun.	Azania (Xhosa)	M
LIBBILA	leeb-bee-lah	Setting sun.	Zambia, Zimbabwe (Tonga)	M
LOLIA	loh-LEE-ah	Shining star.	Nigeria	
LOMO	LOH-moh	Sunshine.	Nigeria	
LUTANDA	loo-TAHN-dah	Star.	Zambia (Bemba)	
LUTONDE	loo-tohn-deh	Star.	DRC (Rega)	F
MACHEO	mah-CHEH-oh	Sunrise.	Kiswahili	
MARU	MAH-roo	Clouds.	Azania (North Sotho)	
MATIMA	mah-TEE-mah	Full moon.	Kiswahili	
MATLAA	maht-LAH-ah	Sunrise.	West Africa	F
MATSATSI	maht-SAHT-see	A child born on a sunny day.	Azania (Nguni)	
MATU	MAH-too	The clouds.	Kenya (Agikuyu)	M
MAWINGU	mah-WEEN-goo	Clouds.	Kiswahili	
MBINGU	m-been-goo	Heaven.	Kenya, Tanzania	
MLENGA LENGA	m-lehg-ah-LENG-ah	Heaven.	Malawi (Ngoni)	M
MUKAM WEZI	moo-kahm-WEH-zee	Moonlight.	Rwanda, Burundi (Kinyarwanda, Kirundi)	
MUNYENYE	moon-yehn-yeh	Star.	Uganda (Ganda)	
MWESHI	MWEH-shee	The moon.	Zambia (Bemba)	
MWEZI	m-weh-zee	The moon.	Uganda (Ganda)	
NAJMA	NAH-jh-mah	Star.	East Africa (Kiswahili)	F
NAKIRE	nnah-tch-ee-reh	Cloud.	Uganda (Ganda)	F
NAKPANGI	nahk-pahn-gee	Star.	Central Africa	F

Name	Pronunciation	Meaning	Origin	Gender
NALEDI	nah-LEH-dee	A star, eternal.	Azania (Zulu)	
NAMALE	nnah-mah-leh	Clouds, associated with wind instruments.	Uganda (Ganda)	F
NEWAN YAMA	neh-wahn-YAH-mah	Wait for the sun.	Cameroon (Mubako)	M
NOMAFU	noh-MAH-foo	She brings the clouds.	Azania (Xhosa)	F
NOMA LANGA	noh-MAH-LAHN-gah	Sunny.	Azania (Xhosa)	F
NUMANTA	noo-mahn-tah	Heaven gives as I give.	Egypt/Khamit	
NURESHA	noo-REH-shah	Heaven is my joy.	Egypt/Khamit	
NYAMA	n-yah-mah	Sun.	Cameroon (Mubako)	M
NYAM GAMSEN	nyahm gahm-sehn	The sun does not recognize anybody.	Cameroon (Mubako)	M
NYARUGURU	ndjh-ah-roo-goo-roo	One from the sky.	Rwanda, Burundi, DRC (Huti, Tutsi, Twa)	M
NYOTA	n-yoh-tah	Star.	Kiswahili	
OKON	OH-kohn	Born after sunset.	West Africa	
OTHA	OH-tah	The sun.	Azania (Xhosa)	
OTHAMELA	oh-tah-MEH-lah	To bask in the sun.	Azania (Zulu)	
RAMSES	RAHM-sehs	Sun born.	Egypt/Khamit	M
RANA	RAH-nah	Sun.	West Africa (Hausa)	
SAMA	SAH-mah	Heaven.	West Africa (Hausa)	F
SANASNU	sah-NAH-snoo	I only know heaven.	Egypt/Khamit	
SANG	SAHNG	Star.	Cameroon (Mungaka)	M
SARRAQA	sah-rrah-kah	The rise of the moon, stars, and sun.	Ethiopia (Amharic)	
SEBUN YENYERI	seh-boon-yehn-YEH-reh	Stars.	Rwanda, Burundi (Kinyarwanda, Kirundi)	M
SEMAINESH	seh-MEEHG-nehsh	You are the sky.	Eritrea	F

Name	Pronunciation	Meaning	Origin	Gender
SEMWEZI	ssehm-weh-eh-zee	The moon; moonlight.	Uganda (Ganda)	M
SHAHAAB	SHAH-haab	Shooting star.	East Africa (Kiswahili)	M
SHAMFA	SHAHM-fah	Sunshine.	Somalia	F
SHAMI	SHAH-mee	Like the sun.	North Africa	F
SHAMIS	shah-mees	Sun.	Sudan	
SHANIRA	shah-NEE-rah	Warmed by the sun.	Zimbabwe (Shona)	
SHEMSA	SHEHM-sah	Sunlight.	East Africa (Kiswahili)	F
SOAMAKIRI	soo-ah-mah-kee-ree	Paradise, heaven.	Nigeria	
SOBILLA	soh-BEEL-lah	The moon is up; she is a light to the man's feet.	Cameroon (Mubako)	F
THORAYA	toh-RAH-yah	Star.	North Africa (Arabic)	
THURAYA	too-RAH-yah	Star.	North Africa (Arabic)	
UZOIGWE	oo-zoh-eeg-weh	Path to sky.	Nigeria (Igbo)	M
UZUNGO	oo-ZOON-goh	The halo around the moon.	Kiswahili	
VEGA	VEH-gah	Shooting star.	North Africa (Arabic)	
WATA	WAH-tah	Moon.	West Africa (Hausa)	
WINGU	ween-goo	Heavenly cloud.	East Africa (Kiswahili)	F
YANIKA	yah-NEE-kah	To dry in the sun.	DRC (Kongo)	F
ZULU	ZOO-loo	Sky.	Azania (Zulu)	M

Change, Growth, and Maturity

To a man who has only a hammer in his tool kit,
every problem looks like a nail. —*Africa*

Name	Pronunciation	Meaning	Origin	Gender
ANANI	a-nah-nee	Increase, thrive, expand.	Azania (Xhosa)	M

Name	Pronunciation	Meaning	Origin	Gender
ASSEFA	ah-SEHF-ah	He has increased our family by coming into the world.	Ethiopia	M
ATILE	ah-TEE-leh	Increasing family.	Azania (Sotho)	
AYANDA	ah-YAHN-dah	They augment the family, another one.	Azania (Zulu)	
BADILINI	BAH-dee-lee-nee	Change.	East Africa (Kiswahili)	M
BAMBELI	bahm-BEH-lee	Substitute.	Azania (Zulu)	
BANDILE	bahn-DEE-leh	They have grown.	Azania (Zulu)	
BAZATOHA	bah-zah-TOH-ah	They will grow.	Rwanda, Burundi (Kinyarwanda, Kirundi)	M
DALMAR	DAHL-mahr	Versatile.	Somalia	
EJODAKE	eh-joh-DAH-keh	Wherever the deficiency is, I will mend.	Nigeria (Ishan)	
FUMIISA	foo-MEE-ee-sah	Enrichment.	Southern Africa (Tsonga)	
KEBEDE	keh-BEH-deh	Getting heavy.	Ethiopia	M
KHEHLE	KEH-leh	The mature one.	Azania (Xhosa)	M
KULU	koo-loo	Grow; mature.	Uganda (Soga)	M
LAKE	LAH-keh	Getting better.	Ethiopia	M
LALE	LAH-lee	Flexible.	East Africa (Kiswahili)	M
MHLUME	mloom-meh	Good growth.	Swaziland	
MUKURIRA	moo-koo-REE-rah	Who grows for.	Rwanda, Burundi (Kinyarwanda, Kirundi)	M
NAHPAGHA	nah-pah-gah	She cannot be otherwise.	Cameroon (Mubako)	F
NAHSEH	nah-seh	It is not yet mature.	Cameroon (Mubako)	F
NKEHLI	n-KEH-lee	The mature one.	Azania	F
PENSIA	pehn-SEE-ah	You have changed.	Cameroon (Mubako)	F
RABUWA	RAH-boo-wah	Grow.	East Africa (Kiswahili)	F
SIBADILI	SEE-bah-dee-lee	I will not change.	East Africa (Kiswahili)	F

Name	Pronunciation	Meaning	Origin	Gender
SIYANDA	see-YAHN-dah	We are growing, increasing.	Azania (Zulu)	F
THUTHUKA	too-TOO-kah	Grow, develop.	Azania	
UMDENI	oom-DEH-nee	Growing family.	Azania (Zulu)	
WAYIGHA	wah-YEE-ghah	Do not change plans.	Cameroon (Mubako)	M
YANDA	YAHN-dah	Increase, expand.	Azania (Xhosa)	M
ZADA	ZAH-dah	To grow.	North Africa (Arabic)	F
ZAIDEE	zah-EE-dee	Blooming, flourishing.	North Africa (Arabic)	
ZIADA	zee-AH-dah	Increase, surplus.	North Africa (Arabic)	F

Character and Reputation

Better you lose time, than character. —Jamaica

Name	Pronunciation	Meaning	Origin	Gender
HALI	HAH-lee	Character.	West Africa (Hausa)	
IRILI	ee-REE-lee	Reputation, honor.	West Africa (Hausa)	
ISIMO	ee-SEE-moh	Character, nature.	Azania (Zulu)	
IWA	EE-wah	Character.	West Africa (Yoruba)	
JALEN	JAH-lehn	You don't need to brag, we already know you.	Nigeria (Ishan)	
KATEKE	kah-TEH-keh	Person who is very pleasant at first, but does not wear well upon longer acquaintance.	Angola (Ovimbundu)	
MBUNDU	m-BOON-doo	Live closely with a person to know their character.	Angola (Ovimbundu)	
SILIKA	see-LEE-kah	Instinct, disposition, character.	Kenya, Tanzania	
VUSI	voo-see	One who restores the family name.	Azania (Xhosa)	M

Charm and Charisma

If a poor person has nothing else,
he has at least a sweet tongue with which to defer
the payment of his debts. —Ghana

Name	Pronunciation	Meaning	Origin	Gender
AVIELELE	ah-vee-eh-leh-leh	Charmer.	Nigeria (Bini)	
BWANGA	BWAHN-gah	Charm, spell.	Zambia (Bemba)	
GERDA	gehr-dah	Snake charmer.	West Africa	
HAIBA	HAH-ee-bah	Charm.	East Africa (Kiswahili)	F
HIRIZI	hee-REE-zee	Charm.	Kiswahili	
ILIZI	ee-LEE-zee	Charm against lions.	Kiswahili	
JEMILA	jeh-MEE-lah	Charming and delightful girl.	East Africa	F
KAATIMOO	kaah-tee-mooh	Charm.	Gambia (Mandinka)	
MARINI	MAH-ree-nee	Attractive, very charming.	Kenya, Tanzania (Kiswahili)	F
OPUNABO	oh-poo-NAH-boh	One with charisma.	Nigeria	
TOROSHA	toh-ROH-shah	To entice away.	Kiswahili	
YUSUFU	yoo-soo-foo	Enchanter.	East Africa	M

Children and Youth

A tree is straightened when it is young. —Africa

Name	Pronunciation	Meaning	Origin	Gender
AKINLABI	ah-keen-LAH-bee	We have a boy.	Nigeria	M
AKINTUNDE	ah-KEEN-toon-deh	A boy has come again.	Nigeria (Yoruba)	M
ANDILE	ahn-DEE-leh	More children.	Azania (Xhosa)	
AZI	AH-zee	Youth.	Nigeria	M

Name	Pronunciation	Meaning	Origin	Gender
BEBI	BEH-bee	Baby.	East Africa (Kiswahili)	F
DYESHA	DYEH-shah	A well-built youth.	Azania (Xhosa)	
GINIKANWA	gee-nee-KAHN-wah	Nothing is greater than a child.	Nigeria (Igbo)	F
IFEYINWA	ee-feh-yeen-wah	Nothing resembles a child.	Nigeria (Igbo)	F
KABALA	kah-bah-lah	Young.	DRC (Rega)	F
KABWANA	kahb-WAH-nah	Young boy.	Malawi	M
KANA	KAH-nah	Small child.	Rwanda, Burundi (Kinyarwanda, Kirundi)	M
KIJANA	KEE-jah-nah	Youthful, young.	Kenya, Tanzania (Kiswahili)	M
KILOLO	kee-LOH-loh	Youth shines upon her.	Kiswahili	F
KIPUSA	kee-POO-sah	Young girl.	Kenya, Tanzania	
MJUKUU	m-JOO-koo	Grandchild.	Kiswahili	
MTOTO	MTOH-toh	Youngster, little boy.	East Africa (Kiswahili)	M
NTONGO	n-tohn-goh	The little girl.	Azania	F
NWADOZILI	n-wah-doh-zee-lee	Child rebuilds.	Nigeria (Igbo)	
NWOHA	n-woh-hah	People's child.	Nigeria (Igbo)	
NWORA	n-woh-rah	People's child.	Nigeria (Igbo)	
NYONYA	n-yohn-yah	To suck the breast.	Kiswahili	
OMOSEDE	oh-MOH-seh-deh	A child counts more than a king.	Benin	F
OMOTAYO	oh-moh-TAH-yoh	A child is worth everything.	Nigeria	
OMOWON	oh-MOH-wohn	Children are dear.	Nigeria (Yoruba)	
POTINGANA	poh-teen-GAH-nah	Baby.	Azania (Zulu)	
SEBUTO	seh-eh-boo-toh	Youthfulness.	Rwanda, Burundi (Kinyarwanda, Kirundi)	M
SHERITI	sheh-REE-tee	Little girl.	Egypt/Khamit	F
TOTO	TOH-toh	Baby.	Kiswahili	

Name	Pronunciation	Meaning	Origin	Gender
UDOGO	oo-DOH-goh	Youthfulness.	Kiswahili	
UJANA	oo-JAH-nah	Youth.	Kiswahili	

Clarity and Confusion

*She who knows a matter
beforehand confuses the liar. —Benin*

Name	Pronunciation	Meaning	Origin	Gender
ADISA	ah-DEE-sah	The clear one.	Nigeria	M
BONAKELE	bah-nah-KEH-leh	It has been made clear.	Azania (Xhosa)	M
DIDEKA	dee-DEH-kah	Be confused.	Azania (Xhosa)	
DHIHIRIKA	dee-hee-REE-kah	Be clear.	Kiswahili	
KOYINDI	koh-yeen-dee	To clarify.	Gambia (Mandinka)	
LWEZI	lweh-ZEE	One who lacks clarity.	Azania	
MARIYAN	mah-ree-yahn	Brilliance, clarity.	North Africa (Arabic)	
NENANI	neh-NAH-nee	Explanation.	Malawi	
NOLWEZI	nohl-WEH-zee	One who lacks clarity.	Azania	F
OBALA	oh-BAH-lah	Out in the open, clearly.	Azania (Zulu)	
SAFA	SAH-fah	Clarity.	North Africa (Arabic)	
SAFIYA	sah-FEE-yah	Clear-minded.	Kiswahili	F
TOLIKI	toh-LEE-kee	Interpreter.	Azania (Xhosa)	

Cleanliness and Purity

It is a nasty bird that messes in its own nest. —Africa

Name	Pronunciation	Meaning	Origin	Gender
ADILI	AH-dee-lee	Pure.	Kenya, Tanzania	

Name	Pronunciation	Meaning	Origin	Gender
ASUKILE	ah-soo-KEE-leh	The Lord has washed me.	Tanzania (Nyakyusa)	M
AYEZA	ah-yeh-zah	He cleanses.	Uganda (Kiga, Nyankore, Nyoro, Toro)	
BASA	BAH-sah	Clean, pure, bright.	Togo	
BUNONO	boo-NOH-noh	The neat one; one who is well-organized.	Azania	
CHINASA	chee-NAH-sah	God cleanses.	Nigeria	
GEZANI	geh-ZAH-nee	Wash yourself.	Zambia (Tumbuka)	M
JUGHA	joo-gah	One who does not want to be smeared with filth.	Cameroon (Mubako)	M
KATUKU	kah-too-koo	The little one who is pure.	Uganda (Soga)	F
MATLAKALA	maht-lah-KAH-lah	One who sweeps the home clean.	Azania (Sotho)	
MBEJA	mBEH-jah	Neat; well-dressed.	Africa (Kiswahili)	M
MUTHERU	MOO-tehh-roo	Cleansed.	Kenya (Agikuyu)	M
NABUKWASI	nah-boo-KWAH-see	Bad housekeeper.	Uganda (Ganda, Luganda)	F
NAKUYA	nnah-koo-yah	That makes dirty.	Uganda (Ganda)	F
NSANZYA	n-sahn-dzjah	Cleaning; washing.	Zambia, Zimbabwe (Tonga)	
NYIRAWERA	n-yee-rah-weh-rah	Clean.	Rwanda, Burundi (Kinyarwanda, Kirundi)	F
OBIOMA	oh-bee-OH-mah	Clean mind, good heart.	Nigeria (Igbo)	
OGESHA	oh-geh-shah	To bathe someone.	Kiswahili	
PESULANI	peh-soo-LAH-nee	Comb your hair.	Zambia (Chewa)	M
SADIO	sah-dee-oh	Pure.	West Africa	F
SAFI	SAH-fee	Pure, neat, clean.	Kenya, Tanzania	F
SAFISHA	sah-FEE-shah	Cleansed, clean.	Kenya, Tanzania	
SAUDI	sah-OO-dee	Clean, neat.	Kenya, Tanzania	
SHOORAI	shoh-oh-RAH-ee	Broom that sweeps clean.	Zimbabwe (Shona)	F

Name	Pronunciation	Meaning	Origin	Gender
TAKASA	tah-KAH-sah	To cleanse.	Kiswahili	
TAKATA	TAH-kah-tah	Pure, clean; become clear.	East Africa (Kiswahili)	M
UNADHIFU	oo-nah-DEE-foo	Neatness.	Kiswahili	
USAFI	oo-SAH-fee	Cleanliness; purity.	Kiswahili	

Colors

A raven desires colorfulness just as an unenterprising man desires cattle. —Namibia

Name	Pronunciation	Meaning	Origin	Gender
ASWAD	ahss-wahd	Black.	North Africa (Arabic)	M
BOMBU	BOHM-boo	Brown, red.	Azania (Xhosa)	
CHUM	CHOOM	Black.	Kiswahili	
FUSA	FOO-sah	Dark brown.	Azania (Xhosa)	
JA	JAH	Red.	West Africa (Hausa)	
KEMOSIRI	keh-moh-SEE-ree	Black.	Egypt/Khamit	M
MONTSHO	MOHN-shoh	Black.	Botswana (Tswana)	M
RANGA	RAHN-gah	Of many colors.	Azania (Xhosa)	
RUKARA	roo-KAH-rah	Black.	Rwanda, Burundi (Kinyarwanda, Kirundi)	
TALE	TAH-leh	Green.	Botswana (Tswana)	
TSHWEU	tch-weh-yoo	White.	Azania (Sotho)	M

Comfort

If a child takes interest in crying, its mother will develop interest in comforting it. —Benin

Name	Pronunciation	Meaning	Origin	Gender
ABADEET	ah-bah-DEET	Comforter.	Eritrea	F
ASITA	ah-SEE-tah	Console, pacify.	Kiswahili	
ASIYA	AH-see-yah	Console.	East Africa (Kiswahili)	F
DAMU	DAH-moo	Sudden relief.	Azania (Zulu)	
DUDUZA	doo-doo-zah	Comfort.	Azania (Zulu)	
DUDUZILE	doo-doo-zee-leh	The comforter.	Azania	
FARAJA	FAH-rah-jah	Relief.	East Africa (Kiswahili)	F
FOPHISA	foh-PEE-sah	Pacifier.	Lesotho (South Sotho)	
HEKELEKA	heh-keh-LEH-kah	Comfort!	Namibia (Ovambo)	
ITUNU	ee-TOO-noo	Consolation.	West Africa (Yoruba)	
LIWAZA	lee-WAH-zah	Consolation.	Kenya, Tanzania	
LIZO	lee-zoh	The one who consoled us.	Azania (Xhosa)	
MDUDUZI	m-doo-DOO-zee	The comforter.	Azania	M
MTHULI	m-TOO-lee	One who relieves.	Azania	M
MTHU THUZELI	M-TOO-TOO-zeh-lee	One who has given us comfort.	Azania (Xhosa)	M
NEPO	NEH-poh	Comforter.	Sierra Leone	
NOMALIZO	noh-mah-lee-zoh	Comforter.	Azania (Xhosa)	F
NUHA	NOO-hah	Consoled.	Kiswahili	
ONAJIN	oh-NAH-jeen	Soothing.	Nigeria (Yoruba)	
PHOLISA	POH-lee-sah	She brings soothing like a salve.	Azania (Xhosa)	F
RAYHA	rah-ee-hah	Small comfort.	Kiswahili	
SAIWA	sah-ee-WAH	Consolation.	East Africa (Kiswahili)	F
TUKITJHI	too-keet-jee	He who solves or attends to problems; to correct or rectify.	Zimbabwe (Ndebele)	M

Name	Pronunciation	Meaning	Origin	Gender
UTULIZI	oo-too-LEE-zee	One who brings comfort.	Kiswahili	
ZINGIRA	ZEHN-GEE-rah	To comfort.	Kiswahili	
ZINZI	ZEHN-zee	Comfortably settled.	Azania (Xhosa)	

Courage and Bravery

Fear is nothing. The thing is courage. —*Azania (Zulu)*

Name	Pronunciation	Meaning	Origin	Gender
ADOFO	ah-DOH-foh	Courageous warrior.	Ghana	M
AKHIWU	ah-KEE-woo	Let us have courage and perseverance.	Nigeria (Ishan)	
AKIN KAWON	ah-keen-KAH-wohn	Bravery pacified them.	Nigeria (Yoruba)	M
AKINS	AH-keens	Brave boy.	Nigeria (Yoruba)	M
ANYAKA	ahn-YAH-kah	Boldness.	Nigeria (Igbo)	M
AWOLO	ah-WOH-loh	Courageous one.	Nigeria (Ishan)	
BASEL	bas-ehl	Brave.	Sudan	M
CHASIRI	chah-SEE-ree	Courage.	Kenya, Tanzania	
DANKE NEYAA	dahn-keh-neh-yaah	Courage.	Gambia (Mandinka)	
DIALLO	DEE-ah-loh	Bold one.	Guinea (Malinke)	M
DIKEJIAKU	dee-keh-jee-AH-koo	The courageous are also the wealth.	Nigeria (Igbo)	
DILA	DEE-lah	Courage.	North Africa	
FATIYAA	fah-tee-yaah	Brave.	Gambia (Mandinka)	
GASIRA	GAH-see-rah	Bold, courageous.	East Africa (Kiswahili)	F
HODARI	hoh-DAH-ree	Courageous; brave; energetic, capable.	Africa (Kiswahili)	M

Name	Pronunciation	Meaning	Origin	Gender
ISIBINDI	ee-see-BEEN-dee	Courageous, fearless.	Azania	
ISOKA	ee-SOH-kah	Courageous, fearless.	Azania	
JABARI	jah-BAH-ree	Brave, almighty, omnipotent.	East Africa (Kiswahili)	M
JAHA	JAH-hah	Courageous.	Azania (Nguni)	
JAHINA	JAH-hee-nah	Brave, courageous.	East Africa (Kiswahili)	M
JARAMOGI	JAH-rah-moh-ghee	Courageous.	Kenya (Agikuyu)	M
JARINTEE	jah-reen-teh	Brave.	Gambia (Mandinka)	
JARUNTAKA	jah-roo-TAH-kah	Courage.	West Africa (Hausa)	
JASIRI	jah-SEE-ree	Fearless.	Kenya, Tanzania	
JUBA	JOO-bah	Fearless.	Africa	M
JUSUJAA	joo-soo-jaah	Fearlessness.	Gambia (Mandinka)	
KAMBUI	kahm-boo-ee	Unafraid; fearless.	East Africa	M
KITA	KEE-tah	Be firm in the face of danger.	Kiswahili	
LAIYA	lah-EE-yah	Brave.	West Africa (Yoruba)	
MARIAM	mah-ree-ahm	Fearless.	North Africa (Arabic)	
MJASIRI	m-jah-SEE-ree	Brave, daring.	Africa (Kiswahili)	M
MPAGI	m-pah-gee	A brave person in the community; pillar of the community.	Uganda (Luganda)	M
MUJASI	moo-jaah-see	Courageous fighter, soldier.	Uganda (Ganda)	M
MUSAOPE	moo-sah-OH-peh	Do not fear, do not be afraid.	Zambia (Chewa)	M
NESIBINDI	neh-see-been-dee	Courageous, fearless.	Azania	
OMUZIRA	oh-moo-ZEE-rah	Brave.	Uganda	
RUBANZA	roo-BAHN-zah	Courageous.	Kiswahili	M
RUTIKANGA	roo-tee-KAHN-gah	The one who is never scared.	Rwanda, Burundi (Kinyarwanda, Kirundi)	
SENTWALI	sehn-TWAH-lee	Brave one.	Rwanda	M

SHUJAA	SHOO-jah	Brave; a hero.	East Africa (Kiswahili)	M
SINAAN	SEE-nahn	Brave.	Kiswahili	M
TAAMITI	tah-MEE-tee	Bravery.	Uganda (Lunyole)	M
USHUJAA	oo-SHOO-jah	Courage.	Kiswahili	
YAFEU	yah-FEH-oh	Bold.	Ghana (Fante)	M
ZUBER	ZOO-behr	Brave.	Kiswahili	M

Daughters and Sons

A new daughter is many voices. —Kenya

Name	Pronunciation	Meaning	Origin	Gender
ADAORA	ah-dah-OH-rah	A daughter for her people.	Nigeria (Igbo)	F
DAIB	DAH-eeb	Outstanding daughter.	East Africa	F
DINKEE	DEEN-keh-eh	Son.	Gambia (Mandinka)	M
DODAKAZI	doh-dah-KAH-zee	Daughter	Africa	F
DODANA	doh-DAH-nah	Son.	Azania (Zulu)	M
INDO DAKAZI	een-doh-dah-KAH-zee	Daughter.	Azania (Zulu)	
MODU	MOH-doo	Son of.	Sierra Leone	M
MORWA	mohr-wah	Son.	Azania (North Sotho)	M
NDODAKAZI	n-doh-dah-KAH-zee	Daughter.	Azania	F
NDODANA	n-doh-DAH-nah	Son.	Azania	M
NTOMBI	n-TOHM-bee	Daughter.	Azania (Zulu)	F
UWIMAMA	oo-wee-MAH-mah	Daughter of God.	Rwanda	F
YARO	YAH-roh	Son.	West Africa (Hausa)	M
ZUBA	zoo-bah	Son.	Rwanda, Burundi, DRC (Huti, Tutsi, Twa)	M

Death and Dying

It is useless to be afraid of death. —*Cameroon*

Name	Pronunciation	Meaning	Origin	Gender
AMETEFE	ah-meh-TEH-feh	Born after father's death.	Ghana (Ewe)	M
AYONDELA	ah-yohn-DEH-lah	We all bend toward death.	Angola (Ovimbundu)	
BYAITAKA	byah-ee-tah-kah	Born to die.	Uganda	F
DEHVA	DEH-vah	You are calling for death.	Cameroon (Mubako)	M
DINDI	DEEN-dee	Grave.	Zambia (Tumbuka)	M
DOHVALLA	doh-VAHL-lah	The grandfather of death.	Cameroon (Mubako)	M
JANVAGHA	jahn-VAH-gah	Feeding death or enemies.	Cameroon (Mubako)	M
KEHVAGHA	keh-VAH-gah	You cannot die in someone's place.	Cameroon (Mubako)	M
KEHVALLA	keh-VAHL-lah	Has taken death.	Cameroon (Mubako)	
KIJITA	kee-jee-tah	A child born after the death of his father.	Cameroon (Mungaka)	M
KUMANDA	koo-MAHN-dah	Graveyard.	Malawi (Ngoni)	M
KUNLE-MUGA	koon-leh-moo-gah	A child whose mother dies after delivery.	Cameroon (Mubako)	F
KUNVAGHA	koon-VAH-gah	Death is recognizable.	Cameroon (Mubako)	
KUNVALLA	koon-VAHL-lah	Cannot recognize death.	Cameroon (Mubako)	
LOVALLA	loh-VAHL-lah	I have made fun of death.	Cameroon (Mubako)	F
MAIBA	MAH-ee-bah	Grave.	Zimbabwe (Shona)	F
MAKAJIA	mah-kah-jee-ah	There is no family without a graveyard.	Cameroon (Mubako)	F
MALALO	mah-LOH-loh	Graveyard.	Zambia (Tumbuka)	M

Name	Pronunciation	Meaning	Origin	Gender
MALANI	mah-LAH-nee	Finish us (a taunt to death).	Zambia (Tumbuka)	M
NAHVALLA	nah-VAHL-lah	Our family is meant for death (name given to child after so many have died in the family).	Cameroon (Mubako)	F
NUVALLA	noo-VAHL-lah	Run away from death.	Cameroon (Mubako)	M
ONEKA	oh-neh-kah	Born to die.	Uganda (Luo)	M
ORUFU	oh-ROO-foo	Death.	Uganda (Nyoro)	
OWOLE	oh-woh-leh	One not expected to live long.	Uganda (Madi)	M
OWUO	oh-WOO-oh	Death is tragic.	Ghana	
PANVAH	PAHN-vah	One who pets death.	Cameroon (Mubako)	M
PENVALLA	pehn-VAHL-lah	Can change death.	Cameroon (Mubako)	
SIFIYE	see-fee-YEH	We are dying.	Zimbabwe (Ndebele)	M
VAANA	VAH-nah	Property of death.	Cameroon (Mubako)	F
VAHLENNA	vah-LEHN-nah	Death has abandoned me.	Cameroon (Mubako)	F
VAJEMIA	vah-jeh-MEE-ah	Death dislikes me.	Cameroon (Mubako)	F
VAKAA	VAH-kah	Too many deaths.	Cameroon (Mubako)	F
VAKIDLA	vah-KEED-lah	Deathbed.	Cameroon (Mubako)	F
VALLA	VAH-lah	Death.	Cameroon (Mubako)	F
VASIGHA	vah-SEE-gah	Death has left this one for me.	Cameroon (Mubako)	F
VISIKU	vee-SEE-koo	A child who is afraid to die.	Ghana	
WUBVALLA	woob-VAHL-lah	You have followed death.	Cameroon (Mubako)	M
YEBA	yeh-bah	I have no room for a grave near my house.	Cameroon (Mubako)	F
YEVALLA	yeh-VAHL-lah	It is bad death.	Cameroon (Mubako)	F

Name	Pronunciation	Meaning	Origin	Gender
YIGHA	YEE-gah	A child born after many others have died; taking care of a grave.	Cameroon (Mubako)	
YIVA	YEE-vah	Do not yield to death.	Cameroon (Mubako)	M
ZANVALLA	zahn-VAHL-lah	Death will see.	Cameroon (Mubako)	

Deception, Betrayal, and Thievery

Even if Christ's death could have been prevented,
Judas would still be a traitor. —*Ethiopia*

Name	Pronunciation	Meaning	Origin	Gender
CHAHMU CHANG	chah-MOO-chahng	You pretend to sympathize with a situation when you are inwardly happy of its being.	Cameroon (Mungaka)	M
CHINAMI	tch-ee-nah-mee	Bluffer.	DRC (Lamba)	
DANGANYO	dahn-GAHN-yoh	Deception.	Kiswahili	
DELIWE	dee-LEE-weh	The forsaken one.	Azania	F
DIMIA	dee-mee-ah	You have plotted against me.	Cameroon (Mubako)	F
DUKKU	DOOK-koo	Bribe.	Gambia (Wolof)	
HADAA	HAH-dah	Trickery.	Kiswahili	
HAINI	hah-EE-nee	A traitor—to betray.	Kiswahili	
JENNA	jehn-nah	I have been deceived.	Cameroon (Mubako)	M
JOMIA	joh-mee-ah	He has deceived me.	Cameroon (Mubako)	
KODMIA	kohd-MEE-ah	I have been caught red-handed.	Cameroon (Mubako)	M
KOMBO	KOHM-boh	Crooked.	Kiswahili	
MUBBI	moob-bee	Thief.	Uganda (Ganda)	M

Name	Pronunciation	Meaning	Origin	Gender
NAHJOMIA	nah-joh-MEE-ah	She has deceived me.	Cameroon (Mubako)	F
NAKYAMU	nnah-tch-aah-moo	That is false.	Uganda (Ganda)	F
NDALE	n-DAH-leh	Trick.	Malawi (Ngoni)	M
NGEGERA	n-geh-geh-rah	Crook.	Rwanda, Burundi, DRC (Huti, Tutsi, Twa)	M
ROOZANI	roh-ZAH-nee	Trick.	Malawi (Ngoni)	M
UIZI	oo-EE-zee	Theft.	Kiswahili	
ULAGHAI	oo-LAH-gah-ee	Deceit.	Kiswahili	
UMATA	oo-MAH-tah	You know what you are saying is untrue.	Nigeria (Ishan)	
UONGO	oo-OHN-goh	Falsehood.	Kiswahili	
YEBILLA	yeh-BEEL-lah	A traitor-one who spoils the village.	Cameroon (Mubako)	M
YEMI	YEHM-mee	Betrays me (i.e. releases the secret).	Cameroon (Mubako)	

Deeds and Actions

There is no beauty but the beauty of action. —*Morocco*

Name	Pronunciation	Meaning	Origin	Gender
AKANMA	ah-KAHN-mah	Doer of beautiful deeds.	Nigeria (Igbo)	F
BASHA	BAH-shah	Act of God.	East Africa (Kiswahili)	F
BEESANGA	beh-eh-sah-ngah	They kill themselves, their actions cut down on the time they will live.	Uganda (Ganda, Kiga, Nyankore)	
BUULEWA	BOO-leh-lwah	Her deeds will involve praise.	Azania (Xhosa)	F
DEZBONG	dehz-bohng	One who does good deeds.	Cameroon (Mungaka)	M

Name	Pronunciation	Meaning	Origin	Gender
EDENAU-SEGBOYE	eh-deh-nah-oo-seh-BOH-yeh	Good deeds are remembered.	Benin	F
EMEKA	eh-MEH-kah	Great deed.	Nigeria	
ISE	EE-seh	Action.	West Africa (Yoruba)	
KWENZILE	kwehn-ZEE-leh	The deed has been done.	Azania	M
MBONU	m-BOH-noo	Action speaks louder than words.	Nigeria	M
NDACHI TANJI	n-dah-chee-TAHN-jee	What have I done?	Malawi (Ngoni)	F
NTWARI	n-twaah-ree	Deeds of courage.	Rwanda, Burundi, DRC (Huti, Tutsi, Twa)	M
SAYID	SAH-yeed	My deeds have caused problems.	Cameroon (Mubako)	M

Dependency and Reliability

The poor man cannot become angry
with those on whom he depends. —*Africa*

Name	Pronunciation	Meaning	Origin	Gender
DANSO	DAN-soh	Reliable.	Ghana (Ashanti)	M
HASAN	HAH-sahn	Reliable, honorable.	North Africa (Arabic)	
JAWANZA	jah-WAHN-zah	This one is dependable.	Central Africa	M
MADHUBUTI	mahd-hoo-BOO-tee	Reliable.	Kiswahili	
SOYAMA	soh-YAHM-ah	Rely on each other.	Azania (Zulu)	M
YAMILE	yah-MEE-leh	One who relies on others.	Azania	F

Determination and Will

*If you are building a house and a nail breaks,
do you stop building, or do you change the nail? —Africa*

Name	Pronunciation	Meaning	Origin	Gender
ADROA	ah-droh-wah	The will of God.	Uganda (Lugbara)	M
AZIMA	ah-ZEE-mah	Resolve, determination.	Kiswahili	
CHITARA	chee-TAH-rah	The will of God.	Nigeria	
CHUKU MERE	choo-koo-MEH-reh	The will of God.	Nigeria	
DHATI	DAH-tee	Determination, free-will.	Kiswahili	
HIARI	HEE-ah-ree	Free will.	East Africa (Kiswahili)	F
IBHEJI	ee-beh-jee	Determination.	Azania (Zulu)	
INSHALLAH	n-shah-AH-lah	God-willing.	Kenya, Tanzania	
JINGA	jehn-gah	Determination.	Cameroon (Mubako)	M
KINAH	kee-NAH	Willful; persistent.	Nigeria (Bobangi)	F
MOYAKHE	moh-YAH-keh	Strong-willed, not easily influenced.	Azania	M
MUNYE YINGA	moon-yeh-YEEN-gah	Who has determination.	Rwanda, Burundi (Kinyarwanda, Kirundi)	M
OBIORA	oh-bee-OH-rah	The will of the people; people's heart.	Nigeria	
PHIMBO	pheem-boh	One with free will.	Azania	
REJALLA	REH-jah-lah	God wills it.	East Africa (Kiswahili)	M
THATO	TAH-toh	Having the will to achieve, determined to succeed.	Azania (Sotho)	
TISHA	tee-shah	Strong-willed.	East Africa (Kiswahili)	F
UTASHI	oo-TAH-shee	Free will.	Kiswahili	F

Name	Pronunciation	Meaning	Origin	Gender
ZAMA	ZAH-mah	Determination.	North Africa (Arabic)	M
ZIMISELE	ZEE-mee-seh-leh	Determined; one who is prepared for anything.	Azania (Xhosa)	

Difference and Distinction

The distance for using the club and the arrow
are not the same. —*Kenya*

Name	Pronunciation	Meaning	Origin	Gender
BALI	BAH-lee	Contrary.	Kiswahili	
CAKAZA	kah-KAH-zah	To scatter.	Azania (Zulu)	
FANANISHA	fah-nah-NEE-shah	To compare.	Kiswahili	
FATA	fah-tah	Different.	Gambia (Mandinka)	
MO	MOH	Distinguish.	West Africa (Yoruba)	
PEYAKANYO	peh-yah-KAHN-yoh	Contrary.	Azania (Sotho)	
SHAREEFA	shah-REE-fah	Imposing, impressive.	North Africa (Arabic)	
SHARIFA	shah-REE-fah	Distinguished.	East Africa (Kiswahili)	F
SHARUFA	shah-ROO-fah	Distinguished, outstanding.	Somalia	
TIBAAGA	tee-baah-gah	They are not equal.	Uganda (Soga)	F
WAJIHI	wah-JEE-hee	Distinguished.	North Africa	
YATO	YAH-toh	Different.	West Africa (Yoruba)	

Dignity and Integrity

If the elders leave you a legacy of dignified language,
you do not abandon it and
speak childish language. —*Ghana*

Name	Pronunciation	Meaning	Origin	Gender
ADHAMA	ahd-AHM-mah	Dignity.	Kenya, Tanzania	
CHITUNDA	chee-TOON-dah	Dignity.	Nigeria	
DEMBEZA	dehm-BEH-zah	Stately, dignified.	Azania (Zulu)	
FOLOYAN	foh-LAH-yahn	To walk in dignity.	Nigeria (Yoruba)	F
JAHI	JAH-hee	Dignity.	East Africa (Kiswahili)	M
NDILEKA	n-dee-leh-kah	To be dignified.	Azania (Xhosa)	M
NOSIDIMA	noh-see-DEE-mah	One who has dignity.	Azania (Xhosa)	F
SERITHI	seh-REE-tee	Dignified.	Azania (North Sotho)	
TUKUFU	too-KOO-foo	Dignified; respected; famous.	Kenya, Tanzania	
WONGA	WOHNG-gah	Man of stature, dignity and power.	Azania (Xhosa)	M

Discipline

If your neighbour comes to your house with an
unmannerly child, do not defer to the child
or he will tear your hat to pieces. —*Ghana*

Name	Pronunciation	Meaning	Origin	Gender
ASINIA	ah-see-nee-ah	Stern.	Nigeria (Yoruba)	M
BONSRA	bohn-srah	One who falls in line.	Ghana	
DUMIA	doo-mee-ah	He has scolded me.	Cameroon (Mubako)	M
GOBAMA KHOSI	goh-bah-mah-koh-see	Tamer of chiefs.	Azania	M
NIZAM	nee-ZAHM	Disciplinarian, arranger.	North Africa (Arabic)	M
PANASE	pah-NAH-seh	One who is treated with strict discipline.	Azania	M
SERHITA	sehr-hee-tah	Discipline give me joy.	Egypt/Khamit	
SERTABA	sehr-TAH-bah	Discipline gives me power.	Egypt/Khamit	

Earth, Land, and World

The chameleon changes color to match the earth,
the earth doesn't change color to match the chameleon. —*Senegal*

Name	Pronunciation	Meaning	Origin	Gender
ADANI	ah-dah-nee	Daughter of the earth.	Nigeria (Igbo)	F
ALA	AH-lah	Earth.	Nigeria (Igbo)	F
ALAKWENU	ah-lah-KWEH-noo	Let the land permit.	Nigeria (Igbo)	
ALAM	AH-lahm	World.	Ethiopia	F
ALAUME	ah-lah-OO-meh	Earth's breath.	New Afrika	
ALEMU	ah-LEH-moo	His world.	Ethiopia	M
ANGOM	ah-ndgh-ohm	Of the soil.	Uganda (Langi)	F
AZIBO	a-ZEE-boh	Earth.	Malawi (Ngoni)	M
BANGI LIZWE	bahn-gee-L EEZ-weh	Possess the land!	Azania (Xhosa)	M
BANKOO	bahn-kooh	Land.	Gambia (Mandinka)	
BULONGO	boo-lohn-goh	Dirt.	Zambia, Zimbabwe (Tonga)	F
BUSI	boo-see	Small worlds.	Uganda (Soga)	M
BYAITAKA	bjah-ee-tah-kah	Born for the soil.	Uganda (Nyoro)	
BYANSI	BYAHN-see	We come with nothing, and shall take nothing away from earth.	Uganda	M
DIALA	dee-AH-lah	Land owner.	Nigeria (Igbo)	M
DUNIA	doo-NEE-ah	The world.	Kiswahili	
DUNIYA	doo-NEE-yah	Earth, planet.	Gambia, West Africa (Mandinka, Hausa)	
DZIKO	ZEE-koh	The world.	Azania (Nguni)	F
EKA	EH-kah	Mother earth.	West Africa	F

Name	Pronunciation	Meaning	Origin	Gender
EZEANI	eh-zee-AH-nee	King of the land.	Nigeria (Igbo)	M
HULLANTA	hoo-lahn-tah	The universe; everything.	Ethiopia (Amharic)	
JAARALA	jah-RAH-lah	Heal earth.	New Afrika	
JANINA	joo-NEE-noo	Garden.	Tunisia	F
JIHAN	JEE-hahn	World.	North Africa (Arabic)	F
KAGUNDA	KAH-gohn-dah	Of the land.	Kenya (Agikuyu)	M
KAHYEBA	kah-yeh-bah	I have bought the land.	Cameroon (Mubako)	F
KENOO	keh-nooh	Land.	Gambia (Mandinka)	
KUTAAKA	koo-tah-kah	Soil.	Uganda (Lugisu)	M
LIZWELICHA	leez-weh-LEE-cha	New world.	Zimbabwe (Ndebele)	M
MAFUANE	mah-FOO-ah-neh	Soil.	Azania (Bachopi)	F
MARET	mah-reht	The earth.	Ethiopia (Amharic)	
MOSADI	moh-SAH-dee	The planter of seed.	Azania (Sotho)	
MWANA-DONGO	MWAH-nah-dohn-goh	Child of the earth.	East Africa (Kiswahili)	F
NANA	NAH-nah	Mother of the earth.	Ghana	
NSIKO	N-see-koh	Uncultivated land.	Uganda (Ganda)	M
NUBONSI	noo-bohn-see	The earth decides all cases because it receives any type of death or body.	Cameroon (Mungaka)	F
NYASSA	n-yahs-sah	The dirt has been mixed.	Cameroon (Mubako)	M
NYIKA	n-yee-kah	The earth.		
ONILE	oh-NEE-leh	Spirit of the earth.	Nigeria (Yoruba)	
SEKASI	sseh-kah-see	Of a small land.	Uganda (Ganda)	M
SHIKOKOLA	shee-koh-KOH-lah	Newly cleared plot of land.	Namibia (Ovambo)	
SIRAGUMA	see-rah-GOO-mah	Earth lives long.	Rwanda, Burundi (Kinyarwanda, Kirundi)	

Name	Pronunciation	Meaning	Origin	Gender
THAMBO	TAHM-boh	Ground.	Malawi (Ngoni)	M
UDONGO	oo-DOHN-goh	Earth.	Kiswahili	
UWA	OO-wah	The world; universe.	Nigeria (Igbo)	M
WAITHAKA	WAH-ee-thah-kah	Of the land.	Kenya (Agikuyu)	M
WAMIA	wah-mee-ah	Gather dirt.	Cameroon (Mubako)	M
ZWEKAZI	swah-KAH-zee	The continent.	Azania	
ZWELAKHE	sweh-LAH-keh	His world.	Azania	M
ZWELIHLE	zweh-LEE-leh	Good land; beautiful world.	Azania (Xhosa)	
ZWELIN ZIMA	sweh-leen-ZEE-mah	Tough world.	Azania	M

Ease

Easy does not always happen. —Africa

Name	Pronunciation	Meaning	Origin	Gender
MAYSARA	MAY-sah-rah	Ease.	East Africa (Kiswahili)	F
MREHE	m-REH-heh	Easy life.	Kenya, Tanzania (Kiswahili)	M
MREKHE	mm-REH-keh	Easy life.	Kenya, Tanzania (Kiswahili)	M
RAHISI	rah-HEE-see	Easy.	Kiswahili	
SAHALANI	sah-hah-LAHN-ee	Ease.	Kiswahili	M
TALHA	TAHL-hah	Easy life.	East Africa (Kiswahili)	F
TEREMA	teh-REH-mah	Be at ease.	Kiswahili	
TEREMESHA	teh-reh-MEH-shah	Set at ease.	Kiswahili	
YUSRA	YOOS-rah	Ease.	Kiswahili	F

Education

As long as a human being lives, she will learn. —Libya

Name	Pronunciation	Meaning	Origin	Gender
ABNET	ahb-NEHT	Example.	Eritrea	F
ARDA	AHR-dah	Studious.	Somalia	F
BAJYI SHURI	bah-djee-tch-oo-ree	They go to school.	Rwanda, Burundi, DRC (Huti, Tutsi, Twa)	M
BARUTI	bah-ROO-tee	Born to be a teacher.	Botswana (Tswana)	M
BONISWA	BOH-nee-swah	The teachable one.	Azania (Xhosa)	F
CAMARA	kah-mah-rah	Teacher; passes on knowledge.	West Africa	
ELEKEVU	eh-leh-KEH-voo	Quick to learn.	Kiswahili	
ELIMISHA	eh-lee-MEE-shah	To educate.	Kiswahili	
FUNDA	FOON-dah	Learn, be teachable.	Azania (Xhosa)	M
JINSI	JEHN-see	How; method; manner.	Kiswahili	
KARAMBA	kah-RAHM-bah	Great teacher.	Gambia	M
KARAMO	kah-RAH-moh	Teacher, trainer, tutor.	Gambia	M
KARU	KAH-roo	Learn.	West Africa (Hausa)	
KASOMA	kah-soh-mah	The little studious one.	Uganda (Ganda)	M
MAKTABA	mahk-TAH-bah	Library.	Kiswahili	
MAKUNGU	MAH-koon-goo	Initiation.	East Africa (Kiswahili)	M
MALANGO	mah-LAHN-goh	Initiation; teaching.	Kiswahili	
MENDO	MEHN-doh	The way.	Azania (Xhosa)	M
MFUNDISI	M-FOON-dee-see	Preacher; the one who teaches.	Azania (Xhosa)	M
MFUNDO	M-FOON-doh	The educated one.	Azania (Xhosa)	M
MORUTISI	moh-roo-TEE-see	Teacher.	Azania (North Sotho)	

Name	Pronunciation	Meaning	Origin	Gender
MWALUMI	mwah-LOO-mee	The great teacher.	Kiswahili	
NAUYIGA	nnah-moo-yee-gah	Learner; neophyte.	Uganda (Ganda)	F
NONO	NOH-noh	Scholar.	Southern Africa	M
SHADIA	shah-DEE-ah	Educated.	North Africa (Arabic)	F
SOMA	SOH-mah	To read; go to school.	Kiswahili	
TALIBAH	tah-LEE-bah	Scholar; seeker.	North Africa (Arabic)	F
TISA	TEE-sah	Teacher.	West Africa (Yoruba)	
YERODIN	yeh-roh-deen	One who is studious.	DRC	M

Effort

A feeble effort will not fulfill the self. —*Dogon*

Name	Pronunciation	Meaning	Origin	Gender
AMALU	ah-MAH-loo	If you don't try, you will not succeed.	Nigeria (Ishan)	
ASIDAHI	AH-see-dah-hee	A wasted effort.	Ghana	F
DIKITA	dee-KEE-tah	Perspiration; striving.	Zimbabwe	M
ENELU	eh-NEH-loo	Those who are trying.	Nigeria (Ishan)	
ITASE	ee-TAH-seh	I did all I can.	Nigeria (Ishan)	
JARIBU	jah-REE-boo	One who tries.	Kiswahili	F
JASHO	JAH-shoh	Sweat, perspire.	Kiswahili	
JIBIDISHA	jeh-bee-DEE-shah	To exert oneself.	Kiswahili	
JITAHIDI	jee-tah-HEE-dee	Make an effort.	Kiswahili	
KUSURU	koo-SOO-roo	Try hard.	Kiswahili	
LINJE	LEEN-jeh	Try it.	Azania, Malawi (Yao)	M
NONZAME	nohn-ZAH-meh	She puts a lot of effort into what she does.	Azania (Xhosa)	F

Name	Pronunciation	Meaning	Origin	Gender
NZAME	n-ZAH-meh	Effort.	Azania (Xhosa)	M
OBODE	oh-BOH-deh	I am beginning to see the results of my efforts.	Nigeria (Ishan)	
SENSENTA	sehn-SEHN-tah	To carry a load with effort.	Zambia (Bemba)	
ZAMA	ZAH-mah	Try.	Azania (Zulu)	F

Enemies and Foes

If you have enemies, then travel with your spear. —Namibia

Name	Pronunciation	Meaning	Origin	Gender
BANOBA	bah-NOH-bah	There are people who hate the parents.	Uganda (Nyoro)	
BASEKE	bah-SEH-keh	Let them laugh.	Uganda (Nyoro)	
BAZIMYA	bah-ZEEM-yah	The annihilator of the enemy.	Rwanda, Burundi (Kinyarwanda, Kirundi)	M
BENDAKI	behn-DAH-kee	What makes people persecute us so?	Uganda (Nyoro)	
BASEKE	bah-SEH-keh	Let them laugh.	Uganda (Nyoro)	
CHIJOHFOM	chee-joh-fohm	Living among enemies.	Cameroon (Mungaka)	M
IRAWAGBON	ee-rah-WAH-bohn	Enemy's attempt to kill her.	Benin	F
JENKAA	jehnk-kah	Enmity is widespread in this world; my enemies are numerous.	Cameroon (Mubako)	
KUSI LANGMIA	koo-see-lahg-MEE-ah	Enemies have surrounded me.	Cameroon (Mubako)	M
MALIDOMA	mah-lee-DOH-mah	Be friends with the stranger or enemy.	Burkina Faso (Dagbara)	
MATISHO	mah-TEE-shoh	Threat.	Kenya	F
MUKYAWE	moo-tch-aah-weh	Hated one, enemy.	Uganda (Ganda)	M
NKUNDA	n-KOON-dah	I love those who hate me.	Uganda (Runyankore)	M

Name	Pronunciation	Meaning	Origin	Gender
NONT SHABA	nohnt-SHAH-bah	Mother of enemies.	Azania (Xhosa)	F
NSEKANABO	n-seh-kah-NAH-boo	I laugh at them.	Uganda (Nyoro)	
TISHO	TEE-shoh	Threat.	Swaziland	F

Energy, Enthusiasm, and Vigor

A bald-headed man will not grow hair
by getting excited. —*Congo*

Name	Pronunciation	Meaning	Origin	Gender
AZIKIWE	ah-zeek-EE-weh	Vigorous.	Nigeria (Igbo)	
BAKALLA	bah-KAHL-lah	Restorer of virility.	Lesotho (South Sotho)	
BELA	BEH-lah	To burst forth, to bubble up.	Azania (Zulu)	
BUBUJIKA	boo-boo-JEE-kah	To bubble up, to burst forth.	Kiswahili	
CHAGA	CHAH-gah	To do vigorously.	Kiswahili	M
DUMEZULU	doo-meh-ZOO-loo	Something big and exciting.	Azania (Zulu)	
FATI	FAH-tee	Robust.	West Africa	M
HIMBARA	heem-bah-rah	Be excited.	Rwanda, Burundi, DRC (Huti, Tutsi, Twa)	M
JUHUDI	joo-HOO-dee	Zeal.	East Africa (Kiswahili)	M
KALI	KAH-lee	Energetic.	Côte d'Ivoire (Senufo)	F
LULAMILE	loo-lah-MEE-leh	The reinvigorated one.	Azania	F
NISHATI	NEE-shah-tee	Full of vigor.	Kenya, Tanzania (Kiswahili)	F
NOLULA MILE	noh-loo-lah-MEE-leh	The reinvigorated one.	Azania	M
NTAMWETE	n-tah-WEH-teh	There is no energy.	Rwanda, Burundi (Kinyarwanda, Kirundi)	

Name	Pronunciation	Meaning	Origin	Gender
NTOM BETSHA	n-tohm-BEHN-ntcha	She is full of life and youthful vigor.	Azania (Xhosa)	F
OJEM BANWANYI	oh-jehm-bahn-wahn-yee	Tireless woman.	Nigeria (Igbo)	F
OJIKE	oh-JEE-kee	Full of energy.	Nigeria	
OMUNTU	oh-MOON-too	An energetic person.	Uganda (Ganda)	
SULUBU	soo-LOO-boo	Energy; vigor.	Kiswahili	
TINDO	TEEN-doh	Active.	Kiswahili	M
UZIMA	OO-zee-MAH	Energetic, vitality.	Kenya, Tanzania (Kiswahili)	F
VUSA	VOO-sah	Invigorate; revive.	Azania (Xhosa)	M
YOLANDA	yoh-LAHN-dah	The go-getter.	Azania	
ZUMUDI	zoo-MOO-dee	Excitement.	West Africa (Hausa)	

Equality and Equity

If the wind blows, it enters at every crevice. —Egypt

Name	Pronunciation	Meaning	Origin	Gender
AKAHARA	ah-kah-HAH-rah	Equality.	Nigeria (Igbo)	F
BAINGANA	bah-ee-ngah-nah	People are equal; all people die and are buried in the ground.	Uganda (Runyoro)	
DAIDAI	dah-ee-DAH-ee	Equal.	West Africa (Hausa)	
DAIDAITO	dah-ee-dah-EE-toh	Equality.	West Africa (Hausa)	
DIDOGBA	dee-DOHG-bah	Equality.	West Africa (Yoruba)	
INENE	ee-NEH-neh	I don't discriminate.	Nigeria (Ishan)	
ITIDAL	ee-tee-DAHL	Symmetry.	East Africa (Kiswahili)	F
SAWA	SAH-wah	Equal.	Kiswahili	
TEKANO	teh-KAH-noh	Equal.	Azania (North Sotho)	

Eternity and Immortality

Eternity gives no answer. —Liberia

Name	Pronunciation	Meaning	Origin	Gender
IDRISSA	ee-DREES-sah	Immortal.	West Africa	M
ISHI	EE-shee	Everlasting; to live.	Kiswahili	
KHALID	KHAH-leed	Eternal.	North Africa (Arabic)	M
KHALIDA	kah-LEEN-dah	Eternal, everlasting.	North Africa (Arabic)	
KIAH	KEE-ah	Always.	DRC (Bobangi)	M
MAKADE	mah-KAH-deh	The eternal one.	Azania	M
MILELE	MEE-leh-leh	Eternity.	East Africa (Kiswahili)	F
MUYAYA	moo-YAH-yah	Forever.	Malawi	
TUMA	TOO-mah	Immortal.	Azania (Sotho)	

Europe and Europeans

*If there had been no poverty in Europe,
then the white man would not have come and
spread his clothes in Africa. —Ghana*

Name	Pronunciation	Meaning	Origin	Gender
FATAKOYOO	fah-tah-koh-yooh	White person.	Gambia (Mandinka)	
ISISE	ee-SEE-seh	People tend to believe in the foreigner more than in one's own.	Nigeria (Ishan)	
NASAARAA	nah-saah-raah	White person; European.	Gambia (Mandinka)	
NSANZA BERA	n-sahn-zah-beh-eh-rah	I join the whites.	Rwanda, Burundi, DRC (Huti, Tutsi, Twa)	
SEKYERU	sseh-tch-ee-eh-roo	White; light skinned.	Uganda (Ganda)	M

Name	Pronunciation	Meaning	Origin	Gender
SHILUMBU	shee-LOOM-boo	White man.	Namibia (Ovambo)	
TUBAB	TOO-bahb	The friendly name for white foreigners.	Gambia	
ULAYA	oo-LAH-yah	Europe.	Kiswahili	

Evil and Wrongdoing

Evil enters like a needle and spreads like an oak tree.
—*Ethiopia*

Name	Pronunciation	Meaning	Origin	Gender
ADAOBE	ah-dah-OH-beh	It is unkind thinking evil.	Nigeria (Ishan)	
DILIZA	dee-LEE-zah	Destroyer of evil.	Kiswahili	
EKWENSI	eh-KWEHN-see	Devil.	Nigeria (Igbo)	M
MKOSAJI	m-koh-SAH-jee	Sinner.	Kiswahili	
NJOKU	n-JOH-koo	Chase off evil.	Nigeria (Igbo)	M
RAANJO	rah-ah-joh	Abstain from sin.	Nigeria (Igbo)	
SHETANI	sheh-tah-nee	Evil spirit.	Kiswahili	
SONOSAKHE	soh-noh-sah-keh	His sin.	Azania (Xhosa)	M
UBAYA	oo-BAH-yah	Evil.	Kiswahili	
ZENBENJO	zeh-behn-joh	Avoid sins.	Nigeria (Igbo)	

Exhaustion and Fatigue

When the load fatigues the head, the shoulder takes over. —*Nigeria*

Name	Pronunciation	Meaning	Origin	Gender
AHUMURE	ah-hoo-moo-reh	May he rest.	Uganda (Kiga, Nyankore)	

Name	Pronunciation	Meaning	Origin	Gender
BAMUA	bah-moo-ah	Daddy is tired.	Cameroon (Mubako)	M
BATACHOKA	bah-tah-CHOH-kah	They will be tired.	Congo	M
BIMMUA	bee-moo-ah	He is tired.	Cameroon (Mubako)	M
KALEMEERA	kah-leh-mee-rah	The one that is heavy.	Uganda (Ganda)	
MTHUNZI	M-TOON-zee	Shade; where we can find rest.	Azania (Xhosa)	M
MTUNZINI	m-toon-ZEE-nee	Place of shade.	Azania (Zulu)	
PHUMLA	POOM-lah	Now we can rest.	Azania (Zulu)	
TURYAH UMURA	too-ree-ah-hoo-moo-rah	We will have rest.	Uganda (Rukiga)	M

Expectation

While a dead tree is expected to collapse,
a live one unexpectedly snaps. —*Nigeria*

Name	Pronunciation	Meaning	Origin	Gender
IZEGBE	ee-ZEH-beh	Long expected child.	Benin	F
LINDA	LEEN-dah	The one we are expecting.	Azania	
MINIYA	MEEHN-ee-yah	I have much expected of her.	Eritrea, Ethiopia (Tigrinya)	F
NTEZA	NTEH-zah	I am expecting.	Burundi	
TAZAMIA	tah-zah-MEE-ah	To expect.	Kiswahili	

Faith, Belief, and Spirituality

All religions are but stepping stones back to God.
—*Native American (Pawnee)*

Name	Pronunciation	Meaning	Origin	Gender
ABILA	ah-bee-lah	Shrine.	Uganda (Acholi, Iteso, Langi)	F
ADDINI	ahd-DEE-nee	Religion.	West Africa (Hausa)	
AFI	ah-FEE	Spiritual things.	West Africa	F
AFIFA	ah-FEE-fah	Spiritual, holy.	West Africa	
AJALA	ah-JAH-lah	Believer in Allah.	West Africa	
ALABATOU	ah-lah-bah-TOH-oo	To worship.	Gambia (Mandinka)	
AMINIFU	ah-mee-NEE-foo	Faith, belief.	Kenya, Tanzania	
ATEKEYE	ah-teh-KEH-yeh	What I prayed for.	Nigeria	
DINI	DEE-nee	Faith, religion.	Kenya, Tanzania (Kiswahili)	M
DUMELA	doo-MEH-lah	To be joyful, to believe, have faith.	Southern Africa (Tsonga)	
EBIYE	eh-BEE-yeh	Test of faith.	Nigeria (Eleme)	
EJIRA	eh-JEE-rah	Believe.	Nigeria (Eleme)	
FANA	FAH-nah	Spiritual joy; spirited day.	Ethiopia	F
IMAMU	ee-MAHM-moo	Spiritual leader; minister, preacher.	West Africa	
IMANI	ee-MAH-nee	Faith, belief, religion.	Kenya, Tanzania (Kiswahili)	
JESUOBO	jeh-soo-OH-boh	Jesus is the magician or miracle worker.	Nigeria (Edo)	M
KABONA	kah-BOH-nah	Priest.	Kenya, Tanzania	M
KAHINI	kah-HEE-nee	Priest, holy person.	Kenya, Tanzania	
KAHLIFAH	kah-lee-fah	Holy child.	Kiswahili	M
KALIF	KAH-leef	Holy boy.	Somalia	M

Name	Pronunciation	Meaning	Origin	Gender
KALIFA	kah-LEE-fah	Chaste, holy.	Somalia	F
KASISI	kah-SEE-see	Priest, minister.	Kenya, Tanzania	M
KEITA	KEH-ee-tah	Worshipper.	West Africa	M
KEMBA	KEHM-bah	She is full of faith.	Central Africa	F
KRISTO	KREE-stoh	Christian.	Kenya, Tanzania	
LINJILA	leen-JEE-lah	Bible.	West Africa (Hausa)	
MAMDALI	mahm-DAH-lee	Muhammad Ali.	North Africa (Arabic)	
MAOMBI	mah-OHM-bee	Prayers.	Congo	F
MKRISTO	m-KREES-toh	A Christian.	Kenya, Tanzania	
MTAWA	m-TAH-wah	Religious, devout person.	Kenya, Tanzania	
MUSIM	MOO-seem	Believer.	Egypt/Khamit	M
NDEMEYE	n-deh-MEH-yeh	I accept, believe.	Rwanda, Burundi (Kinyarwanda, Kirundi)	M
NKOLO	n-KOH-loh	Faith.	Azania (Xhosa)	M
PADIRI	pah-dee-ree	Priest.	Rwanda, Burundi, DRC (Huti, Tutsi, Twa)	M
RUHI	ROO-hee	Spiritual.	North Africa (Arabic)	M
SELASSIE	seh-LAH-see	Trinity.	Ethiopia (Amharic)	M
SIBMABA	seeb-MAH-bah	Religious ecstasy gives me power.	Egypt/Khamit	
SIHURRA	see-huhr-rah	Religious ecstasy increases me.	Egypt/Khamit	
SIKHOLEKO	see-koh-leh-koh	One to believe in.	Azania	M
SIKUZANI	see-koo-ZAH-nee	I did not believe.	East Africa	
SOOSI	SOO-see	Church.	West Africa (Yoruba)	
SUBI	SOO-bee	Faith.	Zambia (Bemba)	

Name	Pronunciation	Meaning	Origin	Gender
TAKATIFU	tah-kah-TEE-foo	Sacred, holy, saintly.	Kenya, Tanzania (Kiswahili)	
TAMANDA	tah-man-dah	Worship.	Azania (Chichewa)	F
TAWA	TAH-wah	A religious person.	Kenya, Tanzania	
TONATENI	toh-nah-TEH-nee	Awake out of sleep, become spiritually awakened!	Namibia (Ovambo)	
TUMELO	too-MEH-loh	Believe.	Azania (North Sotho)	
TUMU SHABE	too-moo-shah-beh	We pray to God.	Uganda (Rukiga)	M
TWESIGYE	tweh-SEE-jeh	Let us trust in God.	Uganda (Rukiga)	F

Fame and Celebrity

First he craved for high profile visibility;
then he begged for oblivious privacy. —*Ethiopia*

Name	Pronunciation	Meaning	Origin	Gender
AHUNSI	ah-HOON-see	My fame will come.	Nigeria (Ishan)	
AIDOO	ah-EE-doh	Achieve recognition.	West Africa	
AKABUDE	ah-kah-BOO-deh	One who may become famous by one's deeds.	Nigeria (Igbo)	
ASATIRA	ah-SAH-tee-rah	Legend, saga.	East Africa (Kiswahili)	F
BUMANYE	boo-mah-ndjh-eh	Fame.	Uganda (Ganda)	M
CHUMA	CHOO-mah	Famous, prominent.	Nigeria	
CLEOPATRA	KLEE-oh-pah-trah	Famous.	Egypt/Khamit	F
DARAJA	dah-RAH-jah	Famous.	Gambia (Wolof)	
DUMA	DOO-mah	Be famous, famous, well-known.	Azania (Xhosa, Zulu)	M
DUNYELWA	doon-YEHL-wah	Famous, renowned person.	Azania (Xhosa)	
MONGO	MOHN-goh	Famous, renowned.	Nigeria (Yoruba)	M

Name	Pronunciation	Meaning	Origin	Gender
NEGAMA	neh-GAH-mah	Famous, prominent.	Azania	
OYINLOLA	oh-yeen-LOH-lah	Fame is as sweet as honey.	Nigeria (Yoruba)	
RWOGERA	rwoh-GEH-rah	The very famous.	Rwanda, Burundi (Kinyarwanda, Kirundi)	M
SIDUMO	SEE-doo-moh	Fame.	Azania (Xhosa)	M
SIFA	SEE- fah	Fame.	Kenya, Tanzania	
SUNA	SOO-nah	Fame.	West Africa (Hausa)	
TUMILE	too-MEE-leh	The one who is famous.	Azania (Sotho)	
TUMO	TOO-moh	Fame.	Lesotho (Basotho)	M
ZIMBIRI	zeem-BEE-ree	To be famous.	Zambia (Tumbuka)	M
ZODUMO	zoh-doo-moh	A celebrity.	Azania (Xhosa)	F
ZUKA	ZOO-kah	Famous, renowned.	Azania (Xhosa)	

Familiarity

She knows best the sun of her own country. —Egypt

Name	Pronunciation	Meaning	Origin	Gender
BOBMIA	bohb-mee-ah	He has met me.	Cameroon (Mubako)	
FOKAZI	foh-KAH-zee	Stranger.	Azania (Zulu)	
LEGGE	lehg-geh	Stranger.	Sudan (Bari)	M
MGENI	mgeh-nee	Visitor.	Kiswahili	
MTANI	m-TAH-nee	A familiar friend.	Kiswahili	
NAKYAZZE	nnah-tch-ahz-zeh	Visitor, that which has come.	Uganda (Ganda)	F
SANA	SAH-nah	Stranger.	Burkina Faso (Mossi)	M
TANIA	tah-NEE-ah	To treat with familiarity.	Kiswahili	
WANGA	WAH-jah	The one from without.	Kenya (Agikuyu)	F

Name	Pronunciation	Meaning	Origin	Gender
XELA	TSEH-lah	Having a great resemblance.	Azania (Xhosa)	
ZIZWE	ZEEZ-weh	A boy born in a foreign land.	East Africa	M

Family and Kinship

Family names are like flowers, they blossom in clusters.

—Africa

Name	Pronunciation	Meaning	Origin	Gender
AFELI	ah-FEH-lee	The house has been established by the first baby in the family.	Togo	
AJEBA	ah-JEH-bah	There is still love needed among relatives.	Nigeria (Ishan)	
AKESI	ah-KEH-see	We are already tied by blood; don't pretend.	Nigeria (Ishan)	
BABALANDA	bah-bah-lahn-tdh-ah	They count those of their womb.	Uganda (Soga)	M
BOLLA	boh-lah	Family relationship (egg).	Cameroon (Mubako)	F
CHIBALE	chee-BAH-leh	Kinship.	Malawi (Ngoni)	M
DAIGA	dah-ee-gah	The village chief's or Fon's family is never lost.	Cameroon (Mubako)	M
DANUWA	dah-noo-wah	Cousin.	West Africa (Hausa)	
DHURIYA	doo-ree-yah	Descendant.	East Africa (Kiswahili)	F
DINNE	DEEN-neh	Husband of her mother.	Nigeria (Igbo)	F
FOLI	FOH-lee	There is strength in the family.	Ghana	
GATSHA	gaht-shah	Part of the family.	Azania	M
GAZINI	gah-ZEE-nee	Blood.	Azania (Zulu)	
IYAYE	ee-YAH-yeh	Family.	West Africa (Hausa)	

Name	Pronunciation	Meaning	Origin	Gender
JAMAA	JAH-mah	Family, relatives.	Kiswahili	
JIRA	JEER-ah	Related by blood.	Eritrea, Ethiopia (Tigrinya)	F
KAHKUNA	kah-koon-nah	Family circle.	Cameroon (Mubako)	
KAMANGENI	kah-man-GEH-nee	Seems to be a family member.	Malawi (Ngoni)	
KONA	koh-nah	Family issues.	Cameroon (Mubako)	M
KUNA	koo-nah	Family relationship.	Cameroon (Mubako)	F
LANDIKHAYA	lahn-dee-khah-yah	Our descendant.	Azania	M
MANJAKAZE	mahn-jah-KAH-zeh	Power of blood.	Mozambique	M
MANJIA	mahn-JEE-ah	Born during family crisis.	Sierra Leone (Mende)	F
MAVYA	mahv-yah	One who begot my husband; parents-in-law.	Kiswahili	
MUGO REWASE	moo-goh-reh-wah-seh	The wife of the father.	Rwanda, Burundi (Kinyarwanda, Kirundi)	F
MUKUNA	moo-koo-nah	Is it good to disown your brother.	Cameroon (Mubako)	F
MULOPA	moo-LOH-pah	Blood.	Zambia (Bemba)	
NABILA	nah-BEE-lah	The family has increased.	Kiswahili	
NAJIA	NAH-jee-ah	Progeny.	East Africa (Kiswahili)	F
NDUGU	n-DOO-goo	Brother or sister.	Azania (Nguni)	
NNADI	n-NAH-dee	The father of one's husband.	Nigeria (Igbo)	M
NUKUNA	noo-KOON-nah	Avoid wicked relatives.	Cameroon (Mubako)	M
NWANNEKA	nwahn-neh-kah	Sisterhood or brotherhood is the most valued companion.	Nigeria (Igbo)	
NWANWA	nwan-wah	Grandchild.	Nigeria (Igbo)	
OBIKE	oh-BEE-keh	Strong household.	Nigeria	

Name	Pronunciation	Meaning	Origin	Gender
ODEDE	oh-DEH-deh	Named for a grandmother or grandfather.	Nigeria (Ishan)	
OGO	OH-goh	Father-in-law.	Nigeria (Igbo)	M
OLUINA	oh-loo-EE-nah	The family of my mother.	Angola (Ovimbundu)	F
SAKUMA	sah-KOO-mah	Look for relatives.	Cameroon (Mubako)	
SHEMEGI	sheh-MEH-gee	Parents of a married couple; describes all members belonging to both sides of the family.	Kiswahili	M
SHEMEJI	sheh-MEH-jee	Brother or sister-in-law.	Kiswahili	
SOLOMZI	soh-lohm-zee	The eye of the family.	Azania	
THEMBI-KHAYA	tehm-bee-khah-yah	One with faith in the family.	Azania	M
UJAMAA	oo-JAH-mah	Family.	Kenya, Tanzania	
UKOO	OO-koo	Kinship.	Kiswahili	
UMUBYEYI	oo-moob-YEH-yee	Parent.	Rwanda, Burundi (Kinyarwanda, Kirundi)	F
USOMO	oo-SOH-moh	Fellowship.	Kiswahili	
WALLA	wahl-lah	She gathers the family together.	Cameroon (Mubako)	F
WANDILE	wahn-DEE-leh	Growing family.	Azania (Nguni)	

Fathers and Fatherhood

*The most important thing a father can do
for his children is to love their mother. —Africa*

Name	Pronunciation	Meaning	Origin	Gender
ALOH BOWOE	ah-loh-boh-whah	Where did it come from (usually given to a child whose father is unknown)?	Cameroon (Mungaka)	
ATE	AH-teh	Father.	Nigeria (Eleme)	M
AWIATE	ah-wee-AH-teh	Father's brother.	Nigeria (Eleme)	M
BABA	BAH-bah	Father (Baba Malik)	Kiswahili	M
BABAFEMI	bah-bah-FEH-mee	Father loves me.	Nigeria (Yoruba)	M
BABATUNDE	bah-bah-TOON-deh	Father has returned.	Nigeria (Yoruba)	M
BABATUNJI	bah-bah-TOON-jee	Father returns again.	Nigeria (Yoruba)	M
BABILA	bah-bee-lah	Daddy is back (name given to male child born after death of the grandfather).	Cameroon (Mubako)	M
BAYAH	bah-yah	Where is the father?	Cameroon (Mungaka)	M
BILLA	bee-lah	Father has been reborn.	Cameroon (Mubako)	M
DAGOGO	dah-GOH-goh	Like father, junior.	Nigeria	M
DOHBILLA	doh-BEEL-lah	Grandfather is back.	Cameroon (Mubako)	M
DOHKEA	doh-KEE-ah	Grandfather has grown up.	Cameroon (Mubako)	M
DOKU	DOH-koo	The father died.	Ghana	M
ETETE	eh-TEH-teh	Great grandfather.	Nigeria (Efik)	M
LADJI	lahd-jee	Father.	Cameroon (Mubako)	M
LEBAGA	leh-BAH-gah	Fatherhood cannot be bought.	Cameroon (Mubako)	M
MAMAKEE	mah-mah-keh	Grandfather.	Gambia (Mandinka)	M
NNAKA	n-NAH-kah	The father is supreme.	Nigeria (Igbo)	M
N'NANNA	n-NAHN-nah	Grandfather.	Nigeria (Igbo)	M
NWAMDI	n-wahm-dee	Father's name lives on.	Nigeria (Igbo)	M
NYAKEH	n-yah-keh	Just like father.	Sierra Leone	M

Name	Pronunciation	Meaning	Origin	Gender
OBINNA	oh-BEEN-nah	Dear to the father; father's heart/mind.	Nigeria (Igbo)	M
OGBONNA	oh-BOHN-nah	Image of his father.	Nigeria (Igbo)	M
OGONA	oh-GOH-nah	Father-in-law.	Nigeria (Igbo)	M
OUPA	ohw-pah	Grandfather.	Azania	M
SANGO	SAHN-goh	Father.	DRC (Bobangi)	M
SOKORO	SOH-koh-roh	Named after a grandfather.	East Africa (Kisii)	M
TANYI	tahn-yee	Father of twins.	Cameroon (Mungaka)	M

Fire, Heat, and Warmth

How easy it is to defeat people who do not kindle fire for themselves. —Kenya

Name	Pronunciation	Meaning	Origin	Gender
BIRA	bee-rah	Warmed up.	Uganda (Ganda)	M
BYOTO	bjoh-toh	Fireplace; hearth.	Uganda (Ganda)	M
DUGGA	DOOG-gah	That which cannot burn.	Cameroon (Mubako)	M
FATAKI	fah-TAH-kee	Fireworks; firecrackers.	Kiswahili	
HARI	HAH-ree	Heat.	Kiswahili	M
INA	EE-nah	Fire.	West Africa (Yoruba)	
KABATSI	kah-BAHT-see	Fire; heat.	Rwanda, Burundi (Kinyarwanda, Kirundi)	M
KAMAA	kah-maah	Fire.	Gambia (Mandinka)	
KAMOTO	kah-moh-toh	That is of the fire.	Rwanda, Burundi, DRC (Huti, Tutsi, Twa)	M
KANDITA	kahn-DEE-tah	Hot, warm.	Gambia	
KYOTO	tch-oh-toh	Hearth, fireplace.	Uganda (Ganda)	M
LAAH	la-ah	Fire.	Cameroon (Mubako)	M

Name	Pronunciation	Meaning	Origin	Gender
LAZE	LAH-zeh	Blaze.	North Africa (Arabic)	M
MAFYA	mahf-yah	Firestones.	Kiswahili	
MASHAL	MAH-shahl	Torch.	East Africa (Kiswahili)	M
MEKA	MEH-kah	Flame.	Kiswahili	
MOKERA	moh-keh-rah	Burning down.	Uganda (Ganda)	M
MOLLO	MOHL-loh	Fire.	Azania (Sotho)	
MOSHI	MOH-shee	Smoke.	Kiswahili	
MOTIRAYO	moh-tee-rah-yoh	Fiery.	Nigeria (Yoruba)	F
MOTO	MOH-toh	Fire, heat.	Kiswahili	
MULILO	moo-LEE-loh	Fire.	Zambia (Bemba)	
MULIRO	moo-lee-roh	Fire.	Uganda (Ganda)	M
MUWALI	moo-WAH-lee	Flame.	Kiswahili	
NAKYOTO	nnah-tch-oh-toh	Fireplace; hearth.	Uganda (Ganda)	F
NULAGHA	noo-LAH-gah	Cannot run from fire.	Cameroon (Mubako)	F
NYIMAK	NYEE-mahk	Little fire.	Sudan (Shulla)	F
OBAYANA	oh-bah-YAH-nah	The king warms himself at the fire.	Nigeria (Yoruba)	M
OKHUYIA	ohk-koo-yee-ah	To burn.	East Africa	M
OLOL	OH-lohl	Flame.	Somalia	M
OLUFE	oh-LOO-feh	Flame.	West Africa (Yoruba)	
OLUYIA	oh-loo-YEE-ah	Fire.	East Africa	M
ONA	oh-nah	Fire.	West Africa	F
RURA	ROO-rah	Roar of fire.	West Africa (Hausa)	
SELUKUMA	sseh-loo-koo-mah	That makes a fire.	Uganda (Ganda)	M
SEMPIIRA	ssehm-pee-rah	A large fire deliberately set for a constructive purpose.	Uganda (Ganda)	M

Name	Pronunciation	Meaning	Origin	Gender
TAAKAA	taah-kaah	Wild fire.	Gambia (Mandinka)	
UKOCHA	oo-KOH-chah	To burn.	Zambia (Bemba)	
USI	OO-see	Smoke.	Malawi (Yao)	M
WOTO	WOH-toh	God of fire.	Zimbabwe, Mozambique, Zambia (Shona)	M

Flowers and Plants

We will be grateful to flowers only if they have born fruits. —Zimbabwe

Name	Pronunciation	Meaning	Origin	Gender
ABBEBA	ahb-BEH-bah	Beautiful flower.	Ethiopia	F
ABLA	AH-blah	A wild rose.	East Africa (Kiswahili)	F
ABOSI	ah-BOH-see	Life plant.	Nigeria (Yoruba)	M
BAILISA	bah-ee-lee-sah	A flower.	Azania (Sotho)	
DENE	DEH-neh	Water lily.	West Africa	
FIRI	fee-ree	To flower.	Gambia (Mandinka)	
FURE	FOO-reh	Blossom.	West Africa (Hausa)	
ILIROZA	ee-lee-ROH-zah	Rose.	Azania (Zulu)	
JAWAYRIA	jah-wah-ee-ree-ah	Rose.	Kiswahili	
JUWAYRIA	JOO-wah-ree-yah	A damask rose.	East Africa (Kiswahili)	F
KINUKA	KEE-noo-kah	A type of flower.	Kenya, Tanzania (Kiswahili)	F
MALAWA	mah-lah-wah	Flowers.	Azania (Ngoni)	M
MBALI	m-bah-LEE	Flower.	Azania (Zulu)	F
MBHALI	mbah-lee	Rose.	Azania (Zulu)	F

Name	Pronunciation	Meaning	Origin	Gender
NAKIMULI	nnah-tch-ee-moo-lee	Flower.	Uganda (Ganda, Soga)	F
NISRIM	nees-reem	Wild rose.	Kiswahili	
ODODO	oh-DOH-doh	Flower.	Nigeria (Ishan)	
PALESA	pah-LEH-sah	Flower.	Azania (Xhosa)	F
PUN	poon	Wild rose.	Sudan (Nuer)	M
ROZI	ROH-zee	Flower, rose.	East Africa (Kiswahili)	F
SEKAMULI	sseh-kah-moo-lee	Small flower.	Uganda (Ganda)	M
TITI	tee-tee	Flower.	Nigeria	
ZAHRA	ZAH-rah	Beautiful flower.	Kiswahili	F
ZAHUR	ZAH-huhr	Flower.	Egypt/Khamit	M
ZAMRAH	ZAHM-rah	Beautiful flower.	North Africa (Arabic)	

Food, Hunger, and Thirst

A shinning face goes with a full belly. —Niger

Name	Pronunciation	Meaning	Origin	Gender
ALAHBI	ah-lah-bee	It shall bear fruit.	Cameroon (Mungaka)	M
ALOLI	ah-LOHL-lee	Grapes.	Egypt/Khamit	F
ASOSO	ah-SOH-soh	Sweet fruit.	Nigeria (Bini)	
BAKANOGA	bah-kah-noh-gah	Fruit picked from the tree.	Uganda (Ganda)	F
BEEDZI	beed-zhee	Child that eats well.	Ghana (Akan)	F
BITALO	bee-TAH-loh	Finger-licking.	Uganda (Ganda, Luganda)	M
CHENZA	CHEHN-zah	Orange, tangerine.	Kiswahili	
CHIHAM-BUANE	chee-ham-boo-AH-neh	Sweet potatoes.	Malawi (Ngoni)	M
DATE	DAH-teh	Sweet potato.	Azania	F

Name	Pronunciation	Meaning	Origin	Gender
FOBELA	foh-BEH-lah	To gulp down, eat large mouthfuls.	Azania (Zulu)	
KABOYI	kah-BOH-yee	Cook.	Rwanda, Burundi (Kinyarwanda, Kirundi)	
KAMAKYA	kah-mah-tch-ah	The end of famine.	Uganda (Ganda)	M
KAMIRA	kah-mee-rah	To milk.	Uganda (Soga)	M
KATUNDA	kah-toon-dah	The passion fruit, fruit of the passion flower.	Uganda (Ganda)	M
KILAJI	kee-LAH-jee	Food.	Kiswahili	
KIRAAYI	kee-raah-yee	Potato.	Rwanda, Burundi, DRC (Huti, Tutsi, Twa)	M
KOKOO	koh-koh	Coconut.	Gambia (Mandinka)	
KONDI	KOHN-dee	Sugar plum.	Sierra Leone, Liberia (Mende)	M
KURUWOO	koo-roo-woh	Kola nut.	Gambia (Mandinka)	
LIMAU	lee-MAH-oo	A lemon.	Kiswahili	
MACHUPA	mah-CHOO-pah	Likes to drink.	Kiswahili	
MALIMAO	mah-lee-mah-oh	Limes.	Kiswahili	M
MARWE	MAHR-weh	Land of thirst.	Sudan (Nuer)	M
MPISHI	m-PEE-shee	A cook.	Kiswahili	
MWANJAA	mwahn-JAAH	Born during famine.	Tanzania (Zaramo)	F
NAMATA	nah-MAH-tah	Milk.	Uganda (Luganda)	F
NATA	nah-tah	Drink.	Botswana	
NAZI	NAH-zee	Coconut.	Kenya	F
NDATE	n-dah-teh	Sweet potato.	Azania	M
NJAA	n-JAH	Hunger.	Kiswahili	
NJALA	ndjh-ah-lah	Famine; hunger.	Uganda (Ganda)	M
NYEMBA	n-YEHM-bah	Beans.	Malawi (Ngoni)	M

Name	Pronunciation	Meaning	Origin	Gender
NZALA	n-zah-lah	Hunger.	Zambia, Zimbabwe (Tonga)	F
OREE	oh-reh-eh	Corncake.	Nigeria (Bini)	M
RIZIKI	ree-ZEE-kee	Food.	Africa (Kiswahili)	M
SENJALA	ssehn-jah-lah	Hunger.	Uganda (Ganda)	M
SIAGI	see-agh-gee	Butter.	Kiswahili	
THELATHINI	teh-lah-tee-nee	Thirsty.	Kiswahili	
TIDYANAWO	teed-yah-NAH-woh	We shall both eat.	Malawi (Ngoni)	F
TUFAHA	too-FAH-hah	Apple.	Kiswahili	F
TUNDA	TOON-dah	Fruit.	Kiswahili	

Force, Aggression, and Destruction

Strategy is better than brute force. —Africa

Name	Pronunciation	Meaning	Origin	Gender
CHINJA	CHEEN-jah	To slaughter.	Kiswahili	
CHINJO	CHEEN-joh	Slaughter; cut.	Kiswahili	F
DEMISSIE	deh-MUH-say	Destroyer.	Ethiopia (Amharic)	M
DIDIMISHA	dee-dee-MEE-shah	To force down.	Kiswahili	
DOJUKO	doh-JOO-koh	Confront.	West Africa (Yoruba)	
EJIKEME	eh-jee-KEH-meh	Cannot be forced.	Nigeria (Igbo)	M
EJINIKE	eh-jeen-NEE-keh	Will not yield to force.	Nigeria (Igbo)	M
EMENIKE	eh-meh-NEE-keh	Force solves no problem.	Nigeria	
FAKHTA	FAHK-tah	Pierce.	East Africa (Kiswahili)	F
GAMI	gah-mee	You have pushed me.	Cameroon (Mubako)	M
GITERA	gee-TEH-rah	The attacker.	Rwanda, Burundi (Kinyarwanda, Kirundi)	

Name	Pronunciation	Meaning	Origin	Gender
HARIBU	hah-REE-boo	To destroy.	Kiswahili	
HASHIM	HAH-sheem	Destroyer.	North Africa (Arabic)	M
JEROBA	jeh-ROH-bah	The breaker.	Azania (Sotho)	
JERUHI	jeh-ROO-hee	To wound.	Kiswahili	
KATTA	kaht-tah	The little one that kills.	Uganda (Ganda)	M
KGANELO	kGAH-NEH-loh	Siege.	Azania (Zulu)	
MJEURI	m-jeh-OO-ree	A violent man.	Kiswahili	
MKAZO	m-KAH-zoh	Force.	Kiswahili	
MUGABE	moo-GAH-bee	The weaponed attacker, slasher.	Kiswahili	
MULUMBA	moo-LOOM-bah	One who attacks.	Uganda (Luganda)	M
MUNYIGA	moon-YEE-gah	One who presses others.	Uganda (Ganda, Mukiga)	M
NKOTANYI	n-koh-TAHN-yee	Great fighter.	Rwanda, Burundi (Kinyarwanda, Kirundi)	M
RORO	ROH-roh	Fierce.	West Africa (Yoruba)	
SHOMARI	shoh-MAH-ree	Forceful.	East Africa (Kiswahili)	M
SUNDAI	soon-DAH-ee	Push.	Zimbabwe (Shona)	
UHARIBIFU	oo-hah-ree-BEE-foo	Destruction.	Kiswahili	

Forgiveness

All errors are amendable. —*Africa*

Name	Pronunciation	Meaning	Origin	Gender
ADHRA	AHD-rah	Apology.	East Africa (Kiswahili)	F
ALIIJAIJO	ah-lee-dzah-ee-dzoh	She will be forgiven.	Uganda (Nyoro)	
DARIJI	dah-REE-jee	Forgive.	West Africa (Yoruba)	

Name	Pronunciation	Meaning	Origin	Gender
GHOFIRI	goh-FEE-ree	Forgiveness, pardon.	Kenya, Tanzania	
GHUFIRA	goo-FEE-rah	Forgiveness, pardon.	Kiswahili	
HISSA	HEES-sah	Forgiveness, pardon.	Kenya, Tanzania	
MASAMAHA	MAH-sah-mah-hah	Forgiveness.	East Africa (Kiswahili)	M
MSAMEHEJI	msah-meh-heh-jee	Forgiving person.	Kiswahili	
MTHETHE LELI	mteh-heh-leh-lee	Forgive them.	Azania	M
MWIZA	MWEE-zah	One who forgives.	Kiswahili	
OSAYABA	oh-sah-YAH-bah	God forgives.	Benin	M
RADHI	RAH-dee	Forgiveness.	Kenya, Tanzania (Kiswahili)	
XOLANI	koh-LAH-nee	Be forgiven.	Azania	M
XOLI	KOH-lee	One who forgives.	Azania	F
XOLILE	koh-LEE-leh	One who forgives.	Azania	

Freedom and Liberation

The nose just wants to breathe. —*Togo*

Name	Pronunciation	Meaning	Origin	Gender
ADINASI	ah-DEE-nah-see	Freeman.	Kenya, Tanzania	
AHUMARE	ah-hoo-moo-reh	May he feel free.	Uganda (Ganda, Kiga, Nyankore)	
AMANDAH	ah-MAHN-dah	Freedom.	Sierra Leone	
ANYABWILE	ahn-yah-BWEE-leh	God has unchained me.	Tanzania (Nyakyusa)	M
BHABHA	BAHB-hah	Struggle for freedom.	Azania (Sotho)	
FOROYAA	foh-roh-yaah	Free.	Gambia (Mandinka)	

Name	Pronunciation	Meaning	Origin	Gender
GAKEHMIA	gah-keh-MEE-ah	The Fon/chief has set me free.	Cameroon (Mubako)	M
HUN	HOON	Free person.	East Africa (Kiswahili)	F
HURI	HOO-ree	Free person.	Kenya, Tanzania	
HURU	HOO-roo	Free.	Kiswahili	
INIFO	ee-NEE-foh	I am free already, I have survived.	Nigeria (Ishan)	
KANANDI	kah-nahn-dee	Free.	Gambia (Mandinka)	
KAUFULU	kah-oo-FOO-loo	Freedom.	Malawi	
KOBUNGYE	koh-boon-gah-yeh	Freedom comes.	Uganda	F
LEBSIA	lehb-see-ah	She has set herself free.	Cameroon (Mubako)	F
NETFA	neht-fah	A free man, woman.	Ethiopia	
NETSENET	neht-sah-NEHT	Freedom.	Eritrea, Ethiopia (Tigrinya)	F
NKULI	n-koo-lee	Freedom.	Azania (Xhosa)	F
NKULU LEKO	n-KOO-LOO-LEH-koh	Freedom, independence.	Azania (Xhosa)	M
NONKU LUEKO	nohn-koo loo-eh-koh	Freedom is here.	Azania	
OMNIRA	ohm-NEE-rah	Liberation, liberty.	West Africa (Yoruba)	
OPIO	oh-pee-oh	Liberated.	DRC	M
TOKO LOGO	TOH-koh LOH-goh	Free.	Azania (North Sotho)	
UHURU	oo-hoo-roo	Freedom.	Kiswahili	M
WADINASI	wah-dee-NAH-see	Freeman.	Kenya, Tanzania	

Friendship and Camaraderie

Hold a friend with both of your hands. —*Niger*

Name	Pronunciation	Meaning	Origin	Gender
ABOKI	ah-BOH-kee	Comrade.	West Africa (Hausa)	
AKIIKI	ah-kee-EE-kee	Friend.	Uganda (Ganda)	M
ANISA	ah-NEE-sah	Friendly.	Kiswahili	
ASHURA	ah-SHOO-rah	Companion.	East Africa (Kiswahili)	F
BANUYE	bah-NOO-yeh	It is good to move in twos.	Ghana (Akan)	
DURNISHA	door-NEE-sha	Intimate friendship.	Kenya, Tanzania	
EGBE	EHG-beh	Comrade.	West Africa (Yoruba)	
ENYI	ahn-yee	Friend, friendship, precious friend.	Nigeria (Igbo)	F
ENYIOMA	ehn-yee-oh-mah	Faithful friend.	Nigeria (Igbo)	
JAMALA	JAH-mah-lah	Friendly, good manner.	East Africa (Kiswahili)	F
KASHKA	kahsh-kah	Friendly.	West Africa	M
KAZENI	kah-ZEH-nee	Companion.	North Africa (Arabic)	
KHALIL	KAH-leel	Friend.	North Africa (Arabic)	M
KIRAFIKI	kee-rah-FEE-kee	Friendly.	Kenya, Tanzania	
KUUME	koo-OO-meh	Friend.	Namibia (Ovambo)	
MACHARIA	mah-chah-REE-ah	An eternal friend.	East Africa	
MUKWANO	moo-kwah-noh	Friendship, friend, romantic love.	Uganda (Ganda)	F
MWENZI	MWEHN-zee	Companion.	Kiswahili	
NAJIA	nah-JEE-ah	Close friend.	North Africa (Arabic)	F
NILAJA	nee-lah-jah	Friendly; peaceful.	Nigeria (Yoruba)	F
OGBO	oh-boh	Friend, mate, twin.	West Africa	
OKOLO	oh-koh-loh	Friendly.	West Africa	F
ORE-OLUWA	OH-reh-oh-LOO-wah	God's friend.	Nigeria (Yoruba)	
RAFIKI	rah-FEE-kee	Trusted friend.	Kenya, Tanzania	

Name	Pronunciation	Meaning	Origin	Gender
RAMOSA	rah-MOH-sah	The friendly one.	Lesotho (Basotho)	F
SADIIKI	sah-DEE-kee	Reliable friend.	Kenya, Tanzania	
SADIKIFU	sah-dee-KEE-foo	Reliable friend.	Kenya, Tanzania	
SOMBELLA	sohm-BEHL-lah	Friendship has ended.	Cameroon (Mubako)	M
SUHUBA	soo-HOO-bah	Friend.	Tanzania (Kiswahili)	M
SUHUMBA	soo-HOOM-bah	Friendship.	Kiswahili	
URAFIKI	oo-rah-FEE-kee	Friendship.	Kenya, Tanzania	
UTANI	oo-TAH-nee	A familiar friendship.		

Future, Fate, and Destiny

Tomorrow is pregnant, who knows what it will deliver? —Nigeria

Name	Pronunciation	Meaning	Origin	Gender
AJALI	ah-JAH-lee	Accident; destiny; fate. the future.	Kiswahili	
AMINA	ah-MEEN-ah	The future.	Nigeria	
ATAYA	ah-TAH-yah	Remember the future when you are talking.	Nigeria (Ishan)	
BAROZI	bah-roh-zee	They are seers.	Uganda (Kiga, Nyankore, Nyoro, Toro)	M
BASHIRI	bah-SHEE-ree	Prediction.		
BIKAYI	bee-kah-yee	It has been ear marked.	Cameroon (Mubako)	M
BOFELO	boh-FEH-loh	Destiny, fate.	Azania (North Sotho)	
BYEMERO	bah-yee-meh-roh	He whose identity is not questioned.	Rwanda, Burundi (Kinyarwanda, Kirundi)	M
ECHIDIIME	eh-chee-DEE-meh	Tomorrow is pregnant.	Nigeria (Igbo)	F
HESSA	HEHS-sah	Karma, fate.	North Africa (Arabic)	

READER/CUSTOMER CARE SURVEY

HEFG

We care about your opinions! Please take a moment to fill out our online Reader Survey at **http://survey.hcibooks.com**.

As a **"THANK YOU"** you will receive a **VALUABLE INSTANT COUPON** towards future book purchases

as well as a **SPECIAL GIFT** available only online! Or, you may mail this card back to us.

(PLEASE PRINT IN ALL CAPS)

First Name	MI.	Last Name

Address		City

State	Zip	Email

1. Gender
- ☐ Female
- ☐ Male

2. Age
- ☐ 8 or younger
- ☐ 9-12
- ☐ 13-16
- ☐ 17-20
- ☐ 21-30
- ☐ 31+

3. Did you receive this book as a gift?
- ☐ Yes
- ☐ No

4. Annual Household Income
- ☐ under $25,000
- ☐ $25,000 - $34,999
- ☐ $35,000 - $49,999
- ☐ $50,000 - $74,999
- ☐ over $75,000

5. What are the ages of the children living in your house?
- ☐ 0 - 14
- ☐ 15+

6. Marital Status
- ☐ Single
- ☐ Married
- ☐ Divorced
- ☐ Widowed

7. How did you find out about the book?
(please choose one)
- ☐ Recommendation
- ☐ Store Display
- ☐ Online
- ☐ Catalog/Mailing
- ☐ Interview/Review

8. Where do you usually buy books?
(please choose one)
- ☐ Bookstore
- ☐ Online
- ☐ Book Club/Mail Order
- ☐ Price Club (Sam's Club, Costco's, etc.)
- ☐ Retail Store (Target, Wal-Mart, etc.)

9. What subject do you enjoy reading about the most?
(please choose one)
- ☐ Parenting/Family
- ☐ Relationships
- ☐ Recovery/Addictions
- ☐ Health/Nutrition
- ☐ Christianity
- ☐ Spirituality/Inspiration
- ☐ Business Self-help
- ☐ Women's Issues
- ☐ Sports

10. What attracts you most to a book?
(please choose one)
- ☐ Title
- ☐ Cover Design
- ☐ Author
- ☐ Content

FOLD HERE

Comments

Name	Pronunciation	Meaning	Origin	Gender
KADDARA	kahd-DAH-rah	Destiny, fate.	West Africa (Hausa)	
MUNGU	MOON-goo	God, fate, destiny.	East Africa (Kiswahili)	M
OBATARE	oh-bah-tah-reh	Destiny.	Nigeria (Urhobo)	
RAMLA	RAHM-lah	Predictor of future, divination.	East Africa (Kiswahili)	
SHIMINEGE	shee-mee-NEH-geh	Let's see the future.	Nigeria (Tiv)	F
TICHA WONNA	tee-CHAH-oh-nah	We shall see.	Zimbabwe (Shona)	M
TONTE	TOHN-teh	Destiny.	Nigeria	

Generosity and Hospitality

A candle burns itself out to give light to others. —Africa

Name	Pronunciation	Meaning	Origin	Gender
BUPE	BOO-peh	Generosity. hospitality.	Zambia (Bemba)	
DANSEH	dahn-seh	He is not selfish.	Cameroon (Mubako)	M
FADIL	FAH-deel	Generous.	North Africa (Arabic)	M
JAWAAD	JAH-waahd	Generous.	Kiswahili	M
KAABO	kah-AH-boh	Welcome.	West Africa (Yoruba)	
KAREEM	KAH-reem	Generous.	Sudan	
KARIBISHA	kah-ree-BEE-shah	To welcome.	Kiswahili	
KARIMA	kah-REE-mah	Generous.	North Africa (Arabic)	F
KARIMU	kah-REE-moo	Generous, philanthropic.	Kenya, Tanzania	
KHANGEZILE	kahn-geh-ZEE-leh	Our hands are open.	Azania (Zulu)	
MBONGO	m-BOHN-goh	My hands are open.	Cameroon (Mungaka)	F
MKARIMU	m-kah-REE-moo	Generous person.	Kiswahili	

Name	Pronunciation	Meaning	Origin	Gender
MPAJI	m-PAH-jee	A generous giver.	Kiswahili	
MTUPENI	m-too-PEH-nee	Not welcome.	East Africa (Kiswahili)	
MUGABI	moo-gah-bee	Generous person; distributor.	Uganda (Ganda)	M
NEEMAKA	neh-MAH-kah	Generous, benevolent.	Kenya, Tanzania	
NESISA	neh-SEE-sah	Generous, benevolent.	Azania	
NYACHAE	NYAH-chah-ay	Generous.	Kenya (Kisii)	M
RERE	REH-reh	Benevolent.	West Africa (Yoruba)	
RIMARI	ree-mah-ree	Very generous.	Nigeria (Igarra)	
SAMIHA	sah-MEE-hah	Magnanimous.	Kiswahili	F
SEMBEZA	ssehm-beh-zah	To welcome.	Uganda	F
UKARIMU	oo-kah-REE-moo	Hospitality.	Kenya, Tanzania (Kiswahili)	

Gentleness

A cow is milked by gentle hands. —Niger

Name	Pronunciation	Meaning	Origin	Gender
AHSAN	ah-SAHN	Gentle, understanding.	North Africa (Arabic)	
ANASA	AH-nah-sah	Gentle, tender.	Kenya, Tanzania	
AWENA	ah-WEH-nah	Gentle.	Kiswahili	
DALILA	dah-LEE-lah	Gentle girl, gentleness is her soul.	East Africa (Kiswahili)	F
LATEEF	lah-TEEF	Gentle, pleasant.	North Africa (Arabic)	M
LATEEFAH	lah-TEE-fah	Gentle, pleasant.	North Africa (Arabic)	F
LATIFAH	LAH-tee-fah	Gentle.	East Africa (Kiswahili)	F
LATIFU	LAH-tee-foo	Gentle.	Kenya, Tanzania (Kiswahili)	F
NIIWA	nee-EE-wah	Gentle.	West Africa (Yoruba)	
OBULO	oh-BOO-loh	Gentleness.	Nigeria (Ishan)	

Name	Pronunciation	Meaning	Origin	Gender
SUHAILAH	soo-HAH-ee-lah	Gentle, easy.	North Africa (Arabic)	F
UPOLE	oo-POH-leh	Gentleness.	Kiswahili	

Geography

Until grief is restored in the West as the starting place where the man and woman might find peace, the culture will continue to abuse and ignore the power of water, and in turn will be fascinated with fire. —*Burkina Faso*

Name	Pronunciation	Meaning	Origin	Gender
DEDAN	DEE-dahn	City-dweller.	Kiswahili	M
DZONGA	D-ZOHN-gah	South.	Southern Africa (Tsonga)	
ENTLA	ehnt-lah	Of the north.	Azania (Xhosa)	
ENYAKATHO	ehn-yah-kah-toh	In the north.	Azania (Zulu)	
KASIKAZI	kah-see-KAH-zee	North.	Kiswahili	
KOTEKOTE	koh-teh-koh-teh	Everywhere.	Kiswahili	
KUSI	KOO-see	South.	Kiswahili	
MZANTSI	mzahnt-see	South.	Azania (Xhosa)	
TSIBIRI	tsee-bee-ree	Island.	West Africa (Hausa)	

Giving and Receiving

If you have, give; if you need, seek. —*Malawi*

Name	Pronunciation	Meaning	Origin	Gender
AFANYIKOB	ah-fahn-yee-cohb	It is God given.	Cameroon (Mungaka)	
AKAMPA	ah-kahm-pah	He (God) gave to me.	Uganda (Kiga, Nyankore, Nyoro, Toro)	
AMKELA	ahm-KEH-lah	Receive.	Southern Africa (Tsonga)	
ANAYIMI	ahn-ah-yee-mee	A child is a gift from God.	Nigeria (Igarra)	

Name	Pronunciation	Meaning	Origin	Gender
ANBEH	an-beh	An unconditional gift.	Cameroon (Mubako)	F
BAKISHISHI	bah-kee-SHEE-shee	Gift.	Kiswahili	
BASELA	bah-SEH-lah	Gift, small present.	Southern Africa (Tsonga)	
BENDA	BEHN-dah	They take.	Rwanda, Burundi (Kinyarwanda, Kirundi)	
BIASHARA	bee-ah-SHAH-rah	Trade.	Azania (Xhosa)	
BUNMI	BOON-mee	My gift.	Nigeria (Yoruba)	F
BWAKIRA	bwah-kee-rah	One who receives.	Rwanda, Burundi, DRC (Huti, Tutsi, Twa)	M
CHIPO	chee-poh	Gift.	East Africa	F
DINEO	dee-NEH-oh	Gift.	Azania (Nguni)	
EBUN	EH-boon	Gift.	West Africa	F
EJAU	eh-jahw	We have received.	Uganda (Itetso)	M
ENEBE	eh-NEH-beh	Effortless gift.	Nigeria (Igarra)	
ENO	EH-noh	Gift.	Nigeria	
ESOHE	eh-SOH-seh	A free gift.	Nigeria (Edo)	F
ESOMO	eh-SOH-moh	A gift of a child.	Nigeria (Edo)	F
ESOSA	eh-SOH-sah	God's gift.	Nigeria (Edo)	F
HADIYA	hah-DEE-yah	God's gift.	North Africa (Arabic)	
HEDIYE	HEH-dee-yeh	Gift.	Kenya, Tanzania (Kiswahili)	F
HIBA	HEE-bah	Gift.	Kiswahili	F
HIDAYA	hee-DAH-yah	Precious gift.	East Africa (Kiswahili)	F
INGABIRE	een-gah-BEE-reh	Gift.	Rwanda, Burundi (Kinyarwanda, Kirundi)	F
JAMAL	JAH-mahl	Gift from God.	North Africa (Arabic)	
KABELO	kah-BEH-loh	Gift, beautiful share.	Azania (Sotho)	
KARAMA	kah-RAH-mah	Gift.	Kiswahili	
KARAMU	kah-RAH-moo	Precious gift.	Kenya, Tanzania	

Name	Pronunciation	Meaning	Origin	Gender
KEFILWE	keh-feel-weh	I receive.	Botswana (Tswana)	F
KIRAWA	kee-RAH-wah	Gift.	Kiswahili	
MAGANO	mah-GAH-noh	Gift, present.	Namibia (Ovambo)	
MARIAMA	mah-ree-AH-mah	Gift from God.	West Africa	
NEO	NEE-oh	Act of God; free gift.	Azania (Sotho)	M
NIKIWE	NEE-KEE-weh	She is a gift to us.	Azania (Xhosa)	F
NONI	noh-nee	Gift of God.	West Africa	F
NTANGA	n-TAHN-gah	I give.	Rwanda, Burundi (Kinyarwanda, Kirundi)	
OJI	OH-jee	Bearer of gifts.	Kiswahili	
OKECHUKU	oh-keh-CHOO-koo	God's gift.	Nigeria (Igbo)	M
OMBENI	ohm-beh-nee	Ask and you shall receive.	Tanzania	M
SAMBA	SAHM-bah	Gift.	Guinea	
SIPHO	see-poh	A great gift.	Azania (Nguni)	
TEMBA	TEHM-bah	Gift.	Azania	
THABATHA	tah-BAH-tah	Take; assume.	Azania	M
TUHFA	TOO-fah	Gift.	Kiswahili	F
UPAJI	oo-PAH-jee	Gift.	Kiswahili	
YAHYA	YAH-ya	God's gift.	East Africa (Kiswahili)	M
YOHANCE	yoh-HAHN-seh	God's gift.	Nigeria (Hausa)	M
ZAWADI	zah-WAH-dee	Gift.	East Africa (Kiswahili)	F
ZIHABANDI	zee-hah-BAHN-dee	They give to others.	Rwanda, Burundi (Kinyarwanda, Kirundi)	
ZIPHO	ZEE-poh	Gifts.	Azania (Xhosa)	M

God

Acts of God are like riddles. —Burundi

Name	Pronunciation	Meaning	Origin	Gender
ABASI	ah-BAH-see	God.	Nigeria	
ABDU	AHB-doo	Worshipper of God.	Kiswahili	M
ABENAWE	ah-beh-nah-weh	May God be with you.	Uganda (Ganda, Kiga, Nyankore)	
AFINYIKOB	ah-feen-yee-cob	God knows.	Cameroon (Mungaka)	
AKHALU	ah-KAH-loo	When you have played your part, leave the rest to God.	Nigeria (Ishan)	
AKIMANA	ah-kee-MAHN-nah	For God.	Rwanda, Burundi (Kinyarwanda, Kirundi)	F
ALAMOUTA	ah-lah-moh-OO-tah	To rely on God.	Gambia (Mandinka)	M
ALIMAYO	ah-lee-mah-yoh	Honor the Gods.	East Africa	M
ALIYIINZA	ah-lee-yeen-zaah	The one who will worship God.	Uganda (Ganda)	F
AMANYA	ah-mah-ndjh-ah	S/he knows God.	Uganda (Kiga, Nyankore, Nyoro, Toro)	
AMAOMEE	ahm-ah-oh-meh-eh	Giver of sufficiency.	Ghana (Akan)	
AMBE	AHM-beh	We begged God for this child.	West Africa	
ANDAL WISYE	ahn-dahl-WEES-yeh	God has shown me the way.	Tanzania (Nyakyusa)	M
ANUUA	ah-NOO-oo-ah	I am one with God.	Egypt/Khamit	
BAYETE	bah-yeh-teh	Between God and man.	Azania	M
BELUCHI	beh-LOOCH-ee	Provided God approves.	Nigeria (Igbo)	M
CHIBUEZE	chee-boo-EH-zeh	God is the king.	Nigeria	
CHIBUZOR	chee-BOO-ZOHR	God is the way.	Nigeria	
CHIDI	CHEE-dee	God is alive.	Nigeria	
CHIEKE	chee-EH-keh	God is the creator.	Nigeria	
CHIKA	CHEE-kah	God is great.	Nigeria	

Name	Pronunciation	Meaning	Origin	Gender
CHIKAEZE	chee-kah-EH-zeh	God is greater than king.	Nigeria (Igbo)	F
CHIKELU	chee-KEH-loo	God created all.	Nigeria	
CHIKEZIE	chee-KEH-zee	God is the creator.	Nigeria	
CHIMA	CHEE-mah	God has the answer.	Africa	
CHIMAKARA	chee-mah-KAH-rah	God knows best.	Nigeria	
CHIMAOBI	chee-mah-OH-bee	God knows the heart.	Nigeria (Igbo)	
CHIMARA	chee-MAH-rah	God knows everything.	Nigeria	
CHIMDI	CHEEM-dee	My God is alive.	Nigeria	
CHIME	CHEE-meh	Power of God.	Nigeria	
CHIMU-ANYA	chee-moo-AHN-yah	God is vigilant.	Nigeria (Igbo)	
CHINAKA	chee-NAH-kah	God decides.	Nigeria (Igbo)	
CHINONSO	chee-NOHN-soh	God is near.	Nigeria (Igbo)	
CHINYERE	cheen-YEH-reh	Gift from God.	Nigeria	
CHIOSA	chee-OH-sah	God of all.	Nigeria (Igbo)	F
CHUKUDI	choo-KOO-dee	God is alive.	Azania	
CHUKUKA	choo-KOO-kah	God is the greatest.	Nigeria	
CHUKUMA	choo-KOO-mah	God has the answer.	Nigeria	
DALI	DAH-lee	The creator.	Azania (Zulu)	
DASSABRE	dahs-sah-breh	He who is above all thanks.	Ghana (Akan)	M
EBERECHI	eh-beh-REH-chee	Grace of God.	Nigeria	
EBI	EH-bee	God bless.	Nigeria	
EFE	EH-feh	God's wealth.	Nigeria (Edo)	M
EFOSA	eh-FOH-sah	God's wealth.	Nigeria (Edo)	M
EKEDI	eh-KEH-dee	The existence of the creator is shown by what he does.	Nigeria (Igbo)	

Name	Pronunciation	Meaning	Origin	Gender
ETUHOLE	eh-too-HOH-leh	He loves us.	Namibia (Ovambo)	
HIMIDI	hee-MEE-dee	Praise be to God.	Kenya, Tanzania	
IFECHI	ee-FEH-chee	God's very own.	Nigeria	
IKENNA	ee-KEHN-nah	God's authority, support, power.	Nigeria (Igbo)	
INE ABASI	ee-neh-ah-bah-see	God's time.	Nigeria (Efik)	
ISOKE	ee-SOH-keh	A satisfying gift from God.	Benin	F
IYAMBERE	ee-yahm-BEH-reh	The one from the first.	Rwanda	M
JEMINE	jeh-MEE-neh	The Lord let me have mine.	Nigeria (Shekiri)	F
JOLAMI	joh-LAH-mee	The Lord has settled me.	Nigeria (Shekiri)	F
JON	JAHN	The Lord's grace.	Ethiopia	
KAMALU	kah-MAH-loo	God of lightning.	Nigeria (Igbo)	M
KAMANA	kah-MAH-nah	Little God.	Rwanda, Burundi (Kinyarwanda, Kirundi)	
KARIAMU	kah-ree-AH-moo	In the image of God.	East Africa	
LAGO	LAH-goh	God.	Côte d'Ivoire	
LEVE	LEH-veh	The high up one.	Sierra Leone (Mende)	
LUNJIWE	loon-JEE-weh	The creator.	Azania	F
MANIRAHO	mah-nee-RAH-hoh	God exists.	Rwanda, Burundi (Kinyarwanda, Kirundi)	
MANZILI	MAHN-zee-lee	Sent by God.	Kenya, Tanzania (Kiswahili)	M
MASALA	mah-SAH-lah	The great mother.	Sudan	F
MATHAPELO	mah-tah-peh-loh	Answer from God.	Azania (Nguni)	
MAWULI	MAH-woo-lee	There is a God.	Ghana (Ewe)	M
MAWUSI	mah-woo-SEE	In the hands of God.	Ghana (Ewe)	F
MENZI	MEHN-zee	The one who creates.	Azania (Xhosa)	M
MNIKELO	MNEE-keh-loh	Dedicated to God.	Azania (Xhosa)	M

Name	Pronunciation	Meaning	Origin	Gender
MUKASA	moo-KAH-sah	God's chief administrator.	Uganda (Luganda)	M
MUNASHE	moo-NAH-sheh	With God.	Zimbabwe (Shona)	
MUSLIMA	MOOH-slee-mah	One who submits to God.	East Africa (Kiswahili)	F
MUTALA BALA	moo-tah-lah-BAH-lah	The limitless one who fills all space.	Zambia, Zimbabwe (Tonga)	
NATANGWE	nah-TAHNG-weh	May God be praised.	Namibia (Ovambo)	
NATHI	NAH-tee	The Lord is with us.	Azania	M
NKECHI	n-KEH-chee	God's very own, chosen by God.	Nigeria	F
NKECHIKA	n-keh-CHEE-kah	God's own is the best.	Nigeria	
NOSA	NOH-sah	What God has said.	Nigeria (Edo)	M
NOSAKHARE	noh-sah-KHAH-reh	What God has said.	Nigeria (Edo)	M
NOSAKHERE	noh-SAH-keh-reh	God's way is the only way.	Benin	M
NUNASSA	noo-NAHS-sah	Only God knows.	Egypt/Khamit	
OBARI	oh-BAH-ree	God.	Nigeria (Eleme)	
ODELI	oh-DEH-lee	Left to God.	Nigeria (Igbo)	
ODWA	OHD-wah	The only one.	Azania (Xhosa)	
OGECHI	oh-geh-chee	God's time is the best.	Nigeria	M
OKERA	oh-KEH-rah	Likeness to God.	Ghana	
OKIMIDE	oh-kee-MEE-deh	My God is here.	Nigeria	
OLUFEMI	oh-loo-FEH-mee	God loves me.	Nigeria (Yoruba)	M
OLUJIMI	oh-loo-JEE-mee	God gave me this.	Nigeria (Yoruba)	M
OLUMEKO	oo-loo-MEH-koh	God.	Nigeria	
OLUSEGUN	oo-loo-SEH-goon	God conquers.	Nigeria	
OLUWA	oh-LOO-wah	Our Lord.	Nigeria (Yoruba)	M
OMUTONZI	oh-moo-TOHN-zee	The Creator, Almighty.	Uganda (Ganda)	

Name	Pronunciation	Meaning	Origin	Gender
ONYEBUCHI	ohn-yeh-boo-chee	God is greater than any human.	Nigeria	
ONYECHI	ohn-yeh-chee	Humans cannot play God.	Nigeria	
ONYEMACHI	ohn-yeh-mah-chee	Nobody can figure out God.	Nigeria	
OSAGBORO	oh-SAH-boh-roh	There is only one God.	Benin	M
OSAHAR	oh-SAH-hahr	God hears.	Benin	M
OSAROBO	oh-sah-ROH-boh	God is the magician or a miracle worker.	Nigeria (Edo)	F
OSASERE	oh-sah-SEH-reh	God is supreme.	Nigeria (Edo)	F
OSAWE	oh-SAH-weh	God says or decides, God has kept me.	Nigeria (Edo)	M
OSAZE	oh-SAH-zeh	Whom God likes.	Benin	M
OSOKWE	oh-soh-kweh	God in agreement.	Benin	M
RUNJI	ROON-jee	Son (based on Trinitarian idea).	Zimbabwe, Mozambique, Zambia (Shona)	
SADE	SAH-deh	Direct from God.	Nigeria (Yoruba)	
SENGHOR	SEHN-gohr	Descendant of the Gods.	Gambia	M
SESE	SEH-seh	God hears; God has heard.	Ghana	
SHEYI	SHEH-yee	See what God did for me.	Nigeria	
SIBOMANA	see-boh-MAH-nah	They are not God.	Rwanda, Burundi (Kinyarwanda, Kirundi)	
SUKU	SOO-koo	He who supplies the needs of his creatures.	Angola (Ovimbundu)	
TAFUI	tah-FOO-ee	To appreciate God.	Togo (Mina)	
TINASHE	tee-nah-tch-eh	God is with us.	Zimbabwe, Mozambique, Zambia (Shona)	

Name	Pronunciation	Meaning	Origin	Gender
TOJU	TOH-joo	The Lord is uppermost.	Nigeria (Shekiri)	F
TOSAN	TOH-sahn	God knows best.	Nigeria (Shekiri)	F
TUTAN KHAMUN	TOOT-ahnk-AH-muhn	Living image of Amum (the air and wind God).	Egypt/Khamit	M
UANASSA	oo-NAHS-sah	Only God knows.	Egypt/Khamit	
UBANI	oo-bah-nee	In praise of God, whose gift of this child is not quantifiable.	Nigeria (Igarra)	
UGOBUN GQONGO		He who bends down even majesties.	Azania (Zulu)	F
UGUGA BADELE	oo-goo-gah-bah-DEH-leh	The irresistible.	Azania (Zulu)	
UNATHI	un-nah-tee	"You (the Lord) are with us."	Azania (Xhosa)	M
YEMAJA	yeh-MAH-yah	Goddess of birth.	Nigeria (Yoruba)	F
ZUMME	zoo-meh	Teach me to follow the right path of God.	Nigeria (Igarra)	

Goodness

Evil does not last, but the good does. —Kenya

Name	Pronunciation	Meaning	Origin	Gender
ABONG	ah-bong	It is good.	Cameroon (Mungaka)	M
ADONO	ah-DOH-noh	A life of doing good.	Nigeria (Ishan)	
ALFRYEA	ahl-FREE-yah	Born during good times.	Ghana (Ewe)	
ANIKA	ah-NEE-kah	Goodness has come.	Ghana (Akan)	
BURAHA	boo-RAH-hah	Goodness, good qualities.	Uganda (Ganda)	

Name	Pronunciation	Meaning	Origin	Gender
EMA	EH-mah	Good.	Africa	F
ENYONYAM	eh-yohn-yahm	It is good for me.	Ghana (Ewe)	
EZIMA	eh-ZEE-mah	Goodness.	Nigeria	
HABINEZA	hah-bee-NEH-zah	Only goodness exists.	Rwanda, Burundi (Kinyarwanda, Kirundi)	M
HASANATI	hah-sah-NAH-tee	Good.	East Africa (Kiswahili)	F
HASINA	hah-SEE-nah	Good.	East Africa (Kiswahili)	F
HERI	HEH-ree	Happiness; goodness.	Kenya, Tanzania (Kiswahili)	M
IFAMA	ee-FAH-mah	Everything is good.	Nigeria (Igbo)	
IFEOMA	ee-feh-OH-mah	A good thing.	Nigeria	M
INGAMBA	ee-gahm-bah	Goodness.	Rwanda, Burundi, DRC (Huti, Tutsi, Twa)	
ISIFISO	ee-see-FEE-soh	Good wishes.	Azania	
LILA	LEE-lah	Good.	Kiswahili	
MEMA	meh-MAH	Goodness.	East Africa (Kiswahili)	F
MZURI	m-ZUHR-ree	I feel good.	Kenya, Tanzania	
NJEMA	n-JEH-mah	Good.	Kenya, Tanzania	
OFOMA	oh-FOH-mah	Good-natured.	Nigeria	
OLOVA	oh-LOH-vah	Good-hearted.	Southern Africa (Tsonga)	
RIDHAA	reed-hah-ah	Goodwill.	Kenya, Tanzania	
SALEHE	sah-LEH-heh	Good news.	East Africa (Kiswahili)	M
SALHA	sahl-hah	Good.	Kiswahili	F
SIWAZURU	see-wah-ZOO-ree	They are not good people.	East Africa (Kiswahili)	F
SONBELLA	sohn-BEHL-lah	Goodness is finished.	Cameroon (Mubako)	M
SONNAH	soh-nah	It is very good.	Cameroon (Mubako)	F
UWAOMA	oo-wah-OH-mah	Good world.	Nigeria (Igbo)	
ZENA	ZEE-nah	Good news.	Ethiopia	M
ZUWENA	zoo-WEH-nah	Good news.	East Africa (Kiswahili)	F

Grace and Graciousness

Beauty without grace, is like rose without smell. —Benin

Name	Pronunciation	Meaning	Origin	Gender
BABALA	bah-BAH-lah	Favor, grace.	Azania (Xhosa)	
JOHANNA	JOH-hah-nah	God's grace.	East Africa (Kiswahili)	F
KEFIWE	keh-FEE-weh	I receive grace.	Botswana	F
KHAIRIYA	kah-ee-REE-yah	Gracious, benevolent.	North Africa (Arabic)	
LUFEFE	loo-FEH-feh	Grace.	Azania (Xhosa)	M
MADAHA	mah-DAH-hah	Graceful.	East Africa (Kiswahili)	F
MAJALIWA	mah-jah-lee-wah	By God's grace.	East Africa (Kiswahili)	M
NAMEVA	nah-MEH-yah	Grace, mother of the earth.	Azania (Sotho)	
NEEMA	neh-EH-mah	Grace.	Kiswahili	
NOMUSA	noh-MOO-sah	With grace; with kindness.	Azania (Zulu)	F
NYASHA	neejh-ah-tch-ah	Grace of God.	Zimbabwe, Mozambique, Zambia (Shona)	
SHAWANA	shah-WAH-nah	Grace.	Kiswahili	F
UFEFE	oo-FEH-FEH	Grace.	Azania	
VUNENE	voo-NEH-neh	Graciousness, virtue.	Southern Africa (Tsonga)	

Gratitude

Ingratitude is the worst of sins. —Egypt

Name	Pronunciation	Meaning	Origin	Gender
ASANTE	AH-sahn-teh	You have been good— thank you.	East Africa (Kiswahili)	M
BONGANI	bohn-gah-nee	Be grateful to God for this child.	Azania (Zulu)	M

Name	Pronunciation	Meaning	Origin	Gender
BONGIN KOSI	bohn-geen-koh-see	Thank the Lord for this child.	Azania (Zulu)	M
BULI	boo-lee	Gratitude.	Azania (Xhosa)	F
CHIMEKA	chee-MEE-kah	Thanks to God.	Nigeria	
CHIMELA	chee-MEH-lah	Thanks to God.	Nigeria	
DZIKA	ZEE-kah	Thanks.	Cameroon (Mungaka)	
JENDAYI	jehn-DAH-yee	Give thanks; to give thanks for this child.	Zimbabwe (Shona)	F
KELECHI	keh-LEH-chee	Thank God; praise the Lord.	Nigeria (Igbo)	
KHENSANI	keh-sah-nee	Thank you for the birth of this child.	Botswana (Tswana)	M
KURON	KOO-rahn	Thanks.	Sudan (Kuku)	M
MARAHABA	MAH-rah-HAH-bah	Thank you.	Kiswahili	F
MODUPE	moh-DOO-peh	Thank God; I am grateful.	Nigeria	
NDANGI	n-DAHN-gee	Thank you.	Namibia (Ovambo)	
NDAPAN DULA	n-dah-pah-DOO-lah	I thank.	Namibia (Ovambo)	
NDATIN DANGI	n-dah-teen-DAH-gee	Thank you.	Namibia (Ovambo)	
NINSIIMA	neen-see-mah	I am thankful to God.	Uganda (Kiga, Nyankore)	
OTHULA	oh-too-lah	To give a gift in thanks.	Azania (Zulu)	
SHAKIR	SHAH-keer	Thankful.	North Africa (Arabic)	M
SHAKUR	SHAH-kuhr	The thankful.	North Africa (Arabic)	
SHAMBE KELA	shahm-beh-KEH-lah	Receive with cupped hands!	Namibia (Ovambo)	
SHUKRANI	shook-rah-nee	Grateful.	Kenya, Tanzania	
SHUKURA	shoo-KOO-rah	Be grateful.	East Africa (Kiswahili)	F
SIBONGILE	see-bon-gee-LEH	Thanks.	Zimbabwe (Ndebele)	F

Name	Pronunciation	Meaning	Origin	Gender
TANGI	TAHN-gee	Thank you.	Namibia (Ovambo)	
TANKISO	tahn-kee-soh	Gratitude.	Azania (Sotho)	M
TATENDA	tah-tehn-dah	We are grateful.	Zimbabwe, Mozambique, Zambia (Shona)	
TEBOGO	TEH-boh-goh	We are grateful, gratitude.	Botswana (Tswana)	M
THANAA	TAHN-nah	Gratitude.	North Africa (Arabic)	
TUMPE	TOOM-peh	Let us thank God for this blessing.	Tanzania (Nyakyusa)	F
ZIKOMO	zee-KOH-moh	Thank you.	Malawi (Ngoni)	M

Greatness and Prominence

Glory does not come by calling. —Kenya

Name	Pronunciation	Meaning	Origin	Gender
AAILYAH	ah-LEE-YAH	Of the highest order.	Africa	
AJIMA	ah-JEE-mah	Greater than.	Nigeria (Eleme)	
ANDITO	ahn-DEE-toh	Great one.	Central Africa	F
BUKEKE	boo-keh-keh	Spectacular.	Azania (Xhosa)	F
DANDALA ZISA	dahn-dah-lah-ZEE-sah	Make prominent; clear.	Azania (Xhosa)	
DIN	deen	Great.	DRC	M
ELONA	eh-LOH-nah	The emery one, the most.	Azania (Xhosa)	
ESONA	eh-SOH-nah	The very one, the most.	Azania (Xhosa)	
FOKAZA	foh-KAH-zah	Great fellow.	Azania (Xhosa)	
JALEEL	JAH-leel	Greatness.	North Africa (Arabic)	M
JALIL	JAH-leel	Greatness; revered.	North Africa (Arabic)	M
JITANGU-LIZA	jee-tahn-goo-LEE-zah	Put oneself forward.	Kiswahili	

Name	Pronunciation	Meaning	Origin	Gender
KUBWA	KOOB-wah	Great.	Kiswahili	
LALILA	lah-LEE-lah	Great.	North Africa (Arabic)	F
LANRE	LAHN-reh	Greatness.	Nigeria	
LOLA	LOH-lah	Greatness; having wealth.	Nigeria (Yoruba)	
MSHAN GAMA	mm-SHAHN-gah-mah	Rising.	East Africa (Kiswahili)	
MUGALU	moo-gah-loo	One that raises.	Uganda (Ganda)	M
NDEJURU	n-deh-JOO-roo	I am on top.	Rwanda, Burundi (Kinyarwanda, Kirundi)	
NONGAYE	non-GAH-yeh	She will be important.	Azania	F
OLA	OH-lah	Greatness, noble man.	Nigeria	F
OLABISI	oh-lah-BEE-see	Greatness delivers.	Nigeria	
OLANIYI	oh-lah-NEE-yee	This is greatness.	Nigeria	
OLATAYO	oh-lah-TAH-yoh	Greatness deserves happiness.	Nigeria	
OLAYINKA	oh-lah-YEEN-kah	Greatness surrounds me.	Nigeria	
OLU	OH-loo	Pre-eminent.	Nigeria (Yoruba)	M
OMAR	OH-mar	The highest.	North Africa (Arabic)	M
ONGAMA	ohn-GAH-mah	To stand out, to tower over.	Azania (Xhosa)	
ONYEKA	ohn-YEH-kah	Who is the greatest?	Nigeria (Igbo)	F
SETOWU	seh-TOH-woo	God is great.	Ghana	
TOMA	TOH-mah	Significant.	Sierra Leone, Liberia (Mende)	M
UKUU	oo-koo-OO-oo	Greatness; strength.	Kiswahili	
VELA	VEH-lah	Prominent one.	Azania (Zulu)	

Harvest and Farming

If you eat all your harvest, you won't have seed for tomorrow. —Africa

Name	Pronunciation	Meaning	Origin	Gender
ALAOPA	ah-lah-OH-pah	Plentiful harvest.	Nigeria (Yoruba)	
DIJI	DEE-jee	Farmer.	Nigeria (Igbo)	M
DYEBO	dJEH-boh	Great harvest, abundance of food.	Azania (Xhosa)	
FULA	FOO-lah	Reap, gather crops from fields or river.	Azania (Zulu)	
IBO	EE-boh	First fruits.	Azania (Xhosa)	
ISIVUNO	ee-see-VOO-noh	Harvest.	Azania (Zulu)	
KIRIMI	KEH-ree-mee	A farmer.	Kenya (Agikuyu)	M
KITAKA	kee-TAH-kah	Good farmer.	Central Africa	M
NAHLESU	nah-leh-soo	A child born on the farm, a gift from the farm.	Cameroon (Mubako)	F
OLAPA	oh-LAH-pah	The glory of plentiful harvest.	Nigeria (Yoruba)	
SEMERE	seh-MEH-reh	Farmer.	Ethiopia	M

Hatred and Dislike

The medicine for hate is separation. —Burkina Faso

Name	Pronunciation	Meaning	Origin	Gender
CHUKI	CHOO-kee	Hatred; resentment.	Kiswahili	
CHUKIA	choo-kee-ah	To hate; dislike.	Kiswahili	
ISABELE	ee-sah-BEH-leh	I can't stand them.	Nigeria (Ishan)	

Name	Pronunciation	Meaning	Origin	Gender
ITIMA	ee-TEE-mah	Spite.	Uganda (Nyoro)	
KUNJEMIA	koon-JEH-mee-ah	My brothers hate me.	Cameroon (Mubako)	F
LWANGO	loo-ahn-goh	Hatred; jealousy.	Uganda (Runyankore)	F
SANGEYA	san-GEH-yah	Hate me.	Zimbabwe (Shona)	F

Health and Wellness

Good health does not spread,
disease does. —Azania

Name	Pronunciation	Meaning	Origin	Gender
AFIYA	ah-FEE-yah	Health.	Tanzania (Kiswahili)	F
AFLA	ahf-lah	Health.	Kiswahili	
BABU	BAH-boo	A healer.	East Africa	
CACANJA	kah-kahn-jah	Medicine man.	East Africa	M
DAKTARI	dahk-TAH-ree	Doctor, healer.	Kenya, Tanzania	
DIBIA	DEE-bee-ah	Healer.	Nigeria (Igbo)	M
GANA	gah-nah	Medicine, my chieftaincy.	Cameroon (Mubako)	M
HAJAMBO	hah-JAHM-boh	He is well.	Kiswahili	
JANA	JAH-nah	Healthy child.	East Africa (Kiswahili)	F
JAARA	jaah-rah	To heal.	Gambia (Mandinka)	
JAARA LILAA	jaah-rah-lee-laah	Healer.	Gambia (Mandinka)	
KAHEMBA	kah-HEHM-bah	Just looking at her will get you well.	Southern Africa	M
KAMUZU	KAH-moo-zoo	Medicine for the ill.	Azania (Nguni)	
KASUJJA	kah-sooj-jah	Small fever.	Uganda (Ganda)	M

Name	Pronunciation	Meaning	Origin	Gender
KEHGANA	keh-GAH-nah	A child born after medical therapy for infertility.	Cameroon (Mubako)	M
KEYAH	KAY-yah	In good health.	Gambia, Guinea, Guinea-Bissau (Mande)	F
KIDAWA	kee-DAH-wah	Medicine.	Kiswahili	
KIZIMA	kee-ZEE-mah	Healthy.	Rwanda, Burundi (Kinyarwanda, Kirundi)	
KOSI	koh-see	To heal.	Gambia (Mandinka)	
LIKITA	lee-KEE-tah	Doctor.	West Africa (Hausa)	
MAGODI	mah-GOH-dee	Herbs, medicines.	Zambia (Tumbuka)	M
MBATHA LALA	m-bah-tah-ah-lah-lah	Great fever.	Azania (Xhosa)	
MBIYEE	m-bee-YEH-eh	Medicine.	Nigeria (Eleme)	
MUGANGA	moo-GAHN-gah	Doctor.	Rwanda, Burundi (Kinyarwanda, Kirundi)	M
NAMABWA	nah-mah-bwah	Sores, open wounds.	Uganda (Ganda, Soga)	M
NAWIRI	nah-WEE-ree	Healthy-looking.	Kenya, Tanzania	
NERANTI	neh-RAHN-tee	Health is victory.	Egypt/Khamit	
NGAKA	NGAH-kah	A healer.	Azania (North Sotho)	
OKIA	oh-kee-yah	Medicine.	Uganda (Itetso)	M
PHILA	PEE-lah	Be in health; live!	Azania (Xhosa)	
RAI	RAH-ee	Health, vigor.	Kiswahili	
SHAKA	SHAH-kah	Stomach disorder.	Azania (Zulu)	
SIGALLA	see-GAHL-lah	When one is in good health one forgets the future.	Cameroon (Mubako)	M
SIHA	SEE-hah	Good health.	Kiswahili	
SIJAMBO	see-JAHM-boh	I am well.	Kiswahili	
SOWO	SOH-woh	Medicine woman.	East Africa	F

Name	Pronunciation	Meaning	Origin	Gender
TURYA-TAMBA	too-ree-ah-tahm-bah	We shall heal.	Uganda (Kiga, Nyankore, Nyoro, Toro)	M
VAGANA	vah-GAH-nah	Medicine for death.	Cameroon (Mubako)	M
YAYA	YAH-yah	Child's nurse.	Kiswahili	F
YEKIZE	yeh-kee-zeh	Heal yourself.	Uganda (Kiga, Nyankore, Nyoro, Toro)	
ZILABA	zee-lah-bah	Born while sick.	Uganda (Luganda)	M
ZO	zoh	Folk or traditional medicine.	Liberia	M

Heart

*The heart has reasons which
scholars cannot understand. —Algeria*

Name	Pronunciation	Meaning	Origin	Gender
AGUNWNYI	ah-goonw-nee-yee	Lion heart.	Nigeria (Igbo)	F
ANISIOBI	ah-nee-see-OH-bee	The inside of my heart.	Nigeria (Igbo)	M
ETIOBI	eh-tee-OH-bee	One heart.	Nigeria (Igbo)	M
IKE-DINOBI	ee-keh-dee-NOH-bee	Heart is strength.	Nigeria (Igbo)	
JIDEOBI	jee-dee-oh-bee	Hold your heart.	Nigeria (Igbo)	
JUSOO	joo-soh	Heart.	Gambia (Mandinka)	
KASUJJU	kah-SOO-joo	Heart.	Uganda	
KIJOO	kee-joh	Heart.	Gambia (Mandinka)	
KISIAH	kee-ZEE-ah	Light-hearted.	West Africa (Bini)	F
KISIBIKA	kee-see-BEE-kah	Heart.	Uganda	
MTIMA	m-TEE-mah	Heart	Malawi (Ngoni)	M
NAMUNA	nah-MOON-nah	Heart.	Uganda	

Name	Pronunciation	Meaning	Origin	Gender
OBI	OH-bee	Heart.	Nigeria (Igbo)	
OBIAGU	oh-bee-ah-goo	Lion's heart.	Nigeria (Igbo)	
OBIAMAKA	oh-bee-ah-mah-kah	Gentle and humble heart.	Nigeria (Igbo)	
OBIANYO	oh-bee-ahn-yoh	May the heart rest.	Nigeria (Igbo)	M
OBIDIKE	oh-bee-DEE-keh	Strong heart.	Nigeria (Igbo)	M
OBIJINDU	oh-bee-jeen-doo	Heart holds life.	Nigeria (Igbo)	
OBINALI	oh-bee-NAH-lee	Heart endures.	Nigeria (Igbo)	
PUMA	POO-mah	Beat of the heart.	Kiswahili	
TUNUKA	too-NOO-kah	To set one's heart on.	Kiswahili	
ZAMOYONI	ZAH-moh-yoh-nee	Of the heart.	East Africa (Kiswahili)	M

Help, Support, and Care

Assistance conquers a lion. —Morocco

Name	Pronunciation	Meaning	Origin	Gender
ADAMEZILI	ah-dah-meh-ZEE-lee	A caring daughter.	Nigeria (Igbo)	F
ADOM	ah-DOHM	Help from God.	Ghana (Akan)	M
AMWA	AHM-wah	To be suckled.	Kiswahili	
ANATHI	ah-NAAH-tee	We have divine support; heaven has heard us.	Azania (Xhosa)	M
ARAZAKI	ah-rah-ZAH-kee	Provider.	Kiswahili	
ASIBO	ah-SEE-boh	The person everyone runs to for assistance.	Nigeria (Ishan)	
AUNI	ah-OO-nee	To help, succor.	Africa	
AYAMA	ah-YAH-mah	Someone to lean on.	Azania (Xhosa)	
BABALLA	bah-BAHL-lah	To take care of.	Lesotho (South Sotho)	
BALELWA	bah-leh-lwah	They are nursed; carried.	DRC (Rega)	F

Name	Pronunciation	Meaning	Origin	Gender
BAWO	BAH-woh	Benefactor, master.	Azania (Xhosa)	
BETSERAI	beht-seh-RAH-ee	Help, assistance.	Zimbabwe (Shona)	M
BYOLEDDE	bjoh-lehd-deh	Cared for.	Uganda (Ganda)	M
DUMAKA	doo-mah-kah	Help out.	Nigeria	M
ELEKELELI	eh-leh-keh-LEH-lee	Helper.	Azania (Zulu)	
FAYEKA	fah-YEH-kah	Fragile.	Southern Africa (Tsonga)	
FOLORUHSO	foh-loh-ROO-soh	Under the care of God.	Nigeria	
FOLUKE	foh-LOO-keh	Placed in God's care, hands.	Nigeria (Yoruba)	
IBOLO	ee-BOH-loh	Supporters.	Nigeria (Ishan)	
IKEOLU	ee-keh-OH-loo	The care of God.	Nigeria (Yoruba)	
INAYA	ee-nah-yah	Providence.	East Africa (Kiswahili)	F
JIHADHARI	jee-hahd-HAH-ree	Take care.	Kiswahili	
KHATHALA	kah-tah-lah	One who cares about others.	Azania (Xhosa)	F
KULEA	koo-LEE-ah	To nurse, to tend.	West Africa	
KWATHA	KWAH-tah	Help!	Namibia (Ovambo)	
LEA	LEH-ah	Raise or bring up a child.	Azania	F
MJIMA	m-JEE-mah	A helpful person.	Kenya, Tanzania	
MODIBO	moh-dee-boh	Helper.	West Africa	M
MSAADA	m-saah-dah	Assistance; help.	East Africa (Kiswahili)	F
MSIZI	m-SEE-zee	The helper.	Azania	M
MTUME	m-TOO-meh	An apostle.	Kenya, Tanzania	
MUGANZA	moo-gahn-zah	Caretaker.	Uganda (Ganda)	M
MUTULU	moo-TOO-loo	Someone who will help you get where you are going.	Azania (Zulu)	
NASRA	NAH-srah	Assistance.	East Africa (Kiswahili)	F
NIKA	NEE-kah	Provide.	Azania (Zulu)	

Name	Pronunciation	Meaning	Origin	Gender
NKATHA	n-kah-tah	The support.	Azania	
NOMSIZO	nohm-see-zoh	The helper.	Azania	F
NONZUZO	nohm-zoo-zoh	One who is a benefit.	Azania	F
NSUNGENI	n-soon-gen-nee	Keep and nurture me.	Zambia (Chewa)	M
NYASAMA	nyah-sah-mah	Helper of man.	DRC	M
ODIA	oh-DEE-ah	He who straightens things; a repairer.	Nigeria (Ishan)	
SIZAKELE	see-zah-KEH-leh	The one who has been helped.	Azania	
SIZANI	see-zah-nee	Come and help; you all help.	Azania (Zulu)	
SIZILE	see-ZEE-leh	He has helped us.	Azania (Xhosa)	M
SIZIWE	SEE-zee-weh	She has received help.	Azania (Xhosa)	F
SORA	SOH-rah	Careful.	West Africa (Yoruba)	
THANDI-ZANI	tahn-dee-ZAH-nee	Let's help the people in the community who are suffering.	Zambia (Chewa)	M
UANGALIFU	oo-ahn-gah-LEE-foo	Carefulness.	Kiswahili	
UWIN TONDA	oo-ween-TOHN-dah	The one who is careful.	Rwanda, Burundi (Kinyarwanda, Kirundi)	
UWITONZE	oo-wee-toh-ohn-zeh	One who is careful.	Rwanda, Burundi, DRC (Huti, Tutsi, Twa)	M
WESESA	weh-seh-SAH	Careless.	Uganda (Musoga)	F
WEZIWE	WEH-zee-weh	She has received help to succeed in life.	Azania (Xhosa)	F
YAMURO	yah-MOO-roh	Help; assistance.	Azania (Xhosa)	M

Heroism

The hero shows his courage in the battlefield, not in the house. —Ghana

Name	Pronunciation	Meaning	Origin	Gender
AKINSANYA	ah-KEEN-sahn-yah	The hero avenges.	Nigeria (Yoruba)	M
AKINSHEYE	ah-KEEN-sheh-yeh	Valor acts honorably.	Nigeria (Yoruba)	M
AKINSHIJU	ah-KEEN-shee-joo	Valor awakes.	Nigeria (Yoruba)	M
AKINWOLE	ah-KEEN-woh-leh	Valor enters the house.	Nigeria (Yoruba)	M
AKINYELE	ah-keen-YEH-leh	Valor benefits the house.	Nigeria (Yoruba)	M
DIALLOBE	dee-ahl-loh-beh	Heroic.	Central Africa	M
KHALIPHA	Kah-LEE-pah	The valiant one.	Azania	F
SHUJAA	SHOO-jah-ah	Hero.	Kiswahili	

History, Heredity, and Tradition

Tradition remains in the ear. —*Ghana*

Name	Pronunciation	Meaning	Origin	Gender
AKADE	ah-KAH-deh	What existed before should be valued.	Nigeria (Ishan)	
AZUBIKE	ah-zoo-BEE-keh	The past is our strength.	Nigeria	
BAKANU	bah-kah-noo	Once bitten twice shy.	Cameroon (Mungaka)	M
FUZILE	foo-ZEE-leh	Heredity.	Azania	F
MILA	MEE-lah	Traditional customs.	Kiswahili	
MOLEFI	moh-LEH-feh	Preserver of tradition.	Southern Africa	
NOMFUZO	nohm-foo-zoh	Heredity.	Azania	F
NTYATYAMBO	nath-yaht-ahm-boh	History.	Azania	F
SEBANANI	seh-eh-bah-naah-nee	Heritage.	Rwanda, Burundi, DRC (Huti, Tutsi, Twa)	M
SENNONO	sseh-noh-noh	Tradition.	Uganda (Ganda)	M
SIFUZILE	see-foo-ZEE-leh	Heredity.	Azania	M

Home and Lodging

The ruin of a nation begins in the homes of its people.
—Ghana

Name	Pronunciation	Meaning	Origin	Gender
AFEALETE	ah-feh-ah-leh-teh	The house is still standing.	Ghana	
BALIKA	bah-lee-kah	They are at home.	Uganda (Ganda)	F
BANDELE	bahn-DEH-leh	Born away from home.	Nigeria (Yoruba)	
BIA	BEE-ah	Home.	East Africa (Kiswahili)	F
BIRARO	bee-RAH-roh	Lodgings.	Rwanda, Burundi (Kinyarwanda, Kirundi)	
BUYISILE	boo-yee-SEE-leh	The spirit which has come home.	Azania	F
DEBILLA	deh-BEEL-lah	Run from your house.	Cameroon (Mubako)	M
DWOKATUA	dwoh-kah-too-wah	Take me home.	Uganda (Acholi)	M
CINGO NGEVA	keen-gohn-geh-vah	Homesick person who will go through anything to get home.	Angola (Ovimbundu)	
EGUMBO	eh-GOOM-boh	House, home.	Namibia (Ovambo)	
EZI	eh-zee	Home; premises.	Nigeria (Igbo)	F
INAANI	ee-NAHN-nee	Who is left at home?	Southern Africa	
JUMBA	JOOM-bah	Large building.	East Africa (Kiswahili)	M
KATHERO	kah-TEH-roh	Born at home.	East Africa	
KHATA	KHAH-tah	Home.	Azania (Zulu)	
KHAYA	KAH-yah	Home.	Azania (Xhosa)	M
KHAYAKAZI	kah-yah-KAH-zee	The great home; she will be refuge to many.	Azania (Xhosa)	F
KITANDA	kee-TAHN-dah	A bed.	Kiswahili	
KOBA	KOH-bah	Kitchen.	Gambia	F
KYATO	tch-aah-loh	Village; large estate.	Uganda (Ganda)	M

Name	Pronunciation	Meaning	Origin	Gender
MAKAO	mah-KAH-oh	Home.	Kiswahili	
MAKHAYA	mah-KAAH-yah	Many homes; home to many.	Azania (Xhosa)	M
MANZI	MAHN-zee	Residence.	East Africa (Kiswahili)	M
MBUYISILE	mboo-yee-see-leh	The spirit which has come home.	Azania	M
MOTILEWA	moh-teel-eh-wah	I am from home.	East Africa	F
MUKANDA	moo-kahn-dah	A permanent dweller.	Uganda (Ganda)	M
MZWANDILE	oom-zwahn-dee-lee	The home has expanded.	Azania (Xhosa)	M
NOKHAYA	noh-kah-yoh	She is a home to many.	Azania (Xhosa)	F
NUBILLA	noo-BEEL-lah	I cannot run away from home.	Cameroon (Mubako)	M
NYINIMU	ndjh-ee-nee-moo	The owner of the house.	Uganda (Ganda)	F
OGBE	OHG-beh	Shelter.	Eritrea, Ethiopia (Tigrinya)	M
SAKHUMZI	sah-KOOM-zee	We are building a home.	Azania (Xhosa)	M
SEKIRIKA	sseh-tch-ee-ree-kah	That is at home.	Uganda (Ganda)	M
SOLONZI	soh-lohn-zee	The eye of the home.	Azania (Xhosa)	M
ULIYEMI	oo-lee-YEH-mee	Home suits me.	Nigeria (Shekiri)	F
ULOMA	oo-loh-mah	Good home.	Nigeria (Igbo)	F
UWAYA	oo-WAH-yah	We are at home.	Nigeria (Ishan)	
WALE	WAH-leh	Come home.	East Africa	F
WUBILLA	woo-BEEL-lah	Cover the house.	Cameroon (Mubako)	F
YAHIMBA	yah-heem-BAH	There is nothing like home.	Nigeria (Tiv)	F
ZWAYI	zwah-yee	The home has expanded.	Azania (Xhosa)	M

Hope

Hope does not disappoint. —Azania

Name	Pronunciation	Meaning	Origin	Gender
AMAL	ah-MAHL	Hope.	Egypt/Khamit	
BAMIDELE	bah-mee-deh-leh	Hope.	Nigeria (Yoruba)	
ELECHI	eh-LEH-chee	Hope in God.	Nigeria	
JIKITA	jee-KEE-tah	Hope, confidence.	Gambia	
KORI	KOH-ree	Hope.	Gambia (Mandinka)	
MWEN-DAPOLE	mwehn-dah-POH-leh	Hopeful.	Tanzania (Nyakyusa)	M
NDEZEYE	n-deh-ZEH-yeh	I hope.	Rwanda, Burundi (Kinyarwanda, Kirundi)	M
NIKU-SUBILA	nee-koo-soo-BEE-lah	Hopeful.	Tanzania (Nyakyusa)	M
NOMA-THEMBA	noh-mah-T EHM-bah	She brings hope.	Azania (Xhosa)	F
RAJI	RAH-jee	Hopeful.	North Africa (Arabic)	M
RAJIA	rah-JEE-ah	Hope.	North Africa (Arabic)	F
SUBIRA	ssoo-bee-rah	Being patiently hopeful.	Rwanda, Burundi, DRC (Huti, Tutsi, Twa)	F
SUUBI	SOO-bee	He brings hope.	Uganda (Ganda)	M
TARAJI	tah-RAH-jee	Hope, faith.	Kenya, Tanzania	
TARAJIKA	tah-rah-JEE-kah	Hope, faith.	Kenya, Tanzania	
TASHIYA	tah-SHEE-ah	Hope for tomorrow.	Namibia	F
TESFAYE	tehs-fah-yeh	My hope.	Ethiopia	M
THEMBA	TEHM-bah	Hope.	Azania (Xhosa)	M
THEMBISA	TEHM-BEE-sah	She gives us hope.	Azania (Xhosa)	F

Name	Pronunciation	Meaning	Origin	Gender
TSHEPO	tch-eh-poh	Endeavor, hope, trust.	Azania (North Sotho)	M
TUKESIGA	too-keh-see-gah	Hopeful.	Uganda (Rukiga)	M
TUMAINI	too-mah-EE-nee	Hope.	Kiswahili	
TUMAINISHA	too-mah-nee-shah	Give hope to.	Kiswahili	

Humanity, People, and Community

Does humanity become civilized all at once? —*Ghana*

Name	Pronunciation	Meaning	Origin	Gender
AANTU	ah-AHN-too	Human being.	Namibia (Ovambo)	
BAIZIRE	bah-ee-zee-reh	They (the people) came.	Uganda (Kiga, Nyankore, Nyoro, Toro)	M
BANTWINI	bahn-twee-nee	Dedicated to the people.	Azania (Xhosa)	M
BOTHO	BOH-toh	Humane person.	Azania (Sotho)	
BUNTU	BOON-too	One with humanity.	Azania	M
INOTU	ee-NOH-too	May I not offend the combined strength of the community.	Nigeria (Ishan)	
ISINTU	ee-SEEN-too	Mankind, humanity.	Azania	
IYORA	ee-YOH-rah	I am not a stranger in this community.	Nigeria (Ishan)	
JIRANI	JEE-rah-nee	Neighbor.	Kenya, Tanzania (Kiswahili)	F
LUNTU	LOON-too	Humanity.	Azania	M
MADU	MAH-doo	Of the people.	Nigeria (Igbo)	M
MTUNDU	M-TOON-doo	People, community.	Malawi (Ngoni)	M
MUSHI	MOO-shee	Group.	Rwanda, Burundi (Kinyarwanda, Kirundi)	M

Name	Pronunciation	Meaning	Origin	Gender
NKUNDIU-SHUTI	n-koon-deen-SHOO-tee	I love people.	Rwanda	M
NOBUNTU	noh-BOON-too	Mother of humanity.	Azania (Xhosa)	F
NOLUNTU	noh-LOON-too	Humanity.	Azania	F
OLAJU	oh-LAH-joo	Civilization.	West Africa (Yoruba)	
OMWAN-CHA	OHM-wahn-chah	He loves people.	East Africa (Kisii)	M
SHENZI	SHEN-zee	Uncivilized.	Kiswahili	
UBUNTU	oo-BOON-too	Humanity, mankind.	Zimbabwe	
UJIRANI	oo-JEE-RAH-nee	Neighborhood.	Kiswahili	

Humility and Modesty

Cover up the good you do—do like the Nile and conceal your sources. —Egypt

Name	Pronunciation	Meaning	Origin	Gender
AKAMDU-WOE	ah-kahn-doo-whah	There is no person without liabilities.	Cameroon (Mungaka)	
BAIINA	bah-ee-nah	It is above me.	Cameroon (Mubako)	M
BAMUKE	bah-moo-keh	Humble yourself.	Uganda (Kiga, Nyankore, Nyoro, Toro)	M
BOBO	BOH-boh	Be humble.	Nigeria (Hausa)	M
DONKOR	dohn-KOR	Humble person.	Ghana (Akan)	M
GOBISA	goh-BEE-sah	Humble.	Azania	
HAYA	HAH-yah	Modesty.	Kiswahili	
LOKUNGA	loh-koon-gah	If you are better off, do not laugh at others.	Cameroon (Mubako)	F
LULAMA	loo-lah-mah	To be meek.	Azania (Xhosa)	M

Name	Pronunciation	Meaning	Origin	Gender
NTOBEKO	n-toh-BEH-koh	Humility.	Azania (Xhosa)	M
PASIGHA	pah-SEE-gah	One who does not force herself onto people for recognition.	Cameroon (Mubako)	F
RIOELU	ree-oh-eh-loo	Don't be ashamed to ask for favors.	Nigeria (Igbo)	
THOBA	TOH-bah	Be humble.	Azania (Xhosa)	M
THOBANI	toh-BAH-nee	Be humble.	Azania (Xhosa)	M
THOBEKA	toh-BEH-kah	The humble one.	Azania (Xhosa)	F
THOZAMA	toh-zah-mah	She is humble.	Azania (Xhosa)	F
TIBIMALO	tee-bee-MAH-loh	Humble, quiet.	Azania (North Sotho)	
UJOR	oo-johr	Modesty.	Nigeria (Igbo)	F

Jealousy, Envy, and Greed

The jealous man loses his flesh
by looking at the fat bellies of others. —*Congo*

Name	Pronunciation	Meaning	Origin	Gender
AFEDELE	ah-feh-DEH-leh	They are jealous of our wealth.	Nigeria (Ishan)	
BAWA	BAH-wah	Greedy, voracious.	Azania (Xhosa)	
DZIKUNU	dZEE-koo-noo	A thing of envy.	Ghana	
EHIOZE	eh-HEE-oh-ZAY	I am above people's jealousy.	Benin	M
HUSUDA	hoo-SOO-dah	Envy.	Kiswahili	
KIJICHO	kee-JEE-choh	Envious.	Kiswahili	F
MLAFI	m-LAH-fee	A greedy person.	Kiswahili	
MONA	MOH-nah	Jealousy.	Swaziland	M
MONIMA	moh-NEE-mah	Do not envy others.	Kenya, Tanzania	

Name	Pronunciation	Meaning	Origin	Gender
MUKODO	moo-koh-doh	Miser, stingy person.	Uganda (Ganda)	M
NKINZI	n-keen-zee	Greed or passion blinds reasoning.	Uganda (Ganda)	F
ODMIA	odh-MEE-ah	They are jealous of me.	Cameroon (Mubako)	F
SANJE	SAHN-jeh	Jealousy.	Zambia (Tumbuka)	M
UMGOLO	oom-GOH-loh	Greed.	Azania (Zulu)	
WEMUSA	weh-moo-SAH	Never satisfied with his possessions.	Uganda (Luganda)	M

Jewels, Metals, and Minerals

The jewel of the house is the child. —Senegal

Name	Pronunciation	Meaning	Origin	Gender
ALMASI	ahl-MAH-see	Precious jewel.	Kenya, Tanzania	
AMBALO	ahm-BAH-loh	Jewel.	Southern Africa (Tsonga)	
BHEDU	BEH-doo	Copper.	Azania (Xhosa)	
BUSANGA	boo-sah-ngah	Pearls.	DRC (Rega)	F
CHISULO	chee-SOO-loh	Steel.	Malawi (Yao)	M
DAEMANE	dah-ee-mah-neh	Diamond.	Lesotho (South Sotho)	
DAYIMANE	day-ee-mah-neh	Diamond.	Azania (Xhosa)	
DURRA	DOOR-rah	Large pearl.	Kiswahili	F
FERUZI	feh-ROO-zee	Turquoise.	Azania (Xhosa)	
ILIGUGU	ee-lee-GOO-goo	Jewel; treasured object.	Azania (Zulu)	
JAUHAR	JAH-ooh-hahr	Jewel.	East Africa (Kiswahili)	F
KIMAMETA	KEE-mah-meh-tah	Diamond mine.	East Africa (Kiswahili)	M
KITO	KEE-toh	Precious jewel.	Kenya, Tanzania	
MARJANI	mahr-JAH-nee	Coral.	Kiswahili	
META	MEH-tah	Sparkling like a rare jewel.	Africa	F

Name	Pronunciation	Meaning	Origin	Gender
ONAEDO	oh-nah-eh-doh	Gold.	Nigeria (Igbo)	F
RABABI	rah-BAH-bee	Silver.	Kiswahili	
SERWAA	sehr-wah	Jewel.	West Africa	F
SHABA	SHAH-bah	Copper.	Kenya	M
SIKA	SEE-kah	Gold.	Ghana (Akan)	
TENAGNE	tah-NAHN-yeh	Gold.	Ethiopia	F
YAKUTI	yah-KOO-tee	Ruby, sapphire.	West Africa	F

Joy and Happiness

A smiling face removes unhappiness. —West Africa

Name	Pronunciation	Meaning	Origin	Gender
ABAYOMI	ah-BAH-yoh-mee	Pleasant meeting, born to bring me joy.	Nigeria (Yoruba)	M
ABEO	ah-beh-OH	Her birth brings happiness.	Nigeria (Yoruba)	F
ABIDEMI	ah-bee-DEH-mee	Born during her father's happiness.	Nigeria (Yoruba)	F
ADEBAYO	ah-deh-BAH-yoh	He came at a joyful time.	Nigeria (Yoruba)	
ADEDAGBO	ah-DEH-dah-boh	Happiness is a crown.	Nigeria (Yoruba)	F
AMADI	ah-MAH-dee	Rejoicing.	Nigeria (Igbo)	F
ANULI	ah-NOO-lee	Daughter who brings happiness.	West Africa	F
AWALI	ah-WAH-lee	Joyful.	Nigeria (Igbo)	
AYO	AH-yoh	Happiness, joyful.	Nigeria	F
AYOBAMI	ah-yoh-BAH-mee	I am blessed with joy.	Nigeria (Yoruba)	F
AYODEJI	ah-yoh-DEH-jee	Joy becomes two.	Nigeria (Yoruba)	
AYODELE	ah-yoh-DEH-leh	Joy enters the house.	Nigeria (Yoruba)	F
AYOFEMI	ah-yoh-FEH-mee	Joy likes me.	Nigeria (Yoruba)	F

Name	Pronunciation	Meaning	Origin	Gender
AYOLUWA	ah-yoh-LOO-wah	Joy of our people.	Nigeria (Yoruba)	F
AYORINDE	ah-yoh-REEN-deh	Joy walks in.	Nigeria (Yoruba)	
BALEWA	bah-leh-wah	Happiness.	Nigeria	M
BAYO	BAH-yoh	Rejoice with me; great joy is found.	Nigeria	F
BISIMWA	bee-see-mwah	Things that are enjoyed.	Congo (Bashi)	M
BITI SURURU	BEE-tee-soo-roo-roo	Daughter of happiness.	East Africa (Kiswahili)	F
CHEKO	CHEH-koh	Good mood, happiness.	Kenya, Tanzania	
DAKARAI	dah-KAH-rah-ee	Child brings joy, happiness.	Zimbabwe (Shona)	M
DAMISI	dah-MEE-see	Sociable, cheerful.	Kenya, Tanzania	
DAYO	DAH-yoh	Joy arrives.	Nigeria (Yoruba)	F
DESTA	DEHS-tah	Happiness.	Ethiopia	
DUROTAYO	doo-roh-TAH-yoh	Stay for joy.	Nigeria (Yoruba)	
DURRA	DOOR-rah	Large pearl.	Kiswahili	F
EBE	EH-beh	Wonderful feeling.	Egypt/Khamit	F
EKUNDAYO	eh-KOON-dah-yoh	Sorrow becomes happiness.	Nigeria (Yoruba)	M
ELAGO	eh-LAH-goh	Happiness.	Namibia (Ovambo)	
ENAMA	eh-NAH-mah	Be content.	Azania (Zulu)	
ENANELA	eh-nah-NEH-lah	Rejoice.	Azania (Zulu)	
ENEME	eh-NEH-meh	Cheerful.	Azania	
ESASA	eh-SAH-sah	Be happy.	Azania (Zulu)	
ETHABA	eh-TAH-bah	Be happy.	Azania (Zulu)	
FABAYO	fah-BAH-yoh	A lucky birth is joy.	Nigeria (Yoruba)	F
FAREEHA	fah-REE-hah	Joyful, happy.	North Africa (Arabic)	
FUMILAYO	foo-mee-LAH-yoh	Give me joy.	Nigeria	
FURAHA	foo-RAH-hah	Joy, gladness, pleasure.	Kiswahili	

Name	Pronunciation	Meaning	Origin	Gender
FURAHISHA	foo-rah-HEE-shah	To delight.	Kiswahili	
GATETE	gah-TEH-teh	Let him enjoy himself.	Rwanda, Burundi (Kinyarwanda, Kirundi)	M
HANA	HAH-nah	Joy.	North Africa (Arabic)	F
HANAA	HAH-nah-ah	Happiness.	East Africa (Kiswahili)	F
HANI	HAH-nee	Joyful, happy.	North Africa (Arabic)	
HANUNI	hah-NOO-nee	Cheerful.	Kiswahili	F
IKETLA	ee-KEHT-lah	Happy, carefree.	Lesotho (South Sotho)	
INJABULO	ehn-jah-boo-loh	Happiness, joy.	Azania (Zulu)	
INSIMI	een-SEE-mee	Cheerfulness, merriment.	Azania	
JABU	jah-boo	Happiness; rejoice (nickname for Jabulisiwe).	Azania (Zulu)	
JABULANI	jah-boo-lah-nee	Be happy! Rejoice!	Azania	M
JABULIE	jah-boo-LEE-eh	She is happy.	Azania (Zulu)	F
JABULILE	jah-boo-LEE-leh	Be happy!	Azania	F
JABULISIWE	jah-boo-lee-see-weh	Happiness.	Azania (Zulu)	F
JAFAR	JAH-far	Happiness.	North Africa (Arabic)	
JAMEELA	jah-MEE-lah	Came to bring happiness for everybody.	North Africa (Arabic)	
JOLA	JOH-lah	One who brings happiness.	Azania	M
JUSULAA	joo-soo-laah	Happy, joyous, glad.	Gambia (Mandinka)	
KAYODE	KAH-yoh-deh	He brought joy.	Nigeria (Yoruba)	M
KONDWANI	kohn-DWAH-nee	Joyful.	Malawi (Ngoni)	M
KUNJUFU	KOON-jooh-foo	Cheerful, friendly.	Kenya, Tanzania (Kiswahili)	M
KYESI	kyeh-see	Joy.	Kenya, Tanzania	
LIMBER	LEEM-behr	Joyfulness.	Nigeria (Tiv)	F
MASARA	MAH-sah-rah	Joy.	East Africa (Kiswahili)	F

Name	Pronunciation	Meaning	Origin	Gender
MHINA	m-HEE-nah	Delightful, agreeable.	East Africa (Kiswahili)	M
MILINA	mee-LEE-nah	Delightful.	East Africa (Kiswahili)	M
MTEREMO	mteh-reh-moh	Cheerful person.	Kenya, Tanzania	
MUFARI	moo-FAH-ree	Cheerfulness.	Zimbabwe	
NAJUMA	nah-joo-mah	Abundantly joyful.	East Africa	
NANDIGOLO	nahn-dee-GOH-loh	Shout of joy.	Namibia (Ovambo)	
NAYO	NAH-yoh	We have joy.	Nigeria (Yoruba)	F
NDINELAGO	n-dee-neh-LAH-goh	I am happy, lucky.	Namibia (Ovambo)	
NELAGO	neh-LAH-goh	Happiness.	Namibia (Ovambo)	
NGOLI	n-GOH-lee	Happiness.	Nigeria (Igbo)	M
NJABULO	njah-boo-loh	Happiness.	Azania (Zulu)	M
NTEREMEZI	n-teh-reh-meh-zee	Friendly, cheerful person.	Kenya, Tanzania (Kiswahili)	F
NZIGIRE	n-zee-gee-reh	I am delighted.	DRC (Bashi)	F
OLABISHI	oh-lah-BEE-shee	Joy is multiplied.	Nigeria	
OLABISI	oh-lah-BEE-see	Joy is multiplied.	Nigeria	
OLEE	oh-lee	Happy moment.	Nigeria	
OLUBAYO	oo-loo-BAH-yoh	Great joy.	Nigeria	
OSEYE	oh-seh-yeh	The happy one.	Benin	F
RAHWA	rah-WAH	Coming out of misery.	Eritrea, Ethiopia (Tigrinya)	F
SAEED	sah-EED	Happy, fortunate.	North Africa (Arabic)	M
SAHASSAAA	sah-has-sah-ah-ah	Submitting to the sage; I have joy.	Egypt/Khamit	M
SANYU	SAHG-yoo	Happiness.	Uganda (Luganda)	M
SARAN	sah-rahn	Joy.	West Africa	F
SEKANI	seh-KAHN-nee	Merriment, joy.	West Africa	
SEKELAGA	seh-keh-LAH-gah	Rejoice; be happy.	Tanzania (Nyakyusa)	F
SENEME	seh-NEH-meh	We are happy.	Azania (Zulu)	

Name	Pronunciation	Meaning	Origin	Gender
SHANGILIA	shahn-gee-LEE-ah	Happy occasion; to shout with joy.	Kenya, Tanzania (Kiswahili)	
SHASHU	SHAH-shoo	Great joy; sweetest joy.	Ethiopia	
SISIMKA	see-SEEM-kah	To tingle with excitement.	Kiswahili	
SODA	SOH-dah	Happiness.	North Africa	F
TAFARA	tah-fah-rah	We are overjoyed.	Zimbabwe, Mozambique, Zambia (Shona)	F
TAKALANI	tah-kah-LAH-nee	Happiness, happy.	Azania (Venda)	
THABANE	tah-BAH-neh	Be joyful.	Azania	M
THABANG	tah-bah-ndgh	Came to bring happiness to everyone, be glad.	Azania (North Sotho)	M
THABO	tah-boh	Joy.	Azania (Sotho)	M
THOKO	TOH-koh	Be happy (for this child's birth).	Azania (Zulu)	F
THOKOZA	toh-koh-zah	Happiness.	Azania (Zulu)	F
THOKOZILE	toh-koh-zee-leh	Happiness.	Azania	
TIME	TEE-meh	Full of happiness.	East Africa (Kiswahili)	F
TITILAYO	tee-tee-lah-YOH	Happiness is eternal.	Nigeria (Yoruba)	F
TSAGE	tsah-geh	Happiness.	Ethopia	F
TSOYO	tchoh-yoh	I'll see this one as my joy.	Nigeria (Shekiri)	F
UJE	oo-jeh	Happiness.	Nigeria (Igarra)	
UZONU	oo-ZOH-noo	Full path of joy.	Nigeria (Igbo)	
VUYA	VOO-yah	Delighted, rejoicing.	Azania (Xhosa)	
VUYANI	voo-YAH-nee	Be happy!	Azania	M
VUYELWA	voo-YEHL-wah	Child that beings great joy.	Azania (Xhosa)	
WEPESI	weh-PEH-see	Happiness.	Kenya, Tanzania	
YENYO	yehn-yoh	Mother is rejoicing.	Nigeria (Yoruba)	
YESIIME	yeh-see-mee	Rejoice; be happy.	Uganda	

Name	Pronunciation	Meaning	Origin	Gender
YOLA	YOH-lah	Delightful, agreeable.	Azania (Xhosa)	
YOLISWA	yoh-lee-swah	She will have a lot of people who will make her happy.	Azania (Xhosa)	F
YUYISWA	yoo-YEES-wah	Child that makes us happy.	Azania (Zulu)	

Justice

You don't expect to win a case
in someone else's village. —*Zambia*

Name	Pronunciation	Meaning	Origin	Gender
ADIL	AH-deel	Just.	North Africa (Arabic)	
AJEBILO	ah-jeh-BEE-loh	Don't judge me in the morning, wait till evening.	Nigeria (Ishan)	
FANELE	fah-NEH-leh	He is justified.	Azania (Xhosa)	M
HAKI	HAH-kee	Justice; right.	Kenya, Tanzania (Kiswahili)	
JAJI	JAH-jee	Judge.	Azania (Xhosa)	
KGOTSO	KGOHT-soh	Justice, peace.	Azania (Sotho)	
MAAT	MAH-aht	Balance.	Egypt/Khamit	
MINKAH	MEEN-kah	Justice.	Ghana (Akan)	M
SHERIA	sheh-REE-ah	Law, justice.	Sudan	M
UKULUNGA	oo-koo-LOON-gah	Justice.	Azania (Zulu)	

Kindness and Niceness

Kindness can pluck the hairs of a lion's mustache. —*Sudan*

Name	Pronunciation	Meaning	Origin	Gender
ADABU	ah-DAH-boo	The polite one.	Kenya, Tanzania	

Name	Pronunciation	Meaning	Origin	Gender
ATAFAR	ah-TAH-fahr	Understanding; kindness.	North Africa (Arabic)	
ATIFAR	ah-TEE-fahr	Understanding, kindness.	North Africa (Arabic)	
BIKO	BEE-koh	Please.	Nigeria (Igbo)	M
BUBELE	boo-BEH-leh	He is the personification of kindness.	Azania (Xhosa)	M
DOMENYO	doh-MEHN-yoh	Kindness is good.	Ghana	
EBERE	eh-BEH-reh	Charity, kindness; mercy.	Nigeria (Igbo)	
FADHILI	fahd-HEE-lee	Kindness, goodwill.	Kenya, Tanzania	
HISANI	hee-SAH-nee	Kind, good-natured.	Kenya, Tanzania	
JAMALA	jah-MAH-lah	Courtesy.	Kiswahili	
KISA	tch-ee-sah	Kindness; mercy.	Uganda (Ganda)	
MJIBU	mm-jee-boo	A nice, pleasant person.	East Africa (Kiswahili)	M
NIFE	NEE-feh	Cordial.	West Africa (Yoruba)	
NOMSA	NOHM-sah	Mother of kindness.	Azania (Xhosa)	F
ONJALI	ohn-JAH-lee	Anyone who is kind and helpful.	Angola (Ovimbundu)	
SARAMA	sah-rah-MAH	Nice, beautiful girl.	West Africa (Bambara)	F
SELEMA	seh-LEH-mah	Be nice and fair to all.	Nigeria	
SISA	SEE-sah	Benevolent; fondness.	Azania	M
TOKO	TOH-koh	Kind, good.	Azania (North Sotho)	
YAMRO	YAHM-broh	Courteous.	Central Africa	M

Leadership

Without leadership, a community disintegrates. —Uganda

Name	Pronunciation	Meaning	Origin	Gender
ABU	AH-boo	Leader.	Sierra Leone	

Name	Pronunciation	Meaning	Origin	Gender
AKIDA	ah-KEE-dah	Leader; officer, captain.	Kenya, Tanzania	
ANDAMA	ahn-DAH-mah	To follow.	Kiswahili	
BALE	bah-lay	Chief.	Nigeria (Yoruba)	M
BONISILE	boh-nee-SEE-leh	The one who led us to see.	Azania	F
CHIEDU	chee-EH-doo	God is the leader.	Nigeria	
CHINEDU	chee-NEH-doo	God leads, God guides.	Nigeria	
DIOP	dee-ohp	Ruler.	Central Africa	M
DONDO	DOHN-doh	The chief man of a place.	Azania (Xhosa)	M
ENDESHA	ehn-DEE-shah	To go on, to guide.	Kiswahili	
ENGAMELI	ehn-gah-meh-lee	President.	Azania (Zulu)	
GASADLA	gah-SAHD-lah	Chieftaincy fits him.	Cameroon (Mubako)	M
GEDE	GEH-deh	Honey guide.	Azania (Zulu)	
GETEYE	geh-TEE-yeh	My master.	Ethiopia (Amharic)	M
HUDA	HOO-dah	Guidance.	Kiswahili	F
INKOSI	n-KOH-see	King, chief, lord.	Azania	M
JAMAADAR	jah-mah-DAHR	Army general.	Kiswahili	M
JUMBE	JOOM-beh	Chief, VIP.	Kenya, Tanzania	
KAGENZA	kah-GEHN-zah	The leader.	Rwanda, Burundi (Kinyarwanda, Kirundi)	M
KAKANFO	kah-kahn-foh	Field marshal.	Nigeria (Yoruba)	M
KARANJA	kah-rahn-jah	Guide.	East Africa	M
KATWE	kaht-weh	Small leader.	Uganda (Ganda)	M
KAZEMDE	kah-ZEHM-deh	Ambassador.	Malawi (Yao)	M
KHALFANI	kahl-FAH-nee	Destined to rule.	Kiswahili	M
KHOKELA	koh-keh-lah	Lead, guide.	Azania (Xhosa)	M
KIONGOZI	KEE-ohn-goh-zee	Leader.	Kenya, Tanzania (Kiswahili)	M

Name	Pronunciation	Meaning	Origin	Gender
KIRAZI	kee-rah-zee	One who knows, guide.	Rwanda, Burundi, DRC (Huti, Tutsi, Twa)	M
MAHDI	MAH-dee	The rightfully guided one.	Sudan (Arabic)	
MALAN DELA	mah-lahn-deh-lah	The follower.	Azania (Zulu)	M
MANDARA	MAHN-dah-rah	Leader.	East Africa (Kiswahili)	M
MASA	MAH-sah	Chief.	Guinea (Toma)	M
MAZI	MAH-zee	Sir; mister.	Nigeria (Igbo)	M
MBWANA	m-BWAH-nah	Master.	East Africa (Kiswahili)	M
MELISIZWE	meh-lee-seez-weh	Leader of the nation.	Azania	M
MILIKI	mee-LEE-kee	To rule over.	Kiswahili	
MUTWARE	moo-TWAH-reh	Chief.	Rwanda, Burundi (Kinyarwanda, Kirundi)	
MWAMI	mwaah-mee	Chief, master, husband.	Uganda (Ganda)	M
NKOSI	n-KOH-see	Ruler, king, chief.	Azania (Zulu)	M
NOLIZWE	noh-LEE-zweh	She will be a world leader.	Azania (Xhosa)	F
OBA	OH-bah	Chief; king/nobility.	Nigeria	M
OGAH	OH-gah	A leader; master.	Nigeria (Ishan)	
RAIS	RAH-ees	President, leader.	Kiswahili	M
RAISA	rah-EE-sah	President.	Kiswahili	
RAS	RAHS	Head.	Ethiopia	M
RHOLI HLAHLA	roh-lee-hlah-lah	One who leads.	Azania	M
SANA	SAH-nah	High rank.	North Africa (Arabic)	F
SHAMBE	SHAHM-beh	Leader.	Kiswahili	M
SHASHE	SHAH-sheh	Without a chief.	Botswana	
SIBONISILE	see-boh-nee-SEE-leh	The one who led us to see.	Azania	M

Name	Pronunciation	Meaning	Origin	Gender
SIYASA	see-YAH-sah	Politics.	Kiswahili	
SUWESI	soo-WEH-see	Govern.	Kiswahili	M
UJANENE	oo-jah-NEH-neh	You are difficult to follow or support.	Nigeria (Ishan)	
UKURU GENZI	oo-koo-roo-GEHN-zee	Leader.	Kenya, Tanzania	
YONGAMA	YOHWN-GAH-mah	Rule, govern.	Azania (Xhosa)	M

Life

Something good is in a long life. —Ghana

Name	Pronunciation	Meaning	Origin	Gender
ACHUWA NIKE	ah-choo-wah-NEE-keh	Life requires one step at a time.	Nigeria (Igbo)	F
ADERO	ah-DEH-roh	Life giver; she who creates life.	Central Africa	F
AISH	AH-eesh	Alive.	North Africa (Arabic)	M
AISHA	ah-EE-shah	Life.	East Africa (Kiswahili)	F
AKHILE	ahk-HEE-lee	It is a long life.	Nigeria (Ishan)	
AMAR	ah-MAH	Long life.	East Africa (Kiswahili)	M
ANIWETA	ah-nee-WEH-tah	Brought by a spirit.	Nigeria	M
ASHA	AH-shah	Life.	East Africa (Kiswahili)	F
AZEMATA	ah-zeh-mah-tah	Life is eternal.	Nigeria (Igarra)	M
BUGINGO	boo-jeen-goh	Life; attributed to God.	Burundi, Rwanda	F
BUJINGO	boo-jeen-goh	Life; attributed to God.	Burundi, Rwanda	M
CHIKWENDU	chee-KWEHN-doo	Life is in God's hands.	Nigeria (Igbo)	
DIMMA	dee-mah	Has come back to life.	Cameroon (Mubako)	M

Name	Pronunciation	Meaning	Origin	Gender
EJINDU	eh-JEEN-doo	Alive.	Nigeria (Igbo)	
EKEBUISI	eh-keh-boo-EE-see	Life is supreme.	Nigeria (Igbo)	
ESHE	EH-sheh	Life, animated, spirited.	East, West Africa	
FUFUKA	foo-FOO-kah	To come to life.	Kiswahili	
GABVASE	gahb-VAH-seh	Does not know death.	Cameroon (Mubako)	M
GILA	GEE-lah	Let this live.	Sierra Leone	
GILO	GEE-loh	Let this live.	Sierra Leone	
HAI	HAH-ee	Alive.	Kiswahili	
IYANDU	ee-YAHN-doo	We are only spending some time before we go to sleep in this world.	Nigeria (Ishan)	
IZUNDU	ee-ZOON-doo	The thought of life; plan for life.	Nigeria (Igbo)	
JANAAN	JAH-nahn	Essence, incarnation.	North Africa (Arabic)	
KABURAME	kah-boo-RAH-meh	May they live longer.	Rwanda, Burundi (Kinyarwanda, Kirundi)	M
KASULE	kah-soo-leh	That spent the night; that remained; that lived; that dwelled.	Uganda (Ganda)	M
KIJAKAZI	kee-jah-KAH-zee	Your life is due to us.	East Africa (Kiswahili)	F
KITWANA	kee-TWAH-nah	Pledged to live.	Kiswahili	F
KOKUMO	KOH-koo-moh	This one will not die.	Nigeria (Yoruba)	F
KUMUZI	koo-MOO-zee	Death has kicked my seat away.	Ghana	
LEHVALLA	leh-VAHL-lah	Death takes people, yet more are born.	Cameroon (Mubako)	F
LITHA	LEE-tah	One who gives meaning to life.	Azania	M
LOLITHA	loh-LEE-tah	One who gives meaning to life.	Azania	F

Name	Pronunciation	Meaning	Origin	Gender
MAISHA	mah-EE-shah	Life.	Kenya, Tanzania	
MAWIYAH	MAH-wee-yah	The essence of life.	North Africa (Arabic)	F
MDAHOMA	mm-DAH-hoh-mah	Long life.	East Africa (Kiswahili)	M
MIWIYAH	mee-WEE-yah	The essence of life.	North Africa (Arabic)	
MOYO	MOH-yoh	Life, well-being, good health.	Malawi	M
MUPASHI	moo-PAH-shee	The soul.	Zambia (Bemba)	
MVITA	mvee-tah	Full of life.	Kiswahili	F
NDUBIA	N-doo-BEE-ah	Let life come.	Nigeria (Igbo)	M
NDUBISI	n-doo-BEE-see	Life is precious; paramount.	Nigeria (Igbo)	
NDUKA	n-DOO-kah	Life is valuable.	Nigeria	
NJU	n-JOO	Life.	Nigeria (Eleme)	
NOLITHA	noh-LEE-tah	One who gives meaning to life.	Azania	F
OKRA	OHK-rah	Soul.	Ghana	M
OKWUNDU	oh-KWOON-doo	Word for life.	Nigeria (Igbo)	
RAYUMA	rah-YOO-mah	Existence, life.	West Africa (Hausa)	
ROHO	ROH-hoh	Spirit; soul.	Kiswahili	M
UJELU	oo-JEH-loo	They have been able to bring you to life.	Nigeria (Ishan)	
UKANDU	oo-KAHN-doo	The question of life.	Nigeria (Igbo)	
UMI	OO-mee	Life.	Malawi (Yao)	M
UTNI	OOT-nee	Life.	Malawi (Yao)	M
UWEME	oo-WEH-meh	Life.	Nigeria (Efik)	
UZONDU	oo-ZOHN-doo	Path for life.	Nigeria (Igbo)	
YAHYA	YAH-yah	Grant someone a long life.	North Africa (Arabic)	M
ZWA	ZWAH	Live.	Azania (Zulu)	
ZWAASHA	swah-AH-shah	Live life.	New Afrika	

Light and Illumination

The person that we know in the daytime, we don't light a lamp to see his face in the night. —Ghana

Name	Pronunciation	Meaning	Origin	Gender
ABRIHET	ahb-roo-HOOT	She emanates light.	Ethiopia	F
AMOWIA	ah-moh-WEE-ah	Giver of light or sun.	Ghana (Akan)	
ANGAA	AHN-gah-ah	Shine; be bright.	Kiswahili	
ASRA	AHS-rah	Brilliant.	East Africa	
AVAN	AH-vahn	Brilliant.	East Africa	
AYAH	ah-YAH	Sparkling, twinkling.	West Africa	
BAINA	bah-EE-nah	Sparkling; bright, glittering	West Africa (Bobangi)	F
BANE	BAH-neh	Candle, light.	Azania (Xhosa)	
BEKEBEKE	beh-keh-BEH-keh	Glittering, shining.	Azania (Nguni)	
BENYA	BEHN-yah	To be bright, to shine.	Azania (Sotho)	
BERHANE	buhr-HAH-nay	My light.	Ethiopia	F
BEYAKANYA	beh-yah-KAHN-yah	People who shine.	Kiswahili	
CHIEDZA	tch-ehd-zah	Dawning; light.	Zimbabwe, Mozambique, Zambia (Shona)	M
CHIONESU	chee-oh-NEH-soo	Guiding light.	Zimbabwe (Shona)	M
DEMEKE	deh-MEH-keh	Getting brighter.	Ethiopia	M
DIYA	DEE-yah	Light.	North Africa (Arabic)	F
KENTA	kehn-tah	Glowing.	Gambia (Mandinka)	
KHANYA	KAHN-yah	Shine.	Azania (Xhosa)	M
KHANYISA	KAHN-YEE-sah	Bring forth light.	Azania (Xhosa)	M
KHANYISILE	kahn-yee-see-leh	Bright.	Azania (Zulu)	
KHANYISWA	kahn-YEE-swah	The illuminated one, she reflects the light.	Azania (Xhosa)	F

Name	Pronunciation	Meaning	Origin	Gender
KIMETA META	kee-meh-tah-MEH-tah	A sparkling light.	Kiswahili	
KUMETA	koo-MEH-tah	To shine, glow.	Kiswahili	
LESEDI	leh-seh-dee	Light.	Azania (Sotho)	M
LITHA	LEE-tah	A bright beam of light.	Azania (Xhosa)	M
MULIKA	moo-LEE-kah	To give light to.	Kiswahili	
MUNIRA	moo-NEE-rah	Radiant.	Kiswahili	
NOLITHA	noh-LEE-tah	Mother of light and warmth.	Azania (Xhosa)	F
NURA	NOO-rah	Brightness.	East Africa (Kiswahili)	F
NURISHA	NOO-ree-shah	Shine light upon.	East Africa (Kiswahili)	F
NURU	NOO-roo	Born in daylight.	East Africa (Kiswahili)	
TULIM BWELU	too-leem-BWEH-loo	We are in the light.	East Africa (Nyakyusa)	M
UNIKA	oo-NEE-kah	Light up.	Malawi (Lomwe)	M
VANGAMA	vahn-GAH-mah	Dazzling, brilliant.	Southern Africa (Tsonga)	
VUTHA	VOO-tah	Blazing, ardent, glowing.	Azania (Xhosa)	
ZAHIRA	zah-HEE-rah	Glittering.	North Africa (Arabic)	

Love, Intimacy, and Affection

Love has to be shown by deeds not words. —Kiswahili

Name	Pronunciation	Meaning	Origin	Gender
ABEKE	ah-BEH-keh	We begged for her to pet her.	Nigeria (Yoruba)	F
ABOKI	ah-boh-kee	A pet name.	Uganda (Nyoro)	
ADA	AH-dah	Lovable daughter.	Nigeria (Igbo)	F

Name	Pronunciation	Meaning	Origin	Gender
AFIIFE	ah-fee-EE-feh	Spiritual love.	New Afrika	
AGALA	ah-gahl-lah	Love.	Uganda (Ganda)	
AHUROLE	ah-hoo-ROH-leh	Loving.	West Africa	
AIJEBA	ah-ee-JEH-bah	Love strengthens relationship.	Nigeria (Ishan)	
AKANKE	ah-kahn-KEH	To meet her is to love her.	Nigeria (Yoruba)	F
AKARALE	ah-kah-RAH-leh	To meet her is to love her.	West Africa	F
AMBATA	ahm-BAH-tah	Embrace.	Kiswahili	
ANGA	AHN-gah	Kiss.	Azania (Zulu)	
ASHIKI	ah-SHEE-kee	Love, passion.	Kenya, Tanzania	
BELEMA	beh-LEH-mah	Love.	Nigeria	
BISA	bee-sah	Greatly loved.	West Africa	F
BUSU	BOO-soo	Kiss.	Kiswahili	
CORO	KOH-roh	Boyfriend; lover.	Gambia (Wolof)	M
DANAI	dah-nah-ee	Love one another.	Rwanda, Burundi, DRC (Huti, Tutsi, Twa)	
DEJENABA	deh-jeh-nah-bah	One who is affectionate.	West Africa	F
DISI	DEE-see	Dear.	Rwanda, Burundi (Kinyarwanda, Kirundi)	M
DJENABA	dhh-jah-NAH-bah	Affectionate.	West Africa	M
DUMISHA	doo-mee-SHAH	Intimate friendship.	East Africa (Kiswahili)	M
EKAEKA	eh-kah-EH-kah	To love very much.	Southern Africa (Tsonga)	
ETAN	EH-tahn	God's love never ceases.	Nigeria (Shekiri)	F
EWOLA	eh-WOH-lah	Love.	Nigeria (Eleme)	
FELA	Feh-lah	Love is saved.	Nigeria (Yoruba)	F
FEMI	FEH-mee	Love me; child to be well loved.	Nigeria (Yoruba)	F

Name	Pronunciation	Meaning	Origin	Gender
FIKRE	FEEK-reh	Love.	Ethiopia	M
FREYA	FREE-yah	Goddess of love.	East Africa (Kiswahili)	F
GABSA	gahb-sah	No lovers.	Cameroon (Mubako)	M
GABSAGA	gahb-sahg-ah	He does not know the lovers.	Cameroon (Mubako)	F
GONZA	gohn-zah	Love.	Uganda (Rutooro)	F
HUBA	HOO-bah	Love, friendship.	East Africa (Kiswahili)	F
IFE	ee-FEH	Love me.	Nigeria (Yoruba)	F
IFEOLU	ee-feh-OH-loo	The love of God.	Nigeria (Yoruba)	
IFETAYO	ee-feh-tah-yoh	Love brings happiness.	West Africa	F
IJNANYA	eej-nahn-yah	Love.	West Africa	F
ISISA	ee-SEE-sah	Love; hospitality.	Azania	
JENEBI	JEH-neh-bee	Affectionate.	East Africa (Kiswahili)	M
JII	jee	To ejaculate.	Gambia (Mandinka)	
JUMOKE	joo-MOH-keh	Everyone loves this child, loved by all.	Nigeria (Yoruba)	
KAI	KAH-ee	Loveable.	West Africa	
KAUNATA	kah-oo-NAH-tah	Love.	West Africa (Hausa)	
KAWERIA	kah-WEH-ree-ah	Loving one; child who gives love.	East Africa (Meru)	F
KENDI	KEHN-dee	The loved one.	Kenya (Meru)	F
KIPENDO	kee-PEHN-doh	Love, affection, devotion.	Kenya, Tanzania	
KONDANA	kohn-DAH-nah	Love.	Zambia	
KUGONZA	koo-GOHN-zah	Love.	Uganda (Rutooro)	F
KUPENDA	koo-PEHN-dah	Love.	Kenya, Tanzania	
KWAGALA	kwah-gah-lah	Liking; loving.	Uganda (Ganda)	F
LERATO	leh-rah-toh	Love.	Azania (Sotho)	M

Name	Pronunciation	Meaning	Origin	Gender
LOLOLI	loh-LOH-lee	There is always love.	Ghana (Ewe)	F
LOLONYO	loh-LOHN-yoh	Love is beautiful.	West Africa	
LOLOVIVI	loh-loh-VEE-vee	There is always love.	West Africa	
MALERATO	mah-leh-RAH-toh	Love.	Botswana (Tswana)	
MAPENDO	mah-PEHN-doh	Love.	East Africa	F
MAPENZI	mah-PEHN-zee	Love, pleasure.	Kiswahili	
MCHUMBA	m-choom-bah	Sweetheart.	East Africa (Kiswahili)	F
MORATUWA	moo-rah-TOO-wah	The most loved one.	Azania (Sotho)	
MPENDA	m-PEHN-dah	Lover.	Kenya (Mwera)	M
MPENZI	m-PEHN-zee	Lover, sweetheart.	Kenya, Tanzania	
MUGANZI	moo-gahn-zee	Darling, favorite, lover, sweetheart.	Uganda (Ganda)	
NAKUBUYA	nah-koo-BOO-yah	Much-loved child.	Azania (Xhosa)	
NANKUNDA	nahn-koon-dah	Someone loves me.	Uganda (Runyankore)	F
NATUKUNDO	nah-too-koon-dah	God loves us.	Uganda (Runyankore)	M
NIMU KUNDA	nee-moo-koon-dah	I love him.	Uganda (Kiga, Nyankore)	F
NOLU THANDO	noh-loo-TAHN-doh	Giver of love.	Azania (Xhosa)	F
NONTANDO	nohn-TAHN-doh	Full of love.	Azania (Nguni)	
PENDA	PEHN-dah	Lover, sweetheart.	Kenya, Tanzania (Kiswahili)	
RAMI	RAH-mee	Love.	Sudan	M
RUDO	ROO-doh	Love.	Zimbabwe (Shona)	M
RUKUNDO	roo-KOON-doh	Love.	Burundi	
RUNGUMA	roon-goo-mah	Embrace.	West Africa (Hausa)	
SALLA	sahl-lah	Sex-friend.	Cameroon (Mubako)	
SUMBATA	soom-BAH-tah	Kiss.	West Africa (Hausa)	

Name	Pronunciation	Meaning	Origin	Gender
TEMMA	teh-mah	My loved one, my heart, lovable.	Cameroon (Mubako)	F
TENE	TEH-neh	Love.	West Africa	F
THANDA	tahn-dah	Love.	Azania	
THANDI	TAHN-dee	Lovable	Azania (Nguni)	
THANDILE	tahn-dee-leh	The one we have loved; the selected one.	Azania (Xhosa)	F
THAN DISWA	tahn-DEES-wah	She who had to be loved.	Azania (Zulu)	F
THANDO	tahn-doh	Love.	Azania (Xhosa)	F
TISHAIFE	tee-shah-EE-feh	Strong-willed love.	New Afrika	
UASHERATI	oo-ah-sheh-RAH-tee	Fornication.	Kiswahili	
UPENZI	oo-PEHN-zee	Lovingness.	Kiswahili	
URUKUNDO	oo-roo-KOON-doh	Love.	Rwanda, Burundi (Kinyarwanda, Kirundi)	
ZONDA	ZOHN-dah	One who is loved greatly.	Azania (Xhosa)	
ZWAIFE	swah-EE-feh	Live love.	New Afrika	

Loyalty and Commitment

Leopard does not eat leopard. —Ghana

Name	Pronunciation	Meaning	Origin	Gender
AHADI	ah-HAD-dee	Promise, vow.	Kenya, Tanzania (Kiswahili)	
AHIDI	ah-HEE-dee	Promise, vow.	Kenya, Tanzania	
AMANA	ah-MAH-nah	Promise, vow.	Kenya, Tanzania	
AMEEN	AH-meen	Loyal, true.	North Africa (Arabic)	
ARNINIKA	ahr-nee-NEE-kah	Faithful, loyal.	Kenya, Tanzania	

Name	Pronunciation	Meaning	Origin	Gender
BAKARI	bah-KAH-ree	Of noble promise.	East Africa (Kiswahili)	M
BAMBISA	bahm-BEE-sah	Pledge, vow.	Zimbabwe	
BIYAYYA	bee-yah-jyah	Loyalty.	West Africa (Hausa)	
BWTEME	bweh-teh-meh	Commitments; promises.	Uganda (Ganda)	M
DINGA	DING-gah	Promise, destiny.	Azania (Xhosa)	M
DORUTIMI	doh-roo-TEE-mee	Stand by me.	Nigeria	
FIDEL	fee-DEHL	Faithful.	Kenya, Tanzania (Kiswahili)	M
FIDELA	FEE-deh-lah	Faithful.	East Africa (Kiswahili)	F
GONI	GOH-nee	A promise.	Azania (Xhosa)	
IDINGA	ee-DEHN-gah	Promise; vow.	Azania	
JANGHA	jahn-gah	Promise.	Cameroon (Mubako)	M
JIKINDI	jee-KEEN-dee	Promise.	Gambia (Mandinka)	
JURODOE	joo-roh-doh-eh	Faithful.	West Africa (Bassa)	M
KHOLIWE	koh-LEE-weh	The devout one.	Azania	F
KHOLWANI	khol-WAH-nee	The devout one.	Azania	M
KIAGA	kee-AH-gah	Promise.	Kenya, Tanzania	
KIDANE	kee-DAH-neh	My covenant; my vow.	Ethiopia, Eritrea	M
MADINGA	MAH-deen-gah	Promises.	Azania (Xhosa)	M
MTUMWA	m-TOOM-wah	Pledged.	East Africa (Kiswahili)	M
NADHIRI	nahd-HEE-ree	Promise, vow.	Kenya, Tanzania	
NATA	NAH-tah	To be faithful.	Kiswahili	F
NDAHIRA	n-dah-HEE-rah	Oath.	Rwanda (Runyarwanda)	M
OMAJE	oh-MAH-jeh	A true, faithful son.	Nigeria (Ishan)	M
REHANI	reh-HAH-nee	Promise, vow.	Kenya, Tanzania (Kiswahili)	F
SADIKI	sah-DEE-kee	Faithful.	East Africa (Kiswahili)	M
SITHEM BISO	see-tehm-bee-soh	Promise.	Azania (Zulu)	

Name	Pronunciation	Meaning	Origin	Gender
THENJISWA	tehn-JEE-swah	She bears a promise.	Azania (Xhosa)	F
TIIFU	tee-ee-FOO	Loyal, faithful.	East Africa (Kiswahili)	M
UBAID	oo-BAH-eed	Faithful.	North Africa (Arabic)	
WAKUFU	wah-KOO-foo	Dedicated, sacred.	Kiswahili	
YELUMA	yeh-LOO-mah	To make a blood pact.	Cameroon (Mubako)	F

Luck and Fortune

The pot and the lid do not break on one day. —DRC

Name	Pronunciation	Meaning	Origin	Gender
AJARUVA	ah-jah-roo-vah	Unfortunate.	Uganda (Alur)	F
AYAN	AH-yahn	Lucky girl.	Somalia	F
BAHATI	bah-HAH-tee	Luck, fortune.	Kiswahili	
BAKHITAH	bah-KEE-tah	Fortunate.	North Africa	F
BAMPIRE	bahm-PEE-reh	May I be fortunate with them.	Rwanda, Burundi (Kinyarwanda, Kirundi)	F
CHEBE	CHEH-beh	Chance, luck, fortune.	Azania (Xhosa)	
CHIBANDA	chee-BAHN-dah	Good luck charm.	Zambia (Bemba)	
DYESE	dJEH-seh	This is my fortune.	Central Africa	F
FAYOLA	fah-YOH-lah	Good fortune walks with honor; lucky.	Nigeria (Yoruba)	F
ISISILA	ee-see-SEE-lah	Good luck.	Azania	
JUMU	JOO-moo	Fate, luck.	Kenya, Tanzania (Kiswahili)	F
KAMBO	KAHM-boh	Unlucky.	Zimbabwe (Shona)	F
KAMPIRA	kahm-PEE-rah	I am lucky.	Rwanda, Burundi (Kinyarwanda, Kirundi)	F
KAMPIRWA	kaahm-pee-rwah	Endowed, lucky, blessed.	Rwanda, Burundi, DRC (Huti, Tutsi, Twa)	F

Name	Pronunciation	Meaning	Origin	Gender
KOHLA	koh-lah	My own problems, ill luck.	Cameroon (Mubako)	M
LUBWA	loo-bwah	Misfortune.	Uganda (Ganda)	M
MASUD	mah-SOOD	Fortunate.	East Africa (Kiswahili)	M
MIKISA	mee-kee-sah	Strokes of luck, blessings.	Uganda (Ganda, Soga)	
MONIFA	MOH-nee-fah	I have my luck.	Nigeria (Yoruba)	F
MUGISA	moo-gee-sah	Luck.	Uganda (Rutooro)	M
MUGISHA	moo-gee-shah	Luck.	Uganda (Rukiga)	M
MUKISA	moo-KEE-sah	Good luck.	Uganda (Luganda)	M
MWAI	MWAH-ee	Good fortune.	Malawi (Ngoni)	M
NAHSANG	nah-sang	A child born under a lucky star.	Cameroon (Mubako)	F
NHLANHLA	nlah-nlah	Lucky.	Azania (Zulu)	M
SAA	SAH-ah	Luck.	West Africa (Hausa)	
SEKAMANA	seh-kah-MAH-nah	Luck.	Rwanda, Burundi (Kinyarwanda, Kirundi)	
SEKAN-DAGU	sseh-kahn-dah-goo	Fortune teller; seer.	Uganda (Ganda)	M
SEKIKWA	sseh-tch-ee-kwah	Having bad luck.	Uganda (Ganda)	M
SEMAHE	seh-eh-mah-heh	One who has luck.	Rwanda, Burundi, DRC (Huti, Tutsi, Twa)	M
SUDI	SOO-dee	Luck.	East Africa (Kiswahili)	M
TADELESH	tah-deh-LEHSH	Lucky.	Eritrea, Ethiopia (Tigrinya)	F
TSOKA	tsoh-ka	Unlucky.	Malawi (Ngoni)	M
UHERI	oo-HEH-ree	Good fortune.	Kenya, Tanzania	
YUMNA	YOOM-nah	Good luck; happiness.	Kiswahili	F

Magic and Witchcraft

If two fight for food, the one with witchcraft always wins. —DRC

Name	Pronunciation	Meaning	Origin	Gender
BUWAA	BOO-wah	Witch.	Gambia (Mandinka)	M
DANKOO	DAHN-koo	Curse.	Gambia (Mandinka)	
DUPA	DOO-pah	To divine, to procure by magic.	Southern Africa (Tsonga)	
EBO	EH-boh	Magic.	Nigeria (Ishan)	
EMI	EH-mee	Ghost.	West Africa (Yoruba)	
JINI	JEE-nee	A genie.	Kiswahili	F
KAMBUNDU	kahm-BOON-doo	Child who is bewitched because the mother had flow of blood during pregnancy.	Angola (Ovimbundu)	
MLOZI	m-LOH-zee	A sorcerer.	Kiswahili	
MULOGO	MOO-loh-goh	A wizard.	Uganda (Musoga)	M
NOLI	NOH-lee	Ghost.	Ghana	
SIHIRI	see-HEE-ree	Witchcraft.	Kiswahili	
UCHAWI	oo-CHAH-wee	Sorcery.	Kiswahili	
WALOGA	wah-LOH-gah	Bewitched.	Uganda (Lunyole)	M

Marriage and Weddings

Marriage is like a ground nut,
you must crack it to see what is inside. —Ghana

Name	Pronunciation	Meaning	Origin	Gender
ARUSI	ah-ROO-see	Born at the time of a wedding.	East Africa (Kiswahili)	F

Name	Pronunciation	Meaning	Origin	Gender
FUNDZU	FOOND-zoo	Tie a knot.	Southern Africa (Tsonga)	
HANGO	HAHN-goh	Wedding.	Namibia (Ovambo)	
HARUSI	hah-ROO-see	Born at time of a wedding.	East Africa (Kiswahili)	F
KABSAH	KAHB-sah	A woman whose bride price was paid in the court because of a dispute.	Cameroon (Mungaka)	F
KEEMAA	keh-maah	Husband.	Gambia (Mandinka)	M
KEHBUMA	keh-BOO-mah	I have succeeded despite problems in my marriage.	Cameroon (Mubako)	M
KEHTEMA	keh-TEH-mah	A well-beloved partner, she will penetrate her husband's heart.	Cameroon (Mubako)	F
MAHARI	mah-HAH-ree	Marriage payment.	Kiswahili	
MUGENI	moo-geh-nee	Bride.	Rwanda, Burundi (Kinyarwanda, Kirundi)	F
MUSU	MOO-soo	Wife; female.	Gambia	F
NAHANGO	nah-HAHN-goh	Wedding.	Namibia (Ovambo)	
NALIAKA	nah-lee-AH-kah	Wedding.	Kenya	
OA	OH-ah	To marry.	Kiswahili	
OBIDIIYA	oh-bee-dee-yah	The heart of the husband.	Nigeria (Igbo)	F
OCHWA	ohc-tch-waah	Husband.	Uganda (Langi)	M
OMASIRI-DIYA	oh-mah-see-ree dee-yah	Loved by the husband.	Nigeria (Igbo)	F
OZA	OH-zah	To marry.	Kiswahili	F
UMUGORE	oo-moo-GOH-reh	A real wife.	Rwanda, Burundi (Kinyarwanda, Kirundi)	F
VATALELE	vah-tah-LEH-leh	A widow who does not intend to remarry.	Angola (Ovimbundu)	

Men and Manhood

Readiness is manly. —*Ghana*

Name	Pronunciation	Meaning	Origin	Gender
BAFANA	bah-FAH-nah	One of the men.	Azania (Zulu)	M
BARIMA	bah-REE-mah	Macho man.	Ghana (Akan)	M
BUGABO	boo-gah-boh	Manliness; bravery.	Rwanda, Burundi, DRC (Huti, Tutsi, Twa)	M
BUSAJJA	boo-sahj-jah	Manhood; manliness; strength.	Uganda (Ganda)	M
BUSAJ JABWABA	boo-sahj-jah-bwah-bah	Masculinity.	Uganda (Ganda)	M
BUSHAIJA	boo-tch-ah-ee-jah	Manhood; manliness; strength.	Africa	M
BWANA	BWAH-nah	Mister, master, gentleman.	Kiswahili	M
DODA	DOH-dah	Man, male; husband.	Azania (Zulu)	M
KAWAYIYO	kwah-YEE-yoh	He is also a man.	Azania (Xhosa)	M
KIUME	KEE-oo-meh	Masculine and strong.	East Africa (Kiswahili)	M
MADODA	MAH-doh-dah	The embodiment of manhood.	Azania (Xhosa)	M
MADU ABUCHI	mah-doo-ah-boo-chee	Men are not Gods.	Nigeria (Igbo)	M
MNSIZWA	mmehm-zeh-lee	Male, masculine.	West Africa (Hausa)	M
NAMIJI	nah-MEE-jee	Male, masculine.	West Africa (Hausa)	M
NDODA	n-DOH-dah	The man.	Azania (Xhosa)	M
NGIYINDODA	ngee-yeen-doh-dah	I am a man.	Azania (Zulu)	M
OKORO	oh-KOH-roh	Man, matured male.	Nigeria (Igbo)	M
OMU SAMANE	oh-mah-sah-MAH-neh	Married man; head of household.	Namibia (Ovambo)	M

Mercy and Compassion

Those who live together must be merciful. —Kenya

Name	Pronunciation	Meaning	Origin	Gender
AANUOLU	ah-noo-OH-loo	The mercy of God.	Nigeria (Yoruba)	
ABELE	ah-BEH-leh	Mercy.	Nigeria	
AMBAKISYE	am-bah-KEES-yeh	God has been merciful to me.	Tanzania (Ndali)	M
ASIF	ah-SEEF	Mercy.	North Africa (Arabic)	
CHILAKA	chee-LAH-kah	Mercilessness, ruthlessness.	Zambia (Bemba)	
EBELE	eh-BEH-leh	Mercy.	Nigeria (Igbo)	F
HALIMA	hah-LEE-mah	Compassionate, kind, gentle.	Kiswahili	
HURUMA	hoo-RAH-mah	Compassion, mercy.	Kiswahili	
HURUMIA	hoo-roo-MEE-ah	Show mercy to.	Kiswahili	
ISONERE	ee-soh-neh-reh	God be merciful to me.	Rwanda, Burundi, DRC (Huti, Tutsi, Twa)	M
ITOHAN	ee-toh-han	Mercy.	Nigeria (Edo)	F
KUFORIJI	koo-fohr-ee-jee	Death please have mercy.	Nigeria	
LALAMIKA	lah-lah-mee-KAH	Pray for mercy.	East Africa (Kiswahili)	F
MAHARI	mah-HAH-ree	One who gives mercy.	Eritrea, Ethiopia (Tigrinya)	M
MBABAZI	m-bah-bah-zee	Grace; mercy.	Uganda (Rukiga)	M
MOHAU	moh-hahw	Mercy of God.	Azania (Sotho)	M
MUSA	MOO-sah	Mercy; grace.	Kiswahili	
NAHENDA	nah-HEHN-dah	Mercy.	Namibia (Ovambo)	
NIYONU	nee-yoh-noo	Compassionate, tender.	Nigeria (Yoruba)	F
NOFEFE	noh-feh-feh	The compassionate one.	Azania (Xhosa)	F
NOMFE SANE	nohm-FEH-sah-neh	Mother of compassion.	Azania (Xhosa)	F
NONCEBA	non-CHEH-bah	Mercy; grace.	Azania (Xhosa)	

Name	Pronunciation	Meaning	Origin	Gender
OLUWA SHANU	oh-loo-wah-SHAH-noo	God shows mercy.	Nigeria (Yoruba)	
RAHEEM	rah-HEEM	Compassionate.	North Africa (Arabic)	M
RAHIM	rah-HEHM	Compassionate.	North Africa (Arabic)	M
RAHIMA	rah-HEEM-mah	Compassionate.	North Africa (Arabic)	F
RAHIMU	rah-HEE-moo	Mercy.	Kenya, Tanzania	
REHEMA	reh-HEH-mah	Compassion; mercy.	Kenya, Tanzania (Kiswahili)	F
TSITSI	tseet-see	Mercy.	Southern Africa	

Messages, Signs, and Omens

The chicken says she cries to let the public know her condition, not that her enemy will release her. —*Nigeria*

Name	Pronunciation	Meaning	Origin	Gender
AGYEI	ahd-JAY-ee	Messenger from God.	Ghana (Akan)	M
ALAMA	ah-LAH-mah	Sign; token.	Kiswahili	
ASHIRIA	ah-shee-REE-ah	To make a sign.	Kiswahili	
BIKA	BEE-kah	Announcement, omen.	Kiswahili	
DALILI	dah-LEE-lee	Sign, omen.	East Africa (Kiswahili)	F
DARA	DAH-rah	Report, message.	Azania (Xhosa)	
DYOLI	dJOH-lee	Secret messenger.	Azania (Xhosa)	
FEELI	feh-EH-lee	Wander, sign, omen.	Kiswahili	
ISHARA	ee-SHAH-rah	A sign; signal; miracle.	Kiswahili	
JUZA	JOO-zah	Notify, announce.	East Africa (Kiswahili)	F
KABARIRA	kah-bah-REE-rah	The messenger.	Rwanda, Burundi (Kinyarwanda, Kirundi)	M
KABONERO	kah-boh-NEH-roh	Sign.	Uganda (Runyankore)	F
KATUMWA	kah-too-mwah	Messenger; the little one that is sent.	Uganda (Ganda)	M

Name	Pronunciation	Meaning	Origin	Gender
KOKAYI	koh-KAH-yee	For the people to hear; summon the people.	Azania (North Sotho)	
MAZWI	MAHZ-wee	One who pronounces a message.	Azania	M
MMEMEZELI	mmehm-zeh-lee	One who announces with authority.	Azania	M
MORITI	moh-REE-tee	Shadow, messenger.	Azania (North Sotho)	
MOROWA	moh-ROH-wah	Messenger.	Azania (Sotho)	
MWITA	MWEE-tah	The summoner; he who announces; the one who is calling.	East Africa (Kiswahili)	M
MYALEZI	myah-leh-zee	One who sends a message.	Azania	M
NGELOSI	n-geh-loh-see	The messenger.	Azania	M
NOSAYINI	noh-sah-YEE-nee	Sign.	Azania (Xhosa)	
NTOMA	ntoh-mah	Messenger.	Central Africa (Bobangi)	M
NTUMVI	n-TOOM-vee	The message of the world.	Cameroon (Mungaka)	M
SIBONISO	see-boh-nee-soh	Sign.	Rwanda, Burundi, DRC (Huti, Tutsi, Twa)	F
TARISHI	TAH-ree-shee	Messenger.	Kenya, Tanzania (Kiswahili)	M
TEKENE	teh-KEH-neh	Sign.	Azania (Sotho)	
TUMMA	toom-mah	Send me.	Cameroon (Mungaka)	
YALEZELA	yah-leh-ZEH-lah	Sending a message.	Azania	M
YALEZILE	yah-leh-ZEE-leh	One who sends a message.	Azania	F
YALEZISA	yah-leh-ZEE-sah	Emphasize the message.	Azania	M
YALEZISILE	yah-leh-zee-SEE-leh	Emphasize the message.	Azania	F
YALEZWA	yah-LEH-zwah	She came with a mission or message.	Azania (Xhosa)	F

Miracles

At home, saints never perform miracles. —Brazil

Name	Pronunciation	Meaning	Origin	Gender
ARUBE	ah-roo-beh	Maker of miracles.	Uganda (Lugbara)	M
ISIMAN GALISO	ee-see-mahn-gah-LEE-soh	Miracle.	Azania (Zulu)	
KIOJA	KEE-oh-jah	Miracle; a marvel.	Kenya, Tanzania (Kiswahili)	F
MALOZA	mah-LOH-zah	Miracle, unexpected.	Zambia (Tumbuka)	F
MANGALISO	mahn-gah-LEE-soh	The miracle.	Azania	M
MIUJIZA	MEE-oo-jee-zah	Miracles.	East Africa (Kiswahili)	M
NUKUNU	noo-KOON-noo	Child of a miracle.	Ghana	

Money, Wealth, Poverty, and Debt

You can't get rich if you look after your relatives properly. —Navajo

Name	Pronunciation	Meaning	Origin	Gender
ABIMBOLA	ah-BEEM-boh-lah	Born to be rich.	Nigeria (Yoruba)	
ABIOLA	ah-BEE-oh-lah	Born into wealth.	Nigeria	M
ADERINOLA	ah-DEH-reenoh-lah-noh-lah	The crown walked toward wealth.	Nigeria (Yoruba)	F
AKOU	ah-KOH-oo	Wealth.	Nigeria (Yoruba)	M
AKUABIA	ah-koo-ah-bee-ah	Wealth has arrived.	Nigeria (Igbo)	
AKUDO	ah-KOO-doo	Wealth is acquired by peaceful means.	Nigeria (Igbo)	
AKUOMA	ah-koo-OH-mah	Good wealth.	Nigeria (Igbo)	
ALABI	ah-LAH-bee	Born into wealth.	Nigeria	
AYOOLA	ah-YOH-oh-lah	Joy in wealth.	Nigeria (Yoruba)	F

Name	Pronunciation	Meaning	Origin	Gender
BANJWA	bbahn-djwah	In debt; under pressure to pay debt.	Uganda (Ganda)	M
BASHAAM	bah-SHAHM	Rich.	East Africa (Kiswahili)	F
BOFUMO	boh-FOO-moh	Wealth, riches.	Azania (Xhosa)	
BYOMERE	bjoh-meh-reh	One who is rich.	Uganda (Ganda)	M
CHANIYA	CHAH-nee-yah	Rich.	East Africa (Kiswahili)	F
DEMOLA	dee-MOH-lah	Made with wealth.	Nigeria (Yoruba)	
EMERE	eh-MEH-reh	Chief of riches.	Nigeria (Eleme)	
ENAKU	eh-NAH-koo	Poverty.	Uganda (Nyoro)	
FAYALO	fah-YAH-loh	Wealth and happiness.	West Africa	
FEZA	FEH-zah	Money.	Africa (Arabic)	F
GAKIRE	gah-KEE-reh	May he or she become rich.	Rwanda, Burundi (Kinyarwanda, Kirundi)	
GHANIA	gah-NEE-ah	Rich.	North Africa (Arabic)	F
JAIFE	jah-EE-feh	Let them be wealthy.	Nigeria (Urhobo)	
JENMIE	jehn-mee-eh	People hate me when I am penniless.	Cameroon (Mubako)	
KAMALI	kah-MAH-lee	Wealth.	Rwanda, Burundi (Kinyarwanda, Kirundi)	M
KATUNGI	kah-toon-jee	Rich person.	Uganda (Runyankore)	M
KAUSIWA	kah-oo-SEE-wah	The poor.	Malawi (Yao)	F
KGWEBO	kGWEH-boh	Wealth.	Azania (Sotho)	
KHUMO	KOO-moh	Richness.	Botswana (Tswana)	
KIAMBU	kee-AHM-boo	This one will be rich.	Kenya	
KOMBO	KOHM-boh	Impoverished.	Kiswahili	M
KOSOKO	koh-SOH-koh	No hoe to dig a grave.	Nigeria (Yoruba)	M
KWASI	KWAH-see	Wealthy, self-sufficient.	Kenya, Tanzania	
KYOME	tch-oh-mee	The one who is rich.	Uganda (Ganda)	M

Name	Pronunciation	Meaning	Origin	Gender
LEFA	leh-fah	Inheritance.	Azania (Sotho)	M
MALI	MAH-lee	Wealth; riches.	Kiswahili	F
MANALA	mah-NAH-lah	The wealthy one.	Zimbabwe (Ndebele)	M
MASKINI	mah-SKEE-nee	Poor.	Tanzania (Kiswahili)	M
MBIYA	m-BEE-yah	Money.	Malawi (Yao)	M
MKWASI	m-KWAH-see	A wealthy person.	Kenya, Tanzania	
MPANDE	m-PAHN-deh	Cowry shell.	Zambia (Bemba)	
MSURI	moo-soo-ree	The rich one.	Tanzania (Chaga)	M
NGO	n-GOH	Wealth.	Nigeria	
ODOZIAKU	oh-doh-zee-ah-koo	Keeper of wealth.	Nigeria (Igbo)	F
OLA	OH-lah	Wealth; riches.	Nigeria (Yoruba)	M
OLAMINA	oh-lah-MEE-nah	This is my wealth.	Nigeria (Yoruba)	
RUTANGA BORO	roo-tahn-gah-boh-roh	Protector of the poor.	Burundi	
SARAFU	sah-RAH-foo	A coin.	Kiswahili	
SOSOBALA	soh-soh-BAH-lah	The rich and contented one.	Azania	
TAANASA	tah-ah-NAH-sah	Lead a life of luxury.	Kiswahili	
TAJIRI	tah-JEE-ree	Rich, wealthy.	Kenya, Tanzania	
UTAJIRI	oo-tah-JEE-ree	Riches, wealth.	Kiswahili	
YAMEOGO	yah-meh-oh-goh	Wealthy.	West Africa	M
YUMJO	YOOM-joh	A debt, something that will bring problems.	Cameroon (Mungaka)	M
YUUTHAR	YOO-tahr	Wealthy; plentiful.	Kiswahili	F
ZUKA	zoo-KAH	Money.	Zimbabwe (Shona)	M

Mothers and Motherhood

A mother cannot die. —DRC

Name	Pronunciation	Meaning	Origin	Gender
A-AA	ah-AAH	Mama.	Nigeria (Eleme)	F
AKA	AH-kah	Mother.	Nigeria (Eleme)	F
AKE MMA	AH-keh m-MAH	Grandmother.	Nigeria (Efik)	F
BIBI	BEE-bee	Grandma.	Kiswahili	F
GOGO	GOH-goh	Grandmother.	Zambia, Zimbabwe (Shona)	F
INE	EE-neh	Mother.	Nigeria (Ishan)	F
IYABO	ee-YAH-boh	Mother has returned.	Nigeria (Yoruba)	F
IYEYE	ee-YEH-yeh	Grandmother.	Nigeria (Ishan	F
JIBOO	jee-boh	New mother.	Gambia (Mandinka)	F
KAH	kah	Grandmother.	Cameroon (Mubako)	F
KUKU	KOO-koo	Grandmother.	Namibia (Ovambo)	F
MAKHULU	mah-KOO-loo	The grandmother.	Azania	F
MAMAWA	MAHM-wah	Small mother.	Liberia	F
MANYI	mahn-yee	The mother of twins.	Cameroon (Mungaka)	F
MUGA	moo-gah	Mother of all.	East Africa	F
NAHBILA	nah-BEE-lah	Mommy is back.	Cameroon (Mubako)	F
NAHWALLA	nah-WAHL-lah	The mother of the family.	Cameroon (Mubako)	F
NINA	NEE-nah	Mother.	East Africa (Kiswahili)	F
NNE	n-NEH	Granny.	Nigeria (Efik)	F
NNEMEKA	n-neh-MEH-kah	Mother has done the greatest.	Nigeria (Igbo)	F
NNENAYA	neh-NAH-yah	Like father's mother.	Nigeria (Igbo)	F
NNENNE	n-NEHN-neh	Mother of mine.	Nigeria (Igbo)	F
NNEORA	n-neh-OH-rah	Mother loved by all.	Nigeria (Igbo)	F
NOFOTO	noh-FOH-toh	Child in the image of her grandmother.	Azania (Xhosa)	F
NOLUNDI	noh-LOON-dee	Mother of horizons.	Azania (Xhosa)	F
NOMALI	NOH-MAH-lee	Mother of riches.	Azania (Xhosa)	F

Name	Pronunciation	Meaning	Origin	Gender
NOMFEZO	nom-FEH-zoh	She leaves nothing unfinished.	Azania (Xhosa)	F
NYANYA	n-yahn-yah	Grandmother.	Kiswahili	F
NYIMENKA	nyee-mehn-kah	Good or sweet mother.	Nigeria (Eleme)	F
SIMANI	see-mah-NEE	Looks like the grandmother.	Sierra Leone	F
SOMO	soh-MOH	Teachings or godmother.	Kiswahili	F
SOMOE	soh-MOH-eh	Her godmother.	East Africa (Kiswahili)	F
UMAYMA	oo-MAH-ee-mah	Little mother.	North Africa (Arabic)	F
UMI	OO-mee	My mother.	Kiswahili	F
UMM	oom	Mother.	North Africa (Arabic)	F
YEAWA	yeh-AH-wah	This belongs to grandma.	Sierra Leone	F
YETUNDE	yeh-TOON-deh	The mother comes back.	Nigeria (Yoruba)	F
YINGI	YEEN-gee	My beloved mother.	Nigeria	

Music, Song, and Dance

The music lover carries the drums. —Ghana

Name	Pronunciation	Meaning	Origin	Gender
ALAYANDE	ah-lah-YAHN-deh	Here comes the master drummer.	Yoruba	
AZALEE	ah-zah-LEE	A singer.	West Africa (Bini)	F
BETI	BEH-tee	Verse of a song.	Kiswahili	F
BINA	BEE-nah	To sing, to dance.	Kiswahili	
BINAH	BEE-nah	A dancer.	West Africa (Bobangi)	F
DANSA	DAHN-sah	Dance.	Azania (Zulu)	
DENKILILAA	dehn-kee-lee-lah-ah	Singing.	Gambia (Mandinka)	
HAYIYA	hah-YEE-yah	Dance with joy.	Azania (Zulu)	
IJO	EE-joh	Dance.	West Africa (Yoruba)	

Name	Pronunciation	Meaning	Origin	Gender
KALIMBA	kah-LEHM-bah	Musical.	Malawi	
KARI	KAH-ree	Rhythm.	West Africa (Hausa)	
KENYATTA	kehn-yaht-tah	Sound of beautiful music; a musician.	Kenya (Agikuyu)	M
KIDA	KEE-dah	Music.	West Africa (Hausa)	
KIGOMA	KEE-goh-mah	Small drum.	East Africa (Kiswahili)	M
LIPENGA	lee-PEHN-gah	Musical.	Malawi	
LUIMBA	loo-EEM-bah	Song.	Uganda (Ganda)	
MAIMBA	mah-EEM-bah	Song.	Malawi	M
MALENGA	MAH-lehn-gah	She sings well.	East Africa (Kiswahili)	F
MALERIGA	mah-leh-REE-gah	Good singer.	Kenya, Tanzania	
MARIMBA	mah-REHM-bah	Mother of music, a musical instrument.	Africa (Bantu)	
MIKINDANI	mee-kee-DAH-nee	Place by the dance.	Tanzania	
MTRIBU	mtree-boo	A musician.	Kiswahili	
MUKONDI	moh-KOHN-dee	A dancer.	Kenya (Agikuyu)	F
MUZIKI	moo-ZEE-kee	Music.	Kiswahili	
MWIMBA	MWEEM-bah	A singer.	Kiswahili	
MWIMBAJI	mweem-BAH-jee	A singer.	Kiswahili	
NIAMBI	nee-ahm-bee	Melody.	Central Africa	F
NYIMBA	n-yeem-bah	Song.	Uganda (Ganda)	
NYIMBO	NYEHM-boh	Song.	East Africa (Kiswahili)	F
PINA	PEE-nah	Song.	Azania (North Sotho)	
RAWA	RAH-wah	Dance.	West Africa (Hausa)	
SAMBA	SAHM-bah	Little drum.	Nigeria (Igbo)	F
SEMA-GOMA	sseh-mah-goh-mah	Drums.	Uganda (Ganda)	M

Name	Pronunciation	Meaning	Origin	Gender
SEMU-ZINYI	sseh-moo-zee-ndjh-ee	Dancer.	Uganda (Ganda)	M
SENDAGO	ssehn-dah-goh	Song; one that sings.	Uganda (Ganda)	M
SHAADIYA	shah-DEE-ah	Singer.	North Africa (Arabic)	
SHADE	shah-DEH	Sweetly singing.	Nigeria (Yoruba)	F
TABALA	tah-BAH-lah	Drum.	Gambia	
UKWE	OOK-weh	Song; rhythm.	Nigeria (Igbo)	M
WAMBUI	wahm-MBOO-ee	Singer of songs.	Kenya (Agikuyu)	F
WIMBO	weem-BOH	Song.	East Africa (Kiswahili)	F
YAHDIMA	yah-DEE-mah	Woman who will make my dancing lively.	Cameroon (Mubako)	F
ZIRAYIDDE	zee-raah-yeed-deh	The drums have sounded.	Uganda (Ganda, Soga)	M

Names and Naming

If you inherit a name you must also adopt its affairs. —Africa

Name	Pronunciation	Meaning	Origin	Gender
AHAEFUEFU	ah-hah-eh-foo-eh-foo	A name never dies.	Nigeria (Igbo)	
BORI	boh-ree	Name.	Gambia (Mandinka)	
HITIMANA	hee-tee-MAH-nah	Only God can name.	Rwanda, Burundi (Kinyarwanda, Kirundi)	M
ISHINA	ee-SHEE-nah	Name.	Zambia (Bemba)	
JATA	jah-tah	Name.	Gambia (Mandinka)	
JINA	JEE-nah	Name.	Kiswahili	
LEBITSO	leh-bee-tcho	Name.	Azania (Sotho)	M
LEENA	leh-EH-nah	Name; that which stays behind you after your death; immortality.	Azania (Sotho)	

Name	Pronunciation	Meaning	Origin	Gender
MAZINA	mah-ZEE-nah	Names.	Rwanda, Burundi (Kinyarwanda, Kirundi)	M
MBU SHANDJE	m-boo-SHAHND-jeh	My namesake.	Namibia (Ovambo)	
OKOH	OH-koh	The usual name for a baby boy before he receives a name.	Nigeria (Ishan)	M
OTITI	oh-TEE-tee	The usual name for a baby girl before she receives a name.	Nigeria (Ishan)	
SOMO	SOH-moh	Namesake (two people refer to each other as *Somo* when they have same name, by coincidence or blood relationship).	Kiswahili	
TAJA	TAH-jah	To mention; to name.	Kiswahili	F
TOOLAA	toh-laah	To name.	Gambia (Mandinka)	
WANYANGA	WAHN-yahn-gah	The name is preserved after death.	East Africa (Luo)	M

Nationhood

The ruin of a nation begins in the homes of its people. —*Ghana*

Name	Pronunciation	Meaning	Origin	Gender
AFURIKA	ah-foo-ree-kah	Africa; African unity or nationalism; during nationalist revolution.	Rwanda, Burundi, DRC (Huti, Tutsi, Twa)	
BANKOO	bahn-koh	Nation.	Gambia (Mandinka)	

Name	Pronunciation	Meaning	Origin	Gender
BENDERA	behn-DEH-rah	Flag, banner (mostly given to those born on Independence Day.)	Africa	M
BONKE	BOHN-keh	He represents the nation.	Azania	M
CHIMU RENGA	tch-ee-moo-rehn-gah	Fighting for one's country.	Zimbabwe, Mozambique, Zambia (Shona)	M
DEMOKRASI	deh-mohk-rah-see	Born during nationalist revolution.	Rwanda, Burundi, DRC (Huti, Tutsi, Twa)	M
KASA	KAH-sah	Country.	West Africa (Hausa)	
KASI	kah-see	Small country.	Uganda (Ganda, Soga)	M
KASOMO	kah-SOH-moh	Flag bearer.	Zambia (Bemba)	
KHULULI SIZWE	koo-loo-lee-see-zweh	Release the nation.	Azania (Zulu)	M
LIYANDA	lee-YAHN-dah	The nation is growing.	Azania (Nguni)	
MMELIZWE	mmeh-leez-weh	Supporter of the nation.	Azania	M
MWANGI	mwahn-gee	Seizes the nation; victorious.	Kenya (Agikuyu)	M
NDEKEZI	n-deh-keh-zee	The country's defender.	Rwanda, Burundi, DRC (Huti, Tutsi, Twa)	M
NOBANTU	noh-BAHN-too	Mother of nations.	Azania (Xhosa)	F
NOLIZWE	noh-leez-WEH	Country.	Azania (Xhosa)	M
NOM MELIZWE	noh-meh-leez-weh	Supporter of the nation.	Azania	F
NOZIZWE	noh-ZEEZ-weh	Mother of nations.	Azania (Nguni)	
RIKONDJA	ree-KOHND-jah	Our nation is struggling.	Southern Africa	
SHILONGO	shee-LOHN-goh	Kingdom; state; country.	Namibia (Ovambo)	
SIZWE	SEEZ-weh	Nation.	Azania (Xhosa)	M
TAIFA	tah-EE-fah	A nation.	Kiswahili	
TYEHIMBA	tah-ee-heem-BAH	We stand as a nation.	Nigeria (Tiv)	M
WATANI	wah-TAH-nee	National; nation.	North Africa (Arabic)	

Nature

The sun tames the goat. —Uganda

Name	Pronunciation	Meaning	Origin	Gender
BODIBA	boh-DEE-bah	Deep place, valley.	Azania (Xhosa)	
BOMBO	BOHM-boh	Mountains.	Azania (Zulu)	
CHAMCHELA	cham-CHEH-lah	A whirlwind.	Kiswahili	
DHORUBA	DOHR-roo-bah	Storm.	Azania (Xhosa)	M
DITHABA	dee-TAH-bah	Mountains.	Azania (North Sotho)	
DUKUDUKU	doo-koo-DOO-koo	Whirlwind, tornado.	Southern Africa (Tsonga)	
EKEAMA	eh-keh-AH-mah	Nature is splendid.	Southern Africa	M
FEFO	FEH-foh	Storm, tempest.	Azania (Sotho)	
FOGHA	FOH-gah	Grass, gift from the bush.	Cameroon (Mubako)	M
ISELE	ee-SEH-leh	Earthquake.	West Africa (Yoruba)	
JANI	JAH-nee	A leaf.	Kiswahili	F
JIRI	GEE-ree	Forest of wild fruits.	Zimbabwe	M
KAMBIHI	kahm-BEE-hee	Whirlwind.	Zambia (Tonga)	
KANYA	KAHN-yah	Ebony.	West Africa (Hausa)	
KASIMU	kah-see-moo	Keeper of the forest.	West Africa	M
KASOZI	kah-SOH-zee	Mountain.	Uganda (Luganda)	M
KAWAIDA	KAH-wah-ee-dah	Natural.	Kenya, Tanzania (Kiswahili)	F
KEAMBI-ROIRO	keh-ahm-bee-ROH-ee-roh	Mountain of blackness.	Kenya (Agikuyu)	M
KIBIRA	tch-ee-bee-rah	Forest.	Uganda (Ganda)	
KONKOO	KOHN-koo	Mountain.	Gambia (Mandinka)	
LAZOLA	LAH-ZOH-lah	The storm has died down.	Azania (Xhosa)	M
LISILE	LEE-SEE-leh	The storms have cleared.	Azania (Xhosa)	M

Name	Pronunciation	Meaning	Origin	Gender
LUNDI	LOON-dee	Horizon.	Azania (Xhosa)	M
MANI	MAH-nee	From the mountain.	Central Africa	M
MANYIKA	mahn-YEE-kah	Meadows.	Zambia (Bemba)	
MATONGO	mah-TOHN-goh	Desert.	Zambia (Bemba)	
MUSISI	moo-see-see	Earthquake.	Uganda (Luganda)	M
MWAMBA	MWAHM-bah	Reef, rock, cliff.	Kiswahili	
MWITI	MWEE-tee	Forest.	Kiswahili	
MYIKA	m-YEE-kah	Desert, wilderness.	Kiswahili	
NAMBUYA	nnahm-boo-yaah	State of chaos; strong wind.	Uganda (Ganda)	F
NAMUKUA	nah-moo-KOO-ah	Baobab tree.	Namibia (Ovambo)	
NEFUNDJA	ne-foond-jah	Flood.	Namibia (Ovambo)	
NKALATI	n-kah-LAH-tee	A very hard tree.	Uganda (Luganda)	M
PORI	POH-ree	Wilderness.	Kiswahili	
SAJIA	sah-JEE-ah	Natural disposition.	North Africa (Arabic)	F
SANGA	sahn-gah	From the valley.	DRC	M
SEFEFO	seh-feh-foh	Storm.	Azania (North Sotho)	
SEKAKANDE	sseh-kah-kahn-deh	The jungle.	Uganda (Ganda)	M
SHAJARA	sha-JAH-rah	Tree.	North Africa (Arabic)	M
SHAMBA	SHAM-bah	Field, plantation.	Kiswahili	
SHARTATI	shahr-tah-tee	Most beautiful mountain.	Ethiopia	
SITAJUWO	see-tah-joo-woh	Baobab tree.	Gambia (Mandinka)	
SOZI	ssoh-zee	Mountain.	Uganda (Ganda)	M
TANGA	tahn-gah	Mountain.	Burkina Faso (Mossi)	M
TETEMEKO	teh-teh-MEH-koh	Earthquake.	Kiswahili	
THABA	TAH-bah	Mountain.	Azania (North Sotho)	
TUFANI	too-FAH-nee	A storm.	Kiswahili	

Name	Pronunciation	Meaning	Origin	Gender
WONYO	wohn-yoh	A deep space, ravine, chasm.	Azania (Xhosa)	
ZAHARA	zah-HAH-rah	From the desert.	North Africa (Arabic)	F

Necessity

He who needs a thing has to go and find it. —*Ghana*

Name	Pronunciation	Meaning	Origin	Gender
DINGANE	deeng-YAH-neh	A person in need.	Azania (Zulu)	M
DINGEKA	deen-GEH-kah	Necessary.	Azania (Zulu)	
HAJA	HAH-jah	Need; request.	Kiswahili	
LAZIMA	lah-ZEE-mah	Necessity.	Kiswahili	
MASILAHI	MAH-see-lah-hee	Necessity.	East Africa (Kiswahili)	M
NONELO	noh-NEH-loh	Mother of sufficiency; all her needs will be met.	Azania (Xhosa)	F
SWELEKA	sweh-LEH-kah	Necessary.	Azania (Zulu)	
UHITAJI	oo-hee-TAH-jee	Need.	Kiswahili	

Newness

An old story does not open the ear as a new one does. —*Benin*

Name	Pronunciation	Meaning	Origin	Gender
KISASA	kee-SAH-sah	New, modern.	Kenya, Tanzania	
SABO	SAH-boh	New.	West Africa (Hausa)	
SHA	SHAH	New.	Azania (Zulu)	
UPYA	OOP-yah	Something new.	Kiswahili	
YALERO	yah-LEH-roh	It is new.	Zambia (Chewa)	M
ZWELITSHA	zweh-LEET-shah	New world.	Azania (Xhosa)	

Noise

You must attend to your business with the vendor in the market, and not to the noise of the market. —Benin

Name	Pronunciation	Meaning	Origin	Gender
ANDI	AHN-dee	Loud noise.	Azania (Xhosa)	
CHINGWELE	cheeng-WEH-leh	Uproar, large commotion.	Zambia (Bemba)	
CHONGO	CHOHN-goh	Noise.	Zambia (Bemba)	
DANDALUKA	dahn-dah-LOO-kah	Call or cry out loud.	Azania (Xhosa)	
DAZULUKA	dah-zoo-LOO-kah	Shout loudly, scream.	Azania (Zulu)	
KELELE	keh-LEH-leh	Noisy.	Kiswahili	
KITAMBILA	kee-tahm-bee-lah	The one that is good at shouting.	DRC (Rega)	M
MAKELELE	mah-keh-LEH-leh	Noise, shouting.	Kenya	F
NAKIYEMBA	nnah-tch-ee-yehn-bah	Talks in a noisy manner.	Uganda (Ganda)	F

Numbers

Numbers can achieve anything. —Ghana

Name	Pronunciation	Meaning	Origin	Gender
ANAN	AH-nahn	Four.	Ghana (Akan)	
BISATU	bee-sah-too	Of three hundred.	Uganda (Ganda)	M
DU	DOO	Ten.	Ghana (Akan)	
GAALI	gah-AH-lee	Two.	Namibia (Ovambo)	
HLAGO	hlah-goh	Five.	Azania (North Sotho)	
IKUMI	ee-koo-mee	Ten.	Uganda (Soga)	M
KUMI	KOO-mee	Ten.	Kiswahili	

Name	Pronunciation	Meaning	Origin	Gender
MBILI	MBEE-lee	Two.	Kiswahili	
MOJA	MOH-jah	One.	Kiswahili	
NANSA	NAHN-sah	Three.	Ghana (Akan)	
NNE	n-neh	Four.	Kiswahili	
SABA	SAH-bah	Seven.	Africa (Kiswahili)	
SEKLARE	sehk-LAH-reh	Three.	Azania (North Sotho)	
SENYANE	sehn-YAHN-neh	Nine.	Azania (North Sotho)	
SESWAI	sehs-wah-ee	Eight.	Azania (North Sotho)	
SIGIDI	see-GHEE-dee	A thousand.	Azania (Zulu)	M
SITA	SEE-tah	Six.	Kiswahili	
TANO	TAH-noh	Five.	Kiswahili	
TATU	TAH-too	Three.	Kiswahili	
THENA SHARA	teh-nah-shah-rah	Twelve.	Kiswahili	
THUMUNI	too-MOO-nee	Eighth.	Kiswahili	
TISA	TEE-sah	Nine.	Kiswahili	
TSHELELA	tsheh-leh-lah	Six.	Azania (North Sotho)	
YESHI	YEH-shee	For a thousand.	Ethiopia (Amharic)	

Obedience

The disobedient fowl obeys in a pot of soup. —Benin

Name	Pronunciation	Meaning	Origin	Gender
AHURRA	ah-hoo-rah	She or he is obedient.	Uganda (Ganda, Kiga, Nyankore)	
ASI	AH-see	To disobey.	Kiswahili	
IDILI	ee-DEE-lee	Well behaved.	Kiswahili	
MTII	M-tEE	An obedient person.	Kiswahili	
NOSIMILO	noh-see-MEE-loh	One who is well behaved.	Azania (Xhosa)	F

Name	Pronunciation	Meaning	Origin	Gender
PULIKA	poo-LEE-kah	Obedience, obey.	Kenya, Tanzania	
SENGONZI	ssehn-gohn-zee	Makes soft, or obedient.	Uganda (Ganda)	M
SIMILO	see-MEE-loh	Well behaved.	Azania (Xhosa)	M
TABIA	tah-BEE-ah	Well-behaved girl.	West Africa	F
THOBELA	toh-BEH-lah	Obey.	Azania (Xhosa)	
THOJA	toh-jah	The obedient one.	Azania (Xhosa)	M
TII	TEE-ee	To obey.	Kiswahili	

Order and Process

Height is not to be hurried. —Zimbabwe

Name	Pronunciation	Meaning	Origin	Gender
AKONO	ah-KOH-noh	It is my turn.	Nigeria (Yoruba)	M
ELENU	eh-LEH-noo	First thing.	Nigeria (Eleme)	
ENDELEA	ehn-deh-LEH-ah	To continue; progress.	Kiswahili	
HAMBISA	hahm-BEE-sah	Progress.	Azania	
KATI	KAH-tee	Middle.	Kiswahili	
KEHINDE	keh-HEEN-deh	Bring up the rear.	Nigeria (Yoruba)	
KWANELE	kwah-NEH-leh	The last one.	Azania (Zulu)	
KWANZA	KWAHN-zah	First.	Kiswahili	
MIZAN	mee-ZAHN	Balance.	Eritrea, Ethiopia (Tigrinya)	F
NTUTHUKO	n-too-too-koh	Progress.	Azania (Zulu)	M
PHAMBI	pahm-bee	In front of, in the lead.	Azania (Zulu)	
SOOKA	soh-oh-kah	Come first.	Uganda (Ganda)	M
TANGO	TAHN-goh	Firstly.	Namibia (Ovambo)	
URAMUKIWE	oo-rah-moo-KEE-weh	Who will be next?	Rwanda, Burundi (Kinyarwanda, Kirundi)	
ZATITI	zah-TEE-tee	Put in order.	Africa	M

Passion and Desire

*Send a boy where he wants to go
and you'll see his best pace. —Niger*

Name	Pronunciation	Meaning	Origin	Gender
ABIYE	ah-BEE-yeh	My wish.	Nigeria	
ADOKIYE	ah-doh-KEE-yeh	My ultimate desire or wish.	Nigeria	
AHISHA-KIYE	ah-hee-tch-ah-kee-yee	Whenever God wants.	Rwanda, Burundi, DRC (Huti, Tutsi, Twa)	
BWEGOMBE	bweh-gohm-beh	Who are desired.	Uganda (Ganda, Soga)	F
DANGAZELA	dahn-gah-ZEH-lah	Intense desire.	Azania (Xhosa)	
DIYAA	dee-yah	Desire.	Gambia (Mandinka)	
DONKOE	DOHN-koh	What we have begged for.	Cameroon (Mungaka)	M
DOUYE	doh-oo-yeh	We got what we wanted.	Nigeria (Igbo)	F
FUNEKA	foo-NEH-kah	To be wanted, desirable.	Azania (Zulu)	
HAMTAKI	hahm-TAH-kee	She or he doesn't want her.	East Africa	F
HARARA	hah-RAH-rah	Passion; body heat.	Kiswahili	
HASHIKI	HAH-shee-kee	Passion.	East Africa (Kiswahili)	F
HAWA	HAH-wah	Longing.	Kiswahili	
HISIA	hee-SEE-ah	Passion, feeling.	Kiswahili	
IJABA	ee-JAH-bah	A wish fulfilled.	Gambia, Nigeria (Hausa)	F
KHUMBO	KOOM-boh	A wish; baby who fulfills a long awaited wish.	Zambia (Tumbuka)	
KOMUN-YAKA	koh-moon-yah-kah	Passionate.	DRC	M
LAFOO	lah-foh	Desire.	Gambia (Mandinka)	
MAIDEYI	mah-EE-deh-yee	What did you want?	Zimbabwe (Shona)	M
MFUNEKO	mfoon-eh-ko	The one who is what is desired.	Azania	M

Name	Pronunciation	Meaning	Origin	Gender
MUREGO	moo-reh-goh	One who has the desire to do something.	Rwanda (Runyarwanda)	M
NOMFUNEKO	nohm-foo-neh-koh	The one who is what is desired.	Azania	F
ONI	oh-NEE	Desired.	Benin	F
PENZIMA	pehn-zee-mah	Desire.	Kenya, Tanzania	
RAJA	RAH-jah	Dreams and desires.	North Africa (Arabic)	
SENNUNGI	ssehn-noon-gee	That is desirable.	Uganda (Ganda)	M
SERAFINA	seh-rah-FEE-nah	Burning passion.	Azania (Xhosa)	F
SHAUKU	shah-OO-koo	Strong desire.	Kiswahili	
SHEKA	SHEH-kah	Be passionate, enthusiastic.	Azania (Zulu)	
SHEMEI	sheh-meh-ee	Desire.	Egypt/Khamit	F
TAKA	TAH-kah	To want; need.	Kiswahili	
TAMAA	tah-MAH-ah	Passion; desire, ambition.	Kiswahili	F
UCHENNWA	oo-CHEHN-wah	Longing for a child.	Nigeria (Igbo)	
UDUAK	oo-DOO-ahk	Desire.	Nigeria	
WEYNI	WEH-ee-nee	Sweet desire.	Africa	

Patience

At the bottom of patience one finds heaven. —West Africa

Name	Pronunciation	Meaning	Origin	Gender
AYUBU	ah-YOO-boo	Patience in suffering.	East Africa (Kiswahili)	M
BADO	BAH-doh	Not yet, wait awhile.	Kiswahili	
BARITONDA	bah-ree-TOHN-dah	They are patient or careful.	Rwanda, Burundi (Kinyarwanda, Kirundi)	M
DUROJAIYE	doo-roh-jah-ee-yeh	Wait and enjoy what the world offers.	Nigeria (Yoruba)	
DZIGBODE	gee-BOH-day	Patience.	Ghana (Ewe)	M

Name	Pronunciation	Meaning	Origin	Gender
GANYANA	gahn-YAH-nah	Born with the gift of patience.	Uganda (Ganda)	M
IME	EE-meh	Patience.	Nigeria (Efik)	
ISINEKE	ee-see-NEH-keh	Patience.	Zimbabwe	
IZIEGBE	ee-zee-ehg-beh	Patience.	Nigeria (Edo)	F
LINDANI	leen-DAH-nee	Wait— be patient.	Azania (Zulu)	M
LINDELA	leen-deh-lah	To wait for something.	Azania (Xhosa)	M
LINDIWE	lehn-dee-weh	The awaited one; waited for.	Azania (Zulu, Xhosa)	F
MONDE	mohn-deh	Patience.	Azania (Xhosa)	M
MWEN DAPOLOE	m-wehn-dah-POH-leh	Takes his time.	Tanzania (Nyakyusa)	M
NDIDI	n-DEE-dee	Patience.	Nigeria (Igbo)	F
NDIDIKA	n-dee-DEE-kah	Patient.	Nigeria (Igbo)	F
NOMANDE	noh-MOHN-deh	Mother of patience.	Azania (Xhosa)	F
OZIGBODI	oh-ZEE-gboh-dee	Patience.	Ghana (Ewe)	F
PELONOMI	peh-loh-NOH-mee	Patience.	Azania (North Sotho)	
SABURI	sah-BOO-ree	Patience.	Kenya, Tanzania	
TEGELELA	teh-geh-LEH-lah	Wait for!	Namibia (Ovambo)	
VUMILIA	voo-mee-LEE-ah	To bear patiently.	Africa	F
YETWARE	yeh-twah-reh	Take your time.	Africa	

Peace and Harmony

*The value of peace is never known
until the peace is disturbed. —Sierra Leone*

Name	Pronunciation	Meaning	Origin	Gender
ADWOA	AHDJ-woh-ah	Peace.	Ghana	
AIYETORO	ah-YEH-toh-roh	Peace on earth.	Nigeria (Yoruba)	F
AMANI	ah-MAH-nee	Peace, security.	Kenya, Tanzania	

Name	Pronunciation	Meaning	Origin	Gender
AMBILI	ahm-BEE-lee	Peace.	Namibia (Ovambo)	
AMINI	ah-MEE-nee	Peaceful person.	Kenya, Tanzania	
BABATU	bah-BAH-too	He is a peacemaker.	Nigeria (Yoruba)	M
BEM	behm	Peace.	Nigeria (Tiv)	M
BUSINGYE	boo-sehn-jeh	Peace.	Uganda (Kiga, Nyankore)	
DEMBE	dehm-beh	Peace.	Uganda	F
EME	EH-meh	Peace.	Nigeria (Efik)	
FERETA	feh-REH-tah	Peace.	Kiswahili	
IKUSEGHAN	ee-KOO-sehg-hahn	Peace surpasses war.	Benin	F
ISITHANGAMI	ee-see-tahn-gah-mee	Peace.	Azania	
JAWARA	jah-WAH-rah	Peace loving.	Gambia, Nigeria (Hausa)	M
KAGISO	kah-GHEE-soh	Peace, let's build together.	Botswana (Tswana)	
KATATTA	kah-tah-tah	The little one that does not kill.	Uganda (Ganda)	M
KAUNAM-BILI	kah-oo-nahm-BEE-lee	There is no peace.	Namibia (Ovambo)	
KAYIROO	kah-yee-roh	Peace.	Gambia (Mandinka)	
KHOTSO	koht-soh	Peace.	Botswana (Tswana)	
MALIZOLE	mah-lee-zoh-leh	Let there be peace.	Azania (Xhosa)	M
MIREMBE	mee-rehm-beh	Times of peace.	Uganda (Ganda)	
MLAMLI	M-LAHM-lee	Peacemaker.	Azania (Xhosa)	M
MUHUMUZA	moo-hoo-moo-zah	He who brings peace and calm.	Uganda (Runyankore)	M
MXOLISI	moo-ksoh-lee-see	The peacemaker.	Azania (Xhosa)	M
NEEMA	neh-ee-mah	Peaceful.	Gambia (Mandinka)	
NOKU THULA	noh-koo-TOO-lah	The mother of peace.	Azania (Xhosa)	F
NWANA	nwah-nah	Peace maker.	Cameroon (Mubako)	M

Name	Pronunciation	Meaning	Origin	Gender
NYIRAMA-HORO	nee-yee-rah-mah-HO-rah	Peaceful.	Rwanda	F
OSENYULU	oh-sehn-YOO-loo	People will always remember peacemakers.	Nigeria (Ishan)	
SAFA	SAH-fah	Serenity of life.	North Africa (Arabic)	F
SAFIA	sah-FEE-ah	Pure; serene.	North Africa (Arabic)	F
SALAAM	sah-lah-ahm	Peace, tranquility.	Kenya, Tanzania	
SALAMA	sah-LAH-mah	Peace, tranquility.	Kenya, Tanzania	
SEKALEMBE	sseh-kah-lehm-beh	Peacemaker.	Uganda (Ganda)	M
SELAM	seh-lahm	Peace.	Ethiopia	
SIKIA	SEE-kee-ah	Harmony.	East Africa (Kiswahili)	F
SULUHU	soo-LOO-hoo	Peacemaker.	Kenya, Tanzania	
UDO	OO-doh	Peace.	Nigeria (Igbo)	M
UDOKA	oo-DOH-kah	Peace is better.	Nigeria (Igbo)	F
UJEMIRIA	oo-jeh-mee-REE-ah	One who is always seeking peace.	Nigeria (Ishan)	
UKUTHULA	oo-koo-TOO-lah	Peace.	Azania	
WAGUA	wah-GOO-ah	I am uniting you, a peacemaker.	Cameroon (Mubako)	F

Perfection

When a thing becomes perfect, it soon fades. —Morocco

Name	Pronunciation	Meaning	Origin	Gender
INYA-MIBWA	ee-ndjh-ah-mee-bwah	Perfect.	Rwanda, Burundi, DRC (Huti, Tutsi, Twa)	M
KAMALI	kah-MAH-lee	Perfection.	West Africa	
KAMILAH	kah-MEE-lah	The perfect one.	North Africa (Arabic)	
KAMILI	kah-MEE-lee	Perfect.	North Africa (Arabic)	

Name	Pronunciation	Meaning	Origin	Gender
KAMILYA	KAH-meel-yah	Perfection.	East Africa (Kiswahili)	F
KARU RANGA	kah-roo-RAHN-gah	Perfect.	Rwanda, Burundi (Kinyarwanda, Kirundi)	M
MAASUMA	maah-SOO-mah	Impeccable.	Kiswahili	F
MATAYE	mah-tah-yeh	Only God is perfect.	Nigeria (Igarra)	
SALAMU	sah-LAH-moo	Perfect.	Kenya, Tanzania	
SALANIU	sah-lah-NEE-oo	Perfect.	Kenya, Tanzania	
SENABIYAH	seh-nah-BEE-yah	The highest aspect of her being is what she is.	Egypt/Khamit	F
TAMIIM	TAH-meem	Perfection.	Kiswahili	M
UKAMILIFU	oo-kah-MEEL-foo	Perfection.	Kiswahili	

Perseverance and Persistence

No journey is ever ended without persistence. —Africa

Name	Pronunciation	Meaning	Origin	Gender
ALINYIIKIRA	ah-lee-ndjh-ee-kee-rah	The one who will diligently persist.	Uganda (Ganda)	F
DAZA	DAH-zah	Obstinate, persistent.	Azania (Zulu)	
EKWE	EHK-weh	Persistence.	Nigeria (Igbo)	M
FENENA	feh-NEH-nah	Persevere.	Azania (Sotho)	
HAMADI	hah-MAH-dee	Tenacity.	Kenya, Tanzania	
IDIHI	ee-DEE-hee	Enthusiasm, perseverance.	East Africa (Kiswahili)	F
KAFUNVU	kah-foon-voo	Persistent, the little one that is self exerting or insistent.	Uganda (Ganda)	M
KAIDI	kah-EE-dee	Stubborn.	Kiswahili	
KAMDIBE	kahm-DEE-beh	Let me endure.	Nigeria (Igbo)	M
KANYIGA	kah-ndjh-ee-gah	The little one that presses.	Uganda (Ganda)	M

Name	Pronunciation	Meaning	Origin	Gender
KARUNVU	kah-foon-voo	Persevering, persistent.	Uganda (Ganda)	M
KASERULA	kah-seh-roo-lah	One who pushes forward bit by bit.	Uganda (Ganda)	
KUDUMU	KOO-doo-moo	Persevering, lasting.	East Africa (Kiswahili)	M
MAKATA	mah-kah-tah	Climbing to the top of a steep mountain; perseverance.	Zimbabwe, Mozambique, Zambia (Shona)	M
NONYA MEKO	non-YAH-MEH-koh	Mother of those who persevere, patience.	Azania (Xhosa)	F
NYAMEKA	nyah-MEH-kah	She will persevere and overcome.	Azania (Xhosa)	F
NYAMEKO	nyah-MEH-koh	Perseverance.	Azania (Xhosa)	M
NYIKIRA	nyee-kee-rah	Perseverance.	Uganda (Ganda)	
SENKONGO	ssehn-koh-mah-goh	Ceaseless.	Uganda (Ganda)	M
SHINGAYI	sheen-GAH-yee	Perseverance.	Azania	
UDUMA	oo-DOO-mah	Perseverance.	Kiswahili	
ZINGISA	zing-GEE-sah	One who perseveres until she receives the expected end.	Azania (Xhosa)	F

Planning and Preparation

People start preparing for the night when the day is still very young. —Ghana

Name	Pronunciation	Meaning	Origin	Gender
ANDILIWA	ahn-dee-LEE-wah	Be ready.	Kiswahili	
BATEGEKA	bah-teh-jeh-kah	People plan.	Uganda (Runyoro)	
GUSI	goo-see	Arm yourself well before anything happens.	Cameroon (Mubako)	F

Name	Pronunciation	Meaning	Origin	Gender
JIANDAA	jee-AHN-dah-ah	To make oneself ready.	Kiswahili	
SHABAHA	shah-BAH-hah	Target, aim.	Africa	M
SHIRI	SHEE-ree	Idea, plan.	West Africa (Hausa)	
SHIRYA	shee-ree-yah	Be ready.	West Africa (Hausa)	
TAYARI	tah-YAH-ree	Always ready.	Kenya, Tanzania	
TAYARISHA	tah-yah-REE-shah	Make ready; prepare.	Kiswahili	
TEGA	TEH-gah	Set; ready.	Kiswahili	

Pleasure, Amusement, and Smiles

Do not stop children having fun otherwise they will also stop your serious work. —Gambia

Name	Pronunciation	Meaning	Origin	Gender
ADUNBI	ah-DOON-bee	Born to be pleasant.	Nigeria (Yoruba)	M
ANISI	ah-NEE-see	Pleasant, pleasing.	Kenya, Tanzania	
ATINU	ah-TEE-noo	Pleasant, desirable.	Nigeria	
BASMA	BAHS-mah	Smile.	Kiswahili	
BAYINA	bah-yee-nah	They tease.	Uganda (Ganda)	
BISIMWA	bee-see-mwah	Things that are enjoyed; things people are pleased with.	DRC (Bashi)	M
CHEKA	CHE-kah	To laugh.	Kiswahili	
CHEKELEA	cheh-keh-LEH-ah	To smile.	Kiswahili	
CHEKESHA	cheh-KEE-shah	To amuse.	Kiswahili	
CHIRESHE	chee-REH-sheh	He mixes speech with little bursts of laughter.	Azania (Xhosa)	
DIKIDA	dee-KEE-dah	Tickle.	Southern Africa (Tsonga)	

Name	Pronunciation	Meaning	Origin	Gender
ENEJE	eh-NEH-jeh	Those laughing at me.	Nigeria (Ishan)	
ENEKAJE	eh-neh-KAH-jeh	Those who laughed first.	Nigeria (Ishan)	
FUMBE	FOOM-beh	Riddle, puzzle.	Azania (Zulu)	
JELE	jeh-leh	To laugh.	Gambia (Mandinka)	
KABASEKE	kah-bah-seh-keh	Let them laugh (or smile at me).	Uganda (Ganda, Kiga, Nyankore)	F
KAMBUYA	kahm-boo-yah	Silliness.	Uganda (Ganda, Soga)	M
KASHORE	KAH-SHO-reh	With humor.	East Africa (Kiswahili)	F
KHOLEKA	koh-LEH-kah	The one I am able to take pleasure in.	Azania (Xhosa)	F
KHOLIWE	KOH-lee-weh	The one I am pleased with.	Azania (Xhosa)	F
KINYEMI	keen-YEH-mee	Pleasant, something good.	Kenya, Tanzania	
KODJO	kohd-joh	Humorous.	West Africa	M
LAABU	LAAH-boo	Entertaining.	Kenya	F
LONYON-GHA	lohn-YOHN-gah	Laugh at matters.	Cameroon (Mubako)	F
MALIHA	MAH-lee-hah	Pleasant.	East Africa (Kiswahili)	F
MORAA	MOH-rah	Fun loving.	East Africa (Kisii)	F
MUSAAZI	moo-SAH-zee	One who jokes.	Uganda (Luganda)	M
MYEMYELA	myehm-yeh-lah	Smile.	Rwanda	
NIBASEKE	nee-BAH-seh-keh	They may laugh.	Rwanda, Burundi (Kinyarwanda, Kirundi)	
NJAKIRI	N-jah-KEE-ree	To be funny.	Nigeria (Igbo)	F
NSEKALIJE	n-seh-kah-lee-jeh	I smile when it comes.	Rwanda, Burundi (Kinyarwanda, Kirundi)	M
NSEKO	n-seh-koh	Laugh; laughter.	Uganda (Ganda)	
NUAHA	NOO-ah-ah	Pleasure.	East Africa (Kiswahili)	F

Name	Pronunciation	Meaning	Origin	Gender
NYAKALLO	nyah-KAH-loh	Merriment.	Lesotho (Basotho)	
NYERO	ndjh-ee-roh	Laughter.	Uganda (Acholi)	M
OCHI	OH-chee	Merriment and joy; laughter.	Nigeria (Igbo)	
OMASIRI	oh-mah-SEE-ree	Pleasant, very pleasing.	Nigeria	
REBERO	reh-BEH-roh	Pleasant sight.	Rwanda, Burundi (Kinyarwanda, Kirundi)	M
RERIIN	reh-REE-een	Laugh.	West Africa (Yoruba)	
RIDHI	REED-hee	To please; content.	Kiswahili	
SARA	SAH-rah	Gives pleasure; joyful.	North Africa	F
SEKAI	seh-kah-yee	Laughter.	Zimbabwe	
SEKAYI	seh-kah-yee	Laugh.	East Africa	F
SIYOLO	see-YOH-loh	Our pleasure.	Azania (Xhosa)	M
SSAAGE	ssaah-geh	That involves joking.	Uganda (Soga)	M
WASA	WAH-sah	Joke.	West Africa (Hausa)	
YOLISA	yoh-lee-sah	She brings pleasure.	Azania (Xhosa)	F

Power

Even an ant can hurt an elephant. —Azania

Name	Pronunciation	Meaning	Origin	Gender
AINRA	AH-een-rah	Lasting power.	East Africa (Kiswahili)	F
AMRI	AHM-ree	Power.	Kiswahili	
AYELE	ah-YEH-leh	Powerful man.	East Africa	
AZA	AH-zah	Powerful, strong.	Kiswahili	
BWAMI	bwaah-mee	Power.	Uganda (Ganda)	M
CHIBUIKE	chee-boo-EE-keh	God is power.	Nigeria	

Name	Pronunciation	Meaning	Origin	Gender
CHIJIKE	chee-JEE-keh	God holds the power.	Nigeria (Igbo)	M
CHIKE	CHEE-keh	Power of God.	Nigeria (Igbo)	M
DIKE	dee-keh	The capable; powerful.	Nigeria (Igbo)	M
EJIKE	eh-JEE-keh	We have the power.	Nigeria	
HAILE	HAH-lee	Powerful.	Ethiopia	
HAULI	HAH-oo-lee	Power, strength.	East Africa (Kiswahili)	M
IKE	EE-keh	Power, authority.	Nigeria	
IKEDIORA	ee-kee-dee-OH-rah	The power of a community.	Nigeria (Igbo)	M
IKEMBA	ee-KEHM-bah	People's power; strength of the people.	Nigeria (Igbo)	M
IKO	EE-koh	Control, power.	West Africa (Hausa)	
JALALI	JAH-lah-lee	Almighty; omnipotent.	East Africa (Kiswahili)	M
MAMLAKA	mahm-LAH-kah	Power, rule.	Africa (Kiswahili)	
MANANI	mah-NAH-nee	Almighty.	Kenya, Tanzania	
MANDLA	MAHND-lah	Power; strength.	Azania (Nguni)	
MANDLAKAZI	mahn-DLAH-KAH-zee	A woman of great power.	Azania (Xhosa)	F
MAWU	MAH-woo	The almighty; omnipotent.	Ghana (Ewe)	
MUKATA	moo-KAH-tah	Powerful, well-respected person.	Zambia (Bemba)	
NABAASA	nah-BAH-sah	Omnipotence.	Uganda (Runyankore)	F
NGUVU	n-GOO-voo	Power.	Azania (Sotho)	
OMARI	oh-MAH-ree	Power, influential.	Kenya, Tanzania	
TWIN AMAANI	tween-ah-MAAH-nee	We are powerful.	Uganda (Rukiga)	F
UBORO	oo-BOH-roh	Powerful; superior.	Kiswahili	
UKEH	OO-keh	Poison; overpowering.	Nigeria (Igbo)	M

Name	Pronunciation	Meaning	Origin	Gender
UWAJIKA	oo-wah-JEE-kah	World power.	Nigeria (Igbo)	
WENIKE	weh-NEE-keh	Power counts.	Nigeria	

Praise

He who praises rain has been rained on. —Tanzania

Name	Pronunciation	Meaning	Origin	Gender
ADHIMISHA	ahd-hee-MEE-shah	Praise, honor.	Kenya, Tanzania	
AHMED	ahk-MEHD	Praiseworthy.	East Africa (Kiswahili)	M
ARIRI	ah-REE-ree	That which is for praise.	Nigeria (Ishan)	
DUMISA	doo-MEE-sah	Praise, worship.	Azania (Xhosa, Zulu)	M
ELERA	eh-LEH-rah	Praise.	Nigeria (Eleme)	
HALALISA	hah-lah-LEE-sah	Compliment, praise.	Azania	
HAMAD	HAH-mahd	He praised.	North Africa (Arabic)	M
HAMIDA	hah-MEE-dah	Praises.	North Africa (Arabic)	
ITORO	ee-TOH-roh	Praise to God.	Nigeria (Efik)	
MUHA MMAD	moo-HAH-mahd	Praised.	East Africa (Kiswahili)	M
NAKITENDE	nnah-tch-ee-tehn-deh	That is praised.	Uganda (Ganda)	F
NNAMEKA	n-nah-MEH-kah	Praise, glory to God.	Nigeria	
OLUTOSIN	oh-loo-TOH-seen	God deserves to be praised.	Nigeria (Yoruba)	M
SUUTA	soo-tah	Praise highly.	Uganda (Soga)	M
TAMANI	tah-MAH-nee	Praise.	Malawi	
TANGENI	tahn-GEH-nee	Praise; thank.	Namibia (Ovambo)	
TENDA	tehn-dah	Speak well of; praise.	Uganda (Ganda)	F
TUMISO	too-MEE-soh	Praise to God.	Azania (Sotho)	

Name	Pronunciation	Meaning	Origin	Gender
TUSIIME	too-see-meh	Let us praise.	Uganda (Kiga, Nyankore, Nyoro, Toro)	
ZUKIE	zoo-kee	The one to be praised.	Azania (Xhosa)	F
ZUKISWA	zoo-kees-wah	The one to be praised.	Azania (Xhosa)	F

Prayer

Prayers and tears don't stop you from dying. —Haiti

Name	Pronunciation	Meaning	Origin	Gender
ASHABA	ah-tch-ah-bah	The one who prays.	Uganda (Nyankore)	M
AYONDU	ah-YOHN-doo	Pray for life.	Nigeria (Igbo)	
DUA	DOO-ah	Prayer; plea.	Kiswahili	
DUSABE	doo-sah-beh	Let us pray.	Rwanda, Burundi, DRC (Huti, Tutsi, Twa)	F
DUWAA	doo-wah	To pray; bless.	Gambia (Mandinka)	
JUBEMI	joo-BEH-mee	The Lord has answered my prayers.	Nigeria (Shekiri)	F
KARAEO	kah-rah-eh-oh	Reply to my prayers.	Azania (Sotho)	
NSEKALIJE	n-seh-kah-lee-jeh	I pray.	Rwanda, Burundi, DRC (Huti, Tutsi, Twa)	
SALA	SAH-lah	Prayer.	Kenya, Tanzania	
TASHIBI	tah-SHEE-bee	Prayer beads.	Kiswahili	
TEKE	TEH-keh	Prayer.	Nigeria	
THAPELO	tah-peh-loh	Prayer.	Azania	

Pride, Confidence, and Vanity

A pearl is only a pearl once it is out of its shell. —Nigeria

Name	Pronunciation	Meaning	Origin	Gender
BONGO	BAHN-goh	My pride.	Azania (Xhosa)	M
BOSILLA	boh-SEE-lah	Pride.	Cameroon (Mubako)	F
CHIMAISI	chee-mah-EE-see	Young; proud.	Kiswahili	M
CHIPALE	chee-PAH-leh	Pride.	Zambia (Bemba)	
DIDAJU	dee-DAH-joo	Confident.	West Africa (Yoruba)	
ETEMI	eh-TEH-mee	I am proud.	Nigeria (Shekiri)	F
GABA	GAH-bah	Our pride.	Azania	F
GUGU	GOO-goo	My pride; my prized possession.	Azania (Xhosa)	M
IMEN	EE-mehn	Confidence, belief.	North Africa (Arabic)	
IYOYA	ee-YOH-yah	I consider myself a pride to this family, community.	Nigeria (Ishan)	
JINAKI	JEE-nah-kee	Think well of oneself.	Kenya, Tanzania (Kiswahili)	F
JINYIMA	jeen-YEE-mah	Be vain.	Kiswahili	
JIONA	jee-OH-nah	To be vain.	Kiswahili	F
JISIFU	jee-SEE-foo	To boast.	Kiswahili	
KAYISHEMA	kah-yee-SHEH-mah	Pride.	Rwanda, Burundi (Kinyarwanda, Kirundi)	M
KIBURI	kee-BOO-ree	Pride, promise.	Kiswahili	
KITAMBI	kee-TAHM-bee	The proud one.	Kenya, Tanzania	
MAYASA	MAH-yah-sah	Walks proudly.	East Africa (Kiswahili)	F
MSIRI	m-SEE-ree	Confidant.	Kiswahili	
NERATSHI	neh-RAHT-shee	Proud, self-assured.	Azania	
NGANGA	n-GAHN-gah	Self-pride.	Nigeria	
NYANGA	n-yahn-gah	Pride.	Cameroon (Mungaka)	M

Name	Pronunciation	Meaning	Origin	Gender
SERU-SHEMA	sseh-roo-tch-eh-mah	Proud one.	Rwanda, Burundi, DRC (Huti, Tutsi, Twa)	M
URENNA	oo-REHN-nah	Father's pride.	Nigeria (Igbo)	
URORO	oo-ROH-roh	Pride.	Nigeria (Igbo)	F
YISSIA	yee-SEE-ah	Take pride in one's self.	Cameroon (Mubako)	M

Prophecy

You do not consult an oracle when you
already know the cause of illness. —*Cameroon*

Name	Pronunciation	Meaning	Origin	Gender
BECCA	BEH-kah	Prophet.	Nigeria (Bobangi)	F
FATEMA	FAH-tee-mah	Daughter of the prophet.	North Africa (Arabic)	F
HAMID	HAH-meed	Prophet.	North Africa (Arabic)	
IDRIIS	EE-drees	Prophet; he studies.	Kenya, Tanzania (Kiswahili)	M
SABOLA	sah-BOH-lah	Prophetess.	Egypt/Khamit	F

Protection and Defense

That which does kill a shepherd
never kills the whole herd. —*Kiswahili*

Name	Pronunciation	Meaning	Origin	Gender
AMNE	AHM-neh	Secure.	Kiswahili	
ANIA	ah-NEE-ah	Defend.	Azania	M
ARINDA	ah-rehn-dah	God protects.	Uganda (Kiga, Nyankore)	
ARISI	ah-REE-see	Guard, protector.	Nigeria (Igbo)	M
ASIM	ah-SEEM	Protector, defender.	North Africa	M

Name	Pronunciation	Meaning	Origin	Gender
BARINDA	bah-rehn-ndah	They wait; they guard against.	Uganda (Ganda, Kiga, Nyankore)	M
BHEKI	BEH-kee	Watchman, caretaker.	Azania (Xhosa)	
BOMA	BOH-mah	Fortress.	Kiswahili	M
BONANI	boh-NAH-nee	To take care of, to guard.	Azania (Nguni)	
DABOBO	dah-BOH-boh	Defend.	West Africa (Yoruba)	
DISH	DEESH	To watch over, to tend.	Southern Africa (Tsonga)	
EGOTO	eh-GOH-toh	Lock (secure).	Nigeria (Eleme)	
HIMAYA	hee-MAH-yah	Protection.	Kiswahili	
HIRSI	HEER-see	Amulet.	Somalia	F
HOMALENI	hoh-mah-LEH-nee	Take up arms and defend self.	Southern Africa	M
JONGUH LANGA	john-GOOH-LAHN-gah	He who watches over his people.	Azania (Xhosa)	M
KAFIL	KAH-feel	Protector, responsible.	Kiswahili	
KALEKEZI	kah-leh-keh-zee	Little elite defender of the country.	Uganda (Ganda, Kiga, Nyankore)	
KALELA	kah-LEH-lah	One who looks after others well.	Zambia (Bemba)	
KAMUKAMA	kah-moo-KAH-mah	Protected by God.	Uganda (Runyankore)	M
KANDIA	kahn-dee-ah	Fortress.	West Africa	M
KANDISA	kahn-DEE-sah	Fortress.	West Africa	M
KANTALA	kahn-TAH-lah	Guard; shepherd.	Gambia	M
KANYAMA	kahn-YAH-mah	Guard.	Central Africa	M
KAREKEZI	kah-reh-KEH-zee	The defender.	Rwanda, Burundi (Kinyarwanda, Kirundi)	M
KELILE	keh-LEE-leh	Protection.	Ethiopia	M
KHUSELWA	KOO-seh-lwah	God will protect her.	Azania (Xhosa)	F

Name	Pronunciation	Meaning	Origin	Gender
KINGIZA	keen-GEE-zah	To protect.	Kiswahili	
LONDA	LOHN-dah	Protect.	Azania (Zulu)	
MAABADE	MAA-bah-deh	Sanctuary.	East Africa (Kiswahili)	M
MAHFUDA	mah-FOO-dah	Protected.	Kiswahili	
MALUSI	mah-LOO-see	Shepherd.	Azania (Xhosa)	M
MASTURA	mahs-TOOR-rah	Protected.	Kiswahili	
MINZI	MEEN-zee	Defender; protector.	East Africa	M
MLINDI	M-LEENN-dee	Watchman.	Azania (Xhosa)	M
MLINZI	m-LEEN-zee	A guard.	Kiswahili	
MMOLOKI	mmoh-loh-kee	Guardian, keeper.	Azania (Sotho)	F
MTUNGA	m-TOON-gah	Shepherd, herdsman.	Azania (Nguni)	M
MULINDWA	moo-LEE-ndoo-ah	The protected one.	Uganda (Rutooro)	M
MWANZA	mwah-zah	Wise protector.	Tanzania	M
NOTHANGO	noh-TAHNG-goh	Watchwoman on the wall; one who forms a buffer against the enemy.	Azania (Xhosa)	F
RULINDA	roo-LEEN-dah	The protector.	Rwanda, Burundi (Kinyarwanda, Kirundi)	M
SELMA	SEHL-mah	Secure.	North Africa (Arabic)	F
STARA	s-TAH-rah	Protected.	East Africa (Kiswahili)	F
SUNGA	SOON-gah	Keep, or look after.	Zambia (Bemba)	
TABARO	tah-BAH-roh	Defense.	Rwanda, Burundi (Kinyarwanda, Kirundi)	M
TAYMURA	tah-ee-moo-rah	Guardian.	Kiswahili	F
TSARE	tsah-reh	Defend.	West Africa (Hausa)	
ULINZI	oo-LEHN-zee	The watchman.	Kiswahili	M
UMZALI	oo-ZAH-lee	Guardian.	Azania (Zulu)	

Name	Pronunciation	Meaning	Origin	Gender
VARASHA	vah-RAH-shah	A sentinel, a watchman.	Azania (Xhosa)	M
VIKELI	vee-KEH-lee	Protector.	Azania (Zulu)	
YERINDA	yeh-ree-ndah	Be careful; protect yourself.	Uganda (Kiga, Nyankore, Nyoro, Toro)	
ZAAHURA	zaah-hoo-rah	Rescue.	Uganda	
ZIMURINDA	zee-moo-REEN-dah	They protect him.	Rwanda, Burundi (Kinyarwanda, Kirundi)	
ZINJA	ZEHN-jah	The protector.	Azania	M

Purpose

Accomplishment of purpose is better than making a profit. —Niger

Name	Pronunciation	Meaning	Origin	Gender
ASHIA	ah-SHEE-ah	Meaningful existence.	East Africa	
ELLA	EHL-lah	To move towards.	Southern Africa (Tsonga)	
MAKUSUDI	mah-koo-SOO-dee	On purpose.	Kiswahili	
NIA	NEE-ah	Purpose.	Kiswahili	
NIAMOJA	nee-ah-moh-JAH	One purpose.	East Africa (Kiswahili)	M
NIARA	NEE-ah-rah	Of high purpose.	East Africa (Kiswahili)	F
NIASHA	nee-AH-shah	Purposeful life.	New Afrika	F
NJONGO	n-JOHN-goh	Our aim or intention.	Azania	M
NOMISHINI	nohm-ee-shee-nee	Mission.	Azania (Xhosa)	
NONJONGO	nohn-john-goh	Our aim or intention.	Azania	F
NYAH	n-yah	Purpose.	East Africa	F
SABABU	sah-BAH-boo	The reason why.	Sierra Leone	M

Questions and Answers

You cannot tell the contents of a parcel until you open it. —Nigeria

Name	Pronunciation	Meaning	Origin	Gender
ABEBI	AH-beh-BEE	We asked for and got her.	Nigeria (Yoruba)	F
ABEJE	ah-BEH-jeh	We asked to have this one.	Nigeria (Yoruba)	
ABENI	ah-BEE-nee	We asked for her, and behold she is ours.	Nigeria (Yoruba)	F
ANOO	ah-NOH-oh	Asking is no offense.	Nigeria (Ishan)	
BUSEJE	boo-seh-jeh	Ask me.	Malawi (Yao)	F
BUZILE	BOOH-zee-leh	We have inquired.	Azania (Xhosa)	M
FUNSANI	foon-SAH-nee	Request.	Malawi (Ngoni)	M
HOJI	HOH-jee	To interrogate.	Kiswahili	
IRIDI	ee-REE-dee	Curiosity.	West Africa (Yoruba)	
JAWABU	jah-WAH-boo	An answer.	Kiswahili	
LUBUSA	loo-boo-sah	The one that questions.	DRC (Rega)	F
MAJIBU	mah-JEE-boo	Answer.	Kiswahili	
MASWALI	mah-SWAH-lee	Questions.	Africa (Kiswahili)	M
POTSISO	poht-SEE-soh	Question.	Azania (North Sotho)	
SABIMAMA	sah-bee-mah-mah	Ask God.	Rwanda, Burundi, DRC (Huti, Tutsi, Twa)	M
SIALA	see-AH-lah	Question.	Kiswahili	
SUM	SOOM	Ask	Tanzania (Nyakyusa)	
SUMA	SOO-mah	Ask.	Tanzania (Nyakyusa)	F
ULIZA	oo-LEE-zah	To question.	Kiswahili	

Quiet and Stillness

Silence does not bring harm. —Africa

Name	Pronunciation	Meaning	Origin	Gender
ADOLE	ah-DOH-leh	Silence is golden.	Nigeria (Ishan)	

Name	Pronunciation	Meaning	Origin	Gender
AFULU	ah-FOO-loo	Quietness.	Nigeria (Ishan)	
BIIKARA	bee-kah-rah	Be quiet; refrain from uttering what one hears.	Uganda (Nyoro)	M
CHIN YERERE	cheen-yeh-REH-reh	A very quiet person.	Azania (Xhosa)	
CWAKA	chwah-KAH	The quiet one.	Azania	M
DZANGA	d-ZAHN-gah	Reserved, shy, silent.	Southern Africa (Tsonga)	
KAFI	kah-fee	Quiet, serene.	Central Africa	F
MBITA	m-BEE-tah	Quiet.	North Africa (Arabic)	
MUKIRI	MOO-kee-ree	Silent one.	Kenya (Agikuyu)	M
MUNYARARI	moon-yah-RAH-ree	A quiet person.	Azania (Xhosa)	
MWENENI	MWEH-NEH-nee	Be quiet!	Namibia (Ovambo)	
NONGONA	nohn-goh-nah	To whisper.	Kiswahili	
NYAMAA	nah-yee-ah-mah-ah	To be quiet.	Kiswahili	
RUJINDIRI	roo-jeen-dee-ree	The one who does not talk.	Rwanda, Burundi, DRC (Huti, Tutsi, Twa)	M
SIATON TOLA	see-yah-tohn-toh-lah	Who is generally quiet.	Zambia, Zimbabwe (Tonga)	M
SIKHU LUMA	see-koo-loo-mah	The one who does not speak.	Azania (Xhosa)	M
SIRISA	see-ree-sah	Cause to be quiet.	Uganda (Ganda)	F
THULANI	too-lah-nee	Be silent (given to a child whose arrival betrays barrenness and silences the enemy).	Azania (Xhosa)	F
TULI	TOO-lee	Quiet.	Kiswahili	

Name	Pronunciation	Meaning	Origin	Gender
ZOLA	ZOH-lah	Humble, quiet.	Azania (Zulu)	
ZOLILE	zoh-lee-leh	The quiet one.	Azania (Zulu)	

Rain, Thunder, and Lightning

One day of rain far surpasses a whole year of drought. —Malawi

Name	Pronunciation	Meaning	Origin	Gender
ARAALI	ah-raah-lee	Strength of thunder.	Uganda (Nyoro, Toro)	M
AYEOLA	ah-yeh-oh-la	Rainbow.	West Africa	F
BANI	BAH-nee	Flash of lightning.	Azania (Zulu)	
BEJIDE	beh-JEE-deh	Child born during rainy time.	Nigeria (Yoruba)	F
BUKUBA	boo-KOO-bah	Thunder.	Rwanda, Burundi (Kinyarwanda, Kirundi)	M
DAJAN	DAH-jahn	Dark sky during a heavy rain.	Kenya, Tanzania (Kiswahili)	M
DUDUMA	doo-DOO-mah	Thunder, rumble.	Azania (Xhosa)	
DUMA	DOO-mah	Lightning, thunder.	Azania (Zulu)	
DUTSWANE	doot-SWAH-neh	Hunt undertaken to bring rain.	Southern Africa (Tsonga)	
DZINDZA	dZEEND-zah	Thunder.	Southern Africa (Tsonga)	
GOWAN	GOH-wohn	Rainmaker.	Nigeria (Tiv)	M
LAZON GOMA	lah-ZOHN-goh-mah	Thunder.	Azania (Xhosa)	M
MANDONDO	mah-DOHN-doh	Rain drops.	Malawi (Ngoni)	
MAPULA	mah-POO-lah	Child born during the rains.	Azania (Sotho)	
MTUNZI	m-TOON-zee	This one is thunderous.	Azania	
MUFUMBI	moo-foom-bee	Continuous rain.	Zambia (Bemba)	

Name	Pronunciation	Meaning	Origin	Gender
MUSOKE	moo-soh-keh	One born while a rainbow is in the sky.	Uganda (Rukonjo)	M
NAFULA	nah-foo-LAH	Born during rainy season.	Uganda (Ganda, Abaluhya)	F
NASHIBU	nah-shee-boo	The mother associated with rainbow.	DRC (Rega)	F
NKUBA	n-koo-bah	Rainfall.	Uganda (Ganda)	M
NOMAZULU	noh-mah-ZOO-loo	A girl born during heavy rainfall.	East Africa	F
NONDU DUMO	non-doo-doo-moh	Mother of thunder.	Azania (Xhosa)	F
NYAMBURA	NYAH-boo-rah	Born of the rain.	Kenya (Agikuyu)	F
NYESHA	nah-yee-shah	To rain.	Kiswahili	
OSUMARE	oh-soo-MAH-reh	Rainbow.	Nigeria (Yoruba)	
PULA	POO-lah	Rain.	Azania (North Sotho)	
RAADI	rah-AH-dee	Thunder.	Kiswahili	
RAPULA	rah-POO-lah	Father of soft rain.	Azania (North Sotho)	
ROBLAI	rohb-lah-ee	The one who brings rain.	Somalia	F
ROBLE	ROHB-leh	Rain maker; one who brings the rains.	Somalia	M
SHANGO	SHAHN-goh	God of thunder.	Nigeria (Yoruba)	
UBONGO	oo-BOHN-goh	Rain.	Kiswahili	
UMEME	oo-MEH-meh	Lightning.	Kiswahili	
VULA	VOO-lah	Rain.	Azania (Zulu)	
YEBSIA	yehb-see-ah	Lightning.	Cameroon (Mubako)	F

Reciprocity

If someone sweats for you, you change his shirt. —Haiti

Name	Pronunciation	Meaning	Origin	Gender
ADANELE	ah-dah-NEH-leh	We are giving them their dues.	Nigeria (Ishan)	
DEDELANA	deh-deh-LAH-nah	Make way for each other.	Azania (Xhosa)	
GUSONGA	goo-SOHN-gah	A bad turn received for a good one done.	Cameroon (Mubako)	M
ROTIMI	roh-TEE-mee	My turn to be long.	Nigeria	

Regret, Guilt, and Shame

Doing one's best drives away regret. —Madagascar

Name	Pronunciation	Meaning	Origin	Gender
DANISO	DAH-nee-soh	He shames the enemy.	Azania (Xhosa)	M
ICALA	ee-KAH-lah	Guilt.	Azania (Zulu)	
JUTA	joo-TAH	To regret.	East Africa (Kiswahili)	M
MAJUTO	mah-JOO-toh	Regret.	Kiswahili	M
MASWABI	mah-swah-bee	Regret.	Azania (Sotho)	M
MORO	MOH-roh	Shameless.	Mali	
SEMMAH	SEHM-mah	She is feeling guilty.	Cameroon (Mubako)	F
UZOYA	oo-ZOH-yah	He came to remove my shame.	Nigeria (Ishan)	
ZIBAKOLE	zee-bah-KOH-leh	Shame will catch up with them.	Zambia (Tumbuka)	F

Remembering and Forgetting

To forget is the same as to throw away. —Africa

Name	Pronunciation	Meaning	Origin	Gender
AHANENE	ah-hah-NEH-neh	If you keep thinking of the past you will be a do-nothing.	Nigeria (Ishan)	
AKHARIA	ah-kah-REE-ah	If you think of the past, you will make mistakes.	Nigeria (Ishan)	
ALINJI JUKIRA	ah-lehn-jee-joo-kee-rah	God will remember me.	Uganda (Ganda)	F
ANENE	ah-NEH-neh	Thinking of the past.	Nigeria (Ishan)	
ATALYEBA	ah-tahl-yeh-bah	The one who will never be forgotten.	Uganda (Ganda, Nyoro)	
AYELE	ah-YEH-leh	That which one will always think about.	Nigeria (Ishan)	
AYELEA	ah-yeh-LEH-ah	Forgetting the past is the only solution.	Nigeria (Ishan)	
BEEBWA	beh-eh-bwah	They forget.	Uganda (Ganda, Kiga, Nyankore)	
CHETA	CHEH-tah	Always remember.	Nigeria	
CHETACHI	cheh-TAH-chee	Always remember God.	Nigeria	
IRIA	ee-REE-ah	I will not think of the past.	Nigeria (Ishan)	
IYERE	ee-YEH-reh	I will always remember the past with this child.	Nigeria (Ishan)	
KANENE	kah-NEH-neh	I have been reminded.	Azania (Xhosa)	M
KIBOBGA	kee-BOHB-gah	I hardly forget what I hear.	Cameroon (Mubako)	M
KIRABIRA	kee-raah-bee-rah	He forgets.	Rwanda, Burundi, DRC (Huti, Tutsi, Twa)	M
KOOFREY	KOH-free	Don't forget me.	Nigeria (Efik)	M
KUFERE	koo-FEH-reh	Never forget.	West Africa	
KUMBUFU	KOOM-boo-foo	Person with excellent memory.	East Africa (Kiswahili)	M

Name	Pronunciation	Meaning	Origin	Gender
KUMBUKA	KOOM-boo-kah	Person with excellent memory.	East Africa (Kiswahili)	M
SEMIA	seh-MEE-ah	I do remember, but it is painful.	Cameroon (Mubako)	F
TAYEBWA	tah-yeh-bwah	God never forgets.	Uganda (Runyankore)	M
TEBALO	teh-BAH-loh	Forget.	Azania (North Sotho)	
TOMORI	TOH-moh-ree	I nursed a child once.	Nigeria (Yoruba)	F
YEVADLA	yeh-VAHD-lah	She has forgotten me.	Cameroon (Mubako)	F

Resolution and Reconciliation

It is better to build bridges than walls. —Kiswahili

Name	Pronunciation	Meaning	Origin	Gender
BIDLOLA	beed-LOH-lah	The child has forced the settlement of the dispute between the parents.	Cameroon (Mubako)	F
BISANGHA	bee-sahn-gah	The issue is resolved.	Cameroon (Mubako)	
BUYISANA	boo-yee-SAH-nah	Reconciled.	Azania (Zulu)	
CAZULULA	kah-zoo-LOO-lah	The untangler.	Azania	M
CENGANI	tseng-AAH-nee	Negotiate.	Azania	M
DALALI	DAH-lah-lee	Broker.	East Africa (Kiswahili)	F
GARAI	GAH-rah-ee	Be settled.	Zimbabwe (Shona)	M
ISILAHI	EE-see-lah-hee	Reconciliation.	East Africa (Kiswahili)	M
IYANGURA	ee-yahn-GOO-rah	To arbitrate.	Zambia (Nyanja)	
LAMLA	LAHM-lah	The mediator.	Azania	M
LAMLILE	lahm-LEE-leh	The mediator.	Azania	F
LUMULA	loo-MOO-lah	The mediator.	Azania	M

Name	Pronunciation	Meaning	Origin	Gender
LUNGI	LOON-gee	One who makes amends.	Azania	F
MASILAHI	MAH-see-lah-hee	Reconciliation.	Kenya, Tanzania	
MUTUA	MOH-too-ah	Reconciles differences.	Kenya (Agikuyu)	M
PATANISHA	pah-tah-NEE-shah	Reconciliation.	Kenya, Tanzania	
SAMIRA	sah-MEE-rah	Reconciler.	Kiswahili	F
SULUHISHA	soo-loo-HEE-shah	To reconcile.	Kiswahili	
YAZALALA	yah-zah-LAH-lah	One who smoothes out, makes even.	Azania (Xhosa)	

Respect, Honor, and Glory

If the elders leave you a legacy of dignified language, you do not abandon it and speak childish language. —*Ghana*

Name	Pronunciation	Meaning	Origin	Gender
AARINOLA	ah-REE-noh-lah	The center of honor.	Nigeria (Yoruba)	
ADAOBI	ah-dah-OH-bee	Honorable daughter.	Nigeria (Igbo)	F
ADEOLA	ah-deh-oh-lah	The crown has honor.	Nigeria (Yoruba)	F
ADETO-KUNBO	ah-DEH-toh-koon-boh	Honor came from over the seas.	Nigeria (Yoruba)	M
ADHINI	ahd-HEE-nee	To honor.	Kiswahili	
ANABE	ah-NAH-bee	One held in honor.	Southern Africa (Tsonga)	
AZISA	ah-ZEE-sah	Honor, esteem, pride.	Kiswahili	
AZUKA	ah-ZOO-kah	Our past glory.	Nigeria	
BEKA	BEH-kah	Honor, respect.	Azania (Xhosa)	
BOLADE	BOH-lah-deh	Honor arrives.	Nigeria (Yoruba)	F
CHAVEKA	chah-VEH-kah	To be honored, feared.	Southern Africa (Tsonga)	
DUMISANI	doo-mee-SAH-nee	One to be honored.	Azania	M

Name	Pronunciation	Meaning	Origin	Gender
DUMISILE	doo-mee-SEE-leh	One to be honored.	Azania	F
DZEHA	dZEH-ha	The one who will be sent to buy the wine (libation).	Ghana	
DZUNISA	dhhZOO-NEE-sah	Praise, glory.	Southern Africa (Tsonga)	
FOLA	FOH-lah	Glory and honor arrive.	Nigeria (Yoruba)	
FOLAMI	FOH-lah-mee	Respect and honor me; breath with honor.	Nigeria (Yoruba)	
HADHI	HAH-dee	Respect, honor.	East Africa (Kiswahili)	F
HALA	HAH-lah	Glorious	East Africa (Kiswahili)	F
HESHIMA	heh-SHEE-mah	Highly esteemed.	Kenya, Tanzania	
HESHIMU	heh-SHEE-moo	Honor, respect.	Kenya, Tanzania	
HISHIMA	hee-SHEE-mah	Honor.	Kiswahili	
HLONIPHILE	hlohn-nee-pee-leh	She has shown respect.	Azania (Zulu)	F
IBAORIMI	ee-bah-oh-REE-mee	I respect the spirit of God within me.	Nigeria (Yoruba)	
JAJA	JAH-jah	Honored; he is honored.	Nigeria (Igbo)	M
JALI	JAH-lee	Respect, honor.	Kenya, Tanzania	
KARAMA	kah-RAH-mah	Honor, respect, esteem.	Kenya, Tanzania	
KULIYAA	koo-lee-yaah	To honor.	Gambia (Mandinka)	
MBEKO	MMBEH-koh	Respect.	Azania (Xhosa)	M
MKEGANI	m-keh-GAH-nee	Child of disrespectful wife.	Tanzania (Zaramo)	F
NEMSI	NEHM-see	Of good reputation, respectable.	East Africa (Kiswahili)	M
NJEMILE	n-jeh-MEE-leh	Upstanding.	Malawi	
NOZUKO	noh-ZOO-koh	Mother of glory.	Azania (Xhosa)	F
NYEMYA	NYEH-meh-yah	Respect, self-esteem.	East Africa (Kiswahili)	F
OLAFEMI	oh-lah-FEH-mee	Honor, or wealth, favors me.	West Africa	

Name	Pronunciation	Meaning	Origin	Gender
OLANIYAN	oh-lah-nee-yahn	Honor surrounds me.	Nigeria	
OMORUYI	oh-moh-ROO-yee	A child lifted on high or respected.	Nigeria (Edo)	M
OTUTO	oh-TOO-toh	Glory.	Nigeria (Igbo)	
RAHIDA	rah-HEE-dah	Honorable, moral.	West Africa	
SHARIFU	shah-REE-foo	Honorable, noble.	Kenya, Tanzania	
SRODA	SROH-doo	Respect.	Ghana	F
SULA	SOO-lah	Disrespectful; to forget about a wrong that has been committed.	Zambia (Bemba)	
TUKUKA	too-KOO-kah	Be worthy of glory.	Kiswahili	
UTUKUFU	oo-too-KOO-foo	Glory.	Kiswahili	
UYI	OO-yee	Respect of God.	Nigeria (Edo)	M
UYIOSA	oo-yee-OH-sah	Respect of God.	Nigeria (Edo)	M
UZUKO	oo-ZOO-koh	Glory.	Azania	
YOBOKA	yoh-BOH-kah	Respect authority.	Rwanda, Burundi (Kinyarwanda, Kirundi)	
ZUKO	ZOO-koh	Glory.	Azania (Xhosa)	M

Responsibility and Self-Sufficiency

A child who is carried on the back
will not know how far the journey is. —*Nigeria*

Name	Pronunciation	Meaning	Origin	Gender
ATEDBOYIH	ah-teed-boh-yee	It is left to him.	Cameroon (Mungaka)	F
DARAKA	dah-RAH-kah	Responsibility.	Kiswahili	
EMA	eh-mah	Stand up and prepare to walk.	Azania (Sotho)	

Name	Pronunciation	Meaning	Origin	Gender
FARRAH	FAHR-rah	One who carries the burden.	North Africa (Arabic)	
FATIMA	fah-TEE-mah	Weaned.	North Africa	F
JILELE	jee-LEH-lee	Be self-reliant.	Zambia (Tumbuka)	M
KAJILELE	kah-jee-LEH-leh	Go and look after yourself; be self-reliant.	Zambia (Tumbuka)	M
KANAIFU	KAH-nah-ee-foo	Self-sufficient person.	Kenya, Tanzania (Kiswahili)	M
MADARAKA	mah-dah-RAH-kah	Responsibility.	Kiswahili	
NNAJIOKE	n-nah-jee-OH-keh	Father holds responsibility.	Nigeria (Igbo)	M
NOBAKHE	noh-BAHK-keh	She takes care of her own.	Azania (Xhosa)	F
NONZENSELE	nohn-zehn-seh-leh	She will do it herself.	Azania (Nguni)	F
NYATANYI	n-yah-tahn-yee	The one who finds his way.	Rwanda, Burundi (Kinyarwanda, Kirundi)	M
OGENE	oh-geh-neh	Call to duty.	Nigeria (Igbo)	F
SENDYOWA	sseh-ehn-djoh-wah	I have a duty.	Uganda (Ganda)	M
ZENZELE	ZEHN-zeh-leh	Do it yourself.	Azania (Xhosa)	M

Reward

Run as hard as a wild beast if you will, but you won't get any reward greater than that destined for you. —Egypt

Name	Pronunciation	Meaning	Origin	Gender
AJABE	ah-jah-beh	One who carries off the prize after a contest.	West Africa	M
AKAMA FULA	ah-kah-mah-FOO-lah	May my work be rewarded.	Nigeria (Yoruba)	M
AMBO-NISYE	am-boh-NEES-yeh	God has rewarded me.	Tanzania (Nyakyusa)	M
AWAD	AH-wahd	Prize, donor.	North Africa (Arabic)	
FAIDA	fah-EE-dah	Benefit; earnings; gain.	North Africa (Arabic)	F

Name	Pronunciation	Meaning	Origin	Gender
IJARA	ee-JAH-rah	The reward.	Kiswahili	
KITUNZI	kee-TOON-zee	Reward.	Kiswahili	M
MALINGE	mah-LING-geh	He is a reward of our efforts; our efforts have been rewarded.	Azania (Xhosa)	M
NAYLA	nay-lah	To gain, benefit.	Azania (Zulu)	
NOM-BUYEKEZO	nohm-BOO-yeh-keh-zoh	She is our reward.	Azania (Xhosa)	F
NZUZO	n-ZOO-zoh	One who is a benefit.	Azania (Xhosa)	M
THAWABU	tah-WAH-boo	Reward.	Kiswahili	
TUNUKIA	too-noo-KEE-ah	Make a present to.	Kiswahili	
TUZA	TOO-zah	To reward.	Kiswahili	
TUZO	TOO-zoh	A prize; present.	Kiswahili	
UMULISA	oo-moo-LEE-sah	Gain.	Rwanda, Burundi (Kinyarwanda, Kirundi)	F
ZUZA	ZOO-zah	Profit or reward.	Azania (Xhosa)	

Righteousness

Better to do what is right than do big things. —Gambia

Name	Pronunciation	Meaning	Origin	Gender
ADIGUN	ah-dee-GOON	Righteous.	Nigeria (Yoruba)	M
ADIO	ah-DEE-oh	Righteous.	Nigeria	M
ADJO	ah-djoh	Be righteous.	Nigeria (Yoruba)	M
HER KHUTI	HEHR-KOO-tee	I uphold righteousness.	Egypt/Khamit	
LUNGA	LOON-gah	The righteous man.	Azania (Xhosa)	M
LUNGISA	LOON-GEE-sah	The righteous one.	Azania (Xhosa)	M
SHAWKI	SHAH-oo-kee	Yearning for right conduct.	North Africa (Arabic)	M

Name	Pronunciation	Meaning	Origin	Gender
TAKIYAH	tah-KEE-yah	Righteous.	North Africa (Arabic)	
UKULUNGA	oo-koo-LOON-gah	Righteous.	Zimbabwe	
YAMINAH	yah-MEE-nah	Right and proper.	North Africa (Arabic)	F

Royalty and Nobility

When a king has good counselors, his reign is peaceful. —*Ghana*

Name	Pronunciation	Meaning	Origin	Gender
ABIADE	ah-bee-ah-DEH	Born of royal parents.	Nigeria (Yoruba)	M
ABUBAKAR	ah-BOO-bah-kahr	Noble.	East Africa (Kiswahili)	M
ADAEZE	ah-dah-EH-ZEH	Princess, king's daughter.	Nigeria (Igbo)	F
ADE	ah-DEH	Royal.	Nigeria (Yoruba)	
ADEAGBO	ah-DEH-ah-boh	He brings royal honor.	Nigeria (Yoruba)	M
ADEBAMGBE	ah-DEH-bam-beh	Royalty dwells with me.	Nigeria (Yoruba)	M
ADEBOMI	ah-deh-boh-MEE	Crown covered my nakedness.	Nigeria (Yoruba)	F
ADEDEJI	ah-deh-DEH-jee	Second to the king.	Nigeria	
ADEDEWE	ah-DEH-deh-weh	The crown is shattered.	Nigeria (Yoruba)	F
ADEDOJA	ah-DEH-doh-jah	The crown becomes a thing of worth.	Nigeria (Yoruba)	F
ADEIFE	ah-deh-EE-feh	The king or crown is loved.	Nigeria	
ADEJOLA	ah-DEH-joh-lah	The crown feeds on honors.	Nigeria (Yoruba)	M
ADELAJA	ah-DEH-lah-jah	The crown settles a quarrel.	Nigeria (Yoruba)	
ADELEKE	ah-DEH-leh-keh	The crown achieves happiness.	Nigeria (Yoruba)	F
ADENIYI	ah-deh-NEE-yee	This is the king or crown.	Nigeria	

Name	Pronunciation	Meaning	Origin	Gender
ADESIMBO	ah-deh-seem-boh	Noble birth.	Nigeria (Yoruba)	F
ADEYEMI	ah-deh-YEHM-mee	Fit to be king.	Nigeria	
ADEYEMO	ah-deh-YEHM-moh	This child will be king.	Nigeria	M
AIDA	ah-ee-dah	Princess.	Ethiopia	F
ALABO	ah-LAH-boh	King.	Nigeria	
ALAYE	ah-LAH-yeh	Kingly, like a king.	Nigeria	
ALIA	ah-LEE-ah	Noble.	North Africa (Arabic)	F
AMEER	AH-MEER	Monarch, prince.	North Africa (Arabic)	M
AMINATA	ah-mee-nah-tah	The princess.	West Africa	F
AMIR	AH-MEER	Leader, prince.	North Africa (Arabic)	
AMIRA	ah-MEER-ah	Princess.	Kiswahili	F
AMIRI	ah-MEER-ree	Prince.	Kiswahili	
ASESIMBA	ah-seh-SEEM-bah	Born noble.	Kiswahili	F
AYINLA	ah-YEEN-lah	Praise the king or crown.	Nigeria	
BADA	bah-dah	Knight.	Nigeria (Yoruba)	M
CHINGANJI	cheen-GAHN-jee	Majesty.	Azania	F
DAMBA	DAHM-bah	King of the world.	Angola	
ENOBA KHARE	eh-noh-bah-KAH-reh	The king's word.	Benin	M
ENZI	EHN-zee	Majesty sovereign, power.	Kiswahili	
EZE	EH-zeh	King.	West Africa	M
EZEOHA	eh-zeh-OH-ah	The people's king.	Nigeria (Igbo)	M
FARI	FAH-ree	The queen.	Gambia (Wolof)	F
GABELLA	gah-behl-lah	The kingship is ended, you have disrespected constituted authority.	Cameroon (Mubako)	M
JALAL	JAH-lahl	Majesty.	North Africa (Arabic)	M

Name	Pronunciation	Meaning	Origin	Gender
JALALA	jah-LAH-lah	Majesty.	North Africa (Arabic)	F
JIBADE	jee-bah-DEH	Born close to royalty.	Nigeria (Yoruba)	M
KABAILA	kah-bah-EE-lah	Person of high social status.	Zambia	
KAMIKAZI	kah-mee-kaah-zee	Queen.	Rwanda, Burundi, DRC (Huti, Tutsi, Twa)	F
KHARI	KAH-ree	Kingly.	West Africa	M
KIBIBI	kee-BEE-bee	Princess; little girl.	Kenya, Tanzania	F
KONATA	koh-nah-tah	Nobleman; man of high station.	West Africa	M
KWINI	KWEE-nee	Queen.	Kiswahili	
MALIA	MAH-lee-ah	Queen.	East Africa (Kiswahili)	F
MALIAKA	mah-LEE-ah-kah	Queen.	Kiswahili	F
MALIK	MAH-leek	King; master; he who owns.	North Africa (Arabic)	M
MALIKA	MAH-lee-kah	Queen.	North Africa (Arabic)	F
MALKIA	mahl-KEE-ah	Queen.	Kiswahili	
MENGESHA	mehn-BEH-shah	Kingdom.	Ethiopia	M
MOROWA	moh-ROH-wah	Queen.	Ghana (Akan)	F
MWINYI	MWEEN-yee	King.	Kiswahili	M
NEGASI	neh-GAH-see	Royalty.	Ethiopia	M
NJINGA	n-JEHN-gah	Queen.	Azania	F
NKOM	n-KOHM	Title, a noble.	Cameroon (Mungaka)	M
NKO SAZANA	n-koh-sah-ZAH-nah	Princess.	Azania (Xhosa)	F
NSILO	n-see-loh	Fortunate prince.	Central Africa	M
NWEZE	n-weh-zeh	Royal child.	Nigeria	
NYAGASSA	n-yah-gahs-sah	I have mixed the kingship.	Cameroon (Mubako)	F

Name	Pronunciation	Meaning	Origin	Gender
OBAFEMI	oh-bah-FEH-mee	The king likes me.	Nigeria (Yoruba)	M
OBATAIYE	oh-bah-tah-ee-yeh	King of the world.	Nigeria (Yoruba)	M
OBENEBA	oh-beh-neh-bah	Child of a king.	Ghana (Akan)	
OMOREDE	oh-moh-REH-deh	Prince.	Benin	M
ONYEKAN	ohn-yeh-kahn	My turn to be king.	Nigeria	
ORIAKU	oh-ree-ah-koo	Princess.	Nigeria (Igbo)	F
OSEI	oh-seh-ee	Noble.	Ghana (Fantei)	M
RWASIBO	rwah-SEE-boh	Elite.	Rwanda, Burundi (Kinyarwanda, Kirundi)	
SERWA	sehr-WAH	Noble woman.	West Africa (Ewe)	F
SHAH	SHAH	King, emperor.	North Africa (Arabic)	M
SURAYYA	suhr-rah-yah	Noble.	Kiswahili	
TAJI	TAH-jee	Crown.	Kiswahili	
THEMA	TAY-mah	Queen.	Central Africa	F
TITA	tee-tah	Prince.	Cameroon (Mubako)	M
TOR	toor	King.	Nigeria (Tiv)	M
TORKWASE	TOHR-kwah-seh	Queen.	Nigeria (Yoruba)	F
UMUNTU	oo-MOON-too	Aristocrat; intellectual; saint.	Azania	
URBI	OOR-bee	Princess.	Benin	F
ZALIKA	zah-LEE-kah	Well-born.	East Africa (Kiswahili)	F
ZAMBO	zahm-boh	Holy prince.	West Africa	M
ZAUDITU	zah-oo-DEE-too	She is the crown.	Ethiopia	F

Sacrifice

We will water the thorn for the sake of the rose. —*Africa*

Name	Pronunciation	Meaning	Origin	Gender
DABIKU	DAH-bee-koo	Sacrifice, offering.	East Africa (Kiswahili)	F
DHABIHU	dah-BEE-hoo	A sacrifice.	Kiswahili	
FADI	FAH-dee	Someone who sacrifices himself to save others.	North Africa (Arabic)	M
GEBRE	GEH-breh	An offering.	Ethiopia (Amharic)	M
KAFARA	KAH-fah-rah	Sacrifice.	Kenya, Tanzania (Kiswahili)	M
KAFELE	kah-FEH-leh	Worthy of sacrifice; worth dying for.	Malawi (Ngoni)	M
NAZAPA	nah-ZAH-pah	Of sacrifice	Central Africa	F
SADAKA	sah-DAH-kah	Offering, sacrifice.	Kenya, Tanzania	
SHAHIDA	shah-hee-DAH	Martyr.	East Africa (Kiswahili)	F
TAMBIKA	tahm-BEE-kah	Offering, sacrifice.	Kenya, Tanzania	

Sadness and Sorrow

Crying a lot does not give you peace of mind. —*Burundi*

Name	Pronunciation	Meaning	Origin	Gender
ALILE	ah-LEE-leh	She weeps.	Malawi (Yao)	F
ALILI	ah-LEE-lee	She who weeps.	Malawi (Yao)	F
APINY	ah-pee-ndjh	In despair.	Uganda (Langi)	F
ASYA	ah-syah	Born during time of grief.	East Africa (Kiswahili)	F
BULOO	BOO-loh	To be blue.	Gambia (Wolof)	
BUUMBA	BOOM-bah	Sorrow.	Zambia (Tonga)	
CHOZI	CHOH-zee	Tear (for those born before or after a funeral).	Zambia	F
DANILE	dah-NEE-leh	Sad.	Azania (Zulu)	
DIKELEDI	dee-KEH-leh-dee	Tears; child born during a time of sorrow.	Botswana, Azania (Tswana, Sotho)	F

Name	Pronunciation	Meaning	Origin	Gender
GALIRA	gah-lee-rah	Who cry; who mourn.	Uganda (Soga)	M
HUZUNISHA	hoo-zoo-NEE-shah	To grieve.	Kiswahili	
KAME	KAH-meh	Desolate.	Kenya, Tanzania (Kiswahili)	M
KANYIKE	kah-ndjh-ee-keh	That is sad.	Uganda (Ganda)	M
KASI	KAH-see	To cry.	Gambia (Mandinka)	
KHUZANI	koo-ZAH-nee	Mourn (family has been victim of frequent deaths).	Zambia (Tumbuka)	M
KOLIRAGA	koh-lee-RAH-gah	Weeping.	Southern Africa	F
KULIRAGA	koo-lee-RAH-gah	Weeping.	Malawi (Yao)	F
LIA	LEE-ah	To cry.	Kiswahili	F
LUL	luhl	To cry.	Sudan (Nuer)	M
MACHOZI	mah-CHOH-zee	Tears.	Africa	F
MAGANYA	mah-gah-ndjh-ah	Sadness.	Rwanda, Burundi, DRC (Huti, Tutsi, Twa)	M
MALLOMOLA	mahl-loh-moh-lah	Sorrow.	Botswana (Tswana)	
MARIASHA	mah-ree-AH-shah	Perfect one; bitter with sorrow.	Egypt/Khamit	F
MASOZI	mah-SOH-zee	Tears.	Azania	
MSIBA	M-SEE-bah	Born during calamity or mourning.	East Africa (Kiswahili)	F
MUHVALLA	moo-vahl-lah	You cannot get tired of grieving.	Cameroon (Mubako)	M
MUKAABYA	moo-kaah-bjah	One who causes them to weep or mourn.	Uganda (Ganda)	M
NAKIRIZE	nnah-tch-ee-ree-zeh	One that has wept.	Uganda (Ganda)	F
NGOLINGA	n-goh-LEENG-gah	Cry-baby; weeping.	Malawi (Yao)	M
OBUJUNE	oh-boo-JOO-neh	Sorrow.	Uganda (Nyoro)	

Name	Pronunciation	Meaning	Origin	Gender
ONYEMA	ohn-yeh-mah	Sorrow.	Nigeria (Yoruba)	
SAGHA	sah-gah	Do not weep over split milk.	Cameroon (Mubako)	F
SELLO	SEHL-loh	A child who cries a lot.	Azania (Sotho)	
WOLOLA	woh-LOH-lah	One who cries all the time.	Azania (Zulu)	

Salvation and Redemption

Devil tempt, but he no force. —Guyana

Name	Pronunciation	Meaning	Origin	Gender
AJUNA	ah-dzoo-nah	God saves.	Uganda (Kiga, Nyankore, Nyoro, Toro)	
CHIDEBE	chee-deh-beh	God saves.	Nigeria (Igbo)	F
HABIMAMA	hah-bee-MAH-nah	It is God who saves.	Rwanda	M
HLENGISWA	hlehn-gee-swah	The redeemed one.	Azania	F
HOLA	HOH-lah	Savior.	Ghana (Ewe)	F
IMOLA	ee-MOH-lah	Rescuer, to bring relief.	Lesotho (South Sotho)	
ISSA	ee-SAH	God is our salvation.	East Africa (Kiswahili)	M
KEHKUNA	keh-KOO-nah	Save the family.	Cameroon (Mubako)	M
KOMBOA	kohm-BOH-ah	Redeemed; redemption.	Kenya, Tanzania (Kiswahili)	
KOYELA	koh-YEH-lah	Save your life, a child born through difficulties.	Cameroon (Mubako)	M
KWOYILA	kwoh-YEE-lah	Save your life, a child born through difficulties.	Cameroon (Mubako)	F
KYA LAMBOKA	kee-ah-lam-BOH-kah	God save me.	Tanzania (Nyakyusa)	F
MASIYA	mah-SEE-yah	Messiah; savior.	Kenya, Tanzania	
MSINDI	m-SEEN-dee	Be saved!	Azania	M

Name	Pronunciation	Meaning	Origin	Gender
MUSA BINGO	moo-sah-been-goh	Savior.	Uganda (Lukonjo)	M
NAJYA	NAH-jyah	Saved.	East Africa (Kiswahili)	F
NEKULILO	neh-koo-LEE-loh	Redeeming, redemption.	Namibia (Ovambo)	
NUILLA	noo-EEL-lah	Try to save your life.	Cameroon (Mubako)	M
NUYILLA	noo-yeel-lah	Save yourself.	Cameroon (Mubako)	M
OKOKA	oh-KOH-kah	To be saved.	Kiswahili	
OLUGBALA	oh-LOO-bah-lah	Savior of the people.	Nigeria (Yoruba)	M
ONGA	OHN-gah	To be saved.	Azania (Zulu)	
OSEGYEFO	oh-sehg-yeh-foh	Savior of the people.	West Africa	
SAILA	sah-EE-lah	Try to save yourself.	Cameroon (Mubako)	M
SINDA	SEEN-dah	Be saved!	Azania	F
SINDILE	seen-DEH-leh	He has been saved.	Azania (Xhosa)	M
SINDISO	seen-DEE-soh	Salvation.	Azania (Xhosa)	M
SINDISWA	sin-DEE-swah	She is being saved.	Azania (Xhosa)	F
WOKOFU	woh-KOH-foo	Salvation, deliverance.	Kiswahili	
YOMI	YOH-mee	Save me.	Nigeria	M
ZOONDU	zoh-OHN-doo	Save life.	Nigeria (Igbo)	

Satisfaction and Contentment

If you cannot get what you like,
you will have to like what you get. —Somalia

Name	Pronunciation	Meaning	Origin	Gender
ANELA	ah-neh-lah	Be satisfied.	Azania (Zulu)	
ANELE	AH-NEH-leh	We are satisfied, enough children.	Azania	M

Name	Pronunciation	Meaning	Origin	Gender
ANELISA	ah-neh-LEE-sah	To satisfy.	Azania (Zulu)	
CHIN WEMWE	cheen-WEHM-weh	Contentment, happiness.	Zambia (Bemba)	
DEKA	DEH-kah	One who pleases; satisfies.	Somalia	
DELANI	dah-LAH-nee	I am content now.	Azania (Xhosa)	M
DIKIWE	dee-KEE-weh	More than satisfied.	West Africa	
DINIZULU	dee-nee-ZOO-loo	The one who satisfies the Zulus.	Azania (Zulu)	
DZELIWE	dZEH-LEE-weh	We are satisfied.	Swaziland	
EJIYA	eh-JEE-yah	I am satisfied with any position in life.	Nigeria (Ishan)	
ENIYA	eh-NEE-yah	My position in life is not bad.	Nigeria (Ishan)	
ESUTHA	eh-SOO-tah	Satisfied with food.	Azania (Zulu)	
FIKILIZA	fee-kee-LEE-zah	To fulfill.	Kiswahili	
JAZA	JAH-zah	To fill.	Kiswahili	F
KANAI	KAH-nah-ee	Contentment; self-satisfied, content.	East Africa (Kiswahili)	F
KHOLISILE	kohl-lee-SEE-leh	The reason to be satisfied.	Azania	M
KHOLISWA	KOH-lee-swah	She brings me satisfaction.	Azania (Xhosa)	F
KIDHI	kee-DEE	Satisfaction.	Kenya, Tanzania (Kiswahili)	F
KINAI	kee-NAH-ee	Satisfied.	Kiswahili	
KINAISHA	kee-nah-EE-shah	To satisfy.	Kiswahili	
KOSHI	KOH-shee	Satisfied, full.	West Africa (Hausa)	F
KUSHIBA	koo-SHEE-bah	To be satisfied.	Kiswahili	
MANELISI	MAH-neh-lee-see	One who brings satisfaction.	Azania (Xhosa)	M
MUKKUTO	mook-koo-toh	Feeling of satisfaction after eating.	Uganda (Ganda)	F

Name	Pronunciation	Meaning	Origin	Gender
MULU	MOO-loo	Fully satisfied.	Ethiopia	F
NAHSADLA	nahd-sah-lah	She befits me, exactly what I have been looking for.	Cameroon (Mubako)	F
NELISA	neh-LEE-sah	She satisfies us.	Azania (Xhosa)	F
NONELE	noh-NEH-leh	She represents all we have asked for.	Azania	F
NYETA	n-yeh-tah	Be hard to please.	Kiswahili	
OLUYEMI	oh-loo-YEH-mee	Fulfillment from God.	Nigeria (Yoruba)	M
RADIA	rah-DEE-ah	Satisfied.	North Africa (Arabic)	F
RIDHA	reed-hah	Contented.	Kiswahili	M
RIDHISHA	REE-dee-shah	Satisfaction.	Kenya, Tanzania (Kiswahili)	F
SANELE	sah-NEH-leh	We have enough.	Azania (Zulu)	M
SEMATTIRE	sseh-maht-tee-reh	Satisfied.	Uganda (Ganda)	M
SEMIRA	seh-MEER-ah	Fulfilled.	Eritrea, Ethiopia (Tigrinya)	F
SHIBE	SHEE-beh	Satisfaction.	Kenya, Tanzania	
SHTHISHA	shee-tee-shah	Very satisfied.	Kenya, Tanzania	
TEKELEA	teh-keh-LEH-ah	To be fulfilled.	Kiswahili	
TOSHA	TOH-shah	To satisfy.	Kiswahili	F
TOSHELEZA	toh-shah-leh-zah	Satisfaction.	East Africa (Kiswahili)	F
URADHI	oo-RAHD-hee	Satisfaction.	Kiswahili	
UTARA	oo-TAH-rah	Satisfaction.	Nigeria (Igbo)	F
ZANELE	zah-NEH-leh	We are satisfied with enough girls.	Azania (Zulu)	F

Searching

If a thing is lost, we start looking for it in the house. —Ghana

Name	Pronunciation	Meaning	Origin	Gender
BATH	bah-sth	To be lost.	Sudan (Nuer)	M
BATHO	Bah-toh	To be lost.	Sudan (Nuer)	M
BETA	BEH-tah	Little child prying.	Azania (Sotho)	
EBIDOU	eh-bee-DOH-oo	Search for what is good.	Nigeria	
FUNANI	foo-NAH-nee	What are we searching for?	Azania (Zulu)	
KASEYEEYE	kah-seh-yeh-eh-yeh	That drifts.	Uganda (Ganda)	M
KONGA	KOHN-gah	Look for, search!	Namibia (Ovambo)	
MACARIA	MAH-shah-ree-ah	Seeker.	Kenya (Agikuyu)	M
NALISANGA	nah-lee-saahn-gah	I found it.	Uganda (Ganda)	F
SAKILA	sah-KEE-lah	Look for, search for.	Zambia (Nsenga)	M
TALIB	TAH-leeb	Seeker.	North Africa (Arabic)	
ZUZIWE	ZOO-zee-weh	One who is sought after.	Azania (Xhosa)	F

Secrets and Concealment

The best way to keep a secret is not to tell it to anyone. —Kiswahili

Name	Pronunciation	Meaning	Origin	Gender
AITANO	ah-ee-TAH-noh	We cannot be revealing ourselves—let's keep our secrets.	Nigeria (Ishan)	
CHISISI	chee-SEE-see	A secret.	Malawi (Yao)	M
DAKUA	dah-KOO-ah	To let out a secret.	Kiswahili	
DANDA LAZA	dahn-dah-LAH-zah	Come into the open.	Azania (Zulu)	
EITARE	eh-ee-TAH-reh	What they had done should not be revealed.	Nigeria (Ishan)	
ESESE	eh-SEH-seh	In a secret place.	Azania (Zulu)	
EWANSIHA	eh-wahn-see-HAH	Secrets are not for sale.	Benin	M

Name	Pronunciation	Meaning	Origin	Gender
GAMSEH	gahm-seh	He is not refusing the secret.	Cameroon (Mubako)	M
ITELE	ee-TEH-leh	I won't say all I have been through.	Nigeria (Ishan)	
ITENA	ee-TEH-nah	I won't speak of these.	Nigeria (Ishan)	
ITENERE	ee-teh-NEH-reh	I won't speak of recent happenings.	Nigeria (Ishan)	
JALLA	jah-lah	The secret has been revealed.	Cameroon (Mubako)	F
KUMPA	KOOM-pah	Secret.	Gambia (Wolof)	
LEMA	leh-mah	Hide my fault.	Cameroon (Mubako)	F
MUA	moo-ah	Hidden.	Cameroon (Mubako)	M
MUKIIBI	moo-kee-bee	One who enters through back doors.	Uganda (Luganda)	M
NIKOKO	nee-KOH-koh	Secret.	West Africa (Yoruba)	
NJAMA	n-JAH-mah	Confidential discussion.	Kiswahili	
NYEMA	n-YEH-mah	I have begged, the secret has been leaked.	Cameroon (Mubako)	F
PEKETU	peh-KEH-too	To reveal a secret.	Azania (Zulu)	
SIRI	SEE-ree	Secret.	Kenya, Tanzania (Kiswahili)	
SITIRI	see-TEE-ree	To conceal.	Kiswahili	
ZIMELA	zee-MEH-lah	One who hides away.	Azania (Xhosa)	

Servitude

If your servants are afraid of you, they do not win victories for you. —Ghana

Name	Pronunciation	Meaning	Origin	Gender
ABDALLA	ahb-DAHL-lah	Servant of God.	East Africa (Kiswahili)	M
ABDUL	AHB-dool	Servant.	North Africa (Arabic)	M

Name	Pronunciation	Meaning	Origin	Gender
ANNU KHEMERA	ahn-noo-keh-meh-rah	One who finds beauty in serving.	Egypt/Khamit	
KASUMBA	kah-soom-bah	A servant.	Uganda (Luganda)	M
MENDI	MEHN-dee	Servant; one who serves the people.	Azania (Xhosa)	M
MENDISWA	MEHN-dee-swah	She will serve.	Azania	F
MUJA	moo-jah	Servant; slave.	Rwanda, Burundi, DRC (Huti, Tutsi, Twa)	M
NGINA	GHEH-nah	One who serves.	Kenya (Agikuyu)	F
NKONZO	n-KOHN-zoh	Service.	Azania	
RAKIRA	rah-KEER-ah	Servant of God.	Egypt/Khamit	F
SEMUDDU	sseh-mood-doo	Servant.	Uganda (Ganda)	M
TEREMESHA	TEH-reh-meh-shah	Always willing to serve others.	Kenya, Tanzania (Kiswahili)	M

Size and Proportion

Better little, than too little. —Burundi

Name	Pronunciation	Meaning	Origin	Gender
AKERELE	ah-KEH-REH-leh	One who, in spite of being small, is strong and tough.	Nigeria (Yoruba)	
ALONGE	ah-LOHN-geh	A tall, skinny boy.	Nigeria (Yoruba)	M
BABAVANA	bah-bah-VAH-nah	Tall, slender person.	Azania (Zulu)	
BUBU-LUNDU	boo-boo-LOON-doo	Fat child of the royal kraal.	Azania (Zulu)	
DOGO	DOH-goh	Little.	Kiswahili	
DOGO	DOH-goh	A tall person.	Nigeria (Hausa)	

Name	Pronunciation	Meaning	Origin	Gender
DONDSHIYA	dohn-SHEE-yah	Tall, muscular person.	Azania (Zulu)	
DUCHA	DOO-chah	Little.	East Africa (Kiswahili)	F
FISHA	FEE-shah	Short.	Azania (Zulu)	
FUPHI	FOO-phee	Short, squat.	Azania (Xhosa)	
FUPI	FOO-pee	Short.	Kiswahili	
GANTU	GAHN-too	Giant.	Uganda (Ganda)	
GHECHE	GEH-cheh	Small thing.	East Africa (Kiswahili)	F
GUNTU	GOON-too	Giant.	Uganda (Ganda)	
ISIGEBENGA	ee-see-geh-BEHN-gah	Giant.	Azania	
JITU	JEE-too	Giant.	Kenya, Tanzania (Kiswahili)	M
JITUJEUSI	JEE-too-jeh-oo-see	A Black giant.	East Africa (Kiswahili)	M
KABIBI	kah-bee-bee	Fat and beautiful child.	Uganda (Ganda)	
KALA	kah-lah	Tall.	West Africa	M
KANIINI	kah-NEE-nee	Small.	Zambia (Tonga)	
KATITO	kah-tee-toh	Little.	Angola (Ovimbundu)	M
KATOU	KAH-toh-oo	Small.	Uganda (Ganda)	F
KHATITI	kah-TEE-tee	Tiny, little.	Kenya	M
KHULU	KOO-loo	The huge one.	Azania	M
KHULUKAZI	koo-loo-KAH-zee	The huge one.	Azania	F
KUMBE LEMBE	koom-beh-LEHM-beh	Poor, thin child.	Angola (Ovimbundu)	
NLA	n-LAH	Big.	West Africa (Yoruba)	
NUSU	NOO-soo	Half.	Azania (Zulu)	
NYASORE	nyah-SOHR-eh	The thin one.	Kenya	M
OYA	OH-yah	A small handful.	Kiswahili	
SERIPA	seh-REE-pah	Half.	Azania (North Sotho)	

Name	Pronunciation	Meaning	Origin	Gender
TINA	TEE-nah	Baby who is smaller than normal, premature.	Zambia (Chewa)	F
UREFU	oo-REH-foo	To be tall, tallness.	Kiswahili	
ZIMUNGA	zee-MOON-gah	A very tall man.	Azania (Xhosa)	M

Slavery and Oppression

The house of the unjust oppressor is destroyed, though it should happen in distant times. —*Egypt*

Name	Pronunciation	Meaning	Origin	Gender
DONKO	DOHN-koh	Slave.	Ghana (Akan)	
LEMEZA	leh-MEH-zah	Oppress.	Kiswahili	
MJAKAZI	m-jah-KAH-zee	Female slave.	East Africa	F
ONEA	oh-NEE-ah	To oppress.	Kiswahili	
SHOKOA	shoh-KOH-ah	Forced labor.	Kiswahili	
SURIA	soo-REE-ah	Concubine.	Kiswahili	

Sleep and Idleness

To sleep is to change. —*Lesotho*

Name	Pronunciation	Meaning	Origin	Gender
CHILALA	chee-LAH-lah	Sleeping.	Zambia (Tonga)	
DANGALA	dahn-GAH-lah	Languid, listless.	Azania (Xhosa)	
DUNDUZELA	doon-doo-ZEH-lah	To lull to sleep.	Azania (Zulu)	
GUSINZIRA	goo-seen-ZEE-rah	To sleep.	Rwanda, Burundi (Kinyarwanda, Kirundi)	
KUBIKIRA	koo-bee-KEE-rah	To put a child to sleep by singing lullaby.	Rwanda, Burundi (Kinyarwanda, Kirundi)	

Name	Pronunciation	Meaning	Origin	Gender
LALA	LAH-lah	To sleep.	Zambia	F
LEPE	LEH-peh	Drowsiness.	Kiswahili	
UKALALA	oo-kah-LAH-lah	Sleep.	Azania (Zulu)	

Softness

To be hard does not mean to be hard as a stone,
and to be soft does not mean to be soft as water. —*Kenya*

Name	Pronunciation	Meaning	Origin	Gender
ANANA	ah-NAHN-nah	Soft.		
ATI	AH-tee	Cushion.	Egypt/Khamit	F
CHEFE	CHEH-feh	Softness, tenderness.	Azania (Zulu)	
CIMILA	tsee-MEE-lah	Soften.	Southern Africa (Tsonga)	
DE	DEH	Soft.	West Africa (Yoruba)	
JEEJEE	jeh-eh-JEH-eh	Softly.	West Africa (Yoruba)	
KANYEREZI	kah-ndjh-eh-reh-zee	Soft to touch; shiny.	Uganda (Ganda)	M
ONAJE	OH-nah-jee	The sensitive one.	Africa	M
ORORO	oh-ROH-oh	Tender, delicate.	Kiswahili	
RAKAYA	rah-KAH-yah	Soft.	Tunisia	F
TEKETEKE	teh-keh-TEH-keh	Soft; tender; yielding.	Kiswahili	
ZINYORO	zee-ndjh-oh-roh	The soft one.	Zimbabwe, Mozambique, Zambia (Shona)	

Solitude, Separation, and Loneliness

What you do on your own does not make you cry. —*Mozambique*

Name	Pronunciation	Meaning	Origin	Gender
ABINO-KENE	ah-bee-noh-kee-neh	She came by herself.	Uganda (Langi)	F
AKALI	ah-KAH-lee	Isolation; segregation.	Niger	F
AVA	AH-vah	To divide.	Southern Africa (Tsonga)	
AYEBALE	ah-yeh-bah-leh	But them; except them.	Uganda (Acholi)	
BAAYO	BAH-yoh	Orphan.	Gambia (Wolof)	
BALIWE	bah-LEE-weh	Rejected.	Azania (Zulu)	
BODWA	bohd-wah	Alone, only.	Azania (North Sotho)	
DINGA	DEHN-gah	To wander, to be without a home.	Azania (Zulu)	
DINGANI	deen-GAH-nee	To be alone.	Zambia (Tumbuka)	M
DUBIWE	doo-BEE-weh	Left alone (refers to the father not visiting the mother when pregnant).	Zambia (Ngoni)	F
DULANI	doo-LAH-nee	Cutting.	Malawi	M
DUNGA	DOON-gah	To fly away, scatter, disperse.	Azania (Xhosa)	M
DUNGU	DOON-goo	To fly away, scatter, disperse.	Azania (Xhosa)	F
ELANA	eh-LAHN-nah	To go somewhere for one another.	Southern Africa (Tsonga)	
FARAGHA	fah-RAH-ghah	Seclusion.	Kiswahili	
FARAKANA	fah-rah-KAH-nah	To be estranged.	Kiswahili	
GABBA	gah-bah	Separated.	Cameroon (Mubako)	M
KALIKEKA	kah-lee-KEH-kah	One who is born, or remains alone.	Zambia (Bemba)	
KALULANDA	kah-loo-LAHN-dah	To be alone; orphaned.	Zambia (Tumbuka)	M
KILEKEN	keel-eh-kehn	Orphan.	Kenya, Tanzania	M
KONGOKA	kohn-GOH-kah	To come apart.	Kiswahili	
KONTAR	KOHN-tar	Only child.	Ghana (Akan)	M
LWANDEKA	lwahn-DEH-kah	Lost all relatives, left alone.	Uganda (Mugwere)	M

Name	Pronunciation	Meaning	Origin	Gender
MALIWA	mah-LEE-wah	He who is rejected.	Zimbabwe (Ndebele)	M
MKIWA	m-KEE-wah	Orphaned child.	Kenya (Kiswahili)	F
MOJA	MOH-jah	One; single.	Kiswahili	
MONOSI	moh-NOH-see	Alone.	Azania (North Sotho)	
MONOSINOSI	moh-noh-see-noh-see	Alone; only.	Azania (North Sotho)	
MPWEKE	mPWEH-keh	Solitary person.	Kiswahili	
MULICHAJE	moo-lee-chah-jeh	To be alone; orphan.	Zambia (Chewa)	F
NDITSHENI	ndeet-sheh-nee	Leave me alone.	Kiswahili	
NGENDAN DUMWE	ngehn-dahn-doom-weh	I walk by myself.	Rwanda, Burundi (Kinyarwanda, Kirundi)	M
NOSI	NOH-see	Alone, only.	Azania (Nguni)	
NYOIKE	NYOH-ee-keh	Stands alone.	Kenya (Agikuyu)	M
PARAD ZANAI	pah-rah-zah-NAH-ee	Keep it aside.	Zimbabwe (Shona)	M
PEKEE	peh-KEH-eh	Alone.	Kiswahili	
SEMANOBE	sseh-mah-noh-beh	One divorced several times.	Uganda (Ganda)	M
SOMA GOLOZA	soh-mah-goh-loh-zah	One who sits solitary.	Azania (Xhosa)	M
TAWANYA	tah-wahn-yah	To scatter.	Kiswahili	
TIHMIA	tee-mee-ah	I have been put aside or pushed to the side.	Cameroon (Mubako)	F
UKIWA	oo-KEE-wah	Loneliness.	Kiswahili	
UMUMA RARUNGU	oo-moo-mah-rah-ROON-goo	The one who kills loneliness.	Rwanda, Burundi (Kinyarwanda, Kirundi)	
UPWEKE	oop-WEH-keh	Loneliness.	Kiswahili	
ZINDOGA	zeen-doh-gah	Lonely one.	Zimbabwe, Mozambique, Zambia (Shona)	
ZONDEKA	zohn-deh-kah	If only they would leave me alone.	Uganda (Kiga, Nyankore, Nyoro, Toro)	

Speed

A human being wants speed, but speed depends on God. —Togo

Name	Pronunciation	Meaning	Origin	Gender
AJIA	ah-jee-AH	Quick, fast.	Kenya, Tanzania (Kiswahili)	F
BALEKA	bah-LEH-kah	A fast runner.	Azania (Xhosa)	
CHAFULU MISA	chah-foo-loo-MEE-sah	Speed, swiftness.	Malawi (Ngoni)	M
DABAZO	dah-BAH-zoh	Rushing away, running off.	Azania (Xhosa)	
KATIBITA	kah-tee-bee-tah	Runner.	DRC (Rega)	M
LUBILO	loo-BEE-loh	Speed.	Zambia (Bemba)	
MBIRO	m-bee-roh	Speed.	Uganda (Ganda)	M
MOTABOGI	moh-tah-boh-gee	A fast runner.	Azania (North Sotho)	
NAMBIRO	nnaahm-bee-roh	Sprinter, good runner.	Uganda (Ganda, Soga)	F
NGOGA	n-GOH-gah	Speed.	Rwanda, Burundi (Kinyarwanda, Kirundi)	M
OSONDU	oh-sohn-doo	To run for one's life.	Nigeria (Igbo)	M
RUTEBUKA	roo-teh-BOO-kah	He who is always fast.	Rwanda, Burundi (Kinyarwanda, Kirundi)	M
SEMBIRO	ssehm-bee-roh	Swiftness; speed.	Uganda (Ganda)	M
SONGO-LOLO	sohn-goh-LOH-loh	The slow one.	Azania	

Strength

The strong don't need clubs. —Senegal

Name	Pronunciation	Meaning	Origin	Gender
ACHI	AH-chee	Strength.	Nigeria (Igbo)	F
AGU	ah-goo	Strong as tiger.	Nigeria (Igbo)	M

Name	Pronunciation	Meaning	Origin	Gender
AGUMA	ah-goo-mah	S/he is always firm.	Uganda (Ganda, Kiga, Nyankore)	
AGUNNA	ah-goon-nah	Strong boy.	Nigeria (Igbo)	
AIWO	ah-EE-woh	No one is strong enough to avoid death.	Nigeria (Ishan)	
AKATA	ah-KAH-tah	Strong headed.	Nigeria (Yoruba)	F
AKERELE	ah-keh-REH-leh	One who is strong in spite of being small.	Nigeria (Yoruba)	
AMSABA	ahm-SAH-bah	I submit to the sage for strength.	Egypt/Khamit	
ANKAMA	ahn-KAH-mah	Strength, firmness.	Namibia (Ovambo)	
ANTANKARA	ahn-tahn-KAH-rah	The people of the rock.	Madagascar	F
AZUKA	ah-ZOO-kah	Back is paramount; spine is important.	Nigeria (Igbo)	M
AZUR	AH-zoor	Strength.	North Africa (Arabic)	F
BALINDA	bah-LEEN-dah	Fortitude, patience, endurance.	Uganda (Rutooro)	M
BITITI	BEE-tee-tee	Strong lady.	East Africa (Kiswahili)	F
BOATEMA	bwoh-TEH-mah	She brings strength.	Ghana	F
BUTARE	boo-TAH-reh	Rock.	Rwanda, Burundi (Kinyarwanda, Kirundi)	M
CHACHA	chah-chah	Strong.	East Africa (Kiswahili)	M
CHANGA	chahn-gah	Iron-like.	Central Africa	M
CHEWA	CHEH-wah	A strong tribe.	Central, Southern Africa	F
CHIMWALA	cheem-WAH-lah	A stone.	Malawi (Yao)	F
DAGE	DAH-geh	Takes a firm stand.	Nigeria (Hausa)	M
DAUDA	dah-OO-dah	Strong.	Sierra Leone	
ETANA	eh-TAH-nah	Robust and strong child.	East Africa (Kiswahili)	F
GOBAND LOVU	goh-bahnd-loh-voh	One who bends elephants; strong one.	Azania	

Name	Pronunciation	Meaning	Origin	Gender
GUGA	GOO-gah	Strong and lasting.	Azania (Xhosa)	
HINDOWAH	heen-doh-wah	Tough man.	Sierra Leone	M
IKECHI	ee-KEH-chee	God's strength.	Nigeria (Igbo)	M
IKECHUKU	ee-keh-CHOO-koo	Power or might of God.	Nigeria	
IKEDI	ee-KEH-dee	God's strength.	Nigeria (Igbo)	M
IKE MUEFUNA	ee-keh-moo-FOO-nah	Let my strength remain; my strength is forever.	Nigeria (Igbo)	M
IKEZUORA	ee-keh-zoo-OH-rah	All strengths are not equal.	Nigeria (Igbo)	M
ILOLA	ee-LOH-lah	To become strong.	Lesotho (South Sotho)	
IMARA	ee-MAH-rah	Stamina, strength.	Kenya, Tanzania (Kiswahili)	
IMARIKA	ee-mah-REE-kah	Be steadfast.	Kenya, Tanzania	
IMARISHA	ee-mah-REE-shah	Make firm.	Kiswahili	
JABALI	JAH-bah-lee	Strong as a rock.	East Africa (Kiswahili)	M
JANGA	jahn-gah	You cannot shake me.	Cameroon (Mubako)	M
JASSIEM	jah-see-ehm	Strong.	North Africa	M
JAYEI	jah-YEH-ee	A woman strong like an elephant.	East Africa	F
JELANI	jeh-LAH-nee	Mighty one.	East Africa (Kiswahili)	M
JENGO	JEHN-goh	Building, strength.	East Africa (Kiswahili)	M
JINJA	JEEN-jah	Stones.	Uganda (Ganda)	
KANI	KAH-nee	Strength, energy.	Kenya, Tanzania (Kiswahili)	M
KATAGWA	kah-tah-gwah	That does not fall or collapse.	Uganda (Ganda)	M
KUTISHA	KOO-tee-shah	Tough, formidable.	Kenya, Tanzania (Kiswahili)	M
KWEHAN GANA	kweh-hahn-gah-nah	Endurance.	Uganda (Rukiga)	F
KWESI	KWEH-see	Overpowering strength.	West Africa	
LWAZI	lwaah-zee	Rock.	Uganda (Ganda)	M

Name	Pronunciation	Meaning	Origin	Gender
MAANYI	maah-ndjh-ee	Strength, power, energy.	Uganda (Ganda)	M
MALUNGO	mah-LOON-goh	Physical and spiritual strength.	Zambia (Chewa)	M
MUJAM BULA	moo-jahm-boo-lah	Strong and aggressive person, a rebel, a rogue.	Uganda (Ganda)	M
MULUGATA	moo-loo-GAH-tah	Strength; powerful.	Ethiopia	M
MWAMBA	MWAHM-bah	Strong.	Tanzania (Nyakyusa)	M
NALYAZI	nnah-ljaah-zee	A large rock.	Uganda (Ganda)	F
NEHANDA	neh-HAHN-dah	Hardiness.	Zimbabwe	F
NGANGO	ngaahn-goh	Strength.	Rwanda, Burundi, DRC (Huti, Tutsi, Twa)	M
NINI	NEE-nee	Stone.	West Africa	F
NKOLE	n-KOH-leh	Strong person.	Zambia (Bemba)	
NOMANDLA	noh-MAHD-lah	Tower of strength.	Azania (Xhosa)	F
NTSIKA	n-TSEE-kah	The pillar.	Azania (Xhosa)	M
OBATA	oh-BAH-tah	Your strength depends upon your struggles.	Nigeria (Ishan)	
OKOROBIA	oh-koh-roh-BEE-ah	Tough guy.	Nigeria	
ORJI	OR-jee	Mighty tree; firm and determined person; mahogany.	Nigeria (Igbo)	M
OTEKA	oh-tee-kah	Strong.	Uganda (Itetso)	M
RAI	RAH-ee	Strength, prudence.	Kiswahili	
RAZINA	rah-ZEE-nah	Strong.	Kiswahili	
RUBUYE	roo-BOO-yeh	Stone.	Rwanda, Burundi (Kinyarwanda, Kirundi)	M
RUNIHURA	roo-nee-HOO-rah	One who smashes to bits.	Rwanda	M
RUTA GARAMA	roo-tah-gah-RAH-mah	The one who doesn't lie down on the back.	Rwanda, Burundi (Kinyarwanda, Kirundi)	M

Name	Pronunciation	Meaning	Origin	Gender
RUTARE	roo-TAH-reh	Rock.	Rwanda, Burundi (Kinyarwanda, Kirundi)	M
TIPILIRE	tee-pee-lee-reh	To endure hardship.	Zambia (Chewa)	F
ZINZO	ZIN-zoh	Stability.	Azania	M
ZUBERI	zoo-BEH-ree	Strong.	East Africa (Kiswahili)	M

Struggle and Resistance

If you are not sleeping in a bed with someone,
you don't struggle for his half of the bed. —Ghana

Name	Pronunciation	Meaning	Origin	Gender
ADOMI	ah-DOH-mee	Life is a struggle.	Nigeria (Ishan)	
AJANI	ah-jah-NEE	Someone possessed through struggle.	Nigeria (Yoruba)	M
ASANI	ah-SAH-nee	Rebellious.	East Africa (Kiswahili)	M
BOFULA	boh-FOO-lah	Struggle.	Azania (North Sotho)	
DEMA	dee-mah	Immunity.	Cameroon (Mubako)	M
HALIFU	hah-LEE-foo	To rebel against.	Kiswahili	
IRAGI	ee-RAH-gee	Revolters.	East Africa	M
IWELA	ee-WEH-lah	To struggle.	Azania (Sotho)	
KAREGA	KAH-reh-gah	A rebel.	Kenya (Agikuyu)	M
KUBA	KOO-bah	Rebellion.	Azania (Zulu)	F
LEHANA	leh-HAH-nah	One who refuses.	Lesotho (Basotho)	M
MAASI	MAAH-see	Rebellion.	Kiswahili	
MPINDUZI	mpehn-doo-zee	A revolutionary.	Kiswahili	
MTORO	m-TOH-roh	Runaway.	East Africa (Kiswahili)	M
MUMIA	moo-MEE-ah	I have refused what you have said.	Cameroon (Mubako)	F

Name	Pronunciation	Meaning	Origin	Gender
NOMZAMO	nohm-zah-moh	Struggle.	Azania (Zulu)	F
REMA	REH-mah	Revolt.	East Africa	F
TSHOKOLO	tsoh-koh-loh	He struggles.	Azania (North Sotho)	M

Success and Achievement

Trials mean success. —Uganda

Name	Pronunciation	Meaning	Origin	Gender
AKOLU	ah-KOH-loo	Success is more likely when there is cooperation.	Nigeria (Ishan)	
AKONTE	ah-KOHN-teh	I made it.	Nigeria	
AMAZUU	ah-mah-ZOO-oo	No success without a struggle.	Nigeria (Ishan)	
BADMIA	bah-mee-ah	He has surpassed me.	Cameroon (Mubako)	M
BAKA	bah-kah	Catch; grasp, grab.	Uganda (Ganda)	M
BARIKA	bah-REE-kah	Bloom; be successful.	Kenya (Kiswahili)	F
BEDIAKO	beh-dee-AH-koh	He overcomes obstacles.	Ghana (Akan)	M
DADAWELE	DAH-DAH-weh-leh	One who will swim safely through life despite challenges; swims through tribulations to success.	Azania (Xhosa)	
DUNDU	DOON-doo	Reaching the top.	Azania (Zulu)	
DUNDU BALA	doon-doo-BAH-lah	Reach the top, climax.	Azania (Zulu)	
FUZIWE	foo-ZEE-weh	She will be a trailblazer.	Azania (Xhosa)	F
FUZU	FOO-zoo	To succeed; win.	Kiswahili	
GAUTA	gah-OO-tah	Golden.	Azania (Sotho)	

Name	Pronunciation	Meaning	Origin	Gender
KATLEGO	kaht-LEH-goh	Success.	Azania (Sotho)	
KOYA	KOH-yah	Happy in success.	Africa	F
LUNGA	LOON-gah	Do well.	Azania (Zulu)	
NAHWOLLA	nah-WOHL-lah	You have crossed the bridge.	Cameroon (Mubako)	F
NDIMA	n-DEE-mah	Evidence of our success.	Azania (Xhosa)	M
OLOYE	oh-LOH-yeh	One who earned the title.	Nigeria	
PHAKAMA	PAH-kah-mah	She will rise to fulfill her calling in life.	Azania (Xhosa)	F
TIOMBE	tee-OHM-beh	An achiever.	Zimbabwe	F
UFANIFU	oo-fah-NEE-foo	Success and prosperity.	Kiswahili	
WINA	WEE-nah	A successful person.	Azania (Zulu)	

Surprise, Mystery, and Wonder

On the hardest rocks, sometimes you'll see beautiful flowers growing. —Haiti

Name	Pronunciation	Meaning	Origin	Gender
AINA	ah-EE-nah	Surrounded by mystery.	Nigeria (Yoruba)	
AJABU	ah-JAH-boo	Wonder, astonishment.	Kiswahili	
ALANIKOE	ah-lah-nee-koh-eh	How did it happen?	Cameroon (Mungaka)	M
ANE	AH-neh	Keep them guessing.	Nigeria (Ishan)	
AYAMISHI	ah-yah-mee-shee	The unexpected child.	Nigeria (Igarra)	
BAGIMBA	bah-jeem-bah	They take by surprise.	Uganda (Ganda, Soga)	M
DIMAKATSO	dee-mah-KAHT-soh	Wonder, astonishment; child who makes wonders.	Azania (North Sotho)	
DUNKUNKA	doon-KOON-kah	A mystery.	Azania (Xhosa)	
ELUMBU	eh-LOOM-boo	Mystery.	Angola (Ovimbundu)	F

Name	Pronunciation	Meaning	Origin	Gender
GYASI	JAH-see	Wonderful.	Ghana (Akan)	M
KADIYE	kah-DEE-yeh	Born suddenly.	Somalia	M
KALAMO	kah-lah-moh	The unexpected.	Central Africa	M
KALEMBE	kah-LEHM-beh	Mystical person.	Zambia (Bemba)	
KALOMO	kah-loh-moh	The unexpected.	Central Africa	M
KEREEN-YAGA	keh-rehn-YAH-gah	Mountain of mystery.	Kenya (Agikuyu)	M
LESA	LEH-sah	Child born unexpectedly.	Zambia (Bemba)	
LISHA	LEE-shah	Mysterious.	West Africa (Hausa)	F
MACHILU	mah-CHEE-loo	A surprise.	Zambia (Tumbuka)	
MANGAKHE	mahn-gah-keh	One who brings surprises.	Azania	M
MASHAMA	mah-SHAH-mah	A surprise, unexpected.	Azania (Nguni)	
MONA	MOH-nah	A great surprise.	North Africa	
NASHWA	NASH-wah	Wonderful feeling.	Egypt/Khamit	F
NDABA	n-DAH-bah	He is a wonder.	Azania	M
NOSIMANGA	noh-see-mahn-ghah	One who brings surprises.	Azania	F
NOURBESE	noor-BEH-seh	A wonderful child.	Benin	F
NUEBESE	noo-beh-seh	A wonderful child.	Benin	
OTHUSA	oh-too-sah	To be surprised.	Azania (Xhosa)	
SIKUDHANI	see-koo-THAH-nee	A surprise; unusual.	East Africa (Kiswahili)	F
SIMAN-GELE	see-MAHNG-geh-leh	We are still surprised.	Azania (Xhosa)	F
STAAJABU	s-TAAH-jah-boo	Surprised; amazement.	East Africa (Kiswahili)	F
WOWU	WOH-woo	One who is a pleasant surprise.	Azania (Zulu)	

Survival

It is survival, not bravery that makes
a man climb a thorny tree. —Uganda

Name	Pronunciation	Meaning	Origin	Gender
ANENI	ah-NEH-nee	We have managed to survive.	Nigeria (Ishan)	
BETTA	BEHT-tah	He will sustain.	Central Africa (Bobangi)	M
JEFAR	JEH-fah	Recovery.	East Africa (Kiswahili)	M
JIBAWO	jee-BAH-woh	Sole survivor.	Sierra Leone (Mende)	M
JILO	JEE-loh	The survivor.	Sierra Leone (Mende)	F
JIMALE	jee-MAH-leh	Survivor.	Somalia	M
KARAMA	kah-raah-mah	The one who lives or survives for a long time.	Rwanda, Burundi, DRC (Huti, Tutsi, Twa)	M
MAZENEEKO	mah-zeh-neh-koh	The only child to survive death amongst all other children.	Rwanda (Runyarwanda)	M
NAFISI	nah-FEE-see	To rescue.	Kenya, Tanzania	
NAMATAKA	nah-mah-TAH-kah	The only survivor.	Uganda (Luganda)	F
NIJIDEKA	n-jeh-deh-kah	Survival is paramount.	West Africa	
NYANJERA	NYAHN-jeh-rah	She survived; born on the way.	East Africa (Kisii)	F

Sweetness

Sweetness walks with bitterness. —Nigeria

Name	Pronunciation	Meaning	Origin	Gender
ASALI	ah-SAH-lee	Nectar, honey.	Kiswahili	
BANURA	bah-noo-rah	They are sweet.	Uganda (Ganda, Kiga, Nyankore)	M

Name	Pronunciation	Meaning	Origin	Gender
BISI	BEE-see	Sweet milk, brandy.	Azania (Xhosa)	F
CHUGUEL	CHOO-goo-ehl	Sugar; sweetness.	Azania (Bachopi)	M
EDE	EH-deh	Sweetness.	Nigeria (Yoruba)	
ITURI	ee-TOO-ree	Sweet-smelling.	Kenya, Tanzania (Kiswahili)	F
KITOTO	kee-TOH-toh	Sweet little child.	Kenya, Tanzania	
LAINI	lah-EE-nee	Sweet and gentle, soft.	Kenya, Tanzania (Kiswahili)	F
MANDISA	mahn-DEE-sah	Sweet, sweet milk, brandy.	Azania (Xhosa)	F
NAMA KAJJO	nnah-mah-kahj-joh	Associated with sugar cane.	Uganda (Ganda)	M
NOTAGI	noh-TAH-gee	Sweet milk, brandy.	Azania (Sotho)	
NULLA	NOOL-lah	As sweet as honey.	Cameroon (Mungaka)	M
NWAKUSO	nwah-koo-soh	Sweet child.	Nigeria (Igbo)	F
OYIN	OH-yeen	Honey.	East Africa	F
RHAMAH	rah-mah	Sweet.	Somalia	
SHAMIM	SHAH-meem	Sweet scent.	Kiswahili	F
SUGA	SOO-gah	Sugar.	West Africa (Yoruba)	
SUKARI	soo-KAH-ree	Sugar.	West Africa (Hausa)	
TAMU	TAH-moo	Sweet, pleasant, nice.	Kenya, Tanzania	
UKI	OO-kee	Honey.	Africa	F
UNA	oo-nah	Sweet as banana.	Nigeria (Igbo)	F

Talking and Listening

Examine what is said, not him who speaks. —*Egypt*

Name	Pronunciation	Meaning	Origin	Gender
ABIKANILE	ah-bee-kah-NEE-leh	Listen.	Malawi (Yao)	F
AKHATA	ah-KAH-tah	If you talk and they don't listen, it is not your fault.	Nigeria (Ishan)	
ASALE	ah-SAH-leh	Speak.	Malawi (Yao)	F
ATASE	ah-TAH-seh	We talked to reach the point.	Nigeria (Ishan)	
BAGAMBA	bah-GAHM-bah	Let them talk; ignore ill talk of enemies.	Uganda (Rutooro)	F
BASEME	bah-SEH-meh	Let them talk.	Central Africa	M
BATASEMA	bah-tah-SEH-mah	They will talk.	Central Africa	M
CHIKU	CHEE-koo	Chatterer.	East Africa (Kiswahili)	F
CIKO	see-koh	The eloquent one.	Azania (Xhosa)	
DOKOZA	doh-KOH-zah	To speak with a deep, gruff voice.	Azania (Xhosa)	
ENETA	eh-NEH-tah	What they are saying does not bother me.	Nigeria (Ishan)	
ENITA	eh-NEE-tah	Watch what you say.	Nigeria (Urhobo)	
FALAZA	fah-LAH-zah	The talkative one.	Azania	M
FALAZILE	fah-lah-ZEE-lee	The talkative one.	Azania	F
FASAHA	fah-sah-hah	Eloquence.	East Africa (Kiswahili)	F
GAMUA	gah-moo-ah	He is tired of talking.	Cameroon (Mubako)	M
GUKAA	goo-kah	The mouth talks a lot.	Cameroon (Mubako)	M
GUSHUA	goo-SHOO-ah	The mouth has redeemed me.	Cameroon (Mubako)	M
HOJIANA	hoh-jee-AH-nah	To discuss.	Kiswahili	
ITARE	ee-TAH-reh	I spoke up when necessary.	Nigeria (Ishan)	
IZOYA	ee-ZOH-yah	I am not bothered by insults.	Nigeria (Ishan)	
KANJOGERA	kaahn-joh-geh-rah	Distinct manner of speaking.	Rwanda, Burundi, DRC (Huti, Tutsi, Twa)	M

Name	Pronunciation	Meaning	Origin	Gender
KARABO	kah-rah-boh	Response.	Botswana (Tswana)	M
KARANGWA	kah-rahn-gwah	The talked about one.	Rwanda, Burundi, DRC (Huti, Tutsi, Twa)	M
KHULUMA	koo-LOOM-mah	Speak!	Azania	M
KIVALLA	kee-VAHL-lah	I have heard and suffered for it.	Cameroon (Mubako)	M
KUJUNDIKA	koo-joon-DEE-kah	To hold something under the tongue.	Rwanda, Burundi (Kinyarwanda, Kirundi)	
KWISISA	kwee-SEE-sah	Listen very closely.	Azania (Sotho)	
LEABUA	LEH-ah-bwa	You speak.	Azania (Sotho)	M
LIU	LEE-oo	Beautiful voice.	Malawi (Ngoni)	
LIYONGO	LEE-yohn-goh	Talks much.	East Africa (Kiswahili)	M
LIZWI	LEEZ-wee	Voice.	Zimbabwe (Ndebele)	M
LULU	LOO-loo	Orator.	Kenya, Tanzania	
MBONGI	MMBOHN-gee	The orator.	Azania (Xhosa)	M
MSEMAJI	mm-SEH-mah-jee	Orator.	East Africa (Kiswahili)	M
MUJABI	moo-jah-bee	One who talks very fast.	Uganda (Ganda)	M
MWARIA	MWAH-ree-ah	One who speaks a lot.	Kenya (Agikuyu)	M
MWAZ WENYI	mwas-WEHN-yee	What have you heard?	Zimbabwe (Shona)	F
NENA	NEH-nah	To speak.	Kiswahili	F
NZA RUBARA	n-zah-roo-bah-rah	I will talk about it and will not die.	Rwanda, Burundi, DRC (Huti, Tutsi, Twa)	M
POPOTA	poh-POH-tah	Talkative.	Zambia (Tonga)	
SEKAMWA	sseh-kah-mwah	A talkative person.	Uganda (Ganda)	M
SEMENI	SEH-meh-nee	Speak.	East Africa (Kiswahili)	F
UJATALO	oo-jah-TAH-loh	You never allow others to get in a word.	Nigeria (Ishan)	

Name	Pronunciation	Meaning	Origin	Gender
UKAH	OO-kah	Conversation, exchanged words.	Nigeria (Igbo)	M
UNUIGBE	OO-noo-HEE-bay	Mouth does not kill.	West Africa (Edo)	M
USENI	oo-seh-nee	Tell me.	Malawi (Yao)	M
VAKELE	vah-KEH-leh	He has been heard.	Azania (Xhosa)	M
VUSIMUZI	voo-see-MOO-zee	What am I saying?	Azania (Venda)	
ZWAKALA	swah-KAH-lah	One who can be heard.	Azania	M
ZWAKALILE	zwah-kah-LEE-leh	One who can be heard.	Azania	F

Thought and Reflection

Thoughts are quicker than gazelles. —Mali

Name	Pronunciation	Meaning	Origin	Gender
BARIBONA	bah-ree-boh-nah	They will eventually see, realize, or experience.	Uganda (Ganda, Kiga, Nyankore)	M
BASIR	BAH-seer	Perceptive.	North Africa (Arabic)	M
BASIRA	bah-SEE-rah	Insight.	Gambia, Nigeria (Hausa)	F
CAMANGA	kah-MAHN-gah	Think, meditate.	Azania (Xhosa)	
DHANI	DAH-nee	To think.	Kiswahili	
ECHERUO	eh-cheh-ROO-oh	Deep thought, reflection.	Nigeria	
FIKARA	fee-KAH-rah	Meditation.	Kiswahili	
FIKIRA	fee-KEE-rah	Thoughts, reflections.	Kiswahili	
FUPUTSA	foo-POOT-sah	Think deeply.	Lesotho (South Sotho)	
IRO	EE-roh	Imagination.	West Africa (Yoruba)	
JI	JEE	Perceive.	West Africa (Hausa)	
KIBASILA	KEE-bah-see-lah	Insight.	East Africa (Kiswahili)	M
KIBASIRA	KEE-bah-see-rah	Insight.	East Africa (Kiswahili)	M

Name	Pronunciation	Meaning	Origin	Gender
KROMA	krohm-mah	Deep thought, reflection.	Nigeria	
MOMAR	MOH-mahr	Philosopher.	Azania	M
NAMBITHA	nahm-BEE-tah	Think it over.	Azania (Xhosa)	F
OTA	OH-tah	Dream.	Kiswahili	
RO	ROH	Imagine.	West Africa (Yoruba)	
RONU	ROH-noo	Contemplate.	West Africa (Yoruba)	
UCHE	OO-cheh	Deep thought, reflection.	Nigeria	
WAZA	WAH-zah	One who reflects; to think.	Kiswahili	
ZANO	ZAH-noh	Idea.	Niger	M
ZINDLA	ZEHND-lah	One who ponders.	Azania (Xhosa)	

Time

Lost time is never found. —Africa

Name	Pronunciation	Meaning	Origin	Gender
AIKERE	ah-ee-KEH-reh	We came early— don't treat us as last come.	Nigeria (Ishan)	
BBANGA	bbahn-gah	Space; room; time.	Uganda (Ganda)	M
DEHKONTEE	deh-kohn-teh-eh	Time will tell.	West Africa (Bassa)	M
DEKONTE	deh-KOHN-teh	Everything has time.	Liberia	
DIRIKI	dee-REE-kee	To be on time.	Kiswahili	M
GABGA	gahb-gah	Who knows tomorrow.	Cameroon (Mubako)	M
HAJUNZA	hah-JOON-zah	Tomorrow.	Zambia (Tonga)	F
IZOLO	ee-ZOH-loh	Yesterday.	Azania (Zulu)	
JANA	JAH-nah	Yesterday.	Kiswahili	F
JUNZA	joon-zah	Tomorrow.	Zambia, Zimbabwe (Tonga)	

Name	Pronunciation	Meaning	Origin	Gender
JUZI	JOO-zee	Day before yesterday.	Kiswahili	
KALE	KAH-leh	Ancient times.	North Africa (Arabic)	
KESHO	KEH-shoh	Tomorrow.	Kiswahili	
KISIKUSIKU	kee-see-koo-SEE-koo	Twilight.	Kiswahili	
LIMA	lee-mah	It is my day or time.	Cameroon (Mubako)	
LONII	lohn-nee	Today.	West Africa (Yoruba)	
MAPEMA	mah-PEH-mah	Early.	Kiswahili	
MARA	MAH-rah	A time.	Kiswahili	F
MINI	MEE-nee	Day.	Azania (Xhosa)	M
MUHANYA	moo-hahn-yah	Daylight, midday.	Zambia (Tumbuka)	
MWASAA	mwa-SAH	Timely.	East Africa (Kiswahili)	F
NOMINI	noh-MEE-nee	Born during daytime.	Azania (Xhosa)	F
RANI	RAH-nee	Dry season.	West Africa (Hausa)	
SIKU	SEE-koo	Day.	Kiswahili	
SONDO	SOHN-doh	Sunday.	Zambia (Tonga)	
SYANDENE	see-ahn-DEH-neh	Punctual.	Tanzania (Nyakyusa)	F
TETE	TEH-teh	Early.	West Africa (Yoruba)	
UBOCHI	oo-BOH-chee	Day.	Nigeria (Igbo)	M
ZAMANI	zah-MAH-nee	Long time ago.	East Africa (Kiswahili)	F

Days—Friday

Name	Pronunciation	Meaning	Origin	Gender
AFIBA	ah-FEE-bah	Born on Friday.	Ghana	M
AFUA	ah-FOO-ah	Born on Friday; forgiveness, mercy.	Ghana (Ewe)	F
AYA	AH-yah	Born on Friday.	Ghana	F

Name	Pronunciation	Meaning	Origin	Gender
COFFIE	koh-FEE	Born on Friday.	Ghana (Ewe)	M
DANJUMA	dahn-joo-MAH	Born on Friday.	Nigeria (Hausa)	M
EFIA	ee-FEE-ah	Friday's child, born on Friday.	West Africa	
FIDA	FEE-dah	Friday.	Ghana (Ga)	
FIFI	fee-FEE	Born on Friday.	Ghana (Fantei)	M
IIJUMAA	ee-JOO-mah	Friday.	Kiswahili	
KOFI	koh-FEE	Born on Friday; growth.	Ghana (Baule)	M
SOHAA	SOH-hah-ah	Friday.	Ghana (Akan)	
YOOFI	yoh-oh-FEE	Born on Friday.	Ghana (Akan)	M

Days—Monday

Name	Pronunciation	Meaning	Origin	Gender
ADIJOBA	ah-dee-JOH-bah	Born on Monday.	Côte d'Ivoire	F
AJO	AH-joh	Born on Monday.	Ghana	M
AKISSI	ah-KEE-see	Born on Monday.	Ghana	F
COUJOE	koh-JOH	Born on Monday.	Ghana (Ewe)	M
DJU	d-JOO	Monday.	Ghana (Ga)	
DWODA	DWOH-dah	Monday.	Ghana (Akan)	
ISNINA	ees-NEE-nah	Born on Monday.	Somalia	F
JOJO	joh-joh	Born on Monday.	Ghana (Fante)	M
KADIA	kah-DEE-ah	Born on Monday.	Cote d'Ivoire	M
KODJO	KOHD-joh	Monday's child.	West Africa	M
KODWO	KOHD-woh	Born on Monday.	Ghana (Twi)	M
KOJO	koh-JOH	Born on Monday.	Ghana (Akan)	M
KWAKU	KWAH-koo	Born on Monday.	Togo	M
MOSU PULOGO	moh-soo-poo-loh-goh	Monday.	Azania (North Sotho)	

Days—Saturday

Name	Pronunciation	Meaning	Origin	Gender
AKPA	AHK-pah	Born on Saturday.	Togo	M
AMA	AH-mah	Born on Saturday.	Ghana (Ewe)	F
ASABE	ah-SAH-beh	Saturday.	North Africa (Arabic)	F
COMMIE	KOH-mee	Born on Saturday.	Ghana (Ewe)	M
KOMLA	KOHM-lah	Born on Saturday.	Benin, Togo	M
KWAME	KWAH-meh	Born on Saturday.	Ghana (Twi)	M
KWAMINA	kwah-MEE-nah	Born on Saturday.	Ghana	M
MEMENDA	meh-MEHN-dah	Saturday.	Ghana (Akan)	
SIBIRI	see-bee-REE	Born on Saturday.	Mali	

Days—Sunday

Name	Pronunciation	Meaning	Origin	Gender
AHADA	ah-HAH-dah	Born on Sunday.	Somalia	F
AKOSUA	ah-KOH-soo-ah	Born on Sunday.	Ghana (Ewe)	F
DANLADI	dahn-LAH-dee	Born on Sunday.	Nigeria (Hausa)	M
ESI	eh-SEE	Born on Sunday.	Ghana (Fantei)	F
JUMAPILI	joo-mah-PEE-leh	Born on Sunday.	Kenya (Mwera)	F
KWESIDA	kweh-SEE-dah	Sunday.	Ghana (Akan)	
QUAASHIE	kwah-SHEE	Born on Sunday.	Ghana (Ewe)	M
SEDE	SEH-deh	Born on Sunday.	Benin	F
SISI	see-SEE	Born on Sunday.	Ghana (Fante)	
SONDAHA	sohn-DAH-hah	Sunday.	Namibia (Ovambo)	
SONDO	sohn-doh	Sunday.	Zambia, Zimbabwe (Tonga)	
SONTAGA	sohn-TAH-gah	Sunday.	Azania (Sotho)	

Name	Pronunciation	Meaning	Origin	Gender
SONTAHA	sohn-TAH-hah	Sunday.	Azania (Sotho)	

Days—Thursday

Name	Pronunciation	Meaning	Origin	Gender
ABA	AH-bah	Born on Thursday.	Ghana (Ewe), Nigeria (Eleme)	F
ALAMISI	ah-lah-MEE-see	Thursday.	Kiswahili	
AYABA	ah-YAH-bah	Born on Thursday.	Togo	F
KHAMIISA	kha-MEE-ee-sha	Born on Thursday.	North Africa (Arabic)	M
KHAMISI	kah-MEE-see	Born on Thursday.	East Africa (Kiswahili)	M
LAMISSA	lah-MEE-sah	Born on Thursday.	Mali	
ULWESINE	ool-weh-SEE-neh	Thursday.	Azania (Zulu)	
YAA	yah-ah	Born on Thursday.	Ghana (Ashanti)	F
YABA	YAH-bah	Born on Thursday.	Cote d'Ivoire	F
YAO	YAH-oh	Born on Thursday.	Ghana (Ewe)	M
YAWO	YAH-woh	Born on Thursday.	Ghana (Akan)	M
YORKOO	yohr-KOH-oh	Born on Thursday.	Ghana (Fante)	M

Days—Tuesday

Name	Pronunciation	Meaning	Origin	Gender
ABENA	ah-bee-NAH	Born on Tuesday.	Nigeria (Eleme)	F
ABRA	AHB-rah	Born on Tuesday.	Benin, Togo	F
ADOWA	ah-doh-WAH	Born on Tuesday.	Ghana	F
ALATA	tah-LAH-tah	Tuesday.	North Africa (Arabic)	M
BOBO	BOH-boh	Born on Tuesday.	Ghana (Fante)	M
COBLAH	koh-BLAH	Born on Tuesday.	Ghana (Ewe)	M
EBO	eh-BOH	Born on Tuesday.	Ghana (Fante)	M

Name	Pronunciation	Meaning	Origin	Gender
JUMAANE	joo-MAAH-neh	Born on Tuesday.	Kiswahili	
TALATU	tah-LAH-too	Tuesday.	North Africa (Arabic)	F

Days—Wednesday

Name	Pronunciation	Meaning	Origin	Gender
ABEEKU	AH-BEE-koo	Born on Wednesday.	Ghana	M
AKOMBA	ah-KOHM-bah	Born on Wednesday.	Côte d'Ivoire	F
AKU	ah-KOO	Born on Wednesday.	Ghana	
AKUA	ah-KOO-ah	Born on Wednesday.	Ghana (Ewe)	F
DABA	DAH-bah	Born on Wednesday.	Senegal	
KAKUA	kah-KOO-ah	Born on Wednesday.	Ghana (Fante)	
KUKUA	koo-KOO-ah	Born on Wednesday.	Ghana (Fante)	F
KWAKOU	kwah-KOO	Born on Wednesday.	Ghana (Ewe)	M
LABORARO	la-boh-RAH-roh	Wednesday.	Azania (North Sotho)	
LARABA	lah-RAH-bah	Wednesday.	West Africa	F
WUKUDA	woo-KOO-dah	Wednesday.	Ghana (Akan)	
YOOKU	yoh-oh-KOO	Born on Wednesday.	Ghana (Fante)	M

Months

Name	Pronunciation	Meaning	Origin	Gender
AGASTI	ah-GAHS-tee	Month of August.	Azania (Xhosa)	
APRELI	ah-PREH-lee	Month of April.	Zimbabwe (Ndebele)	M
APRILI	ah-PREE-lee	Month of April.	Azania (Xhosa)	
ARHOSI	ahr-hoh-ee	Month of August.	Zimbabwe (Ndebele)	M
DISEMBA	dee-SEHM-bah	Month of December.	Azania (Xhosa)	M
FEBRUWARI	feh-broo-WAH-ree	Month of February.	Azania (Xhosa)	
JANABARI	jah-nah-BAH-ree	Month of January.	Zimbabwe (Ndebele)	M

Name	Pronunciation	Meaning	Origin	Gender
JANUWARI	jah-noo-WAH-ree	Month of January.	Azania (Xhosa)	
JULAYI	joo-LAH-yee	Month of July.	Zimbabwe (Ndebele)	M
JUNI	JOO-nee	Month of June.	Zimbabwe (Ndebele)	M
MATSHI	MAHT-shee	Month of March.	Azania (Xhosa)	
MEYI	MEH-yee	Month of May.	Zimbabwe (Ndebele)	M
NAHSONA	nah-sohn-yah	A child born in the month of Sonia (April).	Cameroon (Mubako)	F
NAHSUA	nah-soo-ah	A child born in the month of Gbansoa (September).	Cameroon (Mubako)	F
NAMHLA	nahm-lah	Today.	Azania	
NDASA	ndah-sah	One born in February.	Azania	M
NONDASA	nohn-DAH-sah	One born in February.	Azania	F
NOVEMBA	noh-VEHM-bah	Month of November.	Zimbabwe (Ndebele)	M
OKTOBHA	ohk-toh-bah	Month of October.	Azania (Xhosa)	
SEPTEMBA	sehp-tehm-bah	Month of September.	Azania (Xhosa)	
SILIMELA	see-lee-MEE-lah	One born in June.	Azania	
STEMERE	steh-meh-reh	Month of September.	Zimbabwe (Ndebele)	M

Seasons

Name	Pronunciation	Meaning	Origin	Gender
ABEJIDE	ah-beh-JEE-deh	Born in the wintertime.	Nigeria	
EKWINDLA	eh-KWEEND-lah	In autumn.	Azania (Zulu)	
KHEPHU	KEH-poo	Snow.	Azania (Xhosa)	M
LOLLI	LOHL-lee	Autumn; fall.	Gambia (Wolof)	F
MAREGA	mah-REH-gah	Winter.	Azania (Sotho)	
MARIGA	mah-REE-gah	Winter.	Azania (North Sotho)	
MWAKA	mwaah-kah	Season.	Uganda (Ganda)	M

Name	Pronunciation	Meaning	Origin	Gender
NADIFA	nah-DEEF-ah	Born between two seasons.	Somalia	F
NATHINGE	nah-TEEN-geh	Summer.	Namibia (Ovambo)	
OTUTU	oh-TOO-too	Chill.	West Africa (Yoruba)	
RABIA	rah-BEE-ah	Spring.	North Africa (Arabic)	
SELEMO	seh-LEH-moh	Summer, springtime.	Azania (North Sotho)	
SERAME	seh-RAH-meh	Cold; frost.	Azania	
TUTU	too-too-wahn	Cool, cold.	West Africa (Yoruba)	

Time of Day

Name	Pronunciation	Meaning	Origin	Gender
ALASIRI	ah-lah-SEE-ree	Afternoon.	Kiswahili	
ALFAJIRI	ahl-fah-JEE-ree	Dawn.	Kiswahili	
AMONDI	AH-mohn-dee	Born at dawn.	East Africa (Luo)	F
ANAPA	ah-NAH-pah	Morning; child born at daybreak.	Ghana (Akan)	F
ASUBUHI	ah-soo-BOO-hee	Morning.	Kiswahili	
EKUSENI	eh-koo-SEH-nee	In the morning.	Azania (Zulu)	
FAJA	FAH-jah	Dawn.	Gambia (Wolof)	
ILISASA	ee-lee-SAH-sah	Morning.	Azania (Zulu)	
KIANIA	kee-ah-nee-ah	Dawn.	Kenya (Agikuyu)	
KIANIRA	kee-ah-NAH-rah	The dawn.	Kenya (Agikuyu)	
KWACHA	KWAH-chah	Morning, in the morning.	Malawi (Ngoni)	M
KWAYERA	kwah-YEH-rah	Dawn.	Malawi (Ngoni)	M
LAYLA	LAH-ee-lah	Born at night.	East Africa (Kiswahili)	F
LELA	LEH-lah	Night.	Kiswahili	F
MALEDA	mah-LEH-dah	Dawn.	Ethiopia (Amharic)	
MARINDA	mah-REHN-dah	The evening start.	Zimbabwe (Shona)	
MUROKI	MOO-roh-kee	Comes with the dawn.	Kenya (Agikuyu)	M

Name	Pronunciation	Meaning	Origin	Gender
NDWELE-IFWA	n-dweh-leh-EEF-wah	I came with morning.	Tanzania (Nyakyusa)	M
ODIKONYI	OH-dee-kohn-yee	Born in early morning.	East Africa (Luo)	M
OJI	OH-jee	Darkness.	Nigeria (Igbo)	
OTHIAMBA	oh-tee-ahm-BAH	Born in the afternoon.	Benin	M
OTHIENO	oh-tee-EH-noh	Born at night.	Benin	M
RATYA	RAHT-yah	Dusk, twilight.	Azania (Xhosa)	
SABAH	SAH-bah	Morning.	North Africa (Arabic)	
SAFIYA	sah-fee-yah	Morning.	West Africa (Hausa)	
SEKIRO	sseh-tch-ee-roh	The night.	Uganda (Ganda)	M
SEMAJORO	seh-eh-mah-joh-roh	The one of the nights.	Rwanda, Burundi, DRC (Huti, Tutsi, Twa)	M
SHABA	SHAH-bah	Morning has come.	North Africa	F
SHURUKU	shoo-ROO-koo	Dawn.	Kiswahili	
TUTUSA	too-TOOT-sah	To grope about in the dark.	Kiswahili	
UCHAO	oo-CHAH-oh	Dawn.	Kiswahili	
UGHAO	oog-HAH-oh	Dawn, sunrise.	Kiswahili	
USIKU	oo-SEE-koo	Night has fallen.	Malawi (Ngoni)	M
VINDZUKA	veend-ZOO-kah	One who starts early in the morning.	Southern Africa (Tsonga)	
WEUSI	weh-OO-see	Darkness.	Kiswahili	
ZARARAYE	zah-rah-RAH-yeh	They spent the night.	Rwanda, Burundi (Kinyarwanda, Kirundi)	M

Travel and Journeys

If you travel, you see things with your own eyes. —Ghana

Name	Pronunciation	Meaning	Origin	Gender
ABIONA	ah-bee-OH-nah	Born during journey.	Nigeria (Yoruba)	
ADAODE	ah-dah-OH-deh	We are still far from the end of the journey.	Nigeria (Ishan)	
AJA	AH-jah	Title for female pilgrim.	Gambia	F
BADAWI	BAH-dah-wee	Nomad.	East Africa (Kiswahili)	M
BAGENZI	bah-gehn-ehn-zee	Travelers.	Rwanda, Burundi, DRC (Huti, Tutsi, Twa)	M
BAKATARA	bah-kah-tah-rah	They have wandered all over.	Uganda (Ganda, Kiga, Nyankore)	M
BHADULA	bah-DOO-lah	To wander, roam about.	Azania (Xhosa)	
BHOKE	BOO-keh	He wanders the land.	East Africa	M
BOTEREKWA	boh-teh-reh-kwah	The long winding road.	Zimbabwe, Mozambique, Zambia (Shona)	M
CHAPANJIRA	chah-pahn-JEE-rah	Of the road or journey.	Zambia (Chewa)	F
CHENZIRA	chehn-SEE-rah	Born on the road.	Zimbabwe (Shona)	M
CILOMBO	kee-lohm-boh	Roadside camp (welcome sight for weary travelers, "sight for sore eyes").	Angola (Ovimbundu)	
DAKASA	dah-KAH-sah	Ramble, rove.	Azania (Xhosa)	
DUNGUDELA	doon-goo-DEH-lah	Vagabond, wanderer.	Azania (Xhosa)	
EKOKO	eh-KOH-koh	Continue a journey.	Azania (Xhosa)	
FIKISA	fee-KEE-sah	Accompany to the end of the journey.	Southern Africa (Tsonga)	
FULUMIRANI	foo-loo-mee-RAH-nee	A journey.	Malawi (Ngoni)	M
GETHIL	GEH-teh-ee	Wanderer.	Kenya (Agikuyu)	M
GHEDI	GEHD-ee	Traveler.	Somalia	M
HAJI	HAH-jee	Males born during pilgrimage to Mecca.	Kiswahili	M

Name	Pronunciation	Meaning	Origin	Gender
HAMBA	HAHM-bah	Travel.	Azania (Zulu)	
HAMBILE	hahm-BEE-leh	He has traveled.	Azania (Xhosa)	M
HANZILA	hahn-ZEE-lah	Road, path, way.	Zambia (Tonga)	F
HIJI	HEE-jee	Make a pilgrimage.	Kiswahili	M
IJEDI	ee-JEH-dee	Traveling to get married.	Nigeria (Igbo)	
IJEOMA	ah-jee-OH-mah	Safe journey; a good journey.	Nigeria (Igbo)	F
IZULA	ee-ZOO-lah	Gypsy, nomad.	Azania (Zulu)	
KAMIHANDA	kah-mee-haahn-dah	One associated with roads.	Uganda (Kiga, Nyankore, Nyoro, Toro)	F
KAN YANZIRA	kahn-yahn-ZEE-rah	On the road.	Rwanda, Burundi (Kinyarwanda, Kirundi)	
KATAYIRA	kah-tah-YEE-rah	Not staying in one place.	Uganda (Ganda)	M
KHEN KETHILE	kehn-keh-TEE-leh	The great traveler.	Azania	
KKUBO	k-koo-boh	Path; street, road; way.	Uganda (Ganda)	M
KUSAMIA	koo-sah-MEE-ah	A fruitful journey.	Cameroon (Mubako)	F
LEETO	leh-EH-toh	Journey.	Lesotho (Basotho)	M
LUGENDO	loo-gehn-doh	Journey, trip.	Uganda (Ganda, Soga)	M
LUMPA	LOOM-pah	To travel afar.	Zambia (Bemba)	
MHAMBI	MHAHM-bee	Sojourner, traveler.	Azania (Xhosa)	M
MIWABO	mee-wah-boh	Goings astray, wanderings.	Uganda (Ganda)	F
MMANGA	m-MAHN-gah	Trip; journey.	Kiswahili	F
MOTSAMAI	moht-sah-mah-ee	The traveler.	Lesotho (Basotho)	M
MOYENDA	moh-YEHN-dah	On a journey.	Malawi (Ngoni)	M
MSAFIRI	m-sah-FEE-ree	Traveler, explorer.	Africa	M

Name	Pronunciation	Meaning	Origin	Gender
MUGENZI	moo-gehn-zee	Traveler.	Rwanda, Burundi (Kinyarwanda, Kirundi)	M
MUSHINDO	moo-SHEEN-doh	Footsteps.	Zambia (Bemba)	
NAMAATO	nnah-maah-toh	Boats, canoes, ships.	Uganda (Ganda)	F
NANGILA	nahn-gee-lah	Born while parents traveling.	Uganda (Ganda, Abaluhya)	M
NDLELA	n-deh-LEH-lah	Our journey.	Azania	M
NGENDO	n-gehn-DOH	A traveler.	Kenya (Agikuyu)	F
NJIRAINI	n-JAH-rah-ee-nee	On the road.	Kenya (Agikuyu)	M
NOMAZULU	noh-mah-ZOO-loo	The aimless wanderer.	Azania	F
NOMHAMBI	noh-hahm-bee	The traveler who moves around.	Azania	F
NONDLELA	nohd-LEH-lah	Our journey.	Azania	
NURI	NOO-ree	Gypsy.	Egypt/Khamit	F
NYAGUTHI	NYAH-goo-tee	A traveler.	Kenya (Agikuyu)	F
NYAWELA	nyah-WEH-lah	On a journey.	Sudan (Shulla)	F
NYAWELAN	yah-WEH-lahn	A journey.	Sudan	F
ODE	oh-DEH	Born along the road.	Benin	
SAFARI	sah-FAH-ree	Journey, trip.	Kiswahili	M
SAFARINI	sah-fah-REE-nee	Set on a journey, a trip.	Africa	M
SHANGASE	shahn-GAH-see	The wanderer.	Azania (Zulu)	
SOYAPI	soh-YAH-pee	Travel; visit far places.	Zambia (Tumbuka)	
UZORMA	oo-ZOHR-mah	Good road; safe journey.	Nigeria (Igbo)	M
VAKASA	vah-KAH-sah	To roam or meander, nomad.	Azania (Xhosa)	
WACEERA	WAH-sheh-rah	Wanderer.	Kenya (Agikuyu)	F
WANGERA	WAH-jay-rah	A traveler.	Kenya (Agikuyu)	F
WELILE	weh-LEE-leh	We have crossed over.	Azania (Zulu)	

Name	Pronunciation	Meaning	Origin	Gender
WOBYELLA	wohb-YEHL-lah	Path.	Cameroon (Mubako)	
YANTAZA	yahn-TAH-zah	To ramble about.	Azania (Xhosa)	
ZAMI	ZAH-mee	The long journey.	North Africa	M
ZIARA	zee-AH-rah	A visit.	Kiswahili	
ZULA	ZOO-lah	To wander, roam about.	Azania (Zulu)	
ZULANI	zoo-LAH-nee	The aimless wanderer.	Azania	M
ZURU	ZOO-roo	To visit.	Kiswahili	

Trouble and Adversity

It is crooked wood that shows the best sculptor. —Africa

Name	Pronunciation	Meaning	Origin	Gender
ACHIDRI	ah-tch-ee-dh-ree	I suffered.	Uganda (Lugbara)	M
AKAM BOWHO	ah-kahn-boh-whah	Who does not have a problem.	Cameroon (Mungaka)	M
AKAMMA DAWHO	ah-khan-mah-dah-whah	There is no house without a problem.	Cameroon (Mungaka)	
AKAMYA	ah-kham-yah	Where is there no problem.	Cameroon (Mungaka)	
AYELA	ah-yeh-lah	Vexation; trouble.	Uganda (Acholi)	
BANGABABO	bah-ngah-BAH-boh	Discord in the family.	Rwanda	M
BANU	bah-noo	He is the father of problems.	Cameroon (Mungaka)	M
BULWA	boohl-wah	Trouble.	Uganda (Ganda)	M
BUNGHA	boon-gah	He is hard as a rock, (given to child who is expected to grow up and overcome difficulties in life).	Cameroon (Mubako)	M
CHETE	tch-eh-teh	Our tribulations.	Zimbabwe, Mozambique, Zambia (Shona)	M

Name	Pronunciation	Meaning	Origin	Gender
ENIYE	eh-NEE-yeh	The problems confronting me are enough for me.	Nigeria (Ishan)	
FITINA	fee-TEE-nah	Discord, mischief, strife.	Africa	
GAHMIA	gahm-ee-ah	You have pushed me to the problem.	Cameroon (Mubako)	F
GINNA	geen-nah	I have made my problems worse.	Cameroon (Mubako)	M
HAONIYAO	hah-oh-nee-YAH-oh	Born at the time of a quarrel.	East Africa (Kiswahili)	M
IYAPO	ee-YAH-poh	Many trials; child of many trials.	Nigeria (Yoruba)	M
JELA	JEH-lah	Father in prison at the time of birth.	East Africa (Kiswahili)	M
KATAHALI	kah-tah-HAH-lee	He who has seen trouble.	Angola (Ovimbundu)	M
KATURA	kah-TOOR-ah	Take a burden off my mind.	Zimbabwe	
KEHMIA	keh-mee-ah	You freed me from trouble.	Cameroon (Mubako)	F
KESI	KEH-see	Born when father is in trouble.	East Africa (Kiswahili)	F
KWASA USYA	kwah-sah-OOS-yah	Troubled.	Malawi (Yao)	F
MASUMBUKO	mah-soom-boo-koh	Sufferings.	Africa	M
MATATA	mah-tah-tah	Trouble, tangle.	Rwanda, Burundi, DRC (Huti, Tutsi, Twa)	M
MATSIETSI	maht-see-eht-see	Trouble.	Lesotho (South Sotho)	
MPAKA	mpah-kah	Argument, dispute, strife.	Uganda (Ganda)	M
NAKU	nah-koo	Trouble.	Uganda (Ganda)	
NDAHURA	n-dah-HOO-rah	Agitator.	Uganda (Rutooro)	M
NGONGO	n-GOHN-goh	Name given to girl born into family where there is mourning or sickness.	Angola (Ovimbundu)	F

Name	Pronunciation	Meaning	Origin	Gender
NKAKANU	n-kah-KAH-noo	Perpetual problem.	Cameroon (Mungaka)	M
NNAKU	nnah-koo	Trouble.	Uganda (Ganda)	
NOHLUPHILE	noh-loo-pee-leh	The troublesome one.	Azania	F
NSIKAK ABASI	nsee-kahk-ah-bah-see	What is difficult with God?	Nigeria (Eleme)	
NUSURIKA	NOO-soo-ree-kah	Saved from difficulty.	Kenya, Tanzania (Kiswahili)	F
OJO	OH-joh	Difficult delivery.	Nigeria (Yoruba)	M
OMORE NONIWARA	oh-moh-reh-non-ee-WAH-rah	Meant to suffer.	Benin	F
RWAMA KUBA	rwah-mah-KOO-bah	Trouble.	Rwanda, Burundi (Kinyarwanda, Kirundi)	
SEN DAWULU	ssehn-dah-woo-lah	Agitator.	Uganda (Ganda)	M
SHARI	shah-REE	Adversity.	Kiswahili	
SHIDA	SHEE-dah	With difficulty.	Kiswahili	
SIWATA	see-WAH-too	Born during time of conflict with another group.	East Africa (Kiswahili)	F
TAABU	tah-AH-boo	Troubles; difficulty.	East Africa (Kiswahili)	F
TABALASI	tah-BAH-lah-see	One who works to remove the obstacles.	Azania	M
TABU	TAH-boo	Difficulty.	North Africa (Arabic)	
TAMJO	tahm-joh	A fruit that will bring problems.	Cameroon (Mungaka)	M
TANU	tah-noo	The father of problems.	Cameroon (Mungaka)	M
TIKUNA	tee-koo-nah	Do not push your relationship into trouble.	Cameroon (Mubako)	F
WADMIA	wahd-MEE-ah	She has gathered problems.	Cameroon (Mubako)	F
YAHNU	yah-noo	My own problems.	Cameroon (Mungaka)	

Name	Pronunciation	Meaning	Origin	Gender
ZALIMBA	zah-LEHM-bah	It is difficult.	Malawi	
ZANYIWE	zahn-YEE-weh	She has been tried and has passed the test.	Azania (Xhosa)	F
ZEBENJO	ZEH-BEHN-joh	Avoid sins.	Nigeria (Igbo)	M
ZIKUSOOKA	zee-koo-soh-kah	Better to suffer early in life than later.	Uganda	M

Trust

Befriend many but trust few. —Uganda

Name	Pronunciation	Meaning	Origin	Gender
AMINIKA	ah-mee-NEE-kah	Trustworthy.	Kenya, Tanzania	
AMPAH	AHM-pah	Trust.	Ghana (Akan)	
ANANA	ah-NAHN-nah	Trustworthy.	Kenya, Tanzania	
BECKTEMBA	behk-TEHM-bah	He can be trusted.	Zimbabwe (Ndebele)	M
BEESIGYE	beh-see-jeh	They have trust in God.	Uganda (Rukiga)	M
BWESIGE	bweh-see-geh	Trustworthiness.	Uganda (Ganda, Soga)	F
ETHEMBA	eh-TEHM-bah	Trust, hope.	Azania (Zulu)	
JIKI	jee-kee	Trust.	Gambia (Mandinka)	
MENJIWE	mehn-jee-weh	The trustworthy.	East Africa	F
MWESIGE	mweh-see-geh	Trust.	Uganda (Rutooro)	M
NDIZEYE	n-dee-zeh-yeh	I trust.	Burundi	
NYIMEJIRA	nyee-meh-jee-rah	Trust or believe.	Nigeria (Eleme)	
NZIGIYE	n-zee-gee-yeh	I trust.	Rwanda, Burundi, DRC (Huti, Tutsi, Twa)	M
SADIKIKA	sah-deek-EE-kah	Trustworthy.	Kenya, Tanzania	
SHIRIKA	SHEE-ree-kah	Trusted partner.	East Africa (Kiswahili)	F

Name	Pronunciation	Meaning	Origin	Gender
SITEMBILE	see-tehm-bee-LEH	Trust.	Zimbabwe (Ndebele)	F
THEMBA	TEHM-bah	One who can be trusted, trustworthy.	Azania (Nguni)	
THEMBEKILE	tehm-beh-kee-leh	The trustworthy one.	Azania (Zulu)	
THEMBI	tehm-bee	Trust.	Azania (Zulu)	
THEMBILE	tehm-bee-leh	We trust in you.	Azania (Xhosa)	
THENJIWE	tehn-jee-weh	The trusted one.	Azania (Zulu)	F
WAKILI	wah-KEE-lee	Trustee; hope, confidence.	North Africa	M
WASO	wah-soh	Never trust people.	DRC (Rega)	M
ZITHEMBE	zee-tehm-beh	Trust yourself.	Azania (Zulu)	M

Truth and Honesty

> The truth is like gold: keep it locked up
> and you will find it exactly as you first put it away. —*Senegal*

Name	Pronunciation	Meaning	Origin	Gender
AMINAH	ah-MEE-nah	Honest, faithful.	North Africa (Arabic)	F
ATITA	ah-TEE-tah	God's truth.	Nigeria (Ishan)	
BAYYINA	BAY-ee-nah	Evidence; proof.	East Africa (Kiswahili)	F
HAKIKA	HAH-kee-kah	Truth; certainty.	Kenya, Tanzania (Kiswahili)	F
HOJA	HOH-jah	Proof.	North Africa (Arabic)	
HUJAYJA	hoo-jah-ee-jay	Evidence.	Kiswahili	F
IKAJE	ee-KAH-jeh	Verily. Believe me, it is the truth.	Nigeria (Ishan)	
ISIBILI	ee-see-BEE-lee	Reality, truth.	Azania	
ISIMINYA	ee-see-MEEN-yah	Truth, reality.	Azania	
KWELI	KWEH-lee	Honesty, truth.	Kenya, Tanzania (Kiswahili)	

Name	Pronunciation	Meaning	Origin	Gender
MAAT	mah-AHT	Truth, law, justice.	Egypt/Khamit	F
MSEMA KWELI	msehm-mah-kweh-lee	The truth teller.	Africa	M
MUGA	MOO-gah	Confident of one truth.	Kenya (Agikuyu)	M
MWAMINI	mwah-MEE-nee	Honest, faithful.	East Africa (Kiswahili)	F
NNETI	n-NEH-tee	Truth.	Azania (Sotho)	
NOGHA	noh-ghah	He is blind to the truth.	Cameroon (Mubako)	M
NONYANISO	nohn-yah-NEE-soh	Truth.	Azania	F
NYANISO	nyah-NEE-soh	Truth.	Azania (Xhosa)	M
NYOFU	NYOH-foo	Candid.	East Africa (Kiswahili)	F
THAIR	tah-eer	Honest and clean.	North Africa	M
UDAHE MUKA	oo-dah-heh-moo-kah	One who is never dishonest.	Rwanda, Burundi, DRC (Huti, Tutsi, Twa)	
YAKINI	yah-KEE-nee	Truth, honesty.	Kiswahili	

Twins

The Siamese twin says, "Let a piece of food pass through your throat and a piece through mine, and they will all go into our stomach." —Ghana

Name	Pronunciation	Meaning	Origin	Gender
AGHAN	ah-gahn	Female child in first pair of twins.	Sudan	F
AKWETE	ah-KWEH-teh	Elder of twins.	Ghana (Ga)	F
AKWOKWO	ah-KWO-kwoh	Younger of twins.	Ghana (Ga)	F
ATA	ah-tah	Twin.	Ghana (Fante)	M
BABINI	bah-BEE-nee	There are two of them.	Azania (Xhosa)	M
DOTO	DOH-toh	Second of twins.	Ghana (Ewe)	F

Name	Pronunciation	Meaning	Origin	Gender
KAKRA	KAH-krah	Younger of twins.	Ghana (Fante)	F
KPODO	koph-DOH	Elder of twins.	Ghana (Ewe)	M
NABIRYE	nah-beer-YEH	One who produces twins.	Uganda (Ganda, Luganda)	F
NANJAMBA	nahn-JAHM-bah	Mother of twins.	Angola (Ovimbundu)	
ODION	oh-DEE-ohn	First-born twin.	West Africa	
PATA	PAH-tah	Twin.	Kiswahili	
PHAHLA	pah-lah	One of twins.	Azania (Zulu)	
SAMA	SAH-mah	Male twins, prince, (title conferred officials associate with the Lela cult).	Cameroon (Mubako)	M
TAIWO	tah-EE-woh	First-born twin.	West Africa	
TANKHO	tahn-koh	Predecessor of a set of twins (additional name).	Cameroon (Mubako)	M
TAWIA	tah-WEE-wah	First-born twin.	West Africa	
TAWIAH	TAH-wee-ah	First child after twins.	Ghana (Ga)	F
TSE	tseh	Younger of twins.	Ghana (Ewe)	M
YE	yeh-eh	Elder of twins.	Ghana (Ewe)	F
ZESIRO	zeh-SEE-roh	Elder of twins.	Uganda (Ganda)	M

Unique, Special, and Sacred

A friend who would die with one is rare;
he who would do so accompanies one even to war. —*Benin*

Name	Pronunciation	Meaning	Origin	Gender
ADIMU	AH-DEE-moo	Rare; unobtainable.	East Africa (Kiswahili)	F
AMAZIAH	ah-MAH-zee-ah	Extraordinary.	East Africa (Kiswahili)	F
ASABI	ah-SAH-bee	One of select birth.	Nigeria (Yoruba)	F
BOHLOKWA	boh-LOHK-wah	Special.	Azania (North Sotho)	

Name	Pronunciation	Meaning	Origin	Gender
FAREEDA	fah-REE-dah	One of a kind.	North Africa (Arabic)	F
FARIDA	FAH-ree-dah	Unique.	East Africa (Kiswahili)	F
FIRYALI	FEE-yah-lee	Extraordinary.	East Africa (Kiswahili)	F
HASA	HAH-sah	Special.	Kiswahili	
HUSUSA	hoo-SOO-sah	Special.	Kiswahili	
ITIENI	ee-tee-EHN-nee	The thing that stands apart.	East Africa (Maasai)	F
KANYE	KAHN-yeh	Absolute, special, unique.	Kenya, Tanzania, Azania	
KATAJJWA	kah-tahj-jwah	That is not come by; that is not come upon.	Uganda (Ganda)	M
LELDO	leh-doo	Unique child.	Senegal (Pulssal)	F
MALUUM	MAAH-loom	Something special.	Kenya, Tanzania (Kiswahili)	F
NAMAJALA	nnah-mah-jah-lah	Magnificence.	Uganda (Ganda)	F
NGERI	n-GEH-ree	Special, unique.	Nigeria	
SHANI	SHAH-nee	Curiosity, novelty; amazing child.	East Africa (Kiswahili)	F
TUNU	TOO-noo	Something rare, something new, a new thing.	West Africa	F
TUERE	too-eh-reh	Sacred.	West Africa	F
UNWE	OON-weh	The only one, unique.	Southern Africa (Tsonga)	

Unity, Agreement, and Cooperation

A united family eats from the same plate. —Azania

Name	Pronunciation	Meaning	Origin	Gender
ANAKA	ah-NAH-kah	To share.	Nigeria (Igbo)	F
AZUBUIKE	ah-zoo-boo-EE-keh	Unity is strength.	Nigeria (Igbo)	M
BWAKOBA	bwah-koh-bah	Acted together in concert.	Uganda (Ganda)	M
EBAKATA	eh-bah-KAH-tah	That which we had agreed to.	Nigeria (Ishan)	

Name	Pronunciation	Meaning	Origin	Gender
GABGHA	gahb-gah	Cannot be separated.	Cameroon (Mubako)	M
HADA	HAH-dah	To join, or bring together.	West Africa (Hausa)	
HANGANENI	hahn-gah-neh-nee	Unite!	Namibia (Ovambo)	
IBEBUIKE	ee-beh-boo-EE-keh	Partnership is power.	Nigeria (Igbo)	M
JAMA	JAH-mah	One who brings people together.	Somalia	M
JANGMIA	jahng-mee-ah	He has a deal with me.	Cameroon (Mubako)	
JOZI	JOH-zee	Couple, pair.	Kiswahili	
KASOMBA	kah-sohm-bah	The little one that collects (or brings) together.	Uganda (Ganda)	M
KBELLO	K-BEHL-loh	Something shared.	Azania (Sotho)	
KETASE	keh-TAH-seh	Cooperation.	Zambia (Tumbuka)	F
KOPANO	koh-PAH-noh	Union.	Botswana (Tswana)	M
KOSANA	koh-SAH-nah	To disagree.	Kiswahili	
LUSAMBYA	loo-sahm-bjah	The unifier.	DRC (Rega)	M
MBIZO	m-BEE-zoh	One who calls together the people or nation to discuss matters.	Azania	M
NATHI	NAH-tee	With us.	Kiswahili	
PARA	PAH-rah	A pair.	Azania (Sotho)	
RADHIYA	rah-TEE-yah	Agreeable.	East Africa (Kiswahili)	F
RAZIYA	rah-ZEE-yah	Agreeable; easy to get along with.	East Africa (Kiswahili)	F
RIDHIA	reed-HEE-ah	To approve.	Kiswahili	
SALIHAH	sah-LEE-hah	Agreeable.	North Africa (Arabic)	
SHIME	SHEE-meh	We work together; we pull together.	Kiswahili	
SIHAM	SEE-hahm	Sharing; participation.	Kiswahili	F

Name	Pronunciation	Meaning	Origin	Gender
SIRA	see-rah	May he join together his friends.	Somalia	
SOMBOZA	ssohm-boh-zaah	One who brings together.	Uganda (Ganda)	M
TIZILALE	tee-zee-lah-leh	We shall gather together, meet; unite.	Zambia (Tumbuka)	M
UMOJA	oo-MOH-jah	Unity.	Kiswahili	
UNGAMANA	oon-gah-MAH-nah	Be united.	Kiswahili	
UNGAMA NISHA	oon-gah-mah-NEE-shah	To unite.	Kiswahili	
UNGANA	oon-GAH-nah	To combine.	Kiswahili	
WAGALA	wah-GAH-lah	To be unanimous in doing things; he has shut his mouth.	Cameroon (Mubako)	M
WAKUNA	wah-KOO-nah	Gather.	Cameroon (Mubako)	M
WASALLA	wah-sahl-lah	Gather together.	Cameroon (Mubako)	M
YABA	YAH-bah	Flock.	Azania (Nguni)	
YANJANANI	yahn-jahn-ah-nee	Unite, love, understand each other.	Zambia (Tumbuka)	M

Value, Worth, and Quality

Gold should be sold to the one who knows the value of it. —Africa

Name	Pronunciation	Meaning	Origin	Gender
AALI	AH-Lee	Excellent.	Kenya, Tanzania	
ABOTHI	ah-boh-tee	Child whom parents suspect is not useful, but the parents are wrong.	Uganda (Jopadhola)	F
AIN	ah-EEN	Precious.	North Africa (Arabic)	F
AINKA	ah-EEN-kah	The cherished one.	Nigeria	

Name	Pronunciation	Meaning	Origin	Gender
AKENKE	ah-KEHN-keh	Precious daughter.	Nigeria (Yoruba)	F
AZANA	ah-ZAH-nah	Ultimate.	Azania	
AZIZ	AH-zeez	Precious.	Azania (Zulu)	
BITATURE	bee-tah-too-reh	Those things that will not last long.	Uganda (Kiga, Nyankore, Nyoro, Toro)	M
BOTSANA	boht-SAH-nah	The best.	Azania (Sotho)	
BULUNGI	boo-LOON-gee	Excellent.	Kenya, Tanzania	
DAFINA	DAH-fee-nah	Valuable, precious, treasure.	East Africa (Kiswahili)	F
DULU	DOO-loo	Highly priced, expensive.	Azania (Xhosa)	
FAA	FAAH	Be useful.	Kiswahili	
GHALYELA	GAHL-yeh-lah	Expensive, precious.	East Africa (Kiswahili)	F
HASINA	hah-SEE-nah	First class, excellent, good.	Kiswahili	
ISIMO	ee-SEE-moh	Quality.	Kenya, Tanzania	
JARI	jah-ree	Worthy.	Gambia (Mandinka)	
JOHARI	joh-HAH-ree	Something valuable.	Kenya, Tanzania	
KANZA	KAHN-zah	Treasure.	North Africa (Arabic)	F
KANZI	KAHN-zee	Treasure; valuable.	East Africa (Kiswahili)	F
KAPSALLA	kahp-SAHL-lah	He has gathered trash and thrown them away.	Cameroon (Mubako)	M
KHERI	KEH-ree	Better.	Kiswahili	
KIFAA	kee-FAAH	Useful.	Kenya, Tanzania (Kiswahili)	F
KORO	KOH-roh	A golden child.	West Africa	M
KULULA	koo-LOO-lah	Superior, high quality.	Kenya, Tanzania	
LEOGA	leh-oh-gah	Do not throw it away.	Cameroon (Mubako)	F
MANUFAA	mah-NOO-fah	Usefulness.	Kiswahili	
NABIHA	nah-BEE-hah	Excellent.	North Africa (Arabic)	F
NASTAHILI	nahs-tah-EE-lee	I am worth it; I deserve it.	Africa	M

Name	Pronunciation	Meaning	Origin	Gender
NKERA	n-KEH-rah	I am at my best.	Rwanda, Burundi (Kinyarwanda, Kirundi)	M
NKIRUKA	n-kee-ROO-kah	The best is still to come.	Nigeria (Igbo)	F
NOGOLIDE	noh-GOH-lee-deh	She is as precious as gold.	Azania (Xhosa)	F
NTAWE	n-TAH-weh	It is nothing.	Rwanda, Burundi (Kinyarwanda, Kirundi)	M
OKONA	oh-KOH-nah	The best, the nicest.	East Africa	
OWONA	oh-WOH-nah	The best.	Azania (Xhosa)	
SESOLO	seh-SOH-loh	For nothing, free.	Azania (North Sotho)	
SIKITU	see-kee-too	It is nothing; it's all right.	East Africa	F
THANDE KILE	tahn-deh-KEE-leh	She who is very lovable.	Azania (Nguni)	F
UBORA	oo-BOH-rah	Excellence.	Kenya, Tanzania	
YOKO	YOH-koh	The best of all; abundance of all good things.	Azania (Xhosa)	
ZAHABU	zah-HAH-boo	The golden one.	Ethiopia (Galla)	F
ZITONI	zee-tohn-ee	Cherished.	Rwanda, Burundi, DRC (Huti, Tutsi, Twa)	M
ZUBAIDAH	zoo-BAH-ee-dah	Excellent.	North Africa (Arabic)	F

Victory

Never decide the victory until the war ends. —Africa

Name	Pronunciation	Meaning	Origin	Gender
AASIM	AH-seem	Benefactor, champion.	Africa (Arabic)	
AJAGBE	ah-jahg-BEH	He carries off the prize.	Nigeria (Yoruba)	M
BALARA	bah-LAH-rah	Champion.	Azania (Xhosa)	
CHINYELU	cheen-yeh-loo	One who is invincible.	West Africa	M

Name	Pronunciation	Meaning	Origin	Gender
DIA	DEE-ah	The winner, the best.	West Africa	
DUMA	DOO-mah	Shout of triumph.	Azania (Xhosa)	
EKANG	EH-kahng	He will overcome.	Nigeria	
FAIZAH	FAH-ee-zah	Victorious.	North Africa (Arabic)	F
FENYA	FEHN-yah	Conquer, vanquish.	Lesotho (South Sotho)	
FENYANG	fehn-YANG	Conqueror.	Botswana (Tswana)	M
HEMBA DOON	HEM-bah-doon	The winner; she has earned the prize.	Nigeria (Yoruba)	F
IKINANI	ee-kee-nah-nee	Unbeatable.	Rwanda, Burundi, DRC (Huti, Tutsi, Twa)	M
INTISAR	een-tee-sahr	Victory.	East Africa (Kiswahili)	F
ISIYO SHINDIKA	EE-see-yoh-sheen-dee-kah	Unconquerable.	Kenya, Tanzania (Kiswahili)	M
KALISA	kah-LEE-sah	The winner.	Rwanda, Burundi (Kinyarwanda, Kirundi)	M
KALONJI	kah-lohn-jee	Man of victory.	Central Africa	M
KEFENTSE	keh-FENT-seh	Conqueror.	Botswana, Zimbabwe (Tswana, Shona)	M
KGWETE	KGWEH-teh	The greatest, champion.	Azania (Sotho)	
KOJO	KOH-joh	Unconquerable.	Nigeria (Yoruba)	M
LOYISO	loh-yee-soh	Victory.	Azania (Xhosa)	M
MAHLULI	mah-HLOO-lee	Victory.	Azania (Xhosa)	M
MASIKA	mah-SEE-kah	The invincible.	Uganda (Runyankore)	F
MASIKO	mah-SEE-koh	The invincible.	Uganda (Runyankore)	F
MESHINDI	meh-SHEEN-dee	Winner, victor, conqueror.	Azania (Zulu)	M
MOYISI	moh-yee-see	The conqueror.	Azania (Xhosa)	M
MSINDA	M-sheen-dah	Who triumphs.	East Africa (Kiswahili)	F

Name	Pronunciation	Meaning	Origin	Gender
NASSOR	NAH-sohr	Victorious.	Tanzania (Kiswahili)	M
NJINGA	n-JEHN-gah	The champion.	Azania (Xhosa)	M
NKONKONI	n-kohn-KOH-nee	Champion.	Azania (Zulu)	
NMERI	NMEH-ree	Victory.	Nigeria (Igbo)	M
NTAGANDA	ntah-gaahn-dah	I will not lose.	Rwanda, Burundi, DRC (Huti, Tutsi, Twa)	M
OLUSHE GUN	oh-loo-SHEH-goon	God is the victor.	Nigeria (Yoruba)	
RETTA	REH-tah	S/he has won.	Ethiopia (Amharic)	
SEGUN	seh-goon	Go and conquer.	Nigeria	
SENERTA	seh-nehr-tah	The sage gives me victory.	Egypt/Khamit	
SHASHA	SHAH-shah	Champion.	Zimbabwe	
SHEREHE	sheh-reh-heh	Triumphant.	Kiswahili	
SHINDA	SHEEN-dah	Conqueror, victor.	Kenya, Tanzania	
SIMANGA	see-MAHN-gah	To triumph over.	Kiswahili	
TIWINE	tee-WEE-neh	We will win.	Zambia (Chewa)	F
USHINDI	oo-SHEHN-dee	Victory.	Kenya, Tanzania	
ZAAFIRA	zah-FEE-rah	Triumphant.	North Africa (Arabic)	

War, Fighting, and Quarrels

Let no man say: "Who murdered my father?"
without his hand on his sword. —*West Africa*

Name	Pronunciation	Meaning	Origin	Gender
ABOLAMO	ah-boh-lah-moh	One whose spear shaft (during battle) breaks during its flight.	Uganda (Langi)	M
ABRAFO	ah-BRAH-foh	Warrior.	Ghana	M

Name	Pronunciation	Meaning	Origin	Gender
ADANDE	ah-DAHN-deh	The challenge, the challenger.	Benin	M
AGEL	ah-gehl	One who kills an enemy's flank man during battle.	Uganda (Langi)	M
AGULU	ah-GOO-loo	Fight like a lion.	Nigeria (Igbo)	F
AIKOLU	ah-ee-KOH-loo	Lack of understanding breeds quarrels.	Nigeria (Ishan)	
AJAKAYE	ah-jah-KAH-YEH	A war fought all around the world.	Nigeria (Yoruba)	
AJAMU	ah-jah-MOO	He fights for what he wants.	Nigeria (Yoruba)	M
AJAYI	ah-JAH-yee	We shall fight.	Nigeria	
ALOI	ah-loh-ee	Defeat during war.	Uganda (Langi)	
AMAKANI	ah-mah-KAH-nee	Tendency to argue.	Zambia (Bemba)	
AMANY	ah-mah-ndjh	One who kills without witnesses.	Uganda (Langi)	M
AMI	ah-mee	One who kills without witnesses.	Uganda (Langi)	M
ASHANTI	ah-SHAHN-tee	United in war.	Ghana (Ashanti)	
ASKARI	ahs-KAHR-ee	Warrior.	Kenya, Tanzania	
ASSATA	ahs-SAH-tah	She who struggles, warlike.	West Africa	F
BAD JANGMAN	bah-jahng-mahn	A war fought to demonstrate pride.	Cameroon (Mungaka)	F
BAFAKI	bah-fah-kee	What do they fight or die for?	Uganda (Kiga, Nyankore, Nyoro, Toro)	
BALOGUN	bah-loh-GOON	Warlord.	Nigeria (Yoruba)	M
BAMBATA	bahm-BAH-tah	Great warrior who led rebellion.	Azania (Xhosa)	
BATALA	bah-tah-lah	They lined up for battle.	Uganda (Ganda)	M
BOMANI	boh-MAH-nee	Warrior.	Malawi (Ngoni)	M

Name	Pronunciation	Meaning	Origin	Gender
BUMA	boo-mah	A child born during war.	Cameroon (Mubako)	M
BUTAGI-RAMPUHWE	boo-tah-gee-rahm-poo-weh	Merciless warrior.	Rwanda, Burundi, DRC (Huti, Tutsi, Twa)	M
BUTEEGA	boo-teh-eh-gah	Strategies of ambushing.	Uganda (Ganda)	M
DIOGU	dee-OH-goo	Expert warrior.	Nigeria (Igbo)	
DUULANE	doo-LAH-neh	Warrior, meant to be a warrior.	Somalia	M
EKONG	EH-kohng	Warrior.	Nigeria	
FELA	feh-leh	Warlike.	Nigeria	M
GAAK	gaahk	Quarrel.	Sudan (Nuer)	M
GAIDI	gah-EE-dee	Guerilla fighter.	East Africa	M
GHANA	GAHN-nah	War chief.	Africa	M
GHAZI	GHAH-zee	Warrior.	North Africa (Arabic)	M
GOMBA	GOHM-bah	To quarrel.	Kiswahili	
GWAZA	GWAH-zah	Expert warrior with spear.	Azania (Zulu)	
HARBUU	HAH-boo	Warrior.	East Africa (Kiswahili)	F
HONDO	HOHN-doh	Warrior, fighter, war.	Azania, Zimbabwe (Shona)	M
ISILWI	ee-seel-wee	Fighter.	Azania (Zulu)	
ITA	EE-tah	A war raid.	Kenya (Agikuyu)	M
ITYIARM BIAMO	ee-tee-ahrm-bee-AH-moh	I am against wars.	Nigeria (Tiv)	F
JAGUN	jah-goon	Soldier.	Nigeria (Yoruba)	M
JAMADARI	jah-mah-DAH-ree	Warrior, leader.	Kenya, Tanzania	
JAMBAAR	JAHM-bahr	Warrior.	Gambia (Wolof)	M
JAWAROO	jah-wah-roh	Warrior.	Gambia (Mandinka)	
JELLA	jeh-lah	To shout down an issue.	Cameroon (Mubako)	M
JEMADARI	JEH-mah-dah-ree	Army general.	East Africa (Kiswahili)	M

Name	Pronunciation	Meaning	Origin	Gender
JESHI	JEH-shee	Army.	Africa	M
KADMIA	kahd-mee-ah	I have been ambushed.	Cameroon (Mubako)	
KALWANA	kah-lwaah-nah	The little one that fights.	Uganda (Ganda, Kiga, Nyankore)	M
KAMANZI	kah-MAHN-zee	Courageous warrior.	Rwanda, Burundi (Kinyarwanda, Kirundi)	M
KAMAU	kah-MAH-oo	Quiet warrior.	Kenya (Agikuyu)	M
KANAGGYE	kahn-nahj-jeh	The little one that is of the army.	Uganda (Ganda)	M
KAPALA-KASHA	kah-pah-lah-kah-shah	Fighter.	Zambia (Bemba)	
KARA-SANYI	kah-rah-saah-ndjh-ee	The elite archer.	Rwanda, Burundi, DRC (Huti, Tutsi, Twa)	M
KAREGE	kah-reh-geh	The warrior who is ready to shoot.	Rwanda, Burundi, DRC (Huti, Tutsi, Twa)	M
KARWANA	kahr-wah-nah	One born during war time.	Uganda (Rutooro)	M
KATALO	kah-tah-loh	Small battle or war.	Uganda (Ganda)	M
KESSONGA	kehs-sohn-gah	The leader of the army.	Southern Africa	M
KHALIPHA	kah-LEE-pah	Mighty warrior, the brave one.	Azania (Xhosa)	M
KHANYSANI	kahn-yee-sah-nee	Let there be fight.	Azania	
KIJANI	KEE-jah-nee	Warrior or fearless.	Kenya, Tanzania (Kiswahili)	M
KOBIE	KOH-bee	Warrior.	West Africa	M
KONDO	KOHN-doh	Warlord.	East Africa (Kiswahili)	M
LONGE	LOHN-geh	Young warrior.	Zambia (Bemba)	
LUKATA	loo-KAH-tah	War lord.	Azania	M
LUTALO	LOO-tah-loh	Warrior.	Uganda (Ganda, Luganda)	M
MAGAIDI	mah-gah-EE-dee	Guerilla fighter.	East Africa	M

Name	Pronunciation	Meaning	Origin	Gender
MAJONI	mah-JOH-nee	Soldier.	Azania (Xhosa)	
MASOJA	mah-SOH-jah	Soldiers (for baby born during war).	Zambia (Tumbuka)	M
MORANI	MOH-rah-nee	Warrior.	East Africa (Kisii)	M
MSHINDI	m-SHEEN-dee	Warrior.	Kenya, Tanzania	
MUCHIRI	moo-CHEE-ree	One who likes to argue.	East Africa	M
MUKAN TAGARA	moo-kahn-tah-GAH-rah	Born in time of war.	Rwanda	F
MWAMUILA	mwah-moo-EE-lah	Born during the war.	Tanzania (Zaramo)	F
NGARAMBE	ngah-rahm-beh	Majestic warrior.	Rwanda, Burundi, DRC (Huti, Tutsi, Twa)	M
NJAMA	n-JAH-mah	A council of war.	Kenya (Agikuyu)	M
NJERI	n-jeh-ree	Daughter of a warrior.	Kenya (Agikuyu)	F
NOMPI	nohm-PEE	Mother of war.	Azania (Xhosa)	F
NTALO	ntah-loh	Wars; battles.	Uganda (Ganda)	M
NTAMBARA	n-tahm-BAH-rah	War or fight.	Rwanda, Burundi (Kinyarwanda, Kirundi)	M
NTO	n-TOH	War.	Azania (Zulu)	
NTWA	n-TWAH	War.	Azania (Sotho)	
NYATUI	n-YAH-too-ee	Tiger-fighter; fighter of leopards.	Uganda (Ganda, Abaluhya)	M
OBWANGO	oh-bwah-ndgh-oh	The one who puts his enemy to flight by hurling one spear.	Uganda (Langi)	M
OGUERIMBA	oh-goo-eh-reem-bah	War does not wipe out a people.	Nigeria (Igbo)	
OGUNDU	oh-GOON-doo	Fight for life.	Nigeria (Igbo)	
OJORE	oh-joh-REH	A man of war.	Uganda (Ganda, Ateso)	M
RAAOKWE	rah-ah-ohk-weh	Avoid quarrelling.	Nigeria (Igbo)	

Name	Pronunciation	Meaning	Origin	Gender
RUGAMBA	roo-gahm-bah	Battlefield.	Burundi, Rwanda	M
RUKABU	roo-kah-boo	The warrior who breaks things into pieces.	Rwanda, Burundi, DRC (Huti, Tutsi, Twa)	M
RWAMU	RWAH-moo	War cry.	Rwanda, Burundi (Kinyarwanda, Kirundi)	M
SEKOU	SEH-koo	Fighter.	Guinea	M
SENGABO	sehn-GAH-boh	Army or shield.	Rwanda, Burundi (Kinyarwanda, Kirundi)	M
SOJA	SOH-jah	Soldier.	West Africa (Yoruba)	
TALIRO	tah-lee-roh	A battle.	Uganda (Ganda)	M
TAMAKRO	tah-mahk-roh	One who captures whole cities in battle.	Ghana	
TAPERA	tah-peh-rah	The enemy has all but wiped us out.	Zimbabwe, Mozambique, Zambia (Shona)	M
TARIK	TAH-reek	Muslim general who conquered Spain.	North Africa (Arabic)	M
TWAAMBO	twaahm-boh	Quarreling.	Zambia, Zimbabwe (Tonga)	
VITA	VEE-tah	War.	Kiswahili	
WALUMA	wah-LOOM-mah	I have been surrounded.	Cameroon (Mubako)	M
YERO	yeh-roh	Warrior, born soldier.	DRC	M
YERO	yeh-roh	Warrior, born soldier.	DRC	M
YIADOM	yee-ah-dohm	One who captures whole cities in battle.	Ghana	

Water

You cannot do without water, even if it drowned your child. —*Angola*

Name	Pronunciation	Meaning	Origin	Gender
AFIBA	ah-FEE-bah	By the sea.	Nigeria (Yoruba)	M

Name	Pronunciation	Meaning	Origin	Gender
AMANZI	ah-MAHN-zee	Water.	Azania (Zulu)	
ANDLE	AHND-leh	Sea, ocean.	Azania (Zulu)	
AYISI	ah-YEE-see	Ice.	Southern Africa (Tsonga)	
BAFON	BAH-fohn	Name given to a male child born after death of a family member who was a sub-chief.	Cameroon (Mungaka)	M
BAHARI	bah-HAH-ree	Sea, large lake.	Kiswahili	
BANGA	BAHN-gah	God of clear waters.	DRC (Ngbandi)	
CHANTI	CHAHN-tee	Water spirit.	Azania (Xhosa)	
DABU LAMANZI	dah-boo-lah-MAHN-zee	Crosses the waters.	Azania (Zulu)	
DADA	DAH-dah	Float, swim.	Azania (Xhosa)	
DIBA	DEE-bah	Fountain, spring.	Southern Africa (Tsonga)	
ELA	EH-lah	Flowing river.	Azania (Xhosa)	
FOLIBA	foh-lee-bah	Master of the sea.	Cameroon (Mungaka)	M
FUKU	FOO-koo	Deep water.	Southern Africa (Tsonga)	
JAFARI	jah-FAH-ree	A creek.	East Africa (Kiswahili)	M
JAWOLE	jah-WOH-leh	Clear water.	East Africa	F
JOLIBA	JAHL-ee-bah	Great stream.	West Africa	F
KITHIKA	kee-TEE-kah	Ice.	Azania (Zulu)	
KITITI	kee-TEE-tee	Depths of the ocean.	Kiswahili	
LUBANGI	loo-BAHN-gee	Born in water.	East Africa	F
MADZIMOYO	mahd-zee-MOH-yoh	Water of life.	Azania (Ngoni)	M
MAJI	MAH-jee	Water.	Kiswahili	
MANZI	MAHN-zee	Water.	Azania (Xhosa)	M
MARATHI	mah-RAH-tee	Dew.	Azania (Sotho)	

Name	Pronunciation	Meaning	Origin	Gender
MAZZI	mah-zee	Water.	Azania (Xhosa)	
MBIZI	m-BEE-zee	To drop in water.	Malawi (Lomwe)	M
MESI	MEH-see	Water.	Malawi (Yao)	F
MRASHI	m-rah-shee	Rose water.	East Africa (Kiswahili)	F
NADIA	nah-DEE-ah	Full of dew.	Sudan	
NAMALUBI	nnah-mah-loo-bee	That of the deep waters.	Uganda (Ganda)	
NAMAZZI	nah-mah-zee	Water.	Uganda (Luganda)	F
NZINGA	n-zeen-gah	From the river.	Central Africa	
RUZI	ROO-zee	River.	Rwanda, Burundi, DRC (Huti, Tutsi, Twa)	M
SEMAZZI	sseh-mahz-zee	Water.	Uganda (Ganda)	M
SEMITALA	sseh-mee-tah-lah	Land between two streams.	Uganda (Ganda)	M
SOKONI	soh-koh-nee	From the sea.	DRC	M
UZIWA	oo-ZEE-wah	To be deep, open sea.	Kiswahili	

Weapons

A spear is a big responsibility. —Native American (Navajo)

Name	Pronunciation	Meaning	Origin	Gender
BABOGO	bah-gah-boh	Shields, men, courageous ones.	Rwanda, Burundi, DRC (Huti, Tutsi, Twa)	M
BANGA	bahn-gah	Knife.	East Africa	M
BARUTI	bah-roo-tee	Gunpowder.	Kiswahili	M
BINYELLA	been-yeh-lah	With dagger in hand he is prepared for war.	Cameroon (Mubako)	M
BINZA	BEEN-zah	An expert spearman.	Kiswahili	
BOGALE	boh-GAH-leh	Sharp as a knife, fierce.	Lesotho (South Sotho)	

Name	Pronunciation	Meaning	Origin	Gender
BYAA MUNDU	bjaah-moon-dah	Things associated with the gun.	Uganda (Soga)	M
CHANA	CHAH-nah	A good shot, marksman.	Azania (Xhosa)	
CHAN DAMALI	chan-dah-MAH-lee	Firing range.	Zambia (Bemba)	
CHEMBE	CHEHM-beh	Arrowhead.	Kiswahili	
CHIKUMBU	chee-KOOM-boo	Handle of the sword.	Malawi (Yao)	
CHISONGO	chee-SOHN-goh	Cartridge, bullet.	Zambia (Bemba)	
DINGANA	deen-GAH-nah	Insignia, spear with medicine.	Cameroon (Mubako)	M
DINGHA	deen-gah	Spear.	Cameroon (Mubako)	M
DINO	DEE-noh	An expert spearman, celebration.	Azania (Sotho)	
FUMO	FOO-moh	Lance, spear.	Kiswahili	
GAGA	gaah-gah	Arrow.	Rwanda, Burundi, DRC (Huti, Tutsi, Twa)	M
GATIMU	GAH-tee-moo	A spear.	Kenya (Agikuyu)	M
GAW ABILLA	gahw-ah-BEEL-lah	I am gathering the Fon's spears.	Cameroon (Mubako)	M
HAWU	HAH-woo	Shield.	Azania (Nguni)	
ITIMU	ee-TEE-moo	Spear.	East Africa	M
IZAGALA	ee-zah-GAH-lah	Stick.	Azania (Zulu)	M
JAASI	JAH-see	Sword.	Gambia	M
JOMO	JOH-moh	Burning spear.	Kenya (Agikuyu)	
KABANO	kah-bah-noh	Small arrow.	Rwanda, Burundi, DRC (Huti, Tutsi, Twa)	
KAMATALI	kah-mah-tah-lee	A spear.	Rwanda, Burundi, DRC (Huti, Tutsi, Twa)	M

Name	Pronunciation	Meaning	Origin	Gender
KAMBE	kahm-beh	Knife used for peeling and cutting foods.	Uganda (Ganda)	M
KANORO	KHAN-oh-roo	Sharpens the sword.	Kenya (Agikuyu)	M
KAPENI	kah-PEH-nee	Knife, sharp as a knife.	Malawi (Yao)	M
MAKUZA	mah-KOO-zah	Arrows.	Rwanda, Burundi (Kinyarwanda, Kirundi)	M
MKHONTO	mm-KOHN-toh	The spear, weapon.	Azania (Xhosa)	M
MSHARE	MSHAH-reh	Arrow.	Kiswahili	
MZINGA	m-ZEEN-gah	Cannon.	Kiswahili	
NGABO	ngah-boh	Shield.	Uganda (Ganda)	M
RISASI	ree-SAH-see	Bullet.	Africa	M
SEFU	SEH-foo	Sword.	East Africa (Kiswahili)	M
SILAHA	see-LAH-AH	Weapon.	Africa (Kiswahili)	F
WAITIMU	WAH-ee-tee-moo	Born of the spear.	Kenya (Agikuyu)	M
WARUHIU	WAH-roh-hee-oo	Bears a weapon always.	Kenya (Agikuyu)	M
ZANA	ZAH-nah	Weapons.	Kiswahili	

Wholeness and Completion

No one completes a journey and then goes back
to look for the beginning. —*Ghana*

Name	Pronunciation	Meaning	Origin	Gender
ARIKO	ah-ree-koh	One who fills up.	Uganda (Itetso)	M
AYIHE	ah-YEE-heh	Whole, all.	Namibia (Ovambo)	
BAWEDDE	bah-wehd-deh	They are finished.	Uganda (Ganda)	
ELHASILI	ehl-hah-SEE-lee	Finally, ultimately.	Kiswahili	
FEZA	FEH-zah	Complete your task, accomplish.	Azania (Xhosa)	M

Name	Pronunciation	Meaning	Origin	Gender
FEZEKA	feh-ZEH-kah	The completed one; she does not lack anything.	Azania (Xhosa)	F
FEZEKILE	feh-zeh-KEE-leh	He is finished, fulfilled, complete.	Azania (Xhosa)	M
FEZIWE	feh-ZEE-weh	She is complete.	Azania (Xhosa)	F
FUJO	FOO-joh	Born after parent's separation. She completes the family.	East Africa (Kiswahili)	F
GWOMALA	gwoh-oh-mah-lah	The task you finish (or complete).	Uganda (Ganda)	F
ISE	EE-seh	Amen—may it be so.	Nigeria (Ishan)	
ISHA	EE-shah	To finish.	Kiswahili	
JAPERA	jah-PEH-rah	We are finished, offer thanks, it is done.	Zimbabwe (Shona)	F
KABISA	kah-BEE-sah	Completely, exactly.	Kenya, Tanzania	
KAMA	KAH-mah	Entirely, completely.	Kiswahili	
KAPERA	kah-peh-rah	The little one who becomes finished.	Zimbabwe, Mozambique, Zambia (Shona)	F
KINAYA	KEE-nah-yah	Complete, self-sufficient.	Kenya, Tanzania (Kiswahili)	F
KYOSE	kjoh-seh	All.	DRC (Rega)	M
MNYA MEZELI	mnyah-meh-ZEH-lee	The one who endures to the end.	Azania (Xhosa)	M
MWISHOWE	mwee-SHOH-weh	Finally, conclusively irrevocably, ultimate.	Kiswahili	
NAMALA	nnah-mah-lah	The finisher.	Uganda (Ganda)	M
OSAYIM WESE	oh-sah-eem-WEH-seh	God made me whole.	Benin	M
PEDZI	pehd-zee	The finisher.	Zimbabwe, Mozambique, Zambia (Shona)	F

Name	Pronunciation	Meaning	Origin	Gender
PEYISAI	peh-yee-SAH-ee	Conclusion.	Zimbabwe (Shona)	M
SEKAMA-LIRA	sseh-kah-mah-lee-rah	That finishes, or completes.	Uganda (Ganda)	M
TEMISHE	teh-MEE-sheh	Mine is done.	Nigeria	
TIMIA	tee-MEE-ah	To be completed.	Kiswahili	
WALOWO	wah-LOH-woh	Each and every one.	Azania (Xhosa)	
ZIMA	ZEE-mah	Whole, complete, healthy.	Kiswahili	
ZOONA	zoh-oh-nah	All of them.	Uganda (Kiga, Nyankore, Nyoro, Toro)	

Wisdom, Knowledge, and Intelligence

One head cannot hold all wisdom. —East Africa

Name	Pronunciation	Meaning	Origin	Gender
AJIWHO	ah-gee-whah	Who knows?	Cameroon (Mungaka)	
AKEELAH	ah-KEE-lah	Intelligent.	North Africa (Arabic)	F
AKIL	ah-KEEL	Wise.	North Africa (Arabic)	M
AKILAH	ah-KEE-lah	Intelligent.	North Africa (Arabic)	F
AKILIMALI	ah-kee-MAH-lee	Intelligence is wealth.	West Africa	
AMALYANGO	ah-mahl-YAHN-goh	Intelligence.	Zambia (Bemba)	
AMAZU	ah-MAH-zoo	No one knows everything.	Nigeria (Igbo)	M
ANDINWOH	ahn-deen-whah	Who knows?	Cameroon (Mungaka)	F
ANO	AH-noh	One with knowledge.	Nigeria (Igbo)	M
ATIBA	ah-tee-bah	Understanding.	Nigeria (Yoruba)	M
ATO	ah-toh	This one is brilliant.	Kiswahili	
BANDA	BAHN-dah	Very clever person; birthmark, scar.	Azania (Zulu)	M

Name	Pronunciation	Meaning	Origin	Gender
BARIBONA	ah-ree-boh-nah	They will see, realize, experience.	Uganda (Kiga, Nyankore, Nyoro, Toro)	M
BEHLALE	beh-LAH-leh	Wise.	Azania (North Sotho)	
BIDII	beed-dee	Intelligent.	Kenya, Tanzania	
BOHLALE	boh-LAH-leh	A clever and intelligent child.	Azania (North Sotho)	
BONO	BOH-noh	One who sees and understands.	Azania	
BULUMKO	BOO-loom-koh	He personifies wisdom.	Azania (Xhosa)	M
BUSARA	BOO-sah-rah	Wisdom.	East Africa (Kiswahili)	F
BWENGE	bwehn-geh	Knowledge.	Rwanda, Burundi, DRC (Huti, Tutsi, Twa)	M
CHAGINA	cha-GEE-nah	Tactful, common sense.	Kenya, Tanzania	
DHAKIYA	TAH-kee-yah	Intelligent.	Kenya, Tanzania (Kiswahili)	F
EKEVU	eh-KEH-voo	Intelligent, enlightened.	Kenya, Tanzania	
ELEWA	EH-leh-wah	Very intelligent.	East Africa (Kiswahili)	M
ELIMU	eh-LEE-moo	Science; knowledge.	Kiswahili	M
GABA	gah-bah	I know it.	Cameroon (Mubako)	M
GABSEH	GAHB-zeh	I do not know.	Cameroon (Mubako)	M
GABSIA	gahb-see-ah	I know myself; know yourself.	Cameroon (Mubako)	M
HAFSA	HAHF-sah	Sound judgment.	East Africa (Kiswahili)	F
HAKIM	HAH-keem	Wise.	Sudan	
HAZIKA	hah-ZEE-kah	Enlightened person, intelligent.	North Africa (Arabic)	
HEKIMA	heh-KEE-mah	Clever, wise.	Kenya, Tanzania	
HIKIMA	hee-KEE-mah	Wisdom.	Kiswahili	
IMO	e-moh	Knowledge.	Nigeria (Yoruba)	M

Name	Pronunciation	Meaning	Origin	Gender
KADHI	KAHD-ee	Judge, wise person.	Kenya, Tanzania	
KALAMKA	kah-LAHM-kah	Intelligent, well-informed.	Kenya, Tanzania	
KANGHA	kahn-gah	I am now wise, or intelligent, or mature.	Cameroon (Mubako)	M
KHALIMA	kah-LEE-mah	The clever one.	Azania	
KHALIPHA	kah-LEEP-ah	The intelligent one.	Azania	
LUMKILE	LOOM-keh-leh	The one who has acquired wisdom.	Azania (Xhosa)	M
LUNANGA	loo-nahn-gah	Wisdom.	DRC (Rega)	M
LWAZI	LWAH-zee	Knowledge.	Azania (Xhosa)	M
MAARIFA	mah-ah-REE-rah	Knowledge.	Kenya, Tanzania	
MBUYAZI	mboo-yah-zee	The knowledgeable new arrival.	Azania	
MTAALAMU	m-tah-LAH-moo	Intellectual and scholarly.	Kenya, Tanzania	
MTAFITI	m-tah-FEE-tee	Knowledge seeker.	Kenya, Tanzania	
MUTHONI	MOO-thoh-mee	A scholar.	Kenya (Agikuyu)	M
NDAZI	n-dah-zee	I know.	Rwanda, Burundi, DRC (Huti, Tutsi, Twa)	M
NIMI	NEE-mee	Wisdom.	Nigeria	
NOLWAZI	nohl-WAH-zee	The one with knowledge.	Azania (Zulu)	F
NUWA MANYA	noo-wah-mahg-nah	Omniscient.	Uganda (Runyankore)	M
RAKHETY	rah-KEH-tee	Knowledge; wisdom of God; tears of God.	Egypt/Khamit	F
RASHI	RAH-shee	Sensible.	North Africa (Arabic)	M
RASHIDA	rah-SHEE-dah	Sensible.	North Africa (Arabic)	F
RIBA	REE-bah	Interest.	Kiswahili	F
SAZI	SAAH-zee	The wise man.	Azania (Xhosa)	M

Name	Pronunciation	Meaning	Origin	Gender
SEBA	SEH-bah	To know; to understand.	Azania (Nguni)	M
SHISA	SHEE-sah	Smart.	Azania (Zulu)	
SOLWAYI	sohl-WAH-yee	Knowledge.	Azania (Xhosa)	
SOLWAZI	sohl-WAH-zee	He is knowledge; he possesses wisdom.	Kiswahili	M
TAFITI	tah-FEE-tee	Knowledge seeker.	Kenya, Tanzania	
TAMBUZI	tahm-BOO-zee	Intelligent, informed.	Kenya, Tanzania	
TEHUTI	teh-HOO-tee	Wisdom; the sage.	Egypt/Khamit	
TSABO	tsah-BOH	Knowledge.	Lesotho (Basotho)	F
TUBONJE	too-bohn-dzeh	Understanding.	DRC (Rega)	M
UCHENDU	oo-CHEHN-doo	Mind is life.	Nigeria (Igbo)	
UCHEOMA	oo-cheh-OH-mah	Good mind.	Nigeria (Igbo)	
UKANA	oo-kah-nah	Curiousity.	Nigeria (Igarra)	
UKWAZI	oo-KWAH-zee	Knowledge.	Zimbabwe	
YARA	YAH-rah	Smart.	West Africa (Yoruba)	
ZAKIYA	zah-KEE-yah	Discerning, bright, intelligent.	North Africa (Arabic)	

Women and Womanhood

A woman is more than her breasts; goats also have two. —*Rwanda*

Name	Pronunciation	Meaning	Origin	Gender
BIMKUBWA	behm-KOOB-wah	A great lady.	East Africa (Kiswahili)	F
ESIANKIKI	eh-see-ahn-KEE-kee	Young maiden.	Tanzania	F
FAZI	FAH-zee	Womanhood; a woman, a wife.	Azania (Zulu)	F

Name	Pronunciation	Meaning	Origin	Gender
HAWA	HAH-wah	Eve, wife of Adam.	North Africa (Arabic)	F
IHUOMA	ee-hoo-oh-mah	Maiden.	West Africa	F
JWAHIR	JWAH-heer	Golden woman.	Somalia	F
KAMIA	kah-MEE-ah	Wife of Mohammed.	West Africa	F
KIKE	KEE-keh	Feminine.	Kenya, Tanzania	F
MASSASSI	mahs-SAHS-see	Legendary name for "first woman on earth."	Zimbabwe (Makoni)	F
MUKAZI	moo-kah-zee	Wife, woman, skillful woman.	Uganda (Ganda)	F
MWANA	MWAH-nah	Maiden.	Kiswahili	F
NWAN YIBUEZE	nwahn-yee-boo-eh-zeh	Woman is king.	Nigeria (Igbo)	F
NYALA	n-yah-lah	Women.	East Africa	F
SITI	SEE-tee	Lady.	East Africa (Kiswahili)	F
TAMATA	tah-MAH-tah	Feminine.	West Africa (Hausa)	F
UKE	OO-keh	Womanhood.	Kiswahili	F
ZAJI	ZAH-jee	Woman.	West Africa (Tappa)	F

Words and Writing

All is never said. —Nigeria

Name	Pronunciation	Meaning	Origin	Gender
AKEWI	ah-KEH-wee	Poet.	West Africa (Yoruba)	
ANDIKIA	ahn-dee-KEE-ah	To write.	Kiswahili	
BALA	BAH-lah	To tell or read a story.	Azania (Nguni)	
BEBEZA	beh-BEH-zah	To tell fairy tales.	Azania (Xhosa)	

Name	Pronunciation	Meaning	Origin	Gender
BITONDO	bee-toh-ndoh	Words.	DRC (Rega)	F
EDE	EH-deh	Writer; scribe.	Nigeria (Igbo)	M
HADITHI	hah-DEE-tee	Story.	Kiswahili	
INDABA	een-DAH-bah	Story.	Azania (Zulu)	
INKONDLO	een-kohnd-loh	Poem.	Azania (Zulu)	
ITAN	EE-tahn	Fable.	West Africa (Yoruba)	
JOJO	joh-joh	Storyteller, one who passes down stories.	East Africa	
KWANDIKA	kwahn-dee-kah	To write.	Rwanda, Burundi (Kinyarwanda, Kirundi)	
LASANA	lah-SAH-nah	Poet.	Central Africa	
MAANDIKO	mah-ahn-dee-koh	Writings.	Kiswahili	
MAGAMBO	mah-gahm-boh	Words.	East Africa	M
MAKALANI	mah-kah-LAH-nee	One skilled in writing.	Kenya (Mwera)	M
MANENO	MAH-neh-noh	Words.	East Africa (Kiswahili)	M
MAWAKI	mah-WAH-kee	Poet.	West Africa (Hausa)	
MTUNGAJI	m-toon-gah-jee	An author.	Kiswahili	
MUFUME	moo-foo-meh	One that tells, or recounts a legend.	Uganda (Ganda)	M
MWANDIKA	mwahn-DEE-kah	A writer.	Kiswahili	
NATHARI	NAH-tah-ree	Prose.	East Africa (Kiswahili)	F
RAAWIYA	RAAH-wee-yah	Story teller.	East Africa (Kiswahili)	F
SHAIRI	shah-EE-ree	A poem.	Kiswahili	
WAKA	WAH-kah	Poem.	West Africa (Hausa)	
ZWINYE	ZWEEN-yeh	One word.	Azania (Xhosa)	M

Work and Productivity

Chattering doesn't cook rice. —Niger

Name	Pronunciation	Meaning	Origin	Gender
AFOYA	ah-FOH-yah	Sweat.	Nigeria (Ishan)	
ALUKI	ahl-LOO-kee	Basket weaver.	Azania (Zulu)	
BABAJJA	bah-bahj-jah	They engage in carpentry work.	Uganda (Ganda)	F
BATUMIKE	bah-too-MEE-keh	Let them work.	Central Africa	M
BIGASHYA	bee-bah-shjah	The rower.	Rwanda, Burundi, DRC (Huti, Tutsi, Twa)	M
DAOUDA	dah-oo-dah	Industrious.	West Africa	M
DOBI	DOH-bee	Person who does laundry.	Kiswahili	M
DOOLAA	doh-laah	Worker.	Gambia (Mandinka)	
GACHUZU	gah-tch-oo-zee	Little blacksmith.	Rwanda, Burundi, DRC (Huti, Tutsi, Twa)	M
GAIKA	gah-EE-kah	Wood carver.	Azania	M
IILONGA	ee-ee-LOHN-gah	Work, occupation.	Namibia (Ovambo)	
KAIMU	kah-EE-moo	An agent.	Kiswahili	
KALEI	kah-LEH-ee	One who works for the king.	Angola (Ovimbundu)	M
KAYA	KAH-yah	This child is a laborer.	Ghana (Akan)	M
KAZI	KAH-zee	Work; employment.	Africa (Kiswahili)	F
KAZIJA	KAH-zee-jah	Work comes.	East Africa (Kiswahili)	F
KIMANI	kee-MAH-nee	Sailor.	Kiswahili	M
MAKHI	MAH-kee	The expert builder.	Azania (Xhosa)	M
MIJIZA	mee-JEE-zah	Works with her hands.	East Africa	
MILIMO	mee-lee-moh	Work.	Zambia, Zimbabwe (Tonga)	

Name	Pronunciation	Meaning	Origin	Gender
MIRIMO	mee-REE-moh	Work.	Rwanda, Burundi (Kinyarwanda, Kirundi)	M
MONDLI	mohn-dlee	The provider; feeder.	Azania (Zulu)	M
MOSEGI	moh-seh-gee	Tailor.	Botswana (Tswana)	M
MPOSI	m-POH-see	Blacksmith.	Tanzania (Nyakyusa)	M
MUDADA	moo-DAH-dah	The provider.	Zimbabwe (Shona)	M
NINI	nee-nee	Industrious.	West Africa	F
NYAKIO	NYAH-keh-oh	Hard working.	Kenya (Agikuyu)	F
ODUSINA	oh-doo-SEE-nah	Hard work opens ways.	Nigeria	
OSI	oh-see	A cook.	Nigeria (Igbo)	F
RUBANI	roo-BAH-nee	Pilot.	Kiswahili	M
SEKYEWA	sseh-tch-eh-eh-wah	Volunteer.	Uganda (Ganda)	M
TUMLIGHA	toom-lee-gah	I am not sure I will enjoy the fruit of my labor.	Cameroon (Mubako)	M
YENGE	YEHN-geh	Work.	Sierra Leone	F
ZOLA	ZOH-lah	Productive.	DRC	

Worry and Anxiety

A problem should not be noticed while
it is still far from happening. —*Lesotho*

Name	Pronunciation	Meaning	Origin	Gender
BUCHECHE	boo-tch-eh-tch-eh	Worrisome.	Uganda (Ganda)	M
DANISA	dah-NEE-sah	One who causes worry through disappointing behavior.	Azania	M

Name	Pronunciation	Meaning	Origin	Gender
DANISILE	dah-nee-SEE-leh	One who causes worry through disappointing behavior.	Azania	F
IRIABATA	ee-ree-ah-BAH-tah	I am not worried by talks.	Nigeria (Ishan)	
JUBSIA	joob-see-ah	You are getting worried for nothing.	Cameroon (Mubako)	F
KHA LANGANI	kah-lahn-GAH-nee	What is your worry?	Azania	
KHA THAZILE	kah-tah-ZEE-leh	One who provokes anxiety.	Azania	F
MKHATHAZI	mkah-tah-zee	One who provokes anxiety.	Azania	M
NKATAZO	nkah-tah-zoh	Worry.	Zimbabwe (Zimbabwe, Ndebele)	
NTAKANA	n-tah-KAH-nah	Anxiety; panic.	Azania	M
NYONI	n-yoh-nee	Anxiety; panic.	Azania	

PART 3

It Is Written:
Pronunciation Guide and Phonetics

The pineapple's sweetness is one thing;
and the orange's another.

—*Ghana (Akan)*

nglish speakers frequently find speaking African languages challenging. Naturally, English speakers consider tonal languages such as Igbo and Yoruba to be complicated. Certainly, sounds such as Arabic inflections or the "clicks" found in some Southern African languages (associated with **c, q,** and **x**), are demanding for foreign tongues. Similarly, the **r**'s in several African languages are either rolled a bit more, or are made with a single tongue tap.

Without going into tremendous detail, the information and symbols used in this pronunciation guide are presented to assist English-speaking readers with the phonetic pronunciations of the African names shared in *The African Book of Names*. Please take note of the following:

a	is pronounced as	c<u>a</u>r, f<u>a</u>ther
e	is pronounced as	b<u>e</u>d, p<u>e</u>t
f	is pronounced as	<u>f</u>amous (not as "f" in o<u>f</u>)
g	is pronounced as	<u>g</u>oat, <u>g</u>et, <u>g</u>old (g is rarely softened as in <u>G</u>eorge)
i	is pronounced as	m<u>e</u>, f<u>ee</u>t, k<u>ee</u>p
j	is pronounced as	<u>j</u>et, <u>j</u>ourney
o	is pronounced as	sh<u>o</u>w, g<u>o</u>, gl<u>o</u>be
s	is pronounced as	<u>s</u>oft, <u>s</u>it, <u>s</u>ing (not as "s" in ro<u>s</u>e)
u	is pronounced as	r<u>u</u>de, t<u>oo</u>l, p<u>oo</u>l
w	is pronounced as	<u>w</u>et, <u>w</u>ell
y	is pronounced as	<u>y</u>ell, <u>y</u>ou
z	is pronounced as	<u>z</u>ebra, <u>z</u>est

Based on the information above, the following symbols are used in the text to guide pronunciation:

ah	is pronounced as	c<u>ar</u>, f<u>a</u>ther
ay	is pronounced as	d<u>ay</u>
ee	is pronounced as	m<u>e</u>, f<u>ee</u>t, k<u>ee</u>p
eh	is pronounced as	b<u>e</u>d, p<u>e</u>t
oo	is pronounced as	z<u>oo</u>, b<u>oo</u>, f<u>oo</u>d, p<u>oo</u>l
oh	is pronounced as	sh<u>o</u>w, <u>go</u>, gl<u>o</u>be
tch	is pronounced as	<u>ch</u>urch, or cat<u>ch</u>
uh	is pronounced as	b<u>u</u>t, sh<u>u</u>t

Based on the above, more often than not:

ai	is pronounced as	ah-ee
aoa	is pronounced as	ah-oh-ah
au	is pronounced as	ah-oo
ua	is pronounced as	oo-ah

Further, the following is usually the case:

ch	is pronounced as	<u>ch</u>urch, or mat<u>ch</u>
dh	is pronounced as	<u>th</u>at (pronounced as "th")
th	is pronounced as	<u>t</u>in (in Zulu)
tsh	is pronounced as	<u>ch</u>urch, or mat<u>ch</u>

And further:

◆ In Kiswahili, when an "**m**" is at the beginning of a word, the "**m**" is spoken as its own syllable; so pronounce the "m," and then pronounce the vowel or consonant that follows—do not slide the "m" into the next syllable.
◆ In Kiswahili, the "**r**" is rolled, or made with a single tongue tap.
◆ Double vowels generally indicate an emphasis on the vowel, and so the sound becomes longer than a single vowel.
◆ The consonant "**g**" is not used by most Mandinka, except for borrowed words.

Samaki (2001) explains how to make the various "click" sounds:

♦ For c, press the tip of the tongue against the top of the upper front teeth. Then, withdraw it sharply, while at the same time dropping the back of the tongue from the soft palate. This sound is the sound sometimes used to express exasperation—"tut"—or the sound made when sucking something from the upper teeth.

♦ For q, place the tongue between the teeth ridge and the hard palate (front palate). Then, withdraw the tongue sharply—again, while dropping the back of the tongue from the soft palate. This sound is similar to the sound of a cork being pulled from a bottle.

♦ For x, place the tongue between the teeth ridge and the hard palate, or against the hard palate as if you were going to make the "n" sound. Press one side of the tongue against the side of the jaw. Then, without moving the tip of the tongue from the hard palate, withdraw the side of the tongue sharply from the jaw. This click sound differs from the c, and q sound in that the release or withdrawal of the tongue is from the side of the mouth versus the front of the mouth.

♦ ch, qh, and xh represent aspirated assortments of "simple clicks."

♦ nc, nq, and nx represent "nasalized clicks."

♦ gc, gq, and gx are "simple voiced forms of the clicks."

♦ ngc, ngq, and ngx are "nasalized forms, accompanied by voiced glottal friction."

Please also note the following:

♦ In many African languages, words are written based on what the ear hears, so that many words are actually spelled phonetically.

♦ Most vowels are pronounced fully and not skipped, so in general, where there are two vowels together, pronounce each one.

♦ Lastly, in the names listings, though some African languages have as many as five or six tones, capitalized letters indicate the syllable where emphasis or stress *can* be placed.

This guide emphasizes explanation based on what is most familiar to western English speakers. The more difficult pronunciations will take some practice, and some sounds may not be mastered with only the simple explanations presented here. Respect the pronunciations, but don't become hindered by an inability to immediately master each sound.

Finally, please note that one African name can have several possible pronunciations depending on the tone, pitch, or origin of the name or the accent of the speaker. For example, Kiswahili is spoken in so many African countries that the spelling and pronunciations commonly vary according to local cultural influences. Thus, please do not accept pronunciations as absolute. You are encouraged to seek further assistance from linguists or native speakers of the various languages. I welcome comments, suggestions, and even arguments regarding pronunciation(s).

PART 4

Naming Ceremonies and Traditions

If your sister is in the group of singing girls,
your name always comes into the song.

—Ghana

O nce upon a time in southern Africa, when a child was named, the name and the meaning of the name were painted on a round stone in black or red. This painted stone was kept as long as the person was alive. After the person's death, the stone was ceremoniously broken into two pieces (Samaki 2001). Naming rituals of this type have existed across Africa for centuries.

In traditional African society, naming is as significant as marriage, and therefore many African cultures have naming ceremonies.

Parents can choose from a wide range of naming ceremonies from all over Africa. However, for the past thirty-five years, I and other Blacks in the United States have highlighted significant life passages—naming cere-monies, weddings, graduations, funerals—by observing the House of Umoja's Eight Bowl Ceremony, summarized here[6]:

♦ In preparation for the ritual, decorate a low-lying table with traditional African-centered cultural symbols. Then, use the table as a ceremonial altar.

♦ An elder, either female or male (dressed in authentic African attire), usually leads the ceremony.

♦ This ceremony requires eight bowls, made of wood, glass, clay, or other aesthetically pleasing material.

♦ Place one of the following elements in each of the bowls: wine, honey, lime, salt, cayenne pepper, water, African palm oil, and fresh coconut.

♦ Place the bowls in a circle around the table symbolizing the path of the sun around the earth. If the circle were a clock face, place the elements around the circle counterclockwise in the following manner:

Salt at twelve o'clock
Cayenne pepper at eleven o'clock
Water at nine o'clock
Palm oil at eight o'clock
Coconut at six o'clock
Wine at four o'clock
Honey at three o'clock
Lime at two o'clock

When naming a child, typically the parents sit together in front of the ceremonial leader who gives instruction to the community and reminds the community to be responsible for helping the child learn the lessons of life. The eldest family member in attendance sits up front alongside the child's parents, and holds the child to be named.

The Eight Bowl Ceremony begins with an offering of libation, to remember and honor the community's ancestors. A participant, or the ceremony leader, pours water onto the ground, or into a potted plant. The libation usually involves invoking the names of personal and community ancestors, conveying the purpose of the occasion, and making requests for prosperity and blessing. The libation is not intended to be a solo performance. Rather, there is call and response as attendees verbally compliment the libation. Libation text written by members of the House of Umoja is included here as an example:

Oh Ancestors
Blacker than the skies at midnight
Pyramid builders
Great ancient priests, warriors, and mystic scientists
Give us the inspiration to fight a thousand lions
Give us the enlightenment to unravel the mysteries of
the universe
Give us the sustenance to travel through the trackless
swamps of disharmony
Praised be your Black African names
Help us in our time of need
Oh Ancestors
Umoja (unity)

After the libation, the main part of the ceremony includes the tasting of the eight elements and brief presentations of the life lesson related to each element. The elements are tasted first by the baby (the leader puts the element into the baby's mouth) and parents (or adult to be named) and then by the participants—as all present listen to the lesson from the ceremonial leader:

◆ **Wine**. The wine represents appreciation for tradition and family. As well, wine symbolizes strength in racial or ethnic pride, commitment to household and extended family, and reverence and appreciation for the foundation laid by those who came before.

◆ **Honey**. Honey represents an ability to appreciate and remember the sweetness and goodness of life.

◆ **Lime**. Hurt and betrayal are unavoidable during the life cycle. In this ritual, lime represents an ability to overcome bitterness by retaining dignity, composure, and self-worth, even when feeling hurt by words, actions, or inaction of others.

◆ **Salt**. Salt symbolizes wisdom and balance in making life choices as well as flexibility, creativity, variety, and moral balance in making choices and decisions.

◆ **Cayenne pepper**. Crisis and tragedy are also unavoidable during the life cycle. Cayenne pepper represents resilience in response to critical situations. Cayenne reminds ritual participants to expect unpredictable circumstances and to develop the ability to rebound in the face of crisis.

◆ **Water**. The fluid of life represents a willingness to change. Additionally, water represents spiritual depth and renewal, and coolness in the midst of crises.

◆ **Palm oil**. For this ceremony, palm oil represents reliance on community power. More essentially, the palm oil represents an ability to move towards inevitable death with confidence and grace. This confidence can be born of a cohesive family and community where each person is valued for his contribution.

◆ **Coconut**. Fresh, broken coconut symbolizes assurance of inevitable blessings and unexpected luck. This coconut also represents reliance on that which is greater than oneself and on life benefits that have nothing to do with an individual's own intelligence, skill, or power, but are due solely to the unpredictable goodness of the divine.

The elements' life lessons are interrelated. While it is important for an individual to be steeped in heritage and tradition (wine), it is equally important for a person to be willing to change (water). Children should be surrounded by all the sweetness and joy a family can provide (honey), yet they will not be strangers to bitterness (lime). Power is longed for in life (African palm oil), but must be moderated by wisdom when making decisions (salt). And, while African-descended people are accustomed to experiencing hot and critical times (cayenne pepper), an uneasy expectation can be complimented by the assurance that blessings or good luck will someday surely follow (coconut).

The tasting of elements is often followed by songs, dance, drumming, and of course, feasting (food).

The Eight Bowl Ceremony owes its origin to African culture. Across the African continent, there are commonalities in the substance and concepts associated with naming ceremonies and practices for children:

- The most common waiting period between birth and naming is from three to nine days.
- Most *traditional* African naming ceremonies take place outdoors, representing an African attachment to land. Indoors, the connection to the outdoors can be demonstrated by lifting the child to the sky, or using water (an element of the sky and earth).
- The baby is connected to heaven and earth. This is best illustrated in the classic miniseries *Roots* by the lifting of the baby to the sky and the touching of the baby to the ground.
- The ceremony usually takes place in the morning or midday, but does not normally take place after sunset.
- A sacred space is cleared or prepared for the ceremony.
- Many African ceremonies and rituals begin with bathing, cleansing, or some other act of purification.
- Prayer is involved.
- Ceremonies commonly involve libation, a pouring of a drink as a sacrifice or offering. Liquid is poured onto the earth, into a potted plant, onto some meaningful object, or into another vessel or bowl. Prayers or chants often accompany the pouring of liquid. Water, an element of sky and earth, is often used during the pouring of libations.
- More often than not, a link is made between the living and those who have passed on. Palm wine is often offered to the ancestors.

◆ The essentials of life tend to be represented. For example, salt may represent life; pepper may represent the spice of life; and honey may represent the sweetness of life. Other elements include water (vitality and change), plant (life), soil or earth (humanity's origin), oil (calm), kola nut (longevity), wine (happiness of community), a candle (guiding light), and cowry shells (wealth).

◆ The child is the focus of attention. The child is almost always presented and an announcement of names is made. Usually, people offer prayers and good wishes to the child.

◆ The mother, more often than not, has been in seclusion since childbirth, and the father announces the birth and makes the preparations for the naming ceremony.

◆ The entire community is invited to participate. Many naming ceremonies involve call and response, and the audience is invited to be participatory. Often attendees offer advice, poems, and proverbs and present gifts. Silver bangles, thought to have healing properties (and protect children from illness) are common gifts. Many West African women give babies cowry shells as the first gift. At one time, a cowry shell, used as the main source of currency in West Africa, was worth one eighth of an ounce of gold.

◆ Elders have an active role in the ceremony.

◆ The kola nut is presented, broken, and shared by all. The kola nut is especially important in West Africa, symbolizing good wishes for the newborn, and is a general token of friendship.

◆ Narrative, dance, singing, and the beating of drums and other instruments are almost always included.

◆ Ceremonies tend to culminate with a feast (food is usually brought and prepared by participants).

Appendix A

The African Continent

The stream may prevent you from crossing,
but it cannot prevent your from retracing your steps.
—*Niger, Nigeria (Hausa)*

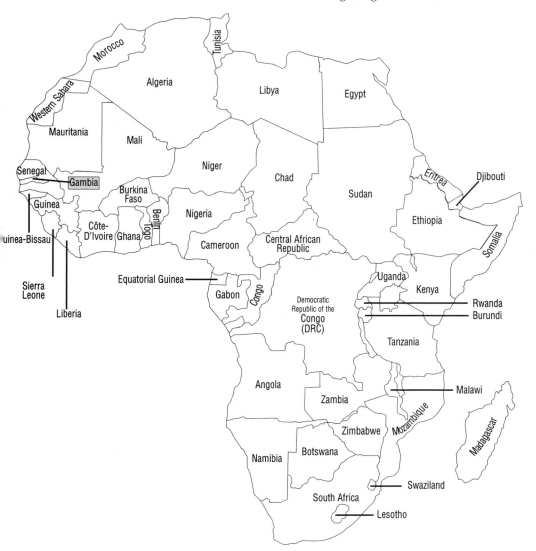

Appendix B

A 200-Year Naming Calendar—Find an African Name Instantly

However far the stream flows, it never forgets its source.

—Nigeria (Yoruba)

INSTRUCTIONS:
1. On the following page, identify the letter corresponding to the year and month of birth.
2. View calendar for that letter to determine the birth day (of week).
3. Choose a African name corresponding to the birth day.

	1888			1889		1890		1891			1892		
1893		1894		1895			1896			1897		1898	
1899		1900		1901		1902		1903			1904		
1905		1906		1907			1908			1909		1910	
1911			1912			1913		1914		1915			1916
		1917		1918		1919			1920			1921	
1922		1923			1924			1925		1926		1927	
	1928			1929		1930		1931			1932		
1933		1934		1935			1936			1937		1938	
1939			1940			1941		1942		1943			1944
		1945		1946		1947			1948			1949	
1950		1951			1952			1953		1954		1955	
	1956			1957		1958		1959			1960		
1961		1962		1963			1964			1965		1966	
1967			1968			1969		1970		1971			1972
		1973		1974		1975			1976			1977	
1978		1979			1980			1981		1982		1983	
	1984			1985		1986		1987			1988		
1989		1990		1991			1992			1993		1994	
1995			1996			1997		1998		1999			2000
		2001		2002		2003			2004			2005	
2006		2007			2008			2009		2010		2011	
	2012			2013		2014		2015			2016		
2017		2018		2019			2020			2021		2022	
2023			2024			2025		2026		2027			2028

Step 1

INSTRUCTIONS: 1. Identify the letter corresponding to the year and month of birth.

January	A	A	B	B	C	C	D	D	E	E	F	F	G	G
February	D	D	E	E	F	F	G	G	A	A	B	B	C	C
March	D	E	E	F	F	G	G	A	A	B	B	C	C	D
April	G	A	A	B	B	C	C	D	D	E	E	F	F	G
May	B	C	C	D	D	E	E	F	F	G	G	A	A	B
June	E	F	F	G	G	A	A	B	B	C	C	D	D	E
July	G	A	A	B	B	C	C	D	D	E	E	F	F	G
August	C	D	D	E	E	F	F	G	G	A	A	B	B	C
September	F	G	G	A	A	B	B	C	C	D	D	E	E	F
October	A	B	B	C	C	D	D	E	E	F	F	G	G	A
November	D	E	E	F	F	G	G	A	A	B	B	C	C	D
December	F	G	G	A	A	B	B	C	C	D	D	E	E	F

Step 2

INSTRUCTIONS: 2.View calendar for that letter to determine the birth day (of week).

A

Sun	Mon	Tues	Wed	Thur	Fri	Sat
1	2	3	4	5	6	7
8	9	10	11	12	13	14
15	16	17	18	19	20	21
22	23	24	25	26	27	28
29	30	31				

E

Sun	Mon	Tues	Wed	Thur	Fri	Sat
				1	2	3
4	5	6	7	8	9	10
11	12	13	14	15	16	17
18	19	20	21	22	23	24
25	26	27	28	29	30	31

B

Sun	Mon	Tues	Wed	Thur	Fri	Sat
	1	2	3	4	5	6
7	8	9	10	11	12	13
14	15	16	17	18	19	20
21	22	23	24	25	26	27
28	29	30	31			

F

Sun	Mon	Tues	Wed	Thur	Fri	Sat
					1	2
3	4	5	6	7	8	9
10	11	12	13	14	15	16
17	18	19	20	21	22	23
24	25	26	27	28	29	30
31						

C

Sun	Mon	Tues	Wed	Thur	Fri	Sat
		1	2	3	4	5
6	7	8	9	10	11	12
13	14	15	16	17	18	19
20	21	22	23	24	25	26
27	28	29	30	31		

G

Sun	Mon	Tues	Wed	Thur	Fri	Sat
						1
2	3	4	5	6	7	8
9	10	11	12	13	14	15
16	17	18	19	20	21	22
23	24	25	26	27	28	29
30	31					

D

Sun	Mon	Tues	Wed	Thur	Fri	Sat
			1	2	3	4
5	6	7	8	9	10	11
12	13	14	15	16	17	18
19	20	21	22	23	24	25
26	27	28	29	30	31	

Step 3   INSTRUCTIONS: 3. Choose an African name corresponding to the birth day.

Days	Female Names	Male Names	Meaning
Sunday	Akosua/Esi/Asi/Kwasiho	Kwasi/Kwesi/Kosi	Under the sun.
Monday	Adwoa/Adzo	Kojo/Kwadwo	Peace.
Tuesday	Abena/Abia	Kobina	Fire.
Wednesday	Akua/Aku	Kwedu/Koku	Fame.
Thursday	Yaa/Awo	Yaw/Yawo	Strength.
Friday	Efua/Afua/Afi	Kofi	Growth.
Saturday	Amma/Abba/Ama	Kwame/Kwami	Most ancient.

Endnotes

If you don't know where you are going,
you should know where you came from.
—*South Carolina, United States*

1. In personal written communication, the use of a lower case "i" for "I" and an upper case "W" in the word "We" is intentional.

2. In personal written communication, my spelling of Afrika with a "k" versus a "c" is intentional. Most traditional languages on the Afrikan continent spell Afrika with a "k," as the "k" is germane to Afrika. Europeans (particularly the Portuguese and British) polluted Afrikan languages by substituting "c" whenever they saw "k" or heard the "k" sound (for instance, Kongo and Congo; Akkra and Accra; Konakri and Conakry). The way Afrikan languages have been scripted, the "c" is only used with "ch" in words like *chakula* (meaning "food" in Kiswahili) or *chimerenga* (meaning "liberation" in Shona). The letter "k" in many written Afrikan languages denotes the hard "c" sound used in the English language (conflict, capitalism, etc.).

3. Kiswashili, one of the most widely spoken languages in Africa, has approximately 100 million speakers. Most Kiswahili speakers are in East and Southeast Africa; however, countries with Kiswahili-speaking communities include, but are not limited to: Sudan, Ethiopia, Somalia, Uganda, Kenya, Democratic Republic of the Congo (DRC), Rwanda, Burundi, Tanzania, Zambia, Malawi, Mozambique, Comoros, and Madagascar.

4. Azania is an alternative name for South Africa.

5. The term *New Afrikan* refers to Blacks in North America. This name recognizes the cultural, racial, and social fusion of various Afrikan ethnic groups and nations (Akan, Ewe, Fante, Fulani, Hausa, Ibo, Mandinka,

335

Yoruba, and several others) into one unique nation in America. The term *New Afrika* refers to the area of the Black belt south now identified as South Carolina, Georgia, Alabama, Mississippi, and Louisiana.

6. *Eight Bowls Full of Life* by Makungu M. Akinyela, Ph.D. (printed with permission)

Bibliography

Nothing occurs that has not occurred. —*Azania (Xhosa)*

detailed bibliography has been included to reference works and, more essentially, to encourage further exploration and study of African naming and culture.

Abell, S. 1992. *African Names and Their Meanings*. New York: Vantage Press.

Adebayo, B. 2005. *Dictionary of African Names, Meanings, Pronunciations and Origin vol. 1:*. Bloomington, IN: Authorhouse.

Adefunmi, O. 1967. *African Names from the Ancient Yoruba Kingdom of Nigeria*. Sheldon, SC: Great Benin Books.

Akinyela, M. 2008. *Eight Bowls Full of Life*. Unpublished manuscript.

Alexandre, P. 1967. *An Introduction to Languages and Language in Africa*. London, England: Heinemann Educational Books.

Amune, P. 1991. *Igarra (Etuno) Names: Origin and Meanings*. Nigeria: Amune Printing Press.

Asante, M. 1991. *The Book of African Names*. Trenton, NJ: Africa World Press.

Babalola, A. 2006. *A Dictionary of Yoruba Personal Names*. Nigeria: West African Book Publishers.

Beattie, J. 1957. "Nyoro Personal Names." The *Uganda Journal*, 21, pp. 99–106.

Bertrand, M., Mullainathan, S. 2003. *Are Emily and Greg More Employable than Lakisha and Jamal? A Field Experiment on Labor Market Discrimination. Working paper*. Cambridge, MA: National Bureau of Economic Research. Retrieved May 28, 2008 from: http://papers.nber.org/papers/w9873.

Borgenicht, J. 2005. *What Not to Name Your Baby*. New York: Simon Spotlight Entertainment.

Chuks-orji, O. 1978. *Names from Africa*. Chicago: Johnson Publishing Company.

Clarke, J.H. 1985, November. *Education for a New Reality in the African World.* Keynote address presented at the Annual Meeting of the National Alliance of Black Educators in Atlanta, Georgia. Retrieved May 10, 2008 from: http://www.africawithin.com/clarke/part20f10.htm.

Cornevin, R. 1954, Summer. "Names among the Bassari." *Southwestern Journal of Anthropology*, 10 (2), pp. 160–163.

Crane, L. 1982. *African Names, People and Places: A Teaching Manual.* Champaign, IL: African Studies Program, University of Illinois at Urbana-Champaign.

Damali, N. 1986. *Golden Names for An African People.* Cedartown, GA: Blackwood Press.

Dinwiddie-Boyd, L. 1994. *Proud Heritage: 11001 Names for Your African-American Baby.* New York: Avon Press.

Dubois, W.E.B. 1947. *The World and Africa: An Inquiry Into the Part Which Africa Has Played in World History.* New York: Viking Press.

Ellefson, C. 1990. *The Melting Pot Book of Baby Names.* White Hall, VA: Betterway Publications.

Enkamit, H. 1993. *African Names: The Ancient Egyptian Keys to Unlocking your Power and Destiny.* Washington, D.C.: Ser Ap-uat Publishers.

Ennis, E. 1945. "Women's Names Among the Ovimbundu of Angola." *African Studies*, 4 (1), pp. 1–8.

Ezeude, E. 2000. *Igbo Names.* Pittsburgh: Dorrance Publishing Co.

Fama, C. 1998. *1,000+ (African) Orisa/Yoruba Names.* San Bernardino, CA: Ile Orunmila Communications.

Faulkner, B. 1994. *What to Name Your African American Baby.* New York: St. Martin's Press.

Gordon, R. (Ed.). 2005. *Ethnologue: Languages of the World*, (15th edition). Dallas: SIL International. Retrieved on June 7, 2008 from: http://www.ethnologue.com/.

Gregersen, E. 1977. *Language in Africa: An Introductory Survey.* New York: Gordon and Breach Science Publishers, Inc.

2003. *Headstart Book of Afrikan Names.* Kingston, Jamaica: Miguel Lorne Publishers.

1965. *Hausa Personal Names*. Washington, D.C.: U.S. Central Intelligence Agency.

Kapwepwe, M. 2002. *Some Bemba Names and Their Meanings*. Lusaka, Zambia: Mulenga Kapwepwe.

Karim, Y. 1976. *Afrikan Names*. Philadelphia: Afram Press.

Keister, L. 1998. *The Complete Guide to African American Baby Names*. New York: The Penguin Group.

Kimenyi, A. 1989. *Kinyarwanda and Kirundi Names: A Semiolinguistic Analysis of Bantu Onomastics*. Lewiston, NY: Edwin Mellen Press.

Koopman, A. 2002. *Zulu Names*. Scottsville, South Africa: University of Natal Press.

Lansky, B. 1991. *The Best Baby Name Book in the Whole World*. New York: Meadowbrook.

Lewin, A. 1996. *Africa is Not a Country: It's a Continent*. Milltown, NJ: Clarendon Publishing Company.

Madubuike, I. 1985. *A Handbook of African names*. Colorado Springs, CO: Three Continents Press.

Mason, T., and Chewas, S. *1999. Baby Names: Real Names with Real Meanings for African Children*. New York: Seaburn Publishing.

Matanda, V. 1998. *Naming Your Child Prophetically*. Grand Rapids, MI: Herald Publications.

Mbiti, J. 1969. *African Religions and Philosophy*. New York, NY: Anchor Books.

Mbiti, J. 1972. African Names of God. *Ibadan Journal of Religious Studies*, 6 (1), pp. 3–14.

McKinzie, H. 1980. *Names from East Africa*. Los Angeles: McKinzie Publishing Co.

Moore, R. (1992). *The Name "Negro": Its Origin and Evil Use*. Baltimore, MD.: Black Classis Press.

Mthembu-Salter, L. 2002. *Call Me by My Name: More than 2000 Xhosa, Zulu, Swazi, and Ndebele Names*. Cape Town, South Africa: Kwela Books.

Murgor, K. (2007, May 28). *African Names VS. European Names*. Kiblog Topical. Retrieved October 10, 2008 from http://arapmurgor.blogspot.com/2007/05/african-names-vs-european-names.html.

Musere, J. and Byakutaga, S. 2000. *African Names and Naming*. Los Angeles, CA: Ariko Publications.

Musere, J. 2000. *Traditional African Names*. Lanham, MD: The Scarecrow Press, Inc.

Njoku, J. 1978. *A Dictionary of Igbo Names, Culture and Proverbs*. Washington, D.C.: University Press of America, Inc.

Nsimbi, M.B. 1980. *Luganda Names, Clans and Totems*. Pasadena, CA: California Instutute of Technology.

Obadina, E. 2007. *Ethnic Groups in Africa*. Philadelphia: Mason Crest Publishers.

Odotei, I. 1989. "What is in a Name? The Social and Historical Significance of Ga Names". *Research Review*, 5, 2, pp. 34–51.

Oduyoye, M. 1972. *Yoruba Names: Their Structure and Meanings*. Ibadan, Nigeria: Daystar Press.

Ogbu, O. 1995. *African-Igbo Names: How to Choose African Names for Yourself or for Your Loved Ones*. Oakland: Boug Publications.

Okojie, C. G. 1980. *What is in a Name?* Lagos, Nigeria: Alumese Palmer.

Onyefulu, I. 2004. *Welcome Dede! An African Naming Ceremony*. London: Frances Lincoln Children's Books.

Osuntoki, C. 1970. *The Book of African Names*. Washington, D.C.: Drum and Spear Press.

Perechi, R. 1996. *What's in a Name: Including African Names and Their Meanings*. Oklahoma City, OK: Sina Investigations and Consulting.

Pongweni, A. 1983. *What's In a Name? A Study of Shona Nomenclature*. Gweru, Zimbabwe: Mambo Press.

Pope, J. 2003, September. *Black Names a Resume Burden?* The Associated Press. Retrieved on September 29, 2003 from: http://www.cbsnews.com/stories/2003/09/29/national/main575685.shtml on 4.11.2008.

Potts, H. 1997. *A Comprehensive Name Index for the American Slave*. Westport, CT: Greenwood Publishing Group.

Ramazani, M. 1995. *African Names: Claiming Your True Heritage*. Manchester, NH: Montecom Publishing.

Robinson, J. 2001. *Pride and Joy: African-American Baby Celebrations*. New York: Pocket Books.

Room, A. 1994. *African Placenames: Origins and Meanings of the Names for over 2000 Natural Features, Towns, Cities, Provinces and Countries*. Jefferson, NC: McFarland and Company Publishers.

Samaki. 2001. *African Names: Reclaim Your Heritage*. Cape Town, South Africa: Struik Publishers.

Sanyika, B. 1975. *Know and Claim Your African Name*. Dayton, OH: Rucker Press Publishing Co.

Saarelma-Maunumaa, M. 2001. Ndalikolule—I was Far Away: Personal names of Wambo Origin in Namibia. *Nomina Africana*, 15 (1and2), pp. 212–223.

Skhosana, P. B. 2002. "Names and Naming Practices Amongst Southern Ndebele Male Persons." *Nomina Africana*, 16 (1and2), pp. 134–145.

Some, S. 1999. *Welcoming Spirit Home: Ancient African Teachings to Celebrate Children and Community*. Novato, CA: New World Library.

Stewart, J. 1993. *African Names: Names from the African Continent for Children and Adults*. New York: Citadel Press.

Stewart, J. 1996. *1001 African Names: First and Last Names from the African Continent*. New York: Citadel Press.

1962. *Swahili Personal Names*. Washington, D.C.: U.S. Central Intelligence Agency.

Tembo, M. 2006. *Zambian Traditional Names: The Meaning of Tumbuka, Chewa, Nsenga, Nogoni, and Tonga Names*. Lusaka, Zambia: Julubbi Enterprises Limited.

Terrell, F. 1988, January. "The Self-Concept Level of Black Adolescents with and without African Names." *Psychology in the Schools*, 25 (1), pp. 65.

2008. *The 2008 World Factbook*. Washington, D.C.: U.S. Central Intelligence Agency.

Titanji, V., Gwanfogbe, M., Nwana, E., Ndangam, G. and Lima, A. 1998. *An Introduction to the Study of Bali Nyonga*. Yaoundé, Cameroon: Stardust Printers.

Van Sertima, I. 1989. *Black Women in Antiquity*. New Brunswick, NJ: Transaction Books.

Wescott, R. 1974. "Bini Names in Nigeria and Georgia." *Linguistics*, 124, pp. 21–32.

Zawawi, S. 1993. *What's in a Name? Unaitwaje?: A Swahili Book of Names.* Trenton, NJ: African World Press.

Zawawi, S. 1998. *African Muslim Names: Images and Identities.* Trenton, NJ: Africa World Press.

About the Author

It is the person who knows how to shoot
whom we put on the track of an animal.

—*Ghana (Akan)*

Askhari Hodari, a practitioner of Black and Africana Studies, regularly studies and travels the African diaspora. She has visited numerous countries in Africa, South America, Latin America, and the Caribbean. Hodari received her bachelor's degree from Spelman College and her doctorate from Howard University. Dr. Hodari is the coauthor of *Lifelines: The Black Book of Proverbs* (Broadway Books).

Certainly, in a text of this type, there will be errors, omissions, oversimplifications, or overgeneralizations. No one named in the acknowledgments section is responsible for mistakes, errors of judgment, misrepresentations, or other failings of this work. Dr. Hodari accepts absolute responsibility.

If you come across an error, or an African name you would like to see included in Dr. Hodari's African name collection, please write her (with "African Book of Names" in the subject line) at: afrikannames@gmail.com.

For a personal name consultation, or to discuss a name not included in this book, please send an e-mail to afrikannames@gmail.com, with "African Name Consultation" in the subject line.

Joys of motherhood

The

ULTIMATE

MOM

Uplifting Stories,
Endearing Photos,
and the Best
Experts' Tips on
the Toughest Job
You'll Ever Love

Maria Bailey
Founder, BlueSuitMom.com

Code #7965 • $14.95

Discover must-know advice, entertaining
stories, and compelling photos for and about the greatest
source of unconditional love.

Mother's intuition

Code #7434 • $14.95

Learn simple communication techniques you
can use to effectively bond with, talk to and hear from
your child in utero.

Hilarious and helpful

STOP SECOND-GUESSING YOURSELF

Momma Said.net PRESENTS

YOURSELF

The Toddler Years

A Field-Tested Guide
to Confident Parenting

Jen Singer | The Internet's Favorite Momma and
Founder of Please Take My Children to Work Day

Code #6535 • $14.95

Get the go-to-guide to the toddler years filled with
practical tips, confessions and 'what works' in real life.